OF CAMEL KINGS
AND OTHER THINGS

Rural Rebels Against Modernity in Late Imperial China

Roxann Prazniak

ROWMAN & LITTLEFIELD PUBLISHERS, INC.
Lanham • Boulder • New York • Oxford

ROWMAN & LITTLEFIELD PUBLISHERS, INC.

Published in the United States of America
by Rowman & Littlefield Publishers, Inc.
4720 Boston Way, Lanham, Maryland 20706

12 Hid's Copse Road
Cumnor Hill, Oxford OX2 9JJ, England

Copyright © 1999 by Rowman & Littlefield Publishers, Inc.

British Library Cataloguing in Publication Information Available

Library of Congress Cataloging-in-Publication Data

Prazniak, Roxann.
    Of camel kings and other things : rural rebels against modernity
in late imperial China / Roxann Prazniak.
        p.   cm.—(State and society in East Asia)
    Includes bibliographical references and index.
    ISBN 0-8476-9006-7 (cloth : alk. paper).—ISBN 0-8476-9007-5
(pbk. : alk. paper)
    1. Peasant uprisings—China—History. 2. China—History—Taiping
Rebellion, 1850–1864. 3. China—History—1861–1912. I. Title.
II. Series.
HD1537.C5P73   1999
951'.034—dc21
                                                        98-23323
                                                        CIP

Printed in the United States of America

♾ ™ The paper used in this publication meets the minimum requirements of
American National Standards for Information Sciences—Permanence of Paper
for Printed Library Materials, ANSI Z39.48–1984.

With love for

Arif,

Nedim, and Murat

Mystery is not what can be hidden deliberately, but rather . . .
the fact that the gamut of the possible can always surprise us.

—John Berger, *Boar Land*, p. 18
[quoted in a letter from Subcomandante Marcos to John Berger,
Chiapas, Mexico, June 1995]

Ballad of the Qu Shiwen Uprising

Recollected by Ding Shiying
of Dadingjia, Zhaoyuan County

Years of turmoil at the end of the Qing,
The Xuantong boy emperor rules over the land.

South of the river and north of the sea, forget all other places;
Let me tell you about Laiyang.

To the west of Laiyang was Qu Shiwen;
To the east of Laiyang was Yu Zhusan.

A monk from the temple became a military man;
Qu became an official of the advance troops.

San Guan was originally a vagabond;
Shao Lianyu is a messenger busy with his delivery.

On a sandbar in the Jiuli River
They pitched their camp.

South to north it was endlessly long;
East to west it was ten *li* wide.

In a battle on Ting Mountain
Several thousand soldiers and officers were killed.

Yejia village had a landlord called Chen Laosan;
We went to his house for grain collection.

Tell how at a signal we went for grain,
We took several tens of *dan* of wheat.

Tell how at a signal to set the fire,
The haystack and house went up in smoke.

Note: *li* = 1/3 mile, *dan* = 50 kilograms

Source: Liu Tongjun, ed. *Xinhai gemingqian Lai Hai Zhao kangjuan yongdong* (Anti-tax movements in Laiyang, Haiyang, and Zhaoyuan before the 1911 Revolution) Beijing: Shehuikexue wenxian chubanshe, 1989, p. 391.

Contents

Illustrations

Maps

Figures

Tables

Acknowledgments

This text had its origins in my studies at the University of California. It has traveled a great distance since those years. At UC Berkeley I was introduced to modern China in courses taught by Franz Schurmann and Frederic Wakeman. Martha Kendall, whose own interests at the time were in the village origins of the Taiping Rebellion, was a most engaging teacher. At UC Davis, Liu Kuang-ching, Don C. Price, and Gary Hamilton were helpful and encouraging during my years of graduate work. In 1983–84, I received a grant from the National Academy of Sciences, Committee on Scholarly Communication with the People's Republic of China. This allowed me to continue my research at a number of archives and libraries and to visit some of the counties in which I was interested. I am most grateful to the staff at each of the following institutions for their assistance and patience: Beijing University Library, Qinghua University Library, the No. 1 Qing Archives in Beijing, the No. 2 Republican Archives in Nanjing, Nanjing University Library, Shandong University Library, and the Shanghai Municipal Library. During the same year, in addition to Chuansha County, I traveled to Laiyang and Haiyang counties where I met with county historians who shared their perspectives and locally collected materials. Mao Jiaqi and Cai Shaoqing of the History Department at Nanjing University kindly offered their assistance with references and introductions throughout this year.

During a sabbatical supported by Hampden-Sydney College, I returned in 1993 to do additional work in Nanjing and Zunhua County. For assistance with the Zunhua trip, which unexpectedly became so crucial, I am thankful to Yu Keping and Xu Xiuli. Also, at Zunhua, I was fortunate to have access to materials in the Zunhua County Historical Archives and to make the acquaintance of Lu Zhanshan and Wang Jiahai, both county historians and longtime observers of the north China political scene.

Several readers have had a hand in improving this manuscript. Philip Huang and Joseph Esherick offered helpful advice in the doctoral stage. Ernest Young read the final draft and made invaluable suggestions. Wan Shuping, Li Qishu, and Thelma Chow helped with translation problems. Richard Kunst did the computer graphics for the glossary and the county maps. Philip Schwartzberg reproduced the all-China map. Scott Horst and Shelli Newhart assisted with a wealth of editorial details. Of course, any errors of fact or judgment are entirely mine.

Last but not least, Arif Dirlik encouraged and supported my efforts and was the source of some of the many minor miracles that made this study possible. Arif's own work has been an inspiration to me throughout this process, and it is to him and my much appreciated stepsons that I dedicate this volume.

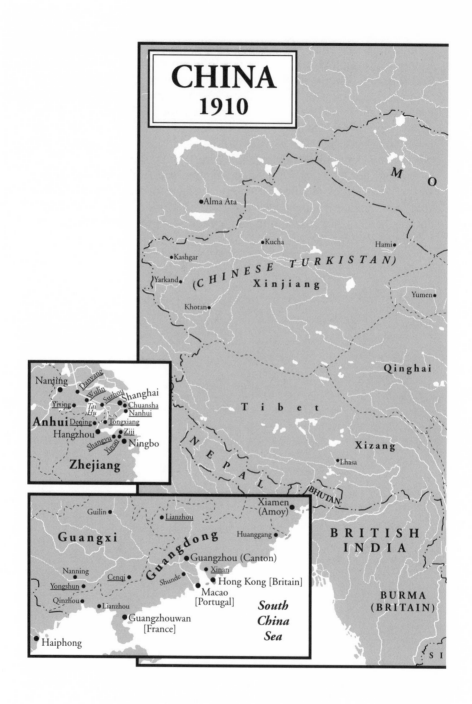

CHINA
1910

M O

•Alma Ata

•Kucha
Hami•

•Kashgar
(C H I N E S E   T U R K I S T A N)
Yarkand•
Xinjiang
Yumen•

Khotan•

Qinghai

T i b e t

N
E
P
A
L
Xizang
•Lhasa

BHUTAN

B R I T I S H
I N D I A

BURMA
(BRITAIN)

Nanjing•
Danyang
Wujin
Suzhou
Shanghai
Yixing•
Tai
Hu
Chuansha
Nanhui
Anhui Deqing• Tongxiang
Hangzhou Ziji
Shangyu Yuyao •Ningbo

Zhejiang

Guilin•
•Lianzhou
Xiamen
(Amoy)
Guangxi
Huanggang•
Guangdong
Nanning• Cenqi
Guangzhou (Canton)
Yongshun• Shunde Xinan
Qinzhou• •Hong Kong [Britain]
•Lianzhou Macao
[Portugal]
•Guangzhouwan
[France] *South
China
Sea*
•Haiphong

SI

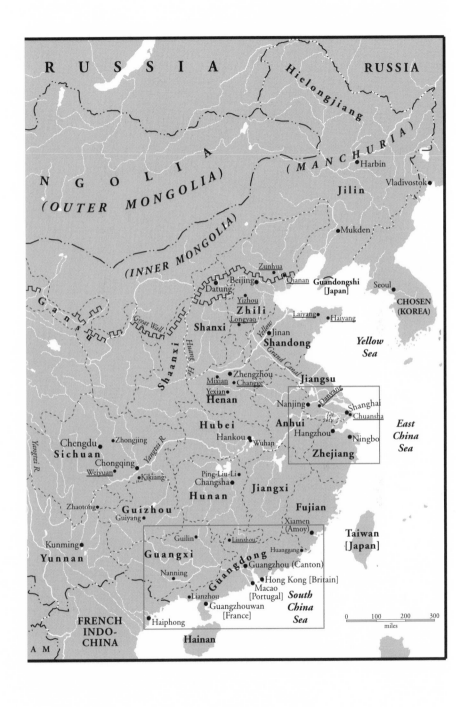

Introduction: Narratives of Resistance and Problems of Suppressed Histories

The dry, hilly landscape of Laiyang county passes through our field of vision framed by the windows of a green, People's Liberation Army, Chinese-made jeep. Seventy-four years ago to this month, one of the most celebrated rural protests of the post-Boxer decade, the Qu Shiwen uprising, took place on this land. In that May of so long ago, villagers organized a major resistance to government reforms, which led eventually to the siege of the county seat by dissident forces. After years of piecing together documentary fragments of stories like the one at Laiyang, I find myself in the spring of 1984 traveling with an entourage of local historians, mostly secondary-school history teachers and Party officials, to the villages and market towns of their own personal and family pasts. I am in search of answers to questions that years of doctoral research have been unable to illuminate, questions about status relations among rebel leaders, economic circumstances of particular families, and reform managers' political connections. As we move across drought-stricken Laiyang county in the heart of the Shandong peninsula, my eyes strain against the glare of a bright midday sun to catch glimpses of figures far and near bent over hard work in fields under a cloudless sky. I had not imagined Laiyang to be this open and rolling, with abrupt rugged hills rising from dusty, almost treeless expanses of light brown earth. The uprising of 1910 took place in a similar time of drought.

At our destination of Malian village, location of a pitched battle between villagers and government troops in June 1910, an aged and weathered farmer, Lü Xunsan, comes in from his work to recount for me what he recalls of the uprising led by Qu Shiwen. Mr. Lü settles into our circle for tea and apples. Although only seven years old at the time of the rebellion, he begins to relate those long ago events. My questions for him meet with silence. He has no answers regarding the amount of land protesters or reformers held or what their ties to groups outside the county might have been. Not only do my questions seem irrelevant to him, more significantly, they interrupt his richly embroidered narrative of the uprising, a narrative which he has committed to memory from his childhood years. Lü shares a surname with Lü Baohuang but tells me he is no direct relation. In late June of 1910, Lü Baohuang posed as a supporter to Qu Shiwen who sought refuge in flight from government troops. Lü Baohuang offered to hide Qu Shiwen in his home, and then locked the front door from the outside and went to Laiyang city to report Qu's capture. Authorities promptly sent troops to arrest Qu. Meanwhile, a hired laborer who knew of Qu Shiwen's support among the people, unlocked the door and told Qu to flee. When the troops arrived, Qu was not to be found. However, the soldiers found Lü Baohuang's son at home and killed him.

What Mr. Lü wants me to know has nothing to do with whether or not Lü Baohuang had commercial ties to the county reformers or exactly how much land he owned. For Lü, the critical memory across all these decades is exactly how Lü Baohuang's son died. He was killed not by a stab to the neck, as had often been erroneously reported Lü tells me, but by a dagger to the stomach, which cut across his guts like this. Lü with his brown, deeply wrinkled, trim face watches my eyes with intensity as he slowly draws his hand holding an imaginary dagger across his stomach. The loss of a son was clearly considered a fitting tragedy for a family that housed a betrayer of Qu Shiwen. Fate works through many agencies to punish with a terrible death, not just a simple fatal blow, even the offspring of those who would betray the leader of a just cause, throwing fear not only into would-be traitors but their relations as well. Lü then goes back to peeling and eating his second apple; he says he knows nothing else of what I ask. When he decides that the interview is over, he stands up and announces to the county official accompanying me that he has to get back to work.

Almost ten years later in the fall of 1993, I am once again traveling with an entourage of Party officials and local historians, mostly secondary-school history teachers, this time by Mitsubishi jeep, compliments of the county party office, down a rural road in Zunhua county, modern Hebei province, known in 1910 as Zhili. Once again I am looking for information that has eluded me, this time about the Camel King who led a tax protest in 1910 and about the Gold Mountain temple, which was the center of antireform activism in Zunhua county. I had almost dropped this case from my research because there were only sketchy details available. But for the sake of thoroughness, and because there were so few well-documented cases, requiring a patchwork methodol-

ogy, Zunhua remained in my reconstructed picture of antireform incidents. It was also a particularly interesting case from the few bits of
information I did have, featuring a cast of colorful characters and sustained collective action over a two-year period. I could not imagine why
it did not show up more often in any of the written records, especially
because it was only ninety miles to the east of Beijing.

When I tell friends at Nanjing University that I am going to Zunhua
to try to find out more about the 1910 tax protest, most pass quickly
over what seems like a remote scholarly interest. Unlike 1984 when
peasant rebellions were still of some interest, be it fading, in academic
circles in 1993 an event even as major as the Taiping Rebellion, a mid-
nineteenth century peasant movement and largest civil war in world
history, holds little interest for history graduate students and many pro-
fessors alike. Instead, almost to a person my friends respond, "Zunhua?
Oh, that's where Wang Guofan is from." I do not recall a Wang Guofan
but soon learn that he was a figure during the early agricultural cooperative movement in the years 1952–54. Mao Zedong drew attention to
Wang's work initiating the organization of cooperatives among his fellow poor peasants of Zunhua.[1] On the basis of the potential Mao saw in
Wang's "Bare Stick Cooperative," he encouraged other rural areas
across the country to take Wang's efforts to collectivize the resources
and labor of poor peasant households as a model for national agricultural progress based on spartan and egalitarian principles of rural organization. In the late 1950s and 1960s, he and Chen Yonggui, leader of
the famed Dazhai Brigade, served on the Party's Central Committee in
Beijing and later on the Politburo as peasant consultants on rural matters. Wang's name is presently on everyone's mind because of a suit he
recently won against Gu Jianzu, author of a semifictional work titled,
Qiongbangzi Wangguo (Kingdom of the Bare Sticks), a play on Wang
Guofan's name and the name of the cooperative he had founded earlier
for those who were "poor as bare sticks." Gu, who had been sent to
Zunhua during the Cultural Revolution for reeducation by the peasants,
evidently hated every minute of his exile from urban life. After 1978
when the county Party officials formally criticized Wang Guofan for
the "errors and mistaken ideas" of his Maoist political line, no longer
in favor once Deng Xiaoping rose to full prominence, Gu let loose his
pent up resentment and published a thinly disguised attack on Wang
Guofan, which Wang and others considered slanderous in the first degree, accusing Wang of political and moral corruption.[2] I decide I would
like to know more about this man Wang in addition to the Camel King.
As it turned out, what at first seemed like two only tangentially related
lives had a link that I could never have expected to uncover.

Lu Zhanshan, vice director of the Zunhua county Party historical research office and former high school history teacher, is delighted that someone is showing interest in the peasant history of Zunhua. After an afternoon of dealing as best he can with my questions about 1910, sharing with me some invaluable unpublished oral histories collected by Party historians in the late 1950s and early 1960s, and then familiarizing me with the history of the communist movement in Zunhua from 1927 to the present, Mr. Lu, a longtime friend of Wang Guofan, announces that Wang has been to town but has already returned home and we must leave immediately if we want to speak with him. Twenty minutes later in the enclosed courtyard of Wang's house, Lu introduces us.

Wang Guofan is relaxed, gentle, and straightforward, a tall man of seventy-five years with a dignified bearing, a slight smile, and an attentive eye. Before long we are gathered in the small sparsely furnished space that is his home around the *kang*, a sitting and sleeping surface heated in winter by warm air vented in from the cooking stove just outside the room. Sitting on a small wooden bench on which he informs us Zhou Enlai sat when he came for a visit once and with some of Mao Zedong's calligraphy and poetry framed on the wall behind him above a row of delicate tea cups with handles, Wang Guofan comments on the contemporary problems of rural China, and Zunhua in particular. He thinks there are too many "western things" these days and that there is a difference between these and modernization. A telephone can be helpful for work, but television for evening entertainment everyday is a distraction he has chosen to live without. In his view, local cadre waste is the main problem China faces. He says there is "too much emphasis on self-interest, not enough attention to the public interest." Wang favors Maoist policies because they encouraged "peasant independence" unlike the current policies that encourage "peasant dependence."

After a while, I change the subject to the Zunhua events of 1910. Wang tells me he is not related to Wang Congman, leader of the tax protest from that time, whose surname he shares. He answers my questions about the protest as readily as if it were yesterday's news. He says the Camel King was a nickname for Wang Congman because he was tall and strong. This had not been clear from my documents. I ask about Li Hailong, who is literally no more than a name I have gleaned from the sparse historical record. Wang Guofan has heard of him. He says that Li Hailong did not attend the magistrate's dinner, at which many rebel leaders were captured, for strategic reasons plotted by the collective leadership of the uprising, not because he was a coward as some have said. Although the temples at the time, including the Gold Mountain, were controlled by the landlords, the villagers used them as meeting places. But how does Wang Guofan know these things? He was born in 1918, eight years after the incidents. I ask him and I am astounded by his answers, not because I think that peasant culture could not have produced such interconnections over the course of Zunhua's rural history (in fact the contrary has been my working assumption) but because such a connection becomes so powerfully explicit at this unexpected moment.

Wang Guofan says that as a child he saw the local traveling shadow-puppet theater, which performed a play about the events of 1910 dedicated to the memory of Yang Xiu, who took full responsibility for the rebellion and consequently spared the lives of the other leaders including Wang Congman. The play was performed into the 1930s and was disrupted by the Japanese Occupation, not to be resumed thereafter. Wang adds that he was very much inspired by the story of the Zunhua uprising of 1910 and the leadership of Yang Xiu and others, and that it was part of his motivation for becoming involved in local rural activism during the early years of the Chinese Communist movement and beyond.

Wang Guofan saw this play—literally the shadow side of Zunhua's history—in the 1930s, and its details and evocative power were still clear in the 1950s and the present—an impressive feat of vivid social memory spanning more than a twenty-year period. I recall from the Laiyang visit a passing reference to a local Beijing-style "Qu Shiwen opera," performed in that county until the time of the Cultural Revolution. How many tales of local activism preserved in local storytelling shaped not only rural culture and society but the ongoing dynamic between local and national politics? How many remembrances from the place-specific personalities and events of the Taiping movement, the Boxer Uprising of 1900, as well as other cases of local activism, built the rural culture of dissident thought and practice in which groups as their own agents of protest acted to challenge the state's version of political and economic modernity in the post-Boxer decade?

As a history of place, this work has certain liabilities and value to which I would like to draw attention from the start.[3] The premise of the study is simple: Those rural residents who opposed government reforms in the decade after the Boxer Uprising acted as their own agents in a context of shifting contemporary politics and a longstanding rural practice of resistance to perceived injustice. Although the specific terms of activism varied from county to county, dissidents were aware of developments and issues in other places, especially in neighboring counties where protest occurred and where they often turned for additional support. When viewed collectively, these protests, which themselves were not coordinated at the provincial or national levels, reveal a common analytical stance. This dissident rural perspective drew on concrete experiences from the protesters' own encounters with the New Policy (*xinzheng*), nationally sponsored county-level political, economic, and educational reforms, as well as ideas and practices conveyed from the earlier eras of interaction with foreign entities and the demands of Chinese landlords and bureaucrats. The rural critique of New Policy reforms from 1901 to 1911 was a unique development of thought and action in the history of Chinese rural dissident practice. The appearance of widespread rural protest on the eve of China's 1911 Revolution was, therefore, neither a cyclic return of timeless dynamics at work within peasant society nor an automatic response to structural changes in the body politic, either locally or nationally. It was an historically conditioned expression in a rural discourse of resistance.

Other works have noted the importance of this decade of rural activism, but none have analyzed these cases as one study or with the level of detail I hope to convey.[4] In both the focus and the detail, new perspectives emerge. Because of its social origins, rural dissent is difficult to study. Documentation is limited and fragmented. If these cases of rural protest were not so numerous and persistent, it would be easy to let them go as historically insignificant. The challenge becomes how to be as thorough as possible in terms of "hard" evidence and to extend historical empathy with caution. The present work argues for an obligation to seek out and render intelligible the integrity of this critical rural perspective, which offered its own views on social and cultural issues regarding economic "development" and political "modernization."

The rural story, in China and elsewhere, in its interactions with industrial capitalism posed important historical and contemporary questions. Consequently, this "history of place" is more than a history of one county or village after another. It suggests a location from which to understand the interactions that render the global, national and regional contingent on place-based conditions. "Place" in this context is more than geographical location, often refered to as "the local." Linked to the specifics of natural environment and land-based labor relations, "place" is also, as the following chapters show, a referent for a shared social analysis with disparate locales.

The Lay of the Land:
Rural Dissident Practice and Social Relations

Each of the five narratives presented in this study is first and foremost a history of a particular geographic environment organized by individuals over time through social and economic relations specific to that place. Each is also part of a rural discourse of dissent. At times hidden, at other times faintly visible, fragmented, or embedded in other political programs, this dissident discourse had its own sources of sustenance deep in the roots of local concerns. Cultural forms that gave expression to rural dissent were grounded in village associations based on productive labor and mutual aid activities. In this environment of often harsh social and natural conditions, the struggle for basic livelihood cultivated great tenacity and vitality among those engaged in strategies of conflict and cooperation. Essential to this capacity for struggle over generations was a level of independent thinking and material resources available to those who would raise dissent. Nothing underlines the strength of loyalties and commitments at the core of this activism more than evidence of the intelligent, thoughtful people who knowingly endangered their lives by accepting leadership in these circumstances. Their motives, actions, and goals distinguish them among various groups charged with transgressions against society. Of the individual leaders of rural protest discussed in this volume, we have a visual document of only one, Qu Shiwen, leader of the movement at Laiyang. A frail looking man in his sixties, with rumpled padded jacket and hair in disarray, Qu looks with intense eyes, a heavy chain around his neck and hands shackled just before his execution by a modernizing state that took photographs of convicted peasant leaders as part of the bureaucratic processing of those who rebelled against government policies. The rural dissent that emerged during this decade offered its own critical perspective on reform and questions of modernization, raising issues of participatory democracy, cultural hegemony, and political economy.

No one case among the five is intended as a model through which the others can be understood. Each narrative is situated in a specific county history, among contemporaneous protests in the proximity, and in relationship to national historical trends. Each is its own story, yet all are part of a scenario with national and global dimensions. The case at Laiyang, for example, reads on the surface like the events in other counties where protest developed. But because more biographical and historical materials were collected on Laiyang, additional layers of understanding are possible to which we simply do not have access in other instances. Protest leader Qu Shiwen's earlier conflicts with individuals who became reform managers at Laiyang and his experiences during the Boxer Uprising are valuable background details that may have had parallels in the biographies of other anti–New Policy leaders about whom we know much less. The case at Laiyang also touches on all the major problems and issues present in the other narratives, though not necessarily to the same degree or in exactly the same way as may be found at Zunhua, Zhili, or Lianzhou, Guangdong. Antiforeign sentiments that some protest leaders intimated only in passing at Laiyang were more fully expressed by protesters at Weiyuan, Sichuan, and Lianzhou, Guangdong. Members of the Tongmenghui (Revolutionary Alliance), founded by Sun Zhongshan (Sun Yat-sen) in 1905, who were residents of Laiyang had no documentable involvement with events there, while in Lianzhou, Tongmenghui members were clearly identified in some accounts of the protest activities. Laiyang women associated with the Tangjia temple were a presence but small voice in the Laiyang events while at Chuansha, Jiangsu, the women of Yugong temple initiated the protest against miscellaneous taxes and confiscation of temple property for reform purposes. In all cases, resistance leadership straddled a line between positions that were extensions of official authority, such as village or subcounty intermediary administrative units, and those that derived authority from place-generated and sometimes heterodox groupings, whether lay Buddhist temples or secret societies. In all cases, the primary issues were taxes, property claims, political conflicts, and cultural challenges related to the post-Boxer New Policy reforms. The specifics of gender, politics, and religion in the configuration of dissent unfolded according to the dynamics of the locale.

Within a framework in which these fragmented histories are deemed meaningful, a number of significant observations become apparent. Protesters generally characterized as *nongmin* (agricultural people), were not exclusively farmers or male or Han Chinese. Small landowners and small businessmen, who seldom took up direct protest leadership in the post-Boxer decade, in some cases gave support from the sidelines or attempted to act as mediators. Women participated in various ways from leadership to support efforts. In some cases, ethnic minorities during the New Policy period came increasingly to have common interests with the Han ethnic majority against state encroachments on local communities. Christian missionary work was related to reform activity. Villagers knew that the reform managers who were quickest to collect new taxes and make other demands were sometimes among the most prominent of the local Christian converts. Anti–New Policy activities were cluster-issue protests distinct from the national revolutionary movement whose goals were primarily industrial and political modernization. There were cases, however, where Tongmenghui members took different sides in the struggles over reforms, creating divisions within the revolutionary position itself.

A rural dialectic of antigovernment and antiforeign issues produced a critique in the post-Boxer years that was an adaptation of the notion that "officials compel the people to rebel" and the idea that foreigners with the consent of officials were "draining the life blood of the people" to build railroads and string telegraph lines across the countryside. In this mix of concerns about both foreign and governmental actions, protesters saw a drift toward definitions of modernity, referred to as the "new style" (*xinshi*), which excluded their own cultural vitality and sense of material well-being in an environment of general austerity. Tension between place-specific authority and nationally linked politics reached a heightened intensity during these years. Upholding concepts of social justice, accountable leadership, and collective action, rural protesters addressing the circumstances of the late Qing political and fiscal crisis drew on a rural culture of protest to produce an antimodernist defense of rural society, critical of government mismanagement, Christian interference in local politics, industrial technologies, and unchecked commercial development.

This is not to say that peasant groups were not open to change. Aspects of what modernity might offer to improve their own conditions were rendered ambiguous at best by the overall unfavorable redistribution of political power and material resources that accompanied the late imperial reforms. Between reformers and dissenters, the social gulf widened. How could someone who considered herself the reincarnation of Guanyin, the Goddess of Mercy, or another person who felt inspired by "spirit boxers" and other rebels of the past be taken seriously as participants in the move toward modernity? What the proponents of reform failed to ask was how such a vocal, large constituency at the foundation of society could be discounted, patronized, and left behind if the path of change was to have lasting integrity and viability.

Scholarship on State and Society:
Locating the Rural Story

The significance of these narratives of rural dissent in the history of late imperial China shifts dramatically depending on location among interpretive frameworks. Earlier decades of scholarship, while recognizing the autonomy of rural protest, placed county histories such as those at Laiyang and Weiyuan on the margins of provincial and national developments. Chinese scholarship in the Marxist tradition produced numerous volumes in the 1950s and 1960s commemorating the 1911 Revolution and the agrarian uprisings that preceeded them. Li Zhuren's study of mass struggles before the 1911 Revolution is but one of the many major works that places rural agitation in relationship to the 1911 Revolution.[5] Although captured in the limited framework of class struggle in the movement toward Chinese Communism, these agrarian rebellions, characterized as lacking in sufficient leadership and organization, nonetheless by their inclusion in histories of 1911 were granted historical significance as an important layer in the analysis of social dynamics at the time and in later decades.[6]

Numerous provincial studies include expanded coverage of county-based activism. Kui Yingtao's *Sichuan jindaishi gao* (Sketches in Sichuan modern history) (1990) surveys rural activism in the post-Boxer decade including a variety of issues and locales with more detailed accounts of some counties than others. Wang Shuhuai's *Zhongguo xiandaihuade quyu yanjiu, Jiangsusheng, 1860–1916* (A regional study of modernization in China: Jiangsu province, 1860–1916) (1984) provides valuable contextual information for the anti–New Policy movements in Jiangsu. Other studies of the 1911 Revolution with a provincial focus include passages on rural protest while giving analytical priority to questions regarding the social origins of county reformers and the nature of this group's expanding political power.[7]

Liu Tongjun's study of Laiyang, Haiyang, and Zhaoyuan counties is a quantum leap in the area of meticulous research giving focus to a wide range of issues surrounding dissident activism on the Shandong peninsula. As Qi Jichang has noted, until Liu's work it was impossible to analyze fully the significance of this most important uprising at Laiyang as well as other anti–New Policy movements, developments that Qi considers to be among the most important events in China's modern history.[8] Jean Chesneaux in early studies and Cai Shaoqing in more recent research have analyzed the organizational and social bases of secret society alliances with rural associations mobilized for political activism. Finally, oral histories provide detail regarding the specifics of geography, custom, and personalities, which considered in the context of other documentation, are invaluable sources of information as well as further questions.

Late-imperial rural dissent in China was not simply reactive but critically reflective of features of political ideology in the process of formation.[9] Despite the clear historical importance of the late imperial protests, these expressions of rural dissent remain largely marginalized in the revolutionary and reformist frames of reference in Chinese history.[10] The result is that scholarship located in these interpretive frameworks tends to proscribe the full historical agency of the anti–New Policy protesters.[11] Some studies focus on patterns of elite domination in counties that did not generate militant opposition to reform.[12] Other studies of radicalism and the modern education movement omit the instances of opposition to new schools that did arise in counties around centers of reform.[13] Perhaps the incompleteness or deficiency of this analysis can be fully recognized only in the last years of the twentieth century when a critique of modernization has come into focus from multiple vantage points including different national and regional locations as well as from consequences to our social and natural environments. In this context, questions about modernity and the nation enable a recognition of autonomous subjectivity to resistance movements that have not previously been considered as potential agents of an alternative modernity.

At another level, the late Qing rural protests can be viewed as instances of collective action against modernist state-building processes, of which there are numerous examples in world history.[14] Studies of European popular activism by Charles Tilly, Eric Hobsbawm, and E. P. Thompson are at the center of this general area of inquiry.[15] James Scott's studies of the principles of moral economy are especially relevant here as well.[16] Within the interaction between state and society itself, the rural story as a suppressed history belongs to what Jurgen Habermas in his writings on civil society and his critique of emerging capitalist state formations has called the "plebian public sphere."[17] Because the rural story is within the suppressed plebian public sphere, and the narratives of resistance are within that sphere, the resistance narratives are themselves doubly suppressed. Consequently, these narratives of resistance represent a deep and neglected critique of state-building processes during the years 1901–1911 and after. Only if the place of late-imperial rural dissent in China is fully excavated to make visible its interconnections with other critical social movements, can its greater significance be understood. Partha Chatterjee has suggested that the concept of "civil society" as a domain from which the majority of the population is excluded should not be rectified to include that population. Instead their separation, he argues, is essential for seeing the emergence of the contemporary opposition between modernity and genuine democracy.[18] Such opposition was clearly present in the concerns raised by the anti–New Policy protest movements.

The rural story of resistance illuminates the national project but is not entirely a part of that project. Situated between the full grasp of historical documentation and the practice of resistance sustained through storytelling and the material realities of daily life, the cases in this study and the critical perspectives they offer occupy territory overlapping written and oral sources of memory. Walter Benjamin distinguished between the consequences of these two patterns of memory, when he defined storytelling as communicable experience embodying counsel for others. "Counsel," Benjamin stressed, "is less an answer to a question than a proposal concerning the continuation of a story which is just unfolding."[19] A story "preserves and concentrates its strength and is capable of *releasing* it even after a long time."[20] Because a story in the oral tradition carries a clear partisan view but does not seek to explain everything, it retains the power of ambiguity, multiple interpretations, astonishment, thoughtfulness and, hence, the power to mobilize action. "The historian," on the other hand, Benjamin continues, "*is bound* to explain in one way or another the happenings with which he deals," and consequently gains certain insights, accuracy and information but loses the power of memory capable of unfolding itself as counsel appropriate to a place-specific living moment.[21]

Partha Chatterjee writes, "In the historical mode of recalling the past, the power to represent one-self is nothing other than political power itself."[22] And as we all know, power through the past extends to the present and into the future in terms of a group's or individual's ability to partake socially in the definition of problems and their solutions. While unconcerned about state-building in terms of national goals, rural protesters were aware that enunciation of their own goals and their concerns was important to their social well-being. For this reason, village dissidents of the New Policy era sought to articulate their place in the shifting network of social relations, and for this reason their part of the revolutionary story of modern China was and is of historic and contemporary significance. It is this articulation that I try to introduce into the historical record here. The conception of revolutionary process that I use in this work places rural dissent in the events preceeding and beyond the 1911 Revolution and argues from the premise that one revolutionary moment contains many revolutionary possibilities. So what peasants did at the end of the Qing may be pertinent not just to grasping problems of the late Qing or the Chinese revolution but the alternatives that stand as a critique of modernity.

Notes

1. Mao Zedong, *Zhongguo nongcun de shehui zhuyi gaochao* (The Socialist High Tide of Chinese Agriculture) (Beijing: Renmin chuban she, 1956), I, 3–5, 16.

2. These developments are covered in a series of articles carried in the *Yangzi wan bao* (The Yangtse Evening Post), November 1993.

3. Works on the geography and sociology of "place" by David Harvey, Neil Smith, Edward Soja, Doreen Massey, and Gillian Rose have drawn attention to the importance of not conflating place-based action with place-bound action. Thinking of social space in terms of the articulation of social relations, Massey writes that, "some of these relations will be, as it were, contained within the place; others will stretch beyond it, tying any particular locality into wider relations and processes in which other places are implicated too." *Space, Place and Gender*, (Minneapolis: University of Minnesota Press, 1994), 120, 141. A place-based analysis of social relations for historical inquiry requires that those relations be conceived of as "open and porous networks" that carry possibilities of perceiving both problems and political potentials in quite different terms than may be posed from other place-based locations in a social setting. (Massey, 121–22)

4. I am indebted to earlier works by Cai Shaoqing, Jean Chesneaux, Joseph Esherick, Winston Hsieh, Liu Tongjun, John Lust, and Edward Rhoads among others.

5. Li Zhuran's *Xinhai geming qiande qunzhong douzheng* (Mass struggles before the 1911 Revolution) (Beijing: Renmin chuban she, 1957) and the *Xinhai geming* in eight volumes compiled by Chai Degeng et al. (Shanghai: Renmin chuban she, 1957) are good examples of work in this genre.

6. See also Winston Hsieh, "Peasant Insurrection and the Marketing Hierarchy in the Canton Delta, 1911," in Mark Elvin and William G. Skinner, *The Chinese City Between Two Worlds* (Stanford: Stanford University Press, 1974), 138. Winston Hsieh writes of well-organized village-level collective action that sometimes coincided with the goals of secret societies and Republican army units operating in the area, but ultimately followed the interests of village communities and their leaders.

7. See Joseph W. Esherick, *Reform and Revolution in China: The 1911 Revolution in Hunan and Hubei* (Berkeley: University of California Press, 1976), 110–11; and Edward J. M. Rhoads, *China's Republican Revolution: The Case of Kwangtung, 1895–1913* (Cambridge: Harvard University Press, 1975), 175–79.

8. Liu Tongjun, ed., *Xinhai gemingqian Lai Hai Zhao kangjuan yongdong* (Anti-tax movements in Laiyang, Haiyang, and Zhaoyuan before the 1911 Revolution) (Beijing: Shehuikexue wenxian chuban she, 1989), 1.

9. For alternative interpretations see, Xiao Gongqin, "Qingmo xinzheng yu Zhongguo xiandaihua yanjiu" (Late Qing New Policy reforms and research on Chinese modernization), in *Zhanlu yu guanli* (Strategy and Management), 1993, no. 1, 61–66; *Xinhai geming sichao* (Research on the 1911 Revolution), ed. Jin Zhongli and Hu Xianwu, volume 2, (Shanghai: Renmin chuban she, 1991), 417–31. Also see Prasenjit Duara *Culture, Power and the State: Rural North China, 1900–42*, (Stanford: Stanford University Press, 1988), 245–48; Duara, *Rescuing History from the Nation: Questioning Narratives of Modern China* (Chicago: University of Chicago Press, 1995). "Knowledge and Power in the Discourse on Modernity," (1991) raises issues regarding the relationship between local political formations and discussions of modernity, but his other works cloud this inquiry.

10. Ralph Thaxton's *Salt of the Earth: The Political Origins of Peasant Protest and Communist Revolution in China* (Berkeley: University of California Press, 1997) is one of the few recent works in China's peasant history.

11. Joan Judge, *Print and Politics: "Shibao" and the Culture of Reform in Late Qing China* (Stanford: Stanford University Press, 1996), 204. Yeh Wenhsin, *Provincial Passages: Culture, Space, and the Origins of Chinese Communism* (Berkeley: University of California Press, 1996), 7. What each of these studies does not sufficiently consider is the symptomatic, limited understanding that their historical subjects carried with respect to the consequences of modernization for many rural groups, even as some of the reformers effectively manipulated for their own purposes an empathetic view of rural suffering under the reforms. Also see, Mary Backus Rankin, *Elite Activism and Political Trans-*

formation in China: Zhejiang Province, 1865–1911 (Stanford: Stanford University Press, 1986), 367, fn. 52; Rhoads, *China's Republican Revolution*, 179.

12. Edward A. McCord, "Local Military Power and Elite Formations: The Liu Family of Xingyi County, Guizhou" 162–188, and Lenore Barkan, "Patterns of Power: Forty Years of Elite Politics in a Chinese county," pp. 191–215 in *Chinese Local Elites and Patterns of Dominance* , ed. Joseph W. Esherick and Mary Backus Rankin, (Berkeley: University of California Press, 1990).

13. Wen-hsin Yeh, *Provincial Passages: Culture, Space, and the Origins of Chinese Communism* (Berkeley: University of California Press, 1996).

14. Boris Porchner, "Popular Uprising as Class War: The Revolt of the Nupieds," in *The Peasantry in the Old Regime* , ed. Isser Woloch (New York: Holt, Rinehart, Winston, 1970), 43; Barbara Alpern Engel, "Women, Men, and the Language of Peasant Resistance, 1870–1907," in *Cultures in Flux: Lower-Class Values, Practices, and Resistance in Late Imperial Russia*, ed. Stephen P. Frank and Mark D. Steinberg, (Princeton: Princeton University Press, 1994), 34.

15. Eric Hobsbawm, *Primitive Rebels: Studies in Archaic Forms of Social Movement in the 19th and 20th Centuries* (New York: Norton, 1965); E. P. Thompson, "Eighteenth-Century English Society: Class Struggle without Class?" *Social History*, 3 (1978); Charles Tilly, *From Mobilization to Revolution* (Reading, Mass.: Addison-Wesley, 1978).

16. James C. Scott, *The Moral Economy of the Peasant* (New Haven: Yale University Press, 1976). Also see Yuji Muramatsu, "Some Themes in Chinese Rebel Ideologies," in *The Confucian Persuasion,* ed. Arthur Wright (Stanford: Stanford University Press, 1960), 256.

17. Jurgen Habermas, *The Structural Transformation of the Public Sphere* (Cambridge: The MIT Press, 1981), xviii. The placement of rural dissent in the works by Rankin and Duara cited earlier are part of the application of concepts of "civil society" to late Qing developments. See also, "Symposium: 'Public Sphere'/'Civil Society' in China?" in *Modern China*, 18, no. 4 (1992) and 19, nos. 1 and 2 (1993). For a reply to this debate, see Arif Dirlik, "Civil Society/ Public Sphere in Modern China: As Critical Concepts versus Heralds of Bourgeois Modernity," *Zhongguo shehui kexue jikan* (Chinese Social Sciences Quarterly), no. 3 (summer, 1993), 10–22 (published simultaneously in Chinese and English). See also, Skocpol, Evan, and Rueschemeyer, who have discussed the dialectics of social dynamics and state-building in *Bringing the State Back In* (New York: Cambridge University Press, 1985), 355.

18. Partha Chatterjee, "Beyond the Nation? Or Within?" in *Economic and Political Weekly*, January 4–11, 1997, 33.

19. Walter Benjamin, "The Storyteller," in *Illuminations*, (London: Fontana, 1992), 86.

20. Ibid., 90 (italics added).

21. Ibid., 96 (italics added).

22. Partha Chatterjee, "Alternative Histories, Alternative Nations: Nationalism and Modern Historiography in Bengal," in *Making Alternative Histories: The Practice of Archaeology and History in Non-Western Settings*, ed. Peter R. Schmidt and Thomas C. Patterson (Santa Fe, N.M.: School of American Research Press, 1995), 229.

1

Anti–New Policy Rural Activism
in Historical Context:Taiping
and Boxer Preludes

> We must have New Policy, but we must also consider the people's
> livelihood . . . otherwise we will have great calamities of *Water
> Margin* type bandits gathering.
> —Dongfang zazhi (Eastern Miscellany)

Textbooks commonly present the Taiping and Boxer (Yihetuan) movements as dramatic national events that were eventually suppressed leaving no significant organizational or ideological traces. From the perspective of the culture of protest, nothing could be farther from the
truth. Major uprisings marked both time and place in a rural memory
of protest that was multilayered and multicentered, commemorating
specific events and leaders. Joseph Esherick has noted that "a glance at
any detailed map of northwestern Shandong will reveal villages called
Yihe (righteous harmony) scattered across the plains."[1] The number of
small towns in Sichuan and other areas called "Taiping" (great peace)
is equally noticeable. Writing on a peasant movement in Hebei and
Sichuan in 1920, Jean Chesneaux notes that groups who took up resistance against "merchants, militarists, and missionaries," utilized names
and expressions charged with history and glamour such as "Taiping"
and "Yihe."[2] Into the recollection of these social dramas, popular culture wove valuable information and inspiration, adaptable under particular circumstances to new experiences and problems.

Those who took up the cause of collective resistance in the post-
Boxer decade did so within this framework of rural history. The heroes
and heroines of *Water Margin* lore, folk religion, and past resistance
movements were all essential reference points for action in the present.
Ma Lishan, a member of the collective leadership popularly known as
the "four mountains" in the resistance at Laiyang, Shandong, was not

15

alone in his boyhood preference for reading stories about the Taiping heroes instead of studying the classics that might lead to social success.[3] Liao Jiumei, leader of a Red Lantern uprising in 1902 that spread to Weiyuan in Sichuan, declared herself to possess the powers of Guanyin (Goddess of Mercy), Sun Wukong (the Monkey King), Guangong (God of War), and Ling Guan (Spirit Official) among others all rolled into one.[4] Song Xunji and Gao Qiwang, involved in the Haiyang protests, were both reportedly avid readers of the *Water Margin* stories and other tales of rural resistance.[5] In his memoirs, educator Huang Yanpei tells of the Taiping stories he and other children listened to in Chuansha, Jiangsu.[6] At Laiyang, Shandong, in 1910, it was Boxer leader Zhu Hongdeng's successful act of defiance against the government in one of the opening battles of the uprising that inspired anti–New Policy leader Qu Shiwen.[7]

Nurtured on Taiping as well as Boxer stories, anti–New Policy protesters understood the dynamics of rural militancy by drawing on collectively preserved stories that not only reflected the ideals of dissident rural leaders and their supporters in defense of the unprivileged against misused authority but also carried practical lessons in how to navigate through the dangerous complexities of local political action. In some instances, protesters even unearthed weapons buried for safekeeping by previous resistance movements. At Zunhua, Zhili (Hebei), in 1907, in an area of the county south of the 1909 anti–New Policy movement, villagers successfully halted plans for a new orchard tax. In addition they demanded that the magistrate provide a memorial plaque for their fallen leader, Qin Erxiong. The plaque not only stated publicly in stone that taxes would not be raised but also honored Qin with the praise that he was among the great men of ancient times who were willing to die for humanity.[8] Local conflicts, Taiping heroes, Boxer leaders, and *Water Margin* episodes were all available in current memory as inspirational and tactical guides.

Perhaps one of the most dramatic cases of continuity between the Taiping Rebellion and the activism of the 1900 decade was the uprising in 1903 in Dongguan and Xianshan counties near Guangzhou led by Hong Quanfu (1834–1910).[9] Hong Quanfu was a leader in the Taiping army and was also a nephew of Hong Xiuquan, principal leader of the Taiping Rebellion. After the defeat of the Taiping armies in 1864, Hong Quanfu went to Hong Kong and from there traveled overseas. In 1901 at the age of sixty-seven, he was working for the Yi He Boating Company in Hong Kong and had regular connections with the Hongmen secret society in the area. Xie Zuantai and Li Jitang contacted Hong in 1902 after the deaths of two friends, Yang Quyun and Shi Jianru, both of whom had been involved in anti-Manchu activism and were murdered in 1901 by agents of the Qing government. Xie's father, Xie Richang, was an overseas merchant in Australia, who had long been a member of the Gelaohui. He had taught his son, who later joined the Furen Literary Society (*Furen wenshe*) and the Renew China Society (*Xingzhong hui*), to be critical of Qing officials.[10]

After a year of preparation in which Hong mobilized overseas Chinese support, and Greenwood (*lüiln*) groups from the North and East River areas joined in the planning, Hong's supporters decided to initiate an uprising by setting off dynamite at the Wanshou temple in Guangzhou. The dissidents picked New Year's Day (January 28) because Qing officials in the area would be preoccupied with celebrations. Triad and Greenwood groups from Dongquan and Xiangshan counties would attack Guangzhou from two directions. Hong Quanfu was senior general in charge of events. Twenty centers scattered throughout the Guangzhou area, including Henan, the region south of the Pearl River, worked with centers in Hong Kong and Guangzhou where the Xinyi Foreign Goods Shop gave cover to the conspirators. As Hong and others converged on Guangzhou, an informer alerted Qing authorities. Hong escaped eventually to Singapore, but twenty others were captured and tortured. Uprising troops on the East River, having received no news of the betrayal, launched their attack as scheduled and without expected support were easily defeated by the Qing army.[11]

The Hong Quanfu uprising was planned independently of Sun Zhongshan's Renew China Society. Xie Zuantai did not have confidence in Sun's leadership. Weapons for the uprising had been purchased from a German armaments company, which, after receiving payment, leaked information to Qing authorities. Planned under the banner of "The Great Ming Supports the Heavenly Kingdom," the Hong Quanfu uprising departed from old-style rural protests but was also at odds with plans for constitutional reform. The literature of the uprising stressed that eventually the European political model that Hong and others believed created division between the sovereign ruler and the people would be overcome and the populace would publicly select a virtuous president (*zongtong*) to manage state affairs.[12] The Taiping Heavenly Kindgom was seen as heir to the Ming rulers and foundation of new-style political reforms yet to be fully articulated.

By 1910, literally hundreds of uprisings related to struggle over the definiton of New Policy (*xinzheng*) reforms had occurred across China, filling the pages of *Eastern Miscellany* (*Dongfang zazhi*), *The Eastern Times* (*Shibao*), *National Customs* (*Guofengbao*) and numerous other periodicals with news items month after month.[13] It is estimated that 1,300 incidents of popular activism were officially recorded in newspaper sources and government records during the decade from 1901 to

1911.[14] In approximately one-third of these incidents, New Policy reforms were the protesters' clearly identifiable primary target. The remaining cases fell into two categories, anti-Christian incidents and price riots. Upon closer examination, the anti–New Policy protests often included anti-Christian sentiments and economic issues beyond taxes related directly to reform measures. Conversely, opposition to New Policy reforms was often in the background of cases that appeared to journalists and others as primarily anti-Christian or market price-related disturbances. Not since the decade of the 1840s, when tax uprisings spread across south and central China, had rural China seen such a precipitous rise in village activism.[15]

Labeling the years between 1901 and 1911 the post-Boxer decade or the pre-Republican Revolution decade gives the same chronological slot two very different orientations. The first periodization stresses the continuing development of dissident rural perspectives on village-level conditions in the context of changing national and international forces. In fact, new Boxer activity addressing these changing circumstances continued into the decade in areas outside of the Boxer movement of 1899–1900. The second periodization emphasizes the movement of Chinese capital toward national political change and international networks of industrial capital. From the latter perspective, which is the standard chronological representation, progressive interest groups, including chambers of commerce, modernized military units, foreign-educated students, and reformist provincial and county political groups were the central actors. Mobilized around their definition of modernist concerns, these groups pushed forward plans for a constitutional monarchy conceived by many as a balance between the feudal (*fengjian*) and bureaucratic (*junxian*) currents of China's political history.[16] Those who moved beyond reform stepped toward republican revolution, which would bring an end to the Chinese imperial order. Under the leadership of Sun Zhongshan (Sun Yat-sen), the Revolutionary Alliance (*Tongmenghui*) was established in 1905 to meet these goals.

The issue of democracy here is a slippery one. Inevitably linked to notions of developmentalism and modernity, the foundational role of restricted democratic political institutions in the history of modern industrial development became the focal point for constitutional reform in China. In 1901, most of the nations of the world that called themselves democratic did not allow full political participation of their adult populations. Yet there was always a debate about inclusion based on democracy's purported allegiance to equality. Issues arose around the problem of how to define citizenship and the terms for admission to this status. In China's case, reformers envisioned a new citizenry of enfranchised political and economic elites who would oversee modernization efforts while remaining attentive to popular sentiments. Within this vision there was a range of views.[17] Influenced primarily by statecraft schools within Chinese political thought and Euro-U.S. models mediated by Japanese approaches, the discussion of local self-government in China included Kang Youwei's notion of citizen (*gongmin*) as degree-holder;[18] Zhao Erxun's idea of commoners and degree-holders alike nominated by peers and selected by the state for subcounty office holding; and Yuan Shikai's position, which prevailed in 1909, of county-level rather than subcounty appointments drawing primarily degree-holders and their associates into the self-govenment councils.[19] The vision of Kang and Yuan regarding voting privileges was similar to the limited franchise allowed at the beginning of England's democratic reforms in 1832. Only with pressure from the working classes did England develop a more democratic political system through expansion of the franchise first to male urban workers in 1867 and male rural workers in 1889. Zhao's position, which lost out to Yuan, was potentially the most democratic of all. Each set of views invariably suggested different routes for political change itself.

The question the rural story raises is this: Does the pre-1911 Revolution interpretive framework with its own chronological structure accurately represent a large sector of village-level experience during these same years? Did rural social relations move toward or away from concepts of self-government in which the views of the common people and the poor would be respected? As the Chinese state proclaimed its attempt to centralize its authority on a base that presupposed a closer relationship between state and society, did the vast majority of rural residents experience inclusion into the new formations of self-government? In fact, national development under the New Policy reforms tended to shift power away from local rural leaders and transferred significant new coercive authority into the hands of their rivals among the lower degree-holders within the political economy of village and county life. Because the rural poor were not actors central to the reforms represented as democratic by some, rural protesters appear simply as obstructionist to the New Policy measures and tangential to the urban momentum among merchants, officials, and others, which culminated in the events of October 1911. In other words, the protesters appear one-dimensional and of little significance to the making and consequences of the 1911 Revolution, or China's turn-of-the-century history in general. Only if the Republican Revolution is considered a process drawing on conditions and perceptions of those conditions throughout all of China rather than an event of limited social and political dimensions is it possible to open the area of study around this pivotal historic moment to include the rural story of popular activism and, thereby, to understand more fully the revolution itself. Viewing the 1911 Revolution from this perspective, historian Cai Shaoqing has commented that "if there had been no organized struggle among the rural people, the 1911 Revolution could not have succeeded so quickly."[20] Cai concludes that because the revolutionaries' alliance with the peasant movement had no political and economic basis among the rural people and their social organizations, the 1911 Revolution failed in the end.[21]

The rural story of opposition to New Policy reforms had its own chronology—its own beginning and interpretive highlights. By definition, where groups begin their story is also a statement about how they understand the causes and origins of a social conflict. Narratives of popular resistance to late-Qing reforms begin with longstanding hardships and grievances of rural groups connected to immediate issues, which provoke a new sense of crisis. Those who became involved in protest sought to protect survival strategies connected to local control of resources and collective decision making. Narratives of national political reform and cultural modernization typically represented popular village culture in negative terms, justifying attempts to "modernize" and transform the organization of rural life in keeping with regionally defined goals under an umbrella of national development. Rural residents who fundamentally opposed the reform process introduced a critical perspective that examined state-building goals in terms of their cost to those who would be expected to pay the most and benefit the least relative both to their ability to pay and to the level of political representation they could expect to gain within the new order. The folk Buddhist vegetarian sisterhood at Chuansha, whose customs were so appalling to local reform-minded students, more effectively mobilized support on behalf of low-income rural women weavers and others in similar socioeconomic groups than would the new self-government offices promoted by the county reformers. Within the framework of an oppositional rural chronology, the activism of the post-Boxer decade, far from celebrating New Policy reform and the prospect of constitutional democracy, was a marker around which coalesced another moment in the memory of popular dissent. Those village inhabitants who militantly opposed the reforms drew together antigovernment grievances of the variety generated during the Taiping Rebellion and antiforeign issues brought to national attention by the Boxer Uprisings into a new rural analysis of China's early twentieth-century crisis.

By 1901–11, Boxers of the 1899–1900 movement, who had grown up on market theater performances about martial heroes,[22] were themselves a part of the repertoire of local drama through which the leaders of the anti–New Policy protests gained their education into the values and codes of conduct befitting those who challenge authority. After

1912, local anti–New Policy leaders were gradually incorporated through storytelling into rural culture. Li Shoushan, a member of the central leadership in the Laiyang protest, who continued to live in the county until his death in 1942, was known as a good-natured, friendly person who in his later years especially enjoyed telling stories to groups of small children who would gather around his house. Very often those stories were about peasant leader Qu Shiwen and how he led rebellion in the neighboring towns.[23] Each new round of stories connected with but also added to village lore. Each case brought with it the particular circumstances and issues of its own historical moment, allowing for continuity and innovation in the popular culture of resistance. Specific items on the agenda of rural dissent during the era of constitutional reform included problems related to taxation and foreign presence, both of which tended to erode the material and cultural foundations of a self-defining and struggling agrarian population. The origins of these issues had roots in a century of experience highlighted by the Taiping and Boxer dissent, alongside of which the movements against New Policy reforms took their place in a legacy of rural protest. I have situated the anti–New Policy activism in the post-Boxer era in order to avoid the teleology of the pre-1911 Revolution framework, which marginalizes these expressions of rural dissent. The post-Boxer periodization is not ideal but permits fuller recognition of the different stances toward the New Policy reforms.

A Century of Rebellion, 1796–1911: Antigovernment and Antiforeign Issues in Rural Political Discourse

The post-Boxer decade of rural protests, while shaped immediately by place-based conditions and personalities, had a lineage with branches touching every major movement of rural dissent for the previous century. Eight years of rural revolt across north and central China, known as the White Lotus Rebellion (1796–1804), was the first signal of widespread discontent in the Qing period (1644–1911).[24] Prior to industrial Western European intervention into the body politic, the White Lotus movement raised a rural agenda in the language of folk Buddhism. Excessive taxation and growing rural impoverishment were the central issues. White Lotus scriptures printed at the end of the sixteenth century and passed from generation to generation within White Lotus families "contained the Eternal Mother's keys to understanding history and truth and were believed to have great value and power."[25] According to these scriptures, the Maitreya Buddha (Buddha of the Future) would come down to earth at some time and lead a "great undertaking" (*dashi*) to bring peace and prosperity to those who lived by justice.[26] Military campaigns to suppress the White Lotus severely strained central government resources already weakened by large-scale cases of administrative graft.

Most groups that adopted the Maitreyist beliefs and practices did not involve themselves in rebellion. This was the case with most heterodox groupings whether they were secret societies or religious sects. When confronted with widespread rural revolt, government officials were quick to see White Lotus activism, when, in fact, the connections to White Lotus teachings could be tangential at most. B. J. Ter Haar in his study of White Lotus teachings notes that a consequence of this governmental readiness to see White Lotus adherents under every rebellion was the stereotyping of all Maitreyist teachings as potentially rebellious, when they were not. "The history of persecution of 'heterodox groups' is, naturally, quite distinct from the history and sociology of religious groups," writes Ter Haar.[27] And yet, this does not mean that at certain times and places this perception of connection between White Lotus teachings and political activism did not have some basis in reality. White Lotus teachings could and did lend themselves to the rural discourse of dissent, just as some sects of Christianity before and after the Protestant Reformation in Western Europe moved between oppositional and nonresistant locations in the body politic.

During the decade of anti–New Policy activism, there were many instances of linkage between White Lotus teachings and rural dissent. From the perspective of White Lotus groups functioning within the range deemed orthodox by official standards, these expressions of White Lotus teachings may have seemed transmogrified versions of teachings, just as Anabaptist views seemed to Luther. But they were certainly within the range of White Lotus interpretations. These connections during the New Policy era were themselves made by multiple sources independent of government records. At Laiyang, Lü Conglü, a student of the classics turned village teacher and later part of the inner circle of tax resistance leaders, seriously studied the Eight Trigram (*bagua*) tradition in connection with issues of strategy.[28] The Eight Trigram Uprising of 1813 drew on these teachings, which were associated with White Lotus beliefs. At Chuansha, the lay Buddhist vegetarian sect that initiated the anti–New Policy reforms created goddess images from the cultural resources available to them through the Buddhist White Lotus practices.[29] These images were in turn at the heart of an identity that could be mobilized for political activism. Perhaps in these cases and other cases we have examples of the sociopolitical thread of dissent in the White Lotus, which becomes more visible as a potential for dissent during a decade when the political focus is squarely on the tension between a new discourse on constitutional government and its contradictions with peasant perceptions of organization and ideology supportive of rural well-being.

Rural martial resistance to foreign presence had one of its first major recorded instances in the events at the village of Sanyuanli in 1841 during the Opium War (1839–42). Lineage leaders and peasants alike mobilized resistance to British military activity through people's militias.[30] In this same area of south China in the aftermath of the Opium War and growing bureaucratic decay, rural activism in the decade of the 1840s gave rise to widespread tax revolts. Directed primarily at county- and subcounty-level tax collectors and their associates, these revolts addressed issues regarding the downward spiral of indebtedness, which led to a rise in tenancy and day labor conditions of livelihood. While the White Lotus rebels had grievances resulting from fiscal and administrative mismanagement, in the 1840s in addition to administrative manipulation of tax records to the detriment of the most financially vulnerable families, overtaxation, high rents, and devalued copper cash were now also connected to China's opium-related imbalance of trade. Left unresolved and worsening, these problems proved a harbinger to the Taiping Rebellion (1851–64), a civil war that devastated central China and placed tax resistance and challenges to government authority squarely on the national political agenda.

Embodying issues of ethnicity, gender, anti-Qing sentiment, and anti-landlordism, the Taiping movement in adapting to post–Opium War conditions expanded the rural discourse. A pro-Qing observer offered this view of the relationship between ethnicity and gender among the Taiping forces.

Among the bandits there are female soldiers, all of whom are relatives of the Taiping kings. Being of vile minorities such as the Yao and the Zhuang, they grew up in caves and run around with bare feet and turbaned heads. They can scale steep cliffs with ease, and their courage surpasses that of men. On the battlefield, they carry weapons and fight at close quarters. Government troops have been defeated by them in battle.[31]

The leader of the Taiping Rebellion, Hong Xiuquan, and the movement's earliest supporters hailed primarily from the Hakka minority communities in south China.[32] Particularly during periods of crisis, farmers of Han ethnicity would have been inclined to identify along class lines and across ethnic boundaries with minorities, such as the Hakkas, who shared common socioeconomic status and grievances against landlords and officials, typically Han by background. For reasons of economic necessity and family demands for farm labor, many rural women regardless of ethnicity did not bind their feet or only partially bound them. Han families among this group might be more comfortable with the Hakka custom of natural feet for women, a custom perceived as repulsive or even barbaric to many upper-class Chinese, men and women alike.

As articulated by its initial rural leaders, Taiping ideology also included adaptations of recently encountered Protestant Christian thought. It was in part the Christian element that allowed Taiping leaders to imagine a revolutionary alternative to state political ideology, but the social experience of ethnic minorities and peasant farmers plus themes from dissident rural culture were the mainstay of the movement's alternative social vision. A Taiping primer for the propagation of Taiping ideology, which counseled believers to worship the Christian God and follow a modified Ten Commandments, never became fully integrated into the village level of the movement especially in central and north China. Many of the leaders of the movement were more involved with local shaman practices and folk ideas about the spiritual realm than about the details of Christian beliefs. What all groups did share was a common perception of the hardships of rural life caused by landlords and officials who used their authority without sufficient regard for the welfare of moderately well-to-do and marginalized rural groups.

Given the animosity with which Christianity was viewed by many participants in rural activism by 1900, it is noteworthy that the first major response to Christianity in the nineteenth century was from a rural area, and it was positive. Taiping leader Hong Xiuquan's claim to be the younger brother of Jesus Christ was, however, an adaptation of Christianity that Protestants and Catholics alike found blasphemous. Differing from later manifestations of Christian presence in China, Taiping Christianity was in the hands of Chinese rural dissidents rather than European and American missionaries and Chinese who sought privilege through foreign associations. By the time Lu Fengqi (1880–1961) was quoting Taiping slogans at Laiyang in 1910, the Christian element in Taiping origins had all but evaporated in the climate of post-Taiping rural China. "All under heaven are one family, enjoy together peace and tranquility," was invoked by Lu not to worship the Christian god but to inspire a movement intended to relieve villagers of the burdens heaped upon them by foreigners and local officials alike.[33]

Beginning in south China in 1851, the Taiping movement left only the most northern parts of the country untouched. Each of the counties in this volume was, at most, within one day's journey from the Taiping front. Prior to the rise of the movement in 1851, Hong Xiuquan, primary leader of the rebellion, went on a tour across Guangdong and

Guangxi in May 1844 taking him through Lianzhou (Lianshan), Guangdong. Hong seems to have gone out of his way to make a stop there on
his journey to preach his ideas and begin the process of gathering support from among those rural inhabitants suffering under new taxes.[34]
Taiping and Nien rebel forces under a coalition headed by Taiping
leader Lai Wenguang passed through Laiyang, Shandong, in 1867. Taiping general Shi Dakai carried out a series of campaigns in 1857
through 1863 in counties on the southern boundary of Weiyuan, Sichuan.[35] In some areas of Sichuan around Tieshan (Iron Mountain)
Boxer forces later fought at the same places where Taiping battles had
previously taken place.[36] Lasting thirteen years, the Taiping civil war
almost brought the Manchu Qing dynasty to a close. After rebels established a capital at Nanjing, conflicts among the rebel leaders along with
the difficulties of coordinating a social movement under conditions of
constant warfare greatly weakened the rebels' efforts to fulfill their revolutionary goals of among other things land redistribution and abolition
of the Chinese classics as a prequisite for political office holding. Foreign intervention on the side of the imperial government was the critical
factor that gave the final advantage to the government's suppression
campaigns. British steamships transported troops down the Yangzi
River just in time to save Shanghai, foreigners and Chinese alike, from
Taiping rebel attack.

Destruction resulting from the civil war between Taiping rebels and
Qing government forces temporarily relieved the mix of pressures produced by administrative corruption, fiscal shortages, and population
growth. In the thirty-five years between 1865 and 1900 as each of these
problems regenerated itself, a new set of experiences also took root in
the rural areas, shaped in part by the introduction of ideas and technologies from European industrial civilization. The unstable administrative
and economic recovery of the post-Taiping years combined with accel-
erated commercialization in the late 1880s and 1890s, characterized by
general growth in cotton market activity and decline in sugar and tea
commodity exchange. Philip Huang's study of the peasant economy in
north China points to a rise of wage labor in the countryside producing
a partial proletarianization of the peasantry during the first three decades of the twentieth century. Under general conditions that Huang describes as "involuted underdevelopment," peasants were left with the
hardships of entrepreneurial commercialization but few of the means
by which to benefit from new market opportunities.[37] Some areas in the
lower Yangzi, a heartland of China's rice agriculture, recorded a shift
from 90 percent owner-cultivators (*zigengnong*) in 1888 to 26 percent
owner-cultivators and 74 percent tenants and part owner-cultivators
(*banzigengnong*) in 1905, continuing to drop to 11.7 percent *zigeng-*

nong with a rise of tenants and *banzigengnong* to 88.3 percent in 1914.[38] Overtaxation, resulting from both domestic and foreign causes, was a critical factor linking changing relations among peasants, state authorities, and local elite members. This pattern of worsening conditions for small owner-cultivators amidst intensifying commercialization characterized rural society across China by 1900.

The Boxer movement of 1899–1900 foregrounded antiforeign issues, but antigovernment sentiments were not entirely absent from rural political discourse in proximity to the Boxer activism. While the preponderance of slogans and official testimony make it clear that anti-Christian and antiforeign pronouncements dominated, the dialectic between antigovernment and antiforeign issues continued to find expression in social analysis during these years. The following is from a purported Boxer poster displayed at Tongzhou, Hebei [Zhili] in 1900:

The Chinese Empire has been celebrated for its sacred teaching. It explained heavenly truth and human duties, and its civilizing influence spread as an ornament over rivers and mountains.

But in an unaccountable manner all this has been changed. For the past five or six generations bad officials have been in office, bureaus have been opened for the sale of office, and only those who had money to pay for it have been allowed to hold position in the government. . . . An Official position can only be obtained at the price of silver. The Emperor covets the riches of his Ministers, these again extort from the lower ranks of the mandarinate and the lower mandarins in turn (by the necessity of their positions) must extort from the people. The whole populace is sunk in wretchedness, and all the officials are spoilers of their food.

The condition of the yamen is unspeakable. In every market and in every guild nothing can be done unless money is spent. The officials are full of schemes none of which are in accordance with the three principles. Having forfeited their heaven-derived disposition they are unreasonable and unregulated. They are all alike—ill-gotten wealth is their one object. . . .

Now in anger the heavenly Powers are sending down multitudes of spirits to earth to make inquiry of all, both high and low. The Emperor himself, the chief offender, has had his succession cut off and is childless. . . .

Greater calamities still have overtaken the nation. Foreign devils come with their teaching, and converts to Christianity, Roman Catholic and Protestant, have become numerous. These churches are without human relations, but being most cunning have attracted all the greedy and covetous as converts, and to an unlimited degree they have practiced oppression, until every good official has been corrupted, and covetous foreign wealth has become their servant. So telegraphs have been established, foreign rifles and guns have been manufactured, and machine-shops have been a delight to their evil nature. Locomotives, balloons, electric lamps, the foreign devils think excellent. Though these foreigners ride in sedans unbefitting their rank, China yet reads them as barbarians of whom God disapproved, and He is sending down spirits and genii for their destruction.

The first of these powers which has already descended is the Light of the Red Lamp, and the Volunteer Associated Fists who will have a fight with the devils.[39]

Translated by missionary Arthur H. Smith, the scope of this analysis is striking. The current problem is clearly considered to predate the arrival of foreigners, and, according to this account, has its origins in the Chinese body politic. The Emperor is the "chief offender," and the bureaucratic officials and their associates are not far behind. The foreigners with their offensive technologies, religions, and covetous ways exacerbate the errosion of social values begun in the early 1600s, possibly with Manchu rule, according to this analysis. If Joseph Esherick is correct in his conclusions that the Boxer movement at its origins was anti-Christian first and foremost, then antiforeign, and not antigovernment or anti-Qing to any significant extent, then technically this poster might not be considered a Boxer source. However, if the Boxer movement were viewed in broader perspective, not just the groups examined by Esherick but also collatoral protests inspired by the Boxer ferment, there certainly were signs of antigovernment challenges at the start of the decade.

Those who initially participated in Boxer activism in 1899–1900 expressed no consistent antigovernment views, but as Boxer activities spread after 1901, this would change. Esherick demonstrates that the Boxers of 1899–1900 consisted of groups of young men who began to study boxing as a way of protecting their families and communities during times of social disorientation. Many became involved in spirit healing in 1898–99 when floods and famine destroyed harvests and led to the spread of cholera and other diseases in western Shandong. In Esherick's judgment, the Boxers' goal was "to restore the sovereignty and revitalize the energies of the Qing—conceived as the representative of Chinese tradition and Chinese culture—and to rid China of the foreigners and their religion. They had no fundamental quarrel with the Qing, or with any Chinese officials for that matter."[40] The fusion of imperial and village perspectives that this suggests denies the space from which a critique of the government could emerge, a critique that becomes quite apparent in the Boxer groups who became active to the west of Hebei and Shandong in the post-1901 period. Esherick writes, "the contradiction of fighting Qing troops under a 'Revive the Qing' flag is in fact not very surprising. History is replete with examples of rebels who conceived themselves as loyal to the monarch; and the Box-

ers were not even rebels."[41] It seems incongruous that people could put
their life on the line in battle against government officials and not think
that at least a part of their quarrel was with some of the Chinese officials. If this did not appear as a contradiction in 1899, it would by 1902.
And if the Boxer groups were not rebels in 1900, they were by 1907.

By 1910, antiofficial sentiments among new Boxer groups were loud
and clear, perhaps a consequence of a retrospective evaluation of the
government's failure to assist the Boxers in 1900 and the additional
experiences of the New Policy era. Boxer activity in Sichuan, after the
suppression of Boxer groups in Zhili and Shandong, was often pre-
sumed to be primarily anti-Christian, but in many cases the emphasis
of these groups had shifted after 1901 to incorporate both antiforeign
and antigovernment protests. Red Lantern groups at Kaixian, Sichuan,
in 1907–8 raised the banner of protest with the intention to, "Destroy
all wine taxes and meat transit stations . . . launch an offensive against
the county seat."[42] Wine was a common retail commodity selected for
taxation in many locales to fund New Policy–related activities. The
meat transit stations were possibly a remnant of the *likin* (goods in
transit) tax introduced to raise government revenue for Taiping suppression campaigns but not always discontinued as intended after the defeat
of the rebels. Grievances piled upon grievances. In other cases, such as
Tongxiang and Shangyu in Zhejiang in 1908, there was genuine confusion by tax protesters about the difference between Christian schools
and government new schools, the latter of which was their primary target.[43] Increasingly into the 1901–11 decade, dissident statements identified local Han Chinese merchants, tax farmers, and landlords along with
their associates in government as the parties primarily responsible for
foreigners' intrusions, whether such intrusions resulted from official
weakness, ineptitude, or collaboration. While the immediate experience
of government mismanagement was at the county level, criticism did
on occasion rise to the national level as well especially under the New
Policy program that linked these levels—foreigner, Han, Manchu, magistrate, and governor—in one project.

The generation that led the New Policy protests was born around the
time of or shortly after the Taiping movement and had grown to matur-
ity by the time of the late Qing commercialization and events of the
Boxer movement. Qu Shiwen was born in 1849 and recalled Boxer
leader Zhu Hongdeng's defeat of government troops as a milestone in
the evolution of his political consciousness. Born in southern Shandong
to a poor landless agricultural laborer, Zhu became a healer and was
known for his effective organizational skills. He was reputedly popular
among poor villagers and become one of the most famous Boxer leaders after joining the spirit boxers.[44] Experience fighting government

troops during the Boxer Uprising and government policies in the aftermath of the Boxer Protocol signed in 1901 resolved much of the ambiguity about those Qing government officials who increasingly seemed in the pocket of foreigners and willing to bring hardship on rural China in order to placate and probably benefit themselves from the foreigners. Many rural residents who themselves had little financial cushion saw the large indemnity that the protocol levied on the government and the reforms the foreigners demanded as evidence of weakness and corruption for which someone would have to pay. In the dialectics of rural political discourse, the experience of the Boxer Uprising and the subsequent New Policy reforms brought into focus rural antigovernment views, which had not been a dominant feature of Boxer activism in 1899–1900.

Structural and Fiscal Challenges of New Policy Reform: Rural Political Economy within National Modernist Policies

Mandated by the Boxer Protocol of 1901, the administrative reforms known as the New Policy (*xinzheng*) immediately raised debate within Chinese political and intellectual circles. The reform process began with an imperial decree issued January 29, 1901, announcing that the government would conduct a review of "all dynastic regulations, national administration, official affairs, matters related to people's livelihood, modern schools, systems of examination, military organization, and financial administration."[45] The decree called for proposals from officials on how to proceed with reform in these areas. Central to this process would be the creation of a constitutional government with appropriate educational, military, and legal supports. The concept of "self-government" (*zizhi*), which was at the heart of the New Policy reforms, had its immediate roots in nineteenth-century discussions about reform, which themselves drew on literature from earlier centuries. Nineteenth-century reformers generally believed that the route to better and more effective government was to close the gap between public opinion and those who set policy. Conceived of as a communications problem, government corruption would be addressed by bringing into official status that ever-growing number of lower-degree holders and educated men who had no legitimate prospects of upward mobility in the political system and were caught in a bottleneck for advancement in the political hierarchy. The language that scholar-officials and intellectuals used to talk about government reform, both in the nineteenth and early twentieth centuries, relied heavily on the concept of "public opinion" (*yulun*). In the aftermath of the devastating Taiping Rebellion, statesman Feng Guifen in the 1880s had raised the notion in an effort to address problems of corruption among county government personnel. He proposed the creation of a new stratum of subcounty officials who would be selected by a consensus among the rural populace, approved by the magistrate's office, and held accountable to officials outside of the county. Feng Guifen imagined a two-tiered system of subcounty leaders, selected by groups of one hundred and one thousand families, respectively. Selected from among commoners, these subcounty officials would be in charge of routine legal affairs and other local matters.[46] Ideally, officials would be selected by village and market town communities (*she* and *xiang* units), allowing the place-based processes of leadership selection to work. Feng hoped this would provide a mechanism for incorporating "public opinion" into the political decision-making process. "Public opinion," however, would remain vaguely defined in terms of who exactly constituted the public.

The context for constitutional reform was a growing sense of urgency shaped by late nineteenth-century Chinese debates about reform as an extension of China's political heritage, the realities of imperialist aggression in East Asia, including the Sino-Japanese War in 1895, foreign intervention in the Boxer movement, and the Russo-Japanese War in 1905. Under these circumstances, it seemed to many that only thoroughgoing constitutional reform could strengthen China's standing in the world. The question was, what kind of reform? Between 1902 and 1905, a series of prototypes for self-government was developed by provincial leaders. Zhao Erxun in Shanxi and Hunan provinces; Zhang Zhidong and Yuan Shikai in Hubei and Zhili; Duanfang in Hubei, Jiangsu, and Hunan; and Cen Chunxua in Shanxi, Sichuan, and Guangdong all sought to begin reform in the areas where they served as provincial governors or other high-ranking posts. Beginning in 1902, Zhao Erxun proposed plans for local self-government that built on and modified some of Feng's views regarding community-selected and government-approved subcounty officials. Zhao's proposal suggested that degree-holders should be allowed to enter these subcounty offices. Both Feng and Zhao agreed that selecting respected, upright individuals for such positions was the most important principle.[47]

While the experimentation with reform started at the provincial level, the national government struggled through these years to centralize policy making. The Empress Dowager Cixi acted as imperial head of state during the last decade of Qing rule until her death in 1908, and the Xuantong emperor reigned for the remaining three years of the dynasty as the last emperor of China. In 1905, conservative factions at court finally authorized five imperial ministers to go abroad for the express purpose of studying modern politics and determining the most appro-

priate forms of consititutional monarchy for China. By 1906, an imperial edict announced plans that would over the next ten years prepare
China for constitutional government. At this point in the national discussion, local self-government became defined as a hierarchy of councils with the county as the smallest unit. Yuan Shikai as governor of
Zhili province appointed on August 29, 1906, the Self-Government Bureau of Tianjin Prefecture. Almost all of its members had studied in
Japan, and as Roger Thompson has noted, they would "emphasize a
Japanese model for reform at the expense of traditional statecraft ideas
for local administrative reform."[48] For all of the pilot plans and materials collected from abroad, the collective decision of the national leaders
was to proceed with an approach that would vest new political authority
in a county elite based on a limited franchise. If all went well, a national
parliament was expected to open in 1917, although it was clear by 1908
that the National Assembly would be a consultative body with no legis-
lative power of its own. For three years between 1906 and 1908, provincial officials sought to adjust general guidelines to specific circumstances in an effort to implement self-government.[49] After bureaucratic
delays around the time of the deaths of the Guangxu emperor and the
Empress Dowager Cixi in 1908, the imperial government finalized regulations for county-level reforms. With many provisional provincial assemblies functioning by 1909, the focus shifted to the final phase of the
New Policy era from 1909 to 1911. This phase called for the establishment of county-level local self-government bureaus, new schools, and
new police offices. A census would be taken to determine voting and
office-holding privileges, and funds and real estate would have to be
designated for the new projects. Neither national policies nor funding
mechanisms were forthcoming from Beijing. The variety of methods
evolved at the county level to undertake these projects reflected the
diverse patterns of place-based political and economic power. Debate
about how to carry out these reforms was fostered by the myriad experiences of reform itself.

Almost immediately, the explosive consequences of the New Policy
measures became apparent. By 1909, the principle of public discussion,
which had been compromised with Yuan Shikai's move toward a Japanese model of reform, would go forward with or without institutional
sanctions and across a wide range of social strata. Liang Qichao, who
had cosponsored the constitutional and educational reforms proposed
by Kang Youwei in 1898, saw the danger of the New Policy reforms
once they were under way. A 1910 article in the journal *National Customs* (*Guofengbao*), whose editorial policy was strongly influenced by
Liang and his supporters, observed that given the extent of popular rural
opposition to reform, intellectuals and others would do well to rethink

their position and consider that reform in the hands of corrupt elites could be robbery—worse than no reform at all.[50] The anarchist journal *Natural Justice* (*Tianyi bao*) also carried articles critical of modernist state policies in the post-Boxer decade.[51] In several issues, anarchist Liu Shipei argued that "autocracy is better than constitutionalism" because the imperial state allowed for greater freedom from political interference. By contrast, the emerging modern nation-state with its political and economic changes seemed nothing less than despotic. While some anarchists saw movement toward constitutional government as progressive, in Liu's view New Policy reforms were an example of excessive enthusiasm for western ways and would only further weaken China. Liu wrote that,

> The ruling elite of the country follows the western way of government excessively. . . . No matter whether this theory was good or not, even if it is earnestly implemented, it can be nothing more than the policy for an ill nation. People have become benefit oriented these days. This seeking after benefits is a convenience for a few people. This is true in every county. . . . Examining the situation after the New Policy, we will find that all those who benefited are capitalists of the new party (*xindang*). Most of the population will be worse off.[52]

Liu's evaluation of the impact of New Policy reforms on rural society accurately described the reality behind the rising tide of rural antireform activism: New schools favored the rich and new local self-government bureaus enhanced the power of the elite groups while both contributed to a concentration of wealth in the hands of the few. When news of the 1906 edict announcing the intention to establish constitutional government was heard throughout China, officials, teachers, journalists, merchants, chamber of commerce members, and degree-holders launched celebrations in Shanghai, Canton, Swatow, Beijing, and Tianjin.[53] There was a shared sense that these reforms would finally empower this new entrepreneurial elite. A similar critique of the modernist project guided village leaders in their defense of rural society and opposition to New Policy measures.

Forces at work within the post-Boxer, pre-1911 Revolution decade were on a collision path. The practice of rural dissent embedded in village culture and organization was a challenge ready to happen to the new notions of constitutional government embedded in the new chambers of commerce and their political networks. In villages with leading families not engaged in injurious reform activities, those recognized as trusted village leaders, *cunzhang*, might represent rural oppositional views against county reform managers and officials. In villages dominated by individuals with interests contrary to dissident demands, resistance was often taken up by leaders of extravillage associations, such as the *lianzhuanghui* (village federation) or *gelaohui* (elder brother association). There was, however, no perfect fit between social status and moral or political outlook. Reform managers without substantial family resources and connections outside their county might be more locally rapacious with regard to village resources, but they might also be more protective of rural livelihood and aware of the need to find an alternative way to meet the crisis born of both domestic and foreign sources. Even in counties where reformers did not themselves burden local taxpayers, the reforms legitimized the actions of others who demanded extra miscellaneous and retail surcharges. Lenore Barkan's study of Rugao county in Jiangsu province demonstrates the effectiveness with which county elite members commanding substantial wealth and higher degree-holding pedigrees could use their own funds to sponsor new schools and a chamber of commerce, successfully moving those who benefited from the reforms toward institutional modernization and capital investments connected to overseas markets, including enterprises as diverse as a steamship company and a ham factory with outlets in the United States.[54] In Rugao county in 1910, even despite conscientious efforts by some to alleviate the potential increased tax burden resulting from reform measures, several thousand rural residents organized to oppose census-taking activities linked specifically to self-government plans.[55] The short- and long-term costs of these reforms and their political ramifications for some rural constituencies inevitably became most apparent through the activities of those who used the reforms to encroach directly and aggressively on rural resources.

By 1900, China's imperial government was managed by a sophisticated bureaucracy with over two thousand years of history. Over the centuries, the Chinese state had evolved into a highly centralized and hierarchical political system. A distinctive feature of the Chinese state was that higher-level degree-holding was normally a prerequisite for appointment to one of the nine thousand statutory posts and roughly thirty thousand additional official assignments.[56] All appointees, whether for national, provincial, or county government positions, were drawn primarily from a pool of degree-holders who had attained at least the provincial (*juren*) or metropolitan (*jinshi*) degree in the imperial examination system. Prior to taking the provincial examination, one was generally required to pass the prefectural (*shengyuan*) degree, which conferred some privileges on the holder but did not entitle him to official appointment.[57] Numerically, the scholar-officials (*shenshi*), including all degree-holders and their immediate family members, were only 1.9 percent of the total population by 1900.[58] Many villages had no degree-holding connections at all. Although governing eighteen provinces and approximately 1,500 counties, the Chinese state itself impinged infrequently on the daily lives of the ordinary people. The county magistrate, the only official who directly governed the populace, was responsible on an average for approximately 300,000 persons. Because of the magistrate's heavy workload and his unfamiliarity with the locale in which he was stationed, the routine business of local government, including record keeping and staffing the yamen offices, became the province of clerks and runners who composed the subbureaucracy. While the local government was highly centralized in its official structure, many of its functions were conducted by persons over whom the state exercised only a minimum of control. Responsibility for tax collection, road repairs, maintenance of a public granary, and so forth were typically farmed out to prominent county families with lower degree-holding status at least and/or financial means.

Once eligibility for office holding under the New Policy was established, reform managers appointed by the magistrate were supposed to hold elections for self-government officials in each of the county's major subdivisions. Officials from the subdivision elected representatives for the countywide self-government bureau. Persons called upon by the magistrate to oversee these proceedings were generally already prominent in local affairs. As discussed above, the quality of county elite members, who formed the pool from which self-government officials were selected, varied from county to county. Variables included the density of degree-holders, the relative influence of lower and higher degree-holders, the strength of the magistrate and his subbureaucracy, and the amount of collusion between merchant degree-holders and yamen personnel. The same self-government officials also oversaw the establishment of new schools and police bureaus.

The Qing government, attempting to make the best of its beleaguered situation, planned to use constitutional reforms to strengthen its own position against the growing power of provincially oriented elite groups, products of both the Taiping suppression and the development of treaty port cities in the aftermath of the Opium War. The government's strategy was flawed by its combination of innovation and business as usual. Through an electoral system, county-level elite members would be endowed with new positions of political, fiscal, and coercive power. In theory, this would have made the new police and self-government heads beholden to central authority for their newfound status. In theory also, through these reforms the central government would finally have converted for its own purposes that huge reservoir of discontented, upwardly mobile but thwarted talent that collected around the halls of county government. While the overall plan was parliamentary, the budgeting process was imperial. The central government provided no central financing for the New Policy institutions. A further erosion of the social foundations of central political authority was the only result. In keeping with traditional methods of government financing, the central government expected the counties themselves to raise the revenue required for self-government bureaus, schools, and police offices. The county as a result often became an arena of intense political strife rather than a base of support for the national government.

The potential sources of conflict were numerous. Would new taxes be levied, thereby increasing the taxpayers' burden, or would self-government officials be given a share of existing revenue, in which case funds already allocated for such public works as local dike repairs would be cut? If new taxes were collected, would they be collected through traditional channels by the clerks and runners, or would new agencies be established for the purpose? There was no attempt to standardize the financing of the New Policy programs, and there were no vehicles for doing so in any event. Economic repercussions of the New Policy reforms placed a growing burden on rural taxpayers. In order to pay for the reforms, miscellaneous taxes and surcharges were significantly increased in most counties. In 1907, the government collected 5.8 million cash (copper coinage) in surcharges, and by 1909–10, surcharges amounted to sixteen million cash annually.[59] This included the new miscellaneous levies on land and property deeds and a great variety of new taxes on such things as pigs, melons, peanuts, and dozens of sundry commodities. A further source of difficulty for rural taxpayers was the introduction in 1900 of a copper coin known as the ten-cash coin (*tongyuan*), which was then heavily depreciated. By 1910, this coin had essentially replaced the previously used copper coin (*zhiqian*), also known as standard cash. Exchange quotations between the silver tael, in which land taxes were calculated, and the old *zhiqian* copper coin were discontinued in the same year.[60]

All of this worked to the disadvantage of rural taxpayers who, when they paid their taxes, found that *tongyuan* were accepted at only 70 percent of the value at which they had received them for goods sold in the marketplace. The few *zhiqian* still in circulation were accepted at only 30 percent of the *tongyuan* rate. Numerous rural disturbances in 1910 demanded that copper cash not be devalued. The real tax burden increased not only because of multiplying surcharges but also because all taxes were collected in devalued copper cash.[61] Unlike the deflationary period that accompanied the pre-Taiping rural disturbances, a time of inflation was the setting for the New Policy antitax movements. Because of inflation, price increases stayed ahead of tax increases until 1906–8. The decline in purchasing power that resulted in these years was felt all the more keenly because the late nineteenth century had been a period of economic stability throughout most of rural China. During the last years of the Qing, taxpayers found their gains of the 1880s and 1890s severely eroded by the demands of reform—sudden tax increases to be paid in a devalued currency at a rate that continued to rise relative to the higher prices that farmers received at market for their goods.[62] Economic uncertainty and portents of further decline made the post-Boxer decade an unsettling time for commoner taxpayers all over China.

A highly commercialized society in which prices were rising and per capita consumption steadily increasing made this growth of nonagricultural taxation possible. In 1853, a tax on goods in transit (*likin*) was established to finance provincial military campaigns against the Taiping. New commercial surcharges were gradually added to the land tax, causing it almost to double between the late eighteenth century and 1908.[63] While the percentage of the total land tax that was set by quota decreased from 80.7 percent in 1753 to 53.1 percent in 1908, the proportion of the land tax that came from commercial surcharges increased from less than 20 percent to approximately 47 percent. Although the absolute amount collected in land taxes nearly doubled over the nineteenth century, land taxes fell from 73.5 percent of the total tax revenue in the late eighteenth century to 35 percent in 1908.[64] After 1906, a new round of surcharges, on such items as wine, oil, thread, and chickens, was visited upon village taxpayers in order to finance New Policy reforms. Many of the additional commercial surcharges and taxes were received through the traditional methods of county tax collection.

The central government's plans to standardize China's chaotic monetary system were unable to alter the local situation either for better or for worse. Provincial mints, which issued their own copper cash, continued to produce coins after a central mint was opened in Tianjin in 1905. The glut of copper cash issued by the provincial mints in order to increase the assets of provincial treasuries contributed significantly to inflation. In 1910, the Qing government drew up the first national budget in China's history, but there was no state apparatus for gaining county and provincial compliance. The central government, acting half-heartedly under pressure from domestic reformers and revolutionaries and in conformity with its own traditional patterns of informal and unsystematic administrative financing, drew up reforms that produced a variety of county-level responses, which it could neither predict nor control. The owner-cultivators in the villages, the small-shop owners and craftsmen in the towns, and the degree-holding merchant households with extensive contacts in the county seat were but a few of the many social groups whose circumstances and expectations wreaked havoc with the central government's plans.

The specifics of each rural area where protest against reforms took shape varied. What linked them together in a strong voice of dissent was the political place they occupied in a matrix of social relations and village networks, which structured privilege and access to material resources during China's early twentieth-century crisis. The contact and support matrix through which protesters organized collective action against New Policy reform managers was a dense and fairly homogeneous marketing network. Thoroughly embedded in the political culture of rural China by the end of the Qing Dynasty, these marketing patterns continued to function without fundamental structural change until a new economic order was introduced in 1949.[65] Dissidence as well as other rural views traveled these lines of communication. According to Skinner's hierarchical typology, three principal levels of commercial activity could be found within the county. These were the central market town, the intermediate market town, and the minor market, or "natural" economic hierarchy of the intervillage networks. The county seat generally functioned either as a central market town or an intermediate market town. Both of these marketplaces were important wholesale centers located at major trade crossroads.[66] Skinner described the standard market town as:

> that type of rural market which met all the normal trade needs of the peasant household; what the household produced but did not consume was normally sold there, and what it consumed but did not produce was normally bought there. The standard market provided for the exchange of goods produced within the market's dependent area, but more importantly it was the starting point for the upward flow of agricultural products and craft items into higher reaches of the marketing system, and also the termination of the downward flow of imported items destined for peasant consumption.[67]

Below the standard market town was a vast area of village and intervillage activity based on social organizations and minor markets for the horizontal exchange of goods. As Skinner notes:

> Extravillage local systems below the level of the standard marketing community were variously structured by higher-order lineages, irrigation societies, crop-watching societies, politico-ritual "alliances" (under a variety of terms including *yüeh, she,* and *hsiang*), and the jurisdiction of particular deities and temples; many if not most were multi-purpose sodalities manifesting more than one organizing principle. It would appear that, in some instances at least, these local systems . . . were not wholly contained within

marketing systems but rather continued the overlapping mode of hierarchical stacking that I have shown to be characteristic of the "natural" economic hierarchy.[68]

A close association existed between a person's political status and
the level of the marketing hierarchy with which one identified one's
economic interests and organizational affiliations. "Political" is used
here in the broadest sense of the term to refer to a degree of control
over individual and group resources, whether they be grain supplies,
tax funds, local schools, or regulation enforcement agencies. One's relationship to the tax collection system was an indicator of political
status in this sense. For example, a small shopkeeper or the head of a
minor household would be most likely to do business at the village and
small market town levels of the marketing hierarchy. Such a person
would belong to intervillage rural organizations such as grain reserve
societies or trade networks, which aided him in his livelihood. Major
household heads and tax farmers, on the other hand, would be more
likely to have business organizations in the county seat or major market
towns. During the New Policy period, antagonisms developed in some
counties among these different status groups over the political and economic issues of who would control and finance institutions introduced
by reforms.

While village leaders (*cunzhang*) could be county elite members,
they would retain the village leadership position only if they continued
to represent the interests of the village over those of the county government. Philip Huang has noted that "as long as a village's political structure remained intact, its elites continued to perceive themselves primarily as leaders of their own community, not as agents of the state."[69] The
county political elite and the village leadership, therefore, tended to
overlap only when the influential families in a particular village identified their interests with those of the county government, or when coer-
cion by a few families had effectively prevented the other households
from selecting a village headman (*cunzhang*) on a consensual basis.
New opportunities created by administrative and economic conditions
in the twentieth century combined to put pressure on village leaders
to follow county-level rather than village-level interests.[70] In general,
however, village leaders did not constitute an elite relative to the
county-seat-based elite, which commanded wealth and political connections far beyond village resources.

While economic interests were an indicator of where in the marketing
hierarchy one had the greatest political leverage, one's residence and
occupation in the marketing hierarchy were only loosely correlated with
political status. A moderately well-to-do landowner, for example, who

lived in a village and did not have connections with the county government, had a much lower political status than that of a landowner of the same economic means who did cultivate ties with the magistrate's office. A wealthy merchant residing in the county seat but lacking county-level political influence would be vulnerable to encroachments by the political elite. Even a degree-holder, who by choice or for lack of means did not assert himself at the magistrate's office, would find himself without this political influence. Residence and occupation were, therefore, not the principal classifiers for political stratification within the county.

None of the sociopolitical groups active within the county formed "classes" with "class consciousness," as the terms are used in nineteenth-century Western European historiography. The main division in Chinese society was not between a class that controlled the means of production and another class that had only its labor to sell but was instead between those social groups that had access to administrative legitimacy for their authority and those groups that drew on the nonofficial, commoner community for their legitimacy in handling disputes over tax collection or other community affairs.

In one sense, the Chinese example resembles the "polite and plebian cultures" of eighteenth-century England, as they have been described by E. P. Thompson in his discussion of class struggle in a society lacking classes as Marx defined them. Thompson finds that those with little political and economic power were able to form their own value systems outside of the dominant ideology of the English gentry. The hegemony of the ruling groups "did not envelop the lives of the poor and it did not prevent them from defending their own modes of work and leisure, and forming their own rituals, their own satisfactions and view of life."[71] Collective experiences of community protest, transmitted through centuries of village popular culture, functioned as a "class consciousness" for the Chinese commoners as well.

In China, where the most powerful groups were defined neither by heredity nor by economic status but rather by admission to and association with the state bureaucracy, the relationship to what Max Weber has called the "means of administration," remained the primary distinction between members of the county political elite and all other interest groups in the county, with the exception of the clerks and runners.[72] Among families lacking influence in the state administration, status groups were differentiated by wealth, which was viewed as a possible springboard to degree-holding status.

The histories of rural dissent that follow indicate a number of important points. First, within the immediate context of the New Policy reforms, there was widespread rural opposition to government intrusion into local society. The depth with which protesters believed these reforms would undermine their well-being was expressed by Laiyang activists who proclaimed, "If we pay the taxes, we'll die of starvation; if we don't pay the taxes, we will be put to death. Since either way we are dead, why not struggle to the death!"[73] Second, given the particular forms in which the reforms were organized, their introduction created opportunities for a new style of self-aggrandizement on the part of local elites, resulting in a new kind of class struggle of the powerful against the rural population. The latter fought back in the process, acquiring a new consciousness of its collective interests. This is not to impute to them a class consciousness in the modern sense of the term but rather to point to a kind of struggle that may be understood best in E. P. Thompson's words as, "class struggle without class," that is to be grasped not in national terms (as the notion of class so often is) but in its many manifestations in place-based activity. And finally, the language of struggle against the New Policy reforms drew on the language of earlier agrarian uprisings and the vision of rural activist practice. In the course of their defense of places, post-Boxer rural activists were to create their own discourse on politics and construct, however tenuously, a collective consciousness that enabled their many struggles against the changes that promised their disenfranchisement.

Notes

Epigraph: *Xinhai geming* (The 1911 revolution) (Shanghai: 1956), vol. 3, 391.

1. Joseph W. Esherick, *The Origins of the Boxer Uprising,* (Berkeley: University of California Press, 1987), 340, parentheses added.

2. Jean Chesneaux, *Secret Societies in China in the Nineteenth and Twentieth Centuries* (Hong Kong: Heinemenn Educational Books, 1971), 169.

3. Liu Tongjun, ed., *Xinhai gemingqian Lai Hai Zhao kangjuan yongdong* (Antitax movements in Laiyang, Haiyang, and Zhaoyuan before the 1911 Revolution) (Beijing: Shehuikexue wenxian chuban she [Social science documentary publications], 1989), 444.

4. Zhang Li, *Sichuan Yihetuan yundong* (Sichuan Boxer movement) (Chengdu: Renmin qubanshe, 1982), 79.

5. Liu Tongjun, *Xinhai gemingqian Lai Hai Zhao kangjuan yongdong*, 450, 452.

6. Huang Yanpei, *Bashi nianlai* (Eighty years past) (Beijing: Wenshi ziliao chuban, 1982), 17.

7. Esherick, *The Origins of the Boxer Uprising*, 241.

8. *Zunhua dongbabao nongmin fankang guoshujuan de douzheng jingguo* (Protest against orchard taxes by the peasants of eight eastern bao in Zunhua county), oral history recorded by Tian Zhihe on April 23, 1961. Zunhua County Party Historical Archives, serial no. 26, document no. A20011.2

9. Jiang Zuyuan, *Jianming Guangdong si* (A concise history of Guang-dong) (Guangdong: Renmin chuban she, 1987), 512.

10. Jiang Zuyuan, *Jianming Guangdong si*, 513.

11. Ibid.

12. Ibid., 514.

13. Although many small protests were not recorded at all, and records such as the *Shilu* (Veritable records of the Qing emperors) note only those cases that came to the attention of the national government, it is generally agreed that this was a decade of widespread rural unrest. Wang Shuhuai had counted thirty-seven cases of anti–New Policy protests in Jiangsu province alone from 1910 to 1911. See his article "Qingmo Jiangsu difang zizhi fengchao" (Riots against local self-government in Jiangsu during the late Qing period), *Bulletin of the Institute of Modern History Academia Sinica*, 6 (June 1977) 319–20.

14. *Xinhai geming si yanjiu beiyao* (Research materials on the 1911 Revolution) (Changsha: Henan chuban she chuban faxing [Henan publishing company], 1991), 82.

15. C. K. Yang, "Some Preliminary Statistical Patterns of Mass Action in Nineteenth-Century China," in *Conflict and Control in Late Imperial China*, ed. Frederic Wakeman Jr. and Carolyn Grant (Berkeley: University of California Press, 1975), 177. Yang's figures are based on material from the *Shilu* (Veritable records of the Qing emperors) only and are, therefore, partial.

16. For a discussion of the late Qing dialogue on local self-government, see Min Tu-ki, *National Polity and Local Power: The Transformation of Late Imperial China*, ed. Philp A. Kuhn and Timothy Brook (Cambridge, Harvard University Press, 1989).

17. For an excellent discussion of these views, see Roger Thompson, "Statecraft and Self-Government: Competing Visions of Community and State in Late Imperial China," in *Modern China*, 14, no. 2 (April 1988): 188–221.

18. Min Tu-ki, *National Polity and Local Power*, 139, 249 fn. 9.

19. Thompson, "Statecraft and Self-Government," 188–89, 207.

20. Cai Shaoqing, "Lun Xinhai geming yu huidang de guanxi" (On the relationship between the 1911 Revolution and secret societies) in *Jinian xinhaigeming qi shizhounian* (Commemorating the seventieth anniversary of the 1911 Revoluton) (Beijing: Zhonghua shuju, 1983), 310.

21. Cai Shaoqing, "Lun Xinhai geming yu huidang de guanxi," 312.

22. Esherick, *The Origins of the Boxer Uprising*, 63–65.

23. Liu Tongjun, *Xinhai gemingqian Lai Hai Zhao kangjuan yongdong*, 439.

24. Susan Naquin, *Millenarian Rebellion in China: The Eight Trigrams Uprising of 1813* (New Haven: Yale University Press, 1976).

25. Naquin, *Millenarian Rebellion in China*, 20.

26. Ibid., 21.

27. B. J. Ter Haar, *The White Lotus Teachings in Chinese Religious History* (New York: E. J. Brill, 1992), 247, 253, 258, 303.

28. Liu Tongjun, *Xinhai gemingqian Lai Hai Zhao kangjuan yongdong*, 437.

29. *Chuansha xianzhi*, 14.10 no. 2, and 14.11, no. 13. Also see, Daniel L. Overmyer, *Folk Buddhist Religion: Dissenting Sects in Late Traditional China* (Cambridge: Harvard University Press, 1976), 135.

30. Frederic Wakeman, *Strangers at the Gate: Social Disorder in South China, 1839–1861* (Berkeley: University of California Press, 1986).

31. Ono Kazuko, *Chinese Women in a Century of Revolution, 1850–1950,* ed. Joshua A. Fogel (Stanford: Stanford University Press, 1989), 8.

32. Technically also Han Chinese, the Hakka groups had immigrated from north China into the south at a later date. Consequently, they were referred to as "guests" by those Han peoples already settled in the Guangdong area for generations. In practice, the Hakkas were treated as an ethnic minority.

33. Liu Tongjun, *Xinhai gemingqian Lai Hai Zhao kangjuan yongdong*, 435.

34. Mou Anjie, *Taiping Tianguo* (Taiping Heavenly Kingdom) (Shanghai: Shanghai renmin chuban she [Shanghai people's publishing house], 1979), 49.

35. Franz Michael, *The Taiping Rebellion* (Seattle: University of Washington Press, 1966), maps 2, 14, 15.

36. Kui Yingtao, *Sichuan jindaishi gao* (Sketches in Sichuan modern history) (Chengdu: Sichuan renmin chuban she, 1990), 347.

37. Philip C. C. Huang, *The Peasant Economy and Social Change in North China* (Stanford: Stanford University Press, 1985), 138–39, 293–302.

38. Wu Yannan, "Xinhai geming yu nongmin wenti" (The 1911 Revolution and the peasant question), in *Jinian xinhai geming qishi zhounian* (Commemorating the seventieth anniversary of the 1911 Revolution) (Beijing: Zhonghua shuju, 1983), 488.

39. Arthur Smith, *China in Convulsion* (New York: Fleming H. Revell, 1901), 201–203.

40. Esherick, *The Origins of the Boxer Uprising,* 253.

41. Ibid.

42. Kui Yingtao, *Sichuan jindaishi gao,* 348–349.

43. *North China Herald,* January 17, 1908; L. R. Barr, Ningpo Intelligence Report, January 1–April 30, 1910, F.O. 228/1762.

44. Esherick, *The Origins of the Boxer Uprising,* 224–25.

45. Douglas R. Reynolds, *China 1898–1912: The Xinzheng Revolution and Japan,* (Cambridge: Council on East Asian Studies, Harvard University, 1993), 201.

46. Thompson, "Statecraft and Self-Government," 196.

47. John H. Fincher, *Chinese Democracy: Statist Reform, The Self-Government Movement and Republican Revolution* (Tokyo: Institute for the Study of Languages and Cultures of Asia and Africa, 1989); Min Tu-ki, *National Polity and Local Power: The Transformation of Late Imperial China,* ed. Philip A. Kuhn and Timothy Brook (Cambridge: Harvard-Yenching Institute Monograph Series, no. 27, 1989).

48. Thompson, "Statecraft and Self-Government," 207.

49. Chuzo Ichiko, "Political and Institutional Reform, 1901–1911," in *Cambridge History of China,* vol. 11, ed. John King Fairbank and Kwang-ching Liu (Cambridge: Cambridge University Press, 1980), 401.

50. *Guofengbao* (National Customs) (Bejing) no. 18, 1910.

51. Arif Dirlik, "Vision and Revolution: Anarchism in Chinese Revolutionary Thought on the Eve of the 1911 Revolution," in *Modern China*, vol. 12, no. 2 (April 1986): 127.

52. Liu Shipei, "Lun xinzheng wei bingming zhi gen" (A discussion of New Policy as the root of the people's suffering), *Tianyi bao* (Natural Justice), nos. 8–10, 1907 in *Wuzhengfu zhuyi sixiang ziliao xuan* (Materials on anarchist thought) (Beijing: Beijing daxue chuban she [Beijing University Publishing], 1984), 108.

53. Report from *Shuntian shibao* cited by Roger Roy Thompson in *Visions of the Future, Realities of the Day: Local Administrative Reform, Electoral Politics, and Traditional Chinese Society on the Eve of the 1911 Revolution* (University Microfilms International, Ann Arbor, Michigan) (Ph.D. dissertation, Yale University, 1985), 138.

54. Lenore Barkan, "Patterns of Power: Forty Years of Elite Politics in a Chinese County," in *Chinese Local Elites and Patterns of Dominance*, ed. Joseph W. Esherick and Mary Backus Rankin (Berkeley: University of California Press, 1990), 204.

55. *Dongfang zazhi* (Eastern Miscellany), 1910, 8/25, no. 8/18062–18063.

56. John King Fairbank, *The United States and China* (Cambridge: Harvard University Press, 1979), 114–15.

57. Some official appointments were made on the basis of recommendations. See Chung-li Chang, *The Chinese Gentry: Studies in Their Role in Nineteenth-Century Chinese Society* (Seattle: University of Washington Press, 1955), 30–31.

58. Ibid., 141.

59. Yeh-chien Wang, *Land Taxation in Imperial China, 1750–1911* (Cambridge: Harvard University Press, 1973), 121.

60. Yeh-chien Wang, *Land Taxation in Imperial China*, 116–17.

61. Ibid.

62. Ibid., 117, 123.

63. Ibid., 52.

64. Ibid., 80–1.

65. Albert Feuerwerker, *Economic Trends in the Republic of China, 1912–1949* (Ann Arbor: Center for Chinese Studies, University of Michigan, 1977), 1–2.

66. G. William Skinner, "Marketing and Social Structure in Rural China, Part I," *Journal of Asian Studies* 24 (1964): 7, 9.

67. Skinner, "Marketing and Social Structure in Rural China, Part I" 6.

68. G. William Skinner, "Cities and the Hierarchy of Local Systems," in *Studies in Chinese Society*, Arthur P. Wolf, ed. (Stanford: Stanford University Press, 1978), 351, n. 48.

69. Philip Huang, *The Peasant Economy and Social Change in North China* (Stanford: Stanford University Press, 1985), 241–42.

70. Huang, *The Peasant Economy and Social Change in North China*, 273–91.

71. E. P. Thompson, "Eighteenth-Century English Society: Class Struggle without Class?" *Social History* 3 (1978): 163.

72. Talcott Parsons, ed., *Max Weber: The Theory of Social and Economic*

Organization, trans. A. M. Henderson and Talcott Parsons (New York: The Free Press, 1964), 63, 340.

73. Ma Gengcun, "Xinhai geming qian de Laiyang kangjuankangshui de douzheng" (The struggle to resist taxes in Laiyang on the eve of the 1911 Revolution), 88.

2

Laiyang, Shandong:
Qu Shiwen and the Four Mountains

Why don't officials take the people as their masters? Why since the institution of the "New Policy" have taxes and exactions brazenly increased even more? It seems that without change in the social system and the political order, all reforms will be to no avail. Only by studying the methods of the Taiping movement and rebellion can radical change be brought about.

—attributed to Lü Conglü, supporter of Qu Shiwen
1910, Laiyang, Shandong

From his father, who enjoyed the confidence of villagers throughout his area during the elder Qu's many years as headman of Taiping *she*, Qu Shiwen (1849–1914) had learned firsthand the values and responsibilities of rural leadership. Inclined from an early age to concern himself with issues of fairness in the struggles of rural residents to sustain their livelihood, Qu Shiwen drew negative attention to himself from those who did not want villagers to have a leader who might interfere with the plans of local power brokers. Perhaps this was the reason that a small incident in the summer of 1891 grew out of proportion and resulted in the suicide of Qu's son, Qu Hongfu. But if those who made trouble for Qu thought this might intimidate him and eliminate his presence as a potential leader of opposition to their manipulations of county affairs, they could not have been more mistaken.

One summer day in 1891 Qu sat at home in Bolin village awaiting the return of his son, Qu Hongfu who had spent the morning tending the family's water buffalo. When the boy arrived for the midday meal, he tethered the buffalo to a tree on the edge of the Lu family property. A slight breeze moved through the warm air as the Qu family members gathered around their modest repast. Unnoticed by anyone, the buffalo pulled free from its post and wandered onto the Zhou family property where it began to eat in the garden. The Zhou family got in touch with

45

the Wang family who they knew were anxious to make trouble for Qu Shiwen. After ruthlessly beating Hongfu, they confiscated the water buffalo. In a court case brought with the help of Wang Qi and Wang Jingyue, Qu was sued for damages amounting to ten strings of cash. If he did not pay, they would kill the water buffalo. Qu Shiwen did not immediately understand the situation. He thought to himself, "What is the big deal? Water buffalo often eat a few greens."[1] But the Wangs had the support of the magistrate; they arrested Qu and brought him to the county jail. The pressure was so great on Qu Hongfu that the boy hung himself. When Qu was released from jail, his son was already lifeless.

Qu was devastated and realized that poor people had no defense against corrupt officials and wealthy gentry. He decided to devote his life to addressing problems of the poor. When Shandong province was astir with the Boxer movement in 1898, Qu Shiwen was encouraged by the first victories of the Boxers against the Qing government troops and was inspired by Zhu Hongdeng (Red Lantern Zhu) to serve the "will of popular feeling (*minqing ming*)."[2]

More than one version of this story of the conflict between the Qus and the Wangs exists. Qu Hongjiang, seventy-nine-year-old nephew of Qu Shiwen, met with county historians in April 1984 at the elementary school building in Bolin village to recount the stories he had heard told in his family about the Qu Shiwen rebellion. In his rendering, Qu's son had stolen a melon, it was Mrs. Zhou who had scolded Qu Hongfu and caused him to lose face, and Qu had initially won a court case against the Zhou family only to have it overturned by Wang Jingyue's intervention with the magistrate. In all accounts, the primary point of the story was that in spite of terrible personal loss, Qu Shiwen's primary concern was with the collective interests of the small farmers who could so easily be ruined by abusive authority.[3] Conflicts between those who represented the interests of poorer villagers against the centralizing authority of local landlords and merchants occurred as early as 1883 over issues surrounding a granary fund and continued into the New Policy era. By 1910, when Wang Qi and his associates moved into full gear to dominate county affairs at the expense of popular well-being, nothing could have stopped Qu Shiwen from accepting leadership of the rural opposition.

Shandong Peninsula: Social and Economic Environment of Protest

Located at the center of Shandong Peninsula on the eastern edge of the North China Plain, Laiyang county shared many geographical and social features of life on this Plain, northern China's most prominent land formation. Extending from the Great Wall in the north to the Huai River in the south and from the Taihuang piedmont in the west to the coastal regions and the central Shandong Mountains in the east, the North China Plain was the cradle of Chinese civilization itself. Over centuries, virtually every acre of the land had been turned into farmland, leaving only a few hilly forested areas and swamplands uncultivated. Evidence of human interaction with the land was visible everywhere. On the plain itself, clumps of trees left standing to shade villages were the only remaining large-sized vegetation. Thousands of small villages dotted the landscape, scattered in a remarkably even-spaced pattern over vast expanses that stretch to the horizon. On the land live people whose primary crops of winter wheat, sorghum, and millet support a lower population density than the rice-growing areas of south China. The human hand has also built the dwellings, long parallel rows of single storied white structures with dark gray tiled roofs, and the many canals and waterways that crisscross the countryside, connecting villages and market towns. Very few major urban centers are located on this plain. It is the heartland of rural China.

In the early twentieth century, before the fall of the Qing Dynasty, roughly 70 percent of the rural households in north China owned all or part of the land they cultivated.[4] Living in nucleated villages, farmers worked their plots in the fields surrounding the clusters of family compounds and village lanes. Family holdings were relatively small, amounting to ten to fifteen *mou* for a family of five, and twenty to thirty *mou* for a moderately well-to-do family. Because the formation of extended family lineages was dependent on large corporate landholdings, villages dominated by such single family networks were not a prominent feature of village life in these northern areas. Tenants who had no ownership title to any land composed about 5 to 10 percent of the households. This number remained the same even as average farm size decreased over the period from 1870 to 1930.[5] Large landowners holding between one and two hundred *mou* or more of land were known as managerial landowners because they employed hired laborers to cultivate the land that they did not work themselves.[6] Through the early twentieth century, the number of landowners in this group declined, and it is estimated that the number of households possessing between one and thirty *mou* of land increased.[7] The general picture was of a strong, small owner-cultivator agrarian society made up primarily of farmers who lived in relative poverty but not deprivation, to draw a distinction made by, among others, Albert Tévoédjrè in his work, *Poverty: The Wealth of Mankind.*[8]

During the period of New Policy reforms, farmers in north China

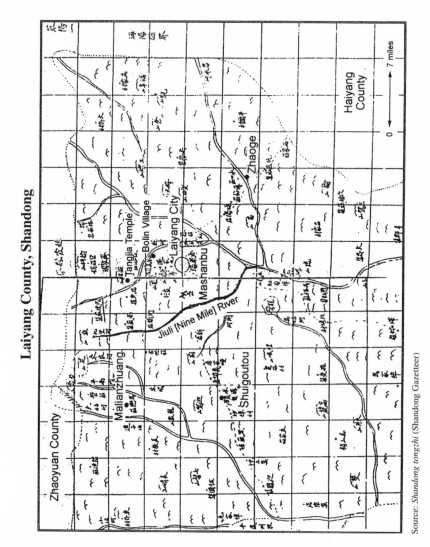

Laiyang County, Shandong

Source: *Shandong tongzhi* (Shandong Gazetteer)

experienced similar increases in taxes and devaluation of copper cash
that plagued many parts of the country. A large number of the antireform movements that developed in response to this situation occurred
in foothill areas in north China situated on borders between low mountains and plains. The economies of the counties in these cases included
wheat, cotton, fruit orchards, and animal husbandry. Yizhou and Longyao in Zhili and Mixian in Henan, where anti–New Policy protests were
recorded were all located along the Taihang piedmont, an active com-

mercial route for the exchange of goods and ideas between the mountainous areas to the west and the central plain to the east. Laiyang county had a composite landscape of low mountain and plains, which produced not only grains but the famous Laiyang pear, a regional specialty. Laiyang was at the crossroads of a moderate flow of traffic that traversed the peninsula. Similarly, Zunhua and Qianan in Zhili, sites of protest against New Policy reforms, rested at the foot of the mountains that formed the northern boundary of the North China Plain. Many of the antireform movements in other parts of the country also occurred in counties of moderate wealth containing foothill areas that provided the basis for a mixed economy as well as relatively well-developed communication and commercial routes and a natural cover for partisan fighters.

Laiyang county was a moderately prosperous agricultural area in which farmers grew wheat, maize, common sorghum, peanuts, melons, and a variety of fruits. Average family size ranged between 4.8 in 1876 and 4.6 in 1922.[9] Eighty percent of the population were owner-cultivators (*zigeng nong*), belonging to households that owned approximately ten *mou* of land each, or two *mou* per person. Ten percent of these cultivators worked land that they did not own in order to supplement the income from their own property. Designated in county historical records as half-owner cultivators (*ban zigeng nong*), they received 60 percent of the produce from the land they worked. There were no tenants without landownership in Laiyang county. The biggest landowners were managerial landowners who constituted 4 to 5 percent of the farming population and held one hundred or fewer *mou* of land apiece.[10] Managerial landowners worked their own land and hired laborers to cultivate acreage beyond what they could manage themselves. Life was hard but good in Laiyang. Between 1876 and 1910, the county's population almost doubled, the number of its households increasing by 90 percent from 57,000 to 109,000.[11]

The Five Dragon River provided easy sea transport connections to Jiangsu, Zhejiang, Fujian, and Guangdong provinces. In addition, Laiyang had commercial ties with the port cities of Yantai and Qingdao and surrounding counties, including Zhaoyuan, Ninghai, Yexian, and Qixia.[12] Both Yantai and Qingdao were sites of brisk trading. Exports through Yantai increased in value from 1, 720, 917 *taels* (silver) in 1898 to 3, 624, 598 in 1908 and 4, 695, 539 in 1913. At Qingdao, the volume of exports rose from 2, 707, 870 *taels* in 1908 to 12, 960, 096 in 1913. Imports through each port ran at a higher volume than exported goods during these years, but by 1919, exports surpassed imports at both places.[13] Foreign goods circulated at Laiyang, and some of those who joined in the protest in 1910 suggested that such goods were connected to problems the local people suffered. When asked by a yamen functionary if he would like an American cigarette, Yu Zhusan [1851–1946] replied, "I don't like foreign products; I only use local goods [*tuhuo*] in order to have dependability and peace of mind."[14] Exports from Laiyang included soybean cakes, pork, and salt. Twenty percent of Laiyang county's population was engaged in trade, many of these people living in the southern part of the county (*xian*), whose location on the coast made its land unsuitable for agriculture but favorable for salt-production.[15] Although fifty to sixty miles from the major commercial centers of Yantai and Qingdao, Laiyang had an active local trade, including dye products, pottery, and other small items, dominated by merchant firms in the county seat. Laiyang merchants also managed money shops, which would remit funds to other locations in China.[16] There was some mining in Laiyang, which included a silver deposit first worked during the Song Dynasty and small deposits of lead, gold, and coal.[17]

In the area of cultural activity, Laiyang was well endowed with temples dedicated to a variety of spirits and deities.[18] Popular religious practice and local Buddhist groups included both formal temple and lay settings. The Tangjia temple and the Sanguan temple, which played key roles in the Laiyang uprising, were thoroughly embedded in the family and market networks of rural life. Local interest in the Eight Diagrams, connected to White Lotus and Nian activism, along with remnants of Boxer views and practice were parts of Laiyang's rich mixture of rural political culture. In addition, by 1905 there were five to six thousand Christians in Laiyang county.[19] In 1882, an American missionary followed by a German in 1901 worked in the area establishing small congregations of Christians but no missionary settlements. Christianity never directly entered into the issues raised by the Laiyang protesters.

Secular Rural Organization:
Lianzhuanghui, the Federated Village Alliance

Laiyang county itself was divided administratively into 11 large rural divisions (*xiang*), which were subdivided into a total of 108 intermediate rural divisions (*she*), each of which contained approximately one to two dozen villages (*cun*).[20] Community leaders known as intermediate rural division headmen (*shezhang*) and village headmen (*cunzhang*) managed local affairs on the villagers' behalf. *Shezhang* were selected by the villagers from among the wealthier villagers, the commoner elders, or the "honest rural residents" to organize such rural projects as commoner-established granaries.[21] Village headmen were selected by villagers to act as the villagers' advocates in official matters and to manage village affairs.[22] Although they carried out yamen directives, both the *she* and *cun* headmen were responsible primarily to the villagers who selected them and who could replace them. Because it was serious business to approach the yamen with petitions and complaints, *she* and *cun* leaders were most likely to act only when several communities simultaneously sought redress for grievances. While the *she* and *cun* headmen were individuals of local influence, owing either to their wealth or to their public esteem, the divisions within these groups of rural leaders depended on their relationship to those who congregated in the magistrate's chambers.

The five-month long movement in 1910 against the expanding economic and political authority of the Laiyang reform managers was organized by a rural alliance of predominantly small and middle landowning cultivators. The organizational network through which tens of thousands of people mobilized and coordinated plans was the *lianzhaunghui* (village federation). Thirty villages to the northwest of Laiyang city were the original core of this intervillage association.[23] A common feature of rural society in north China, *lianzhuanghui* functioned as village federations and had a long history as part of the tradition of self-defense and political mobilization among subsistence farmers. The *lianzhuanghui* coexisted with and drew support from semiofficial administrative structures and religious sect activity in the county without being tied to either. *Lianzhuanghui* brought together households across village boundaries. In the uprising at Laiyang, both *cunzhang* (village headmen) and *shezhang* (*she* headmen) participated as representatives of their fellow villagers and under central leadership that drew authority from the transvillage and trans-*she* organization of the *lianzhuanghui*. In addition to the agriculturists who were the mainstay of the participants and the leadership, others also joined from the ranks of the craftsmen, small merchants, rural intellectuals without official status, wanderers without property, and a few from among the rich peasants, and small and middle landlords.[24]

The first organizational meeting leading to the Laiyang uprising was on April 21, 1910. More than twenty people representing villages in the area northwest of Laiyang city gathered at Tangjia temple to discuss local problems. A drought in the county threatened the livelihood of near subsistence farmers, and they sought relief from the public granary (*shecang*) to which their families had contributed to provide for themselves in just such times of hardship. The granary at Laiyang had a long history. First built during the Ming Dynasty, the structure that housed the collected grain was attacked by Nian rebels in 1861 and successfully protected by people's militias (*mintuan*) called into action by the county magistrate. Composed primarily of men between the ages of sixteen and fifty, the *mintuan* were mobilized in the rural areas and included women organized into groups of three hundred (ten units with thirty women each).[25] After a series of droughts in the late 1870s, the granary was replenished in 1881. Three *shezhang* took the initiative in this project: Qu Laowu, *shezhang* of Taiping *she,* resident of Bolin village and father of Qu Shiwen; Yu Chunling, *shezhang* of Yongzhuang *she* and father of Yu Zhusan; and Jiang Ershou, *shezhang* and wealthy grain merchant of Shiqiao *she.* Each household in the areas represented by the three *shezhang* contributed in grain or money the equivalent of two *dou* [one deciliter] of grain amounting to 5,592 *shih* and 4 *dou.* Qu Shiwen, in his early twenties at the time, helped his father and the other *shezhang* to organize the granary collection. Because people could see that he worked day and night for the common good, they came at this time to trust and respect him.[26]

Then in 1883, Yu Zanyang and Zhang Xiangmo, both local power brokers with commercial interests in the county seat, succeeded with the aid of the county magistrate in having the grain transferred to the academy (*shuyuan*) inside the city.[27] As a consequence, the *shezhang* lost control of the grain, which was later sold by the county notables and the money deposited in pawnshops they owned. At the rate of 300 cash (*wen*) per *dou* of grain, 16,777 strings of big cash (*daqian*) should have been deposited, but from the beginning, only 13,044 strings were in the account. Not even in 1899, when a censor's memorial regarding the granary fund resulted in the resignation of the local magistrate, did the *shezhang* regain control of the reserves. By 1903, only 4,000 strings of the original 13,044 strings of cash remained in the fund, and these were deposited in three merchant firms owned by Yu Zanyang, Zhang Xiangmo, and Wang Qi, the last a rising star among the local elite with closest ties to the magistrate's office.[28] In short, when the peasants needed to draw on their savings, the funds no longer existed. In addition to this grievance, the same group that had embezzled the granary fund became the managers of New Policy reforms at Laiyang and had in recent years begun to make demands for new miscellaneous taxes to fund their reform projects. Far from constituting the growth of a "civil society," the New Policy reforms in this instance and others merely extended national political legitimacy to local tax-farmers and commercial elites who through their own combination of privatization schemes and political privilege had been misappropriating public funds for over two decades.

Among those present at the May Tangjia temple meeting in addition to Qu Shiwen were Yu Zhusan, Li Shoushan (1857–1942), Qian Jingshan (1875–1923), and Ma Xiaoshan (1874–1910) who collectively became known as the Four Mountains representing farmers of four of the eleven *xiang* in Laiyang county. Yu Zhusan, whose father had helped revive the public granary in 1881, came from a landlord family that went back many generations in Laiyang. A *shezhang* himself, Yu and his family had always distributed some of their own grain to families in need, and in 1910 the numbers of such families were especially high. Yu had the respect of villagers and was treated well by the yamen functionaries who hoped, despite their knowledge of his temperament and empathy with the commoners, that they could win him to their side in mollifying the protesters. Because they could not and because Yu continued to speak out against the ruinous tax plans of the yamen functionaries, they considered Yu "a thorn in the flesh."[29] During the uprising, Yu Zhusan organized the protesters to the east of the city while Qu Shiwen headed the western front. Li Shoushan was an agriculturist who also did woodwork, repairing agricultural tools, to supplement his income. He could not read or write but was a storyteller. Well respected in the northwest region of the county, Li commanded up to twenty thousand volunteers along the western road to Malianzhuang during the siege of Laiyang city.[30] Qian Jingshan owned a house, three *jian* in size and seven *mou* of land. When Jin heard of the move to resist taxes in 1910, he went to consult with the *shezhang* of his area. The *shezhang* was unwilling to join in the revolt, so Jin said he would take up leadership. He became the commander of the routes to the north of Laiyang city.[31] Ma Xiaoshan was the son of a newly prosperous landlord family. Educated and an avid reader of Taiping stories, Lishan as an adolescent often queried his parents about why some people were wealthy and some poor. His father, according to accounts, did not know what to say, and his mother, known for her good-heartedness, responded sympathetically. In 1910 Ma became involved in the rebellion led by Qu Shiwen. He helped organize the areas to the south of Laiyang city. In December 1910, he along with Qu's son and sixteen others were executed for their role in the rebellion.[32]

Also present at the Tangjia temple meeting were Lu Fengqi (1880–1961) and Lü Conglü (1860–1925) both of whom were very close to the collective leadership of Qu Shiwen and the Four Mountains. Born into a poor family and orphaned at a very young age, Lu Fengqi was raised in a Buddhist monastery and as an adult continued to live and study there. When he heard of the antitax meeting at Tangjia temple, he compared Qu's cause with that of the Taiping quoting a Taiping saying that "all under heaven are one family, together everyone should enjoy peace and tranquillity."[33] He represented the Buddhist monks and nuns at Laiyang in their opposition to new taxes and was a commander along with Qu Shiwen in coordinating the movements of the Four Mountains. The child of a well-to-do agricultural family, Lü Conglü was sent by his parents when he was six years old to a private school. His mother

曲詩文在牢獄中的遺像

Qu Shiwen (prison photo)

Source: Liu Tongjun, *Zinhai gamingqian Lai Hai Zhao kangjuan yongdong* (Antitax movements in Laiyang, Haiyang, and Zhaoyuan before the 1911 Revolution) Beijing: Shehui kexue wenxian chuban she, 1989.

and father counseled him that study was the most important activity a person could undertake. They made it clear to the young Conglü that they hoped he would do well and bring credit to the Lü family by becoming an official. When Conglü turned twenty in 1880, however, he chose not to take the imperial examinations because of the official corruption he saw around him. At the same time, he was troubled by the suffering of farmers who had such difficult lives. Instead of sitting for the imperial examinations, he decided to become a village teacher. He researched the Eight Diagrams (*bagua*), associated with divination and White Lotus and Nian thought,[34] and studied military strategy (*zhenfa*). Popularly known as "the people's intellectual" (*baixing de haoxiucai*), Lü met Qu Shiwen at the home of one of his students where they all talked and drank wine together and later joined in resistance in 1910.[35]

By the time of the next meeting at Tangjia temple on April 27, fifty to sixty people joined together to make plans. In order to get the *lianzhuanghui* completely functioning, Qu was appointed commander-in-chief (*zongzhuhui*), Yu Zhusan was made responsible for liaison work.[36] A *chuanpai*, message board, was circulated calling for one person from each family to participate in the protest. Gongs sounded throughout the countryside to call people together. On May 21, Qu and thirty village headmen (*cunzhang*) entered the city to request that grain be distributed and that an accounting be made of the public granary fund. A little over one week later, fifty to sixty *shezhang* and *cunzhang* approached a prefect's sedan chair as he left the city after conferring with the magistrate. The *shezhang* hoped to present a petition on the villagers' behalf in connection with grievances over the granary and miscellaneous taxes. While Qu and Yu are described in most sources as *shezhang*, this may not have been a formal appointment by this time.[37] Whatever the formalities, however, Qu and the Four Mountains worked with and through the *cun* and *she* leaders without necessarily being such leaders themselves, and were popularly recognized as playing the role of protector of the public granary. Not all *she* and *cun* headmen supported the protest. Most notably Gao Yufeng, a *shezhang* from the southwestern part of the county, allied himself with Wang Qi, and in one instance, some village headmen organized a counterdemonstration to support Wang Qi and his associates.

Because *cunzhang* and *shezhang* positions were vital to rural order, from both the official and the village views, and because they possessed a swing quality in terms of allegiance and perceived self-interests, these particular organizational features of Chinese rural society were crucial to the rapid and effective mobilization of villagers for protest activity. Having interests connected to state policies by virtue of the fact that their positions were essential to the hierarchy linking local society to the imperial bureaucracy, both village and *she* headmen were also most attuned to local conditions and problems. While village leaders could represent a villagewide consensus, and in the case of the thirty *cunzhang* who mobilized the *lianzhuanghui* in 1910 did, the goal of the village federation was to form a class-based organization of subsistence farmers and their supporters that could draw on both village and family units to mobilize for political activism. The *chuanpai* was addressed specifically to households not village leaders. The decision to join or not join was made at the family level first. The fact that some whole villages had leaders who initiated the protest at Laiyang is evidence that village leadership was often a product of oppositional consensus among villagers and not, as some have argued, primarily an extension of scholar-official authority.

While varying in size, socioeconomic composition, wealth, and physical description, villages shared a common position at the bottom of the marketing hierarchy. They were also the most basic social, economic, and political unit, outside of the family, in rural society. A variety of characteristics have been attributed to the dynamics of village life in the nineteenth and twentieth centuries. Kung-chuan Hsiao described the rural scene as one in which villagers and their commoner leaders were passive recipients of a "Confucian ideology" stressing obedience and compliance with authority. He argued that barely literate commoners were prone to spasmodic outbursts of violence under the guidance either of criminal fringe elements within the rural society or of literati members who were disaffected with local government authority. Leaders of commoner background, according to this view, were capable of generating collective violence on their own, but they could not manage sustained, large-scale protests without literati leadership.[38] Hsiao explained:

> It is difficult to find an instance in which associative efforts were coordinated by a village-wide organization for the welfare of all inhabitants. Most of the organizations were set up only for special purposes and often merely to meet temporary emergencies. Their membership usually included only a segment of the inhabitants of a given village. Commoners were not precluded from participation or even leadership in village undertakings, but the gentry usually dominated them. It was the gentry that determined to a large extent the pattern and direction of organized village life.[39]

Hsiao cited the uprising at Sanyuanli in May 1841 to illustrate the means by which an otherwise passive peasantry could be incited to violence and to show how crucial literati leadership was in building a coordinated, sustained attack lasting several days. Hsiao used "literati" and "gentry" to refer to the scholar-official class (*shenshi*).[40] This issue was also considered by Albert Feuerwerker, who noted that without literati leadership, village-initiated uprisings had next to no organization at all.[41]

These constructions do not provide an adequate understanding of the frequency and vitality with which rural society gave rise to protest movements. To begin, it is unlikely that scholar-official *(shenshi)* domination of village life was as thorough as Hsiao and others have suggested. Estimates indicate that there were between 1.1 and 1.4 million degree-holders of all ranks in a mid-nineteenth-century population of roughly 450 million people.[42] Using these figures, even if all the degree-holders resided in villages, which they did not, Hsiao's picture of scholar-official domination of village leadership could apply to no more than half of China's 2.25 million villages. Furthermore, while there were degree-holders in each province and county, their distribution was uneven. In north China, for example, degree-holders were sparsely distributed. Laiyang county had only one prominent literati family during the nineteenth century, in addition to a small number of lower degree-holders.[43] Zhang Yufa in his study of Shandong's modernization calculates 2,900 degree-holders for Shandong province throughout the Qing Dynasty, with Laiyang in the twenty to twenty-nine degree-holder range and neighboring Haiyang and Zhaoyuan counties, where disturbances also developed in 1910, in the one to nine degree-holder range for the entire dynasty.[44] In the lower Yangzi, where the density of degree-holders was greater, many gentry members had business interests outside of the county and consequently were not concerned with village affairs. It is equally unlikely that the scholar-official's ideology was as pervasive as Hsiao suggests. Village and elite cultures influenced each other, but they were also identifiable as separate realms of thought and action. Robert Redfield has written, "Village culture is the local expression of a larger civilization."[45] I would go even further and argue that local expression often drew on its own insights and resources to generate some of the cultural and political possibilities out of which the "larger civilization" itself was made. Villagers interpreted social expectations to meet their own needs, and the results were often quite different from the scholar-official's views. The "right" to rebel against unjust authority, a principle from Meng Zi (Mencius), was more likely to be invoked by commoner taxpayers with accumulated grievances against local landlords and merchants than it was to be seen by scholar-officials as a legitimate justification for collective commoner violence. Without the presence of degree-holders, whose primary group allegiance was to their connections with state authority, villagers produced their own leadership and their own standards for selecting persons who, if the need arose, would represent their interests against outside authority. A federation of villages mobilized through such rural leaders at Laiyang.

The criteria used to select village headmen indicate the extent to which headmen were often first among equals in their communities. Property qualifications for the position of village headman varied from one village to another. In some areas, where ten *mou* was the average landholding, the same amount was required as a qualification for village headman. In these cases, there was little difference in status between the headman and his fellow villagers.[46] Wealth, status, and ability were all considerations used in selecting a leader, but the manner in which these factors were weighed varied a great deal from one village to another. In a poor or moderately well-to-do village in which there were no significant differences in economic status among families, the selection of a leader might rely more heavily on age. In a village with greater socioeconomic differences among residents, those persons with greater wealth or education might be heavily represented in village leadership.[47] In villages that had large numbers of lower degree-holders, *shengyuan* or *jiansheng* who were considered sympathetic to the commoner villagers might be selected as village headmen. Hsiao-tung Fei, studying Gaixiangong village in Jiangsu, southwest of Lake Tai, concluded that "headmanship is not connected with any privileged 'class'," and that wealth alone did not lead to prestige or power.[48]

The greater the diversity of economic and social status groups within a village, the lower were the chances for strong village solidarity. Allegiance to the village community was expected of each headman, but the social divisions within the village determined the percentage of the population that he represented. Depending on the issues that arose, however, a diversified village community could find itself united against a common enemy whose own support drew heavily from the county or subprefectural government offices. Also, families of near subsistence status within a village could join a call from a *lianzhuanghui* leader even if their local headman did not participate. As the leader of the *lianzhuanghui* at Laiyang, Qu Shiwen distributed information through the *cun* and *she* leaders, but his notices called upon families to send a representative to support the protest. Qu did not act until he saw that a core of village leaders was united in its views and determination to take action.[49]

Less tangible criteria, including impressions of the candidate's past behavior, were also applied to the selection of the village headman. Ideally, the headman was "brave and wise, righteous and unselfish, experienced in affairs outside the village, and much praised by his fellow villagers."[50] Fei found that in Gaixiangong village, "the basis of the headmanship lies in public recognition and support in the leadership in community affairs, and in *being the representative of the community against the outside world* [emphasis added]."[51] The position of village headman involved public service rather than high-level political leverage. For this reason, headmen were sought who possessed "a willingness to take on the task of leadership and an enjoyment of the responsibilities that accompany it."[52] These responsibilities included knowing other people's business, building local contacts, and settling disputes in keeping with the village consensus. If the village headman did not represent the village consensus or the dominant consensus in a strongly differentiated village, he would not continue to enjoy the support that sanctioned his authority. This self-correcting mechanism ensured that the village headman was closely in tune with his fellow villagers' views.

With these criteria in mind, villagers selected their headman from among themselves, and these individuals were then recognized by the county magistrate's office as *cunzhang*.[53] Writing on Weihaiwei village in Shandong, not far from Laiyang county, R. F. Johnston observed that:

> When important matters arise, affecting the interests of the whole village, they discuss them in the headman's house, or in a temple, or in the village street under the shade of an old tree. Nothing is discussed with closed doors. The whole village, including the women and children, may as a rule attend a meeting of the elders, and any one who wishes to air his views may do so, irrespective of his age or position in the village. The elders have few privileges that their fellow-villagers do not share, and the headman himself is only *primus inter pares.* His authority, like that of the elders, is chiefly derived from his position as head of the family clan.[54]

At such meetings, village headmen were selected, local issues were discussed, and the performance of the headman was periodically reevaluated.

Some observers of Chinese society in the final years of the Qing Dynasty detected a shift in the way in which village headmen were selected. In 1883, missionaries had observed the open manner in which headmen were selected in villagewide meetings. They attributed the headman's great influence to the fact that he represented popular sentiment against the claims of higher authority.[55] While noting that these circumstances remained unchanged, contributors to the *China Mission Year Book* for 1912, a Shanghai missionary publication, believed that the recent political turmoil of late Qing China had accentuated the villagers' need to have headmen who represented their interests. As one writer observed:

The leadership of the clan in China is usually hereditary, and the village eldership rests largely upon age. But whoever is the nominal head, in the clan or village where everyone is known, the man who comes to real authority is the one who represents the dominant sentiment of the community. The responsibility of the leaders for his followers is so heavy, and the difficulties of resisting oppression by higher officials so great, that the Chinese exercise the power of recall over inefficient clan leaders and keep to the front their strong, representative man. . . . The present upheaval in China shows a decided trend in favor of the democratic rather than the hereditary principle in the selection of these local officials. In southern China where clanship especially prevails, centuries of experience have inclined the Chinese in the present crisis to repudiate the hereditary method of selecting rulers, and to support the democratic principle.[56]

Although these missionaries were excessively enthusiastic about finding well-springs of democracy in China, their observations regarding the maintenance of effective leadership based on a village consensus are confirmed by the findings of other village studies in various regions of China. This shift beginning in the 1880s and continuing into the 1900s also suggests that these positions of rural leadership were more contested from all directions during the post-Boxer era of social transformation.

Village headmen who accepted leadership roles in local protest movements did so at considerable risk to themselves. Official government policy in the event of a major disturbance was to capture the leaders and punish them severely, while showing leniency toward the other participants, provided that they returned to their work and vowed not to be "misled" again by "bad elements" who stirred up trouble for no good reason. Even when high officials considered the protesters' cause to be just and took steps to redress their grievances, protest leaders could still expect to pay for their role, perhaps with their lives. The logic followed by officials maintained that although the disturbance may have been justified, the peace had been broken, so someone on each side had to be punished. Their intention was to discourage other rural people from readily assuming leadership positions in opposition to authority.

The marketing structure of rural China provided natural channels for intervillage communication. As Martin C. Yang has observed, "Although there is no clear-cut line of demarcation, each market town has a definite and recognizable area, and looks upon the people of certain villages as its primary customers; in turn, it is regarded by the villagers as their own."[57] Villagers sold their goods at periodic markets and purchased items that they did not produce themselves. In north China, dirt roads and footpaths connected the villages with market towns, to which a villager could travel and return in the same day. In many parts of the lower Yangzi region, waterways served the function of roads. At Laiyang, Bolin village, Qu Shiwen's home, was a market town as were other key areas in the uprising, including Malianzhuang, Hetoudian, and Shuiguotou, also known as a Boxer meeting place.

Such market town networks functioned as important vehicles for weaving together an intervillage consensus on local issues. In market town teahouses and wineshops, people gathered informally on market days to exchange news and discuss local issues, and shared with their families on their return home what they had seen and heard. Among the frequent topics of conversation were the family members who had married into other villages. Disputes among villagers over money, land, chickens, or any number of things were also popular topics; these disputes were often mediated by village leaders who "held court" in the teahouses. In this setting, a local leader could gain a reputation for being fair and impartial, and his services would be sought by other villagers. Typical of accounts of village life throughout China is Martin Yang's description of teahouse activities in the area of Shandong just south of Laiyang and west of Haiyang:

> Most of the leaders in a Chinese rural community have leisure time, which they are apt to spend in the wineshops or the teahouses in the market town. They talk or argue in the stores on current affairs or historical events and discuss community problems. Many community programs, good and bad, come out of such informal gatherings and many problems have been solved, wisely or not, in these discussions. . . . Teahouses and wineshops generate rumors which are widely spread. There is an old saying that statesmen should listen to the talk in these hidden corners. Public opinion and social attitudes take form in them and there are numerous historical tales of Chinese officials who visited them in disguise in order to discover what the common man was saying about current affairs.[58]

Village leaders in the market towns at Laiyang certainly discussed the embezzlement of public granary funds by local elite members and related matters. Through market town networks rural residents distributed information and gathered collective views.

Transformations of Local Authority in the Post-Boxer Decade: Commercialization and County Reform Managers

Domestic possibilities shaped by both local and international conditions in the post-Boxer decade presented families with surplus resources and new options—educating children in subjects not previously a part of the classical learning, establishing factories, studying new approaches to agriculture as did Zhang Mianting, who in 1909 traveled at his own expense to Tokyo Imperial University.[59] To what end these new possibilities were put depended largely on the moral imperatives to which groups involved subscribed. Structural economic and administrative shifts generated more opportunities for excessive greed, which overwhelmed those whose impetus to change was motivated by just social intentions. China was becoming a society that gave less and less social and philosophical support to the Qu Shiwens, Yu Zhusans, and Ma Xiaoshans of the villages and towns.

The leadership of the Laiyang county New Policy reform managers, based in the county seat, derived its legitimacy and support not from the farmers who were the majority of the rural population, but from the magistrate's office and from the commercial networks that the reform leadership formed around that office. Although this network had its nucleus in the county seat, it extended into the countryside as well, including among its members both lower degree-holders by purchase and their associates in the rural areas, often rural managers *(dongshi)* appointed by the magistrate's office. Business and political associations were the ties that formed the network. Its members are often referred to collectively in the Laiyang sources as *shendong* (literally, official/manager), *fushen* (literally, person of wealth/official), or *dongshi* (literally, manager/scholar), indicating the merging of degree and non-degree-holding status into one power block. On occasion, the distinction between the reform managers and the rural leadership overlaps as in the case of Gao Yufeng, a *shezhang* who acted in concert with the reformers. Despite such exceptions, however, the pattern remained clear as to which group represented which interests. The county political elite's influence with the magistrate's office distinguished it from other economic elites in the county and enabled it gradually to develop a network of merchant firms through which it monopolized control of the land tax collection as well as other business enterprises.

A long history of unresolved grievances preceded the outbreak of hostilities at Laiyang. The case of the embezzled granary fund has already been noted above. The two members of the political elite most responsible for the expropriation of the granary fund were Yu Zanyang and Zhang Xiangmo. In about 1890, Yu was appointed country manager *(dongshi* or *shendong)* by the yamen to oversee county-village affairs. He held this post for the next twenty years, except for a few months during the brief term of Magistrate Ye, who dismissed Yu for corrupt practices. Yu held no degree, but he derived so much power through his contact with the magistrate's office that he was known among the people of Laiyang as the "second magistrate." In addition to managing a merchant firm, he was also a contractor for lawsuits *(songsou)*. Zhang, a country manager appointed by the magistrate, was known for his ability to block yamen investigation of his manipulation of local legal and financial matters.[60] An early reform in 1899 established a county post office with twenty-two branch offices, fourteen around the county and eight outside of the county.[61]

In 1901, Yu and Zhang were joined by Wang Qi, who eventually became the central figure in the network of county-based merchant firms that managed New Policy reforms. Wang was a poor relation of an influential family, which according to the county gazetteer was the only prominent family active in Laiyang in the nineteenth century. His

TABLE 2.1
Leaders and Associates of the Laiyang Political Elite

Name	Degree	Status
Wang Qi	*Xiushi*[a] and *juren* (*xiaolian*)	Owner of the Gong Shun and Yuan Shun merchant firms; principal merchant tax farmer
Yu Zanyang	None	Owner of the Fu Yuan merchant firm; country manager (*dong-shi*); merchant tax farmer
Wei Longzhang	None	Owner of the Fu Xiang Yi merchant firm; yamen clerk; merchant tax farmer
Wang Jingyue	*Shengyuan (zeng sheng)*	Head of the Laiyang county police bureau
Wang Chi	*Xiushi*	Brother and associate of Wang Qi
Wang Tinglan	*Shengyuan (fu gongsheng)*	Son of and rural tax collector for Wang Jingyue
Gao Yufeng	None	Intermediate rural division headman (*shezhang*)
Ge Guixing	*Shengyuan (sui gongsheng)*	Education society director (*jiaoyu hui zhang*) involved in management of new school funds
Zhang Xiangmo	None	Country manager (*dongshi*)
Song Weikun	None	Rural agent for Wang Jingyue

Sources: Shandong Lujing tongxiang hui (Shandong landsmann's association), ed. "Laiyang shibian di tiaocha baogaoshu" (An investigative report on the Laiyang disturbances), *Shandong jindai shi ziliao* (Sources on Shandong's modern history), Jinan: Shandong renmin chuban she, 1958: 10–11; Imperial Edict in *Shandong jindai shi ziliao* (Sources in Shandong's modern history), Jinan: Shandong renmin chuban she, 1958: 58; *Dongfang zazhi* No. 6, 1910.
a. The *xiushi* was comparable to the *xiucai* or *shengyuan*; see *Cihai*, Encyclopedia of Terms and Phrases, revised edition, Taibei, 1968: 2130. It is possible that *xiushi* was a euphemism for the purchased *jiansheng* degree. Also see Chung-li Chang, *The Chinese Gentry: Studies on Their Role in Nineteenth Century Chinese Society*, Seattle: University of Washington Press, 1955: glossary.

cousin Wang Xu was vice president of the Board of Justice in Beijing, and his brother Wang Chi was a lower degree-holder (*xiushi*).[62] In 1901, Wang Qi purchased a *xiushi* degree, moved to Laiyang city from Bolin village, and opened several businesses, including the Yuan Shun general store, the Gong Shun money shop, and the Yuan Feng clothing store. Wang Qi brought new prominence to that group that had greatest influence with the magistrate's office.

By cultivating ties with the magistrate's office, the Laiyang political elite gradually developed a network of merchant firms through which by around 1902 they monopolized the tax farming of the land tax, as well as other business enterprises.[63] All taxes were collected through the Gong Shun and Yuan Shun firms owned by Wang Qu, the Fu Yuan firm reopened by Yu Zanyang with 3,100 strongs of cash he had collected ostensibly for reforms, the Fu Xiang Yi firm owned by Wei Longzhang, a former clerk in charge of taxes, and the De He firm of unknown ownership.[64] With the support of the magistrate, Wang had also broken the control of the Gong Ju firm, owned by a city merchant, over the opium trade in Laiyang, and had begun to manage the entire business through his own Gong Shun office. The opium trade was licensed by the yamen; Wang's having been granted this license was another indication of his growing influence with the magistrate. In addition, Wang cornered the market on brushwood sales in an area to the northwest of Laiyang, thereby controlling supplies and prices to the detriment of the consumer, for whom supply and demand had previously resulted in a more equitable distribution of this vital commodity.[65] With the benefit neither of elections nor of other formalities, the network of commercial tax farmers took over the management of New Policy reforms, including the establishment of self-government bureaus, schools, and police offices. Finally in 1910, Wang Qi augmented his bureaucratic status by purchasing a *juren* degree, which was apparently being sold despite the abolition of the examination system.[66] In the same year, under the auspices of the magistrate's office, Laiyang established a chamber of commerce with fifteen *dongshi* positions to carry out the work of the chamber.[67]

It was common practice in traditional China for degree-holders to be charged periodically with the responsibility of raising funds for public works projects. Because of the limited funds officially made available for local government services, the magistrate depended heavily on the resources and influence of local degree-holders to raise this revenue. When dikes in a county were in need of repair or materials were needed to construct a poorhouse or foundling home, the magistrate generally appointed several members of the local elite to oversee the funding and management of the project. The project managers collected the fees, which were levied on commoners and local elite members alike, and determined the distribution and use of these funds once they were received. It was also common for local elite members to be charged with management of the county granary.[68] Through these various means, some members of the local elite had always been involved in county finances and administration on an informal, limited basis. In addition to their control of the county grain reserves, Yu Zanyang and Zhang Xiangmo owned pawnshops that were major financial centers in the county.[69] The influence in local affairs that the rural managers derived from these economic assets made them powerful allies of the magistrate in conducting the financial and administrative affairs of local government. In 1902, the Laiyang magistrate, to ensure the collection of taxes and to benefit his longtime administrative assistants, granted Yu Zanyang, Wang Qi, a recent addition to the county elite, and Wei Longzhang, a former yamen clerk, a countywide monopoly of land tax collection.[70] These persons coordinated their land tax collection efforts through the same network of commercial firms and pawnshops that had previously managed other fund-raising projects for the magistrate.

The organizational capacity of local elite members who served as rural managers and project directors resulted from networks of family and business ties that crossed rural-urban boundaries. Family ties usually included fathers, sons, and brothers rather than extended family, lineage relations. The most influential elite members resided nearest the administrative authority in the city. Other persons who identified their own family or business interests with the city elite maintained residences in the rural areas. Far from being exclusively or primarily an urban group, the political elite drew strength from the traditional patterns of residential and occupational diversity. This is illustrated by the example of Wang Qi, the principal tax farmer in Laiyang since 1902. Upon establishing these enterprises, he moved from a village just outside of the county seat, where many of his family members continued to reside. This village was also the home of his arch-opponent, Qu Shiwen. Other associates of the tax-farming network, including some degree-holders, resided outside of the city.

New Policy reforms from 1906 to 1911 introduced a new stage in the relations among local commercial networks, degree-holders, and county officials. Traditional relations between local government and county elite members spawned stiff competition among commercial firms for the advantages derived from magisterial support. As rural project directors and rural managers, some county elite members had a foothold in the local fiscal and administrative apparatus, but they still did not possess official political status in the bureaucratic hierarchy. The barrier to higher political status was formidable. It was controlled and reinforced by the institutional dictates of the imperial examination system and the limited number of official, bureaucratic slots. New Policy reforms significantly altered the institutional arrangements of local government by introducing additional institutions that carried with them opportunities to occupy official government posts. By becoming local self-government representatives or police bureau headmen, elite members hoped to gain formal political recognition matching the considerable economic leverage that many of them already exercised in local administration.

Members of the county elite who became reform managers combined their traditional roles in the local economy with new authority made possible by the establishment of reform institutions. In many counties, for example, the founding of police bureaus gave elite members coercive power, which strengthened their roles as tax farmers, merchants, or rural managers. At Laiyang, Shandong, reform managers successfully established new police bureaus. With this additional authority, the new political elite was able to expand the activities and influence of its commercial networks. Police bureaus were used to enforce the collection of new taxes, which were then deposited in money shops owned by the reform managers.

The development of monopolistic control over local resources by one group was a problem intensified by the New Policy reforms. Wang Qi, for example, continued to build his commercial "empire" of pawnships and merchant establishments by using his newly gained political influence to deprive other merchant firm owners of economic favors. Shortly after 1902, he obtained control of the government-licensed monopoly of the local opium trade, which had previously been shared with the Gong Ju firm. He also monopolized the brushwood business northwest of Laiyang city, pushing smaller salesmen out of the market and raising prices for consumers.[71] All this was accomplished before he became the leader of reform at Laiyang. Once the reforms were introduced in 1906, Wang and his associates extended their monopolistic methods to the implementation of New Policy as well.

Under the auspices of New Policy, the Laiyang reform managers initiated a project in 1909, which they envisioned would develop the county as a commercial center and concentrate further economic power in their hands. Laiyang's location in the vicinity of the treaty port of Yantai had prompted some demand for local handicraft items but had had very little impact on the domestic economy in the interior of this region.[72] The plans of Wang Qi and others to construct a kiln and produce bricks and tiles were conceived with the local market in mind. In clearing a public cemetery for the construction site, many graves were destroyed. Consequently, once the kiln was in operation, people refused to purchase the kiln products because the bricks might contain the bones and spirits of ancestors whose graves had been disturbed. With no convenient commercial contacts through which they could arrange to sell the bricks and tiles outside of the county, the political elite's only solution was to raise additional taxes, ostensibly to pay for the repair of a Confucian temple, but actually to recoup the losses on their investment.[73] In other counties, New Policy programs contributed to a shift toward greater concentration of economic power in the hands of a few, even in those districts where no one group had a firm control of local affairs prior to the advent of reforms.

The magistrate's or subprefect's support was crucial in establishing the new political authority of the reform manager's urban-rural network. In no county or subprefecture did the reform elite function without the sanction of the local government official. His authority and the bureaucracy it represented were still the sole source of political legitimacy for all administrative and fiscal policies. This was true in all cases, including those in which the magistrate only half-heartedly supported the reform managers or relinquished his control of the reforms altogether. The magistrate, more than anyone else in the county, set the stage on which groups competed for influence over reform policies. At Laiyang, the magistrate actively put the management of reforms into the hands of a single county elite network, which consequently was able to monopolize the reform institutions. A conscientious magistrate or subprefect could prevent or check excessive corruption in the implementation of New Policy programs. While Magistrate Zhu of Laiyang gave the elite a free hand in the management of taxation and reform institutions, an earlier magistrate had dismissed key members of the elite for corrupt practices. If this magistrate had held office during the New Policy period, developments at Laiyang might have taken a different course.[74]

The addition of political authority to the commercial influence already exerted by prominent county elite members created more conflict than economic power alone could generate. Approval from the magistrate's office and the possession of at least a purchased lower degree by some of its members were crucial to the emergence of the new political elite. Once the most influential members of the local elite gained a major competitive edge over their opponents by becoming New Policy reform managers, the dynamics of county-village politics were altered. As a result of the introduction of reforms, the traditional elite divided into the reform managers and members of the nonreform elite. With the reform managers, a new spectrum of county political authority came into existence, ranging from those merchants and degree-holders who had major financial and political interests outside of the county and were only mildly interested in the reforms to local elite members whose assets were concentrated within the county and who vigorously pursued the new opportunities made possible by the reform programs. While the reform managers generally developed antagonistic relationships with the commoner taxpayers, those members of the elite who did not become active in reform programs were generally either neutral toward or supportive of the commoners' grievances. The nonreform elite's neutrality with respect to the protest was often genuine, but it was sometimes a guise for this group's own interest in ousting the reform managers and taking control of reform institutions themselves. When taking a genuinely supportive position, members of the nonreform elite could act as spokesmen for or leaders of the tax protests. However, their participation was never essential to the initiation or development of protest against the reform managers, the magistrate, or the yamen subbureaucracy.

Mobilizing Protest:
From Petition to Seige

Financial exactions, largely in the form of new miscellaneous taxes, and the loss of control of subsistence resources to which such exactions contributed were at the heart of the Laiyang and other anti–New Policy protests. During a period of drought and rural hardship, the issue of the embezzled granary fund initiated protest that linked the rise of local corruption to the New Policy reforms through the individuals and their networks responsible for both. Between 1906 and 1910, a series of new taxes compounded the economic and political pressure on subsistence livelihood. The first of the taxes was a temple levy (*miaojuan*), collected ostensibly for new schools. The next year in 1907, a retail tax on shops (*pujuan*) raised revenue for a police bureau. This meant higher prices for items such as oil, dyes, thread, hemp, and tobacco. To this in 1908 was added a theater tax (*xijuan*) for self-government expenses.[75] Among the non-reform-related new taxes was the deed tax (*tianfu fujuan*), which was paid on each change in ownership of property. Approximately 50,000 to 60,000 strings of cash were collected in deed taxes after their drastic increase in 1909–10 from .036 to .096 cash per tael of assessed land value, with an additional flat fee of 250 cash per transaction.[76] In an area with a large number of owner cultivators, the financial burden generated was widespread as was the attendant resentment over the misuse of such funds. The temple tax, for example, levied in 1909 was allegedly intended to finance the task of restoring the local temple to Kong zi (Confucius). In fact, it was a plan designed to make up the losses of the ill-fated business venture of Wang Qi, Yu Zanyang,

Wang Jingyue, and Zhang Xiangmo that was mentioned above. The building materials used on the reconstruction project were manufactured in the men's graveyard kiln. Under magistrate Zhu Huaizhi's official sanction, the temple tax was imposed on each of the county's 108 *she*, large *she* paying 336 strings of cash, medium *she* 124 strings, and small *she* 112 strings. Thirteen thousand strings were collected, but the carpenters and masons who worked on the project estimated that only five or six thousand strings had been spent for materials and labor by the time the work was abandoned. The unspent taxes collected were deposited in Wang Qi's Gong Shun banking firm.[77]

In addition to the numerous new taxes levied by the merchant tax farmers after 1906, manipulation of the exchange rate between taels and cash added further to the already heavy burden of taxation. Western mints introduced into China in the 1880s had begun to create difficulties fully felt by the 1890s. The situation only worsened as further exactions were demanded of the rural population to pay first for the Boxer indemnity and then the New Policy reforms that followed as a consequence. David Faure has described the process this way. The western mints

> produced cash of a lower copper content, which rapidly displaced the standard cash that was in use. They also produced a new copper subsidiary coinage, which depreciated almost immediately upon its appearance. This was followed by a silver subsidiary coinage which also depreciated. As one should expect, the debasement of the currency ushered in price inflation.[78]

Officially the merchant firms were supposed to collect the land tax and all miscellaneous taxes half in copper cash (*tongyuan*) at only 70 percent of their market value, and half in standard cash (*zhiqian*) at a rate of 3,158 cash per tael. They preferred, however, to compel the collection of taxes entirely in copper cash, because by forcing down the value of copper cash in relation to the silver tael, in which land taxes were reckoned, they could make a higher profit.[79] Faure has argued that currency depreciation and the resulting inflation beginning in the mid-1890s were the single most significant factors contributing to rural hardship. Speaking about national conditions in relation to the rural activism in Jiangsu and Gongdong, Faure writes:

> The depreciation of the currency was quite unexpected; not for centuries had any government the ability to depreciate its currency on the scale that the late Qing government did towards the last years of the dynasty. Coming as it did at a time of government financial stringency, the sudden depreciations upset long-established standards in commodity prices and rent, as well as in tax. . . . In a sense, it may be said that the changes that can

be documented from 1870 to 1937 were external to the operation of the farm.[80]

The taxpayers, to whom this nightmare seemed endless, faced still more difficulties as the result of a countywide census called for by self-government reforms in late 1909. Taking advantage of the opportunity, local constables (*dibao*) and yamen runners (*yayi*) demanded cash payments from the households they surveyed. *Dibao* Zhao Renshao, for example, collected thirty cash from each household in the twenty-five villages of Xiguan *she*, far in excess of the amount he needed to cover his own expenses. Acting on behalf of five of the villages, village headman Zhao Naipan filed a complaint at the yamen, in response to which the magistrate ordered the *dibao* to return the money he had collected. In the remaining twenty villages, and in Baima *she* where two head runners had collected a poll tax, no action was taken against the runners, although village headmen had petitioned the magistrate for redress of the villagers' grievances. Once the uprising was under way several months later, the collection of poll taxes ceased.[81]

The meeting at Tangjia temple on April 21, 1910, mentioned above was called to review the people's common grievances, including new miscellaneous taxes, embezzled grain funds, and poll taxes recently collected by the census takers. At the meeting, Qu Shiwen expressed his view that, "the government is going to tax people, cattle, houses, hemp, and potatoes."[82] Qu's words carred significant weight. Qu was generally known as an "old peasant (*nongmin*) of about sixty years of age who was illiterate and had no powerful position or wealth to rely on, but who upon giving the signal could get ten thousand people to gather."[83] Yu Zhusan was a "moderately wealthy" peasant whom his fellow villagers regarded as "upright, and vigorously righteous." He was also literate, and wrote many of the leaflets and proclamations that accompanied various stages of the protest movement.[84] Over the years, Yu had repeatedly resisted taxes, frequently incurring the hostility of Yu Zanyang, a principal member of the county political elite.[85] After further discussion at Tangjia temple, Yu Zhusan proposed that "oppressive taxes which are irregular (*kejuan*) should be resisted and not paid." He personally refused to pay taxes and issued a statement encouraging others to join him.[86] Qu and Yu both posted their statements in the villages and towns of the county, and then sought support from villagers in organizing a village federation.[87] Eventually this alliance coordinated the activities of as many as fifty thousand participants.[88]

On May 21, one month after the meeting at Tangjia temple and after tax resistance notices had been posted, one thousand people from the area southwest of Laiyang city gathered at the Guandi temple to announce that they would go to the city to demand grain. The villagers carried sacks with them, and their numbers grew as they marched toward the county seat. By the time they reached the magistrate's yamen, the crowd was nearly ten thousand people. Qu Shiwen and thirty village and *she* headmen entered the city to request that grain be distributed and that an accounting be made of the public granary fund. Attempting at first to win the support of the magistrate, the protesters raised the slogan, "chou shen bu chou guan" (literally, hate the gentry; don't hate the officials).[89] For three hours Magistrate Zhu Huaizhi, seeing that the situation was tense, spoke to the crowd, which presented him with the following demands: (1) that the unofficial poll tax (*ding shui* or *renkou shui*) of three yuan per person be abolished, (2) that the theater tax be reduced, (3) that the "worthless" yamen gatekeepers and runners, and rural managers (*shendong* and *xiangzhang*) who "make meat and fish out of the people" be replaced, (4) that copper cash should not be devalued in relation to the tael in collecting the land tax, and (5) that those who could not immediately repay should not be allowed to borrow from the public granary fund.[90] The magistrate, unable to leave the crowd and hoping that it would disperse, agreed to summon the persons concerned and have them render account for the granary fund within ten days. He also promised that any shortages in the fund would be made up, and he specifically requested Yu Zhusan to work on the granary fund problem since he enjoyed the respect of the people.

Inspired by the apparent success of Qu Shiwen and the other village headmen, more than one thousand monks and priests gathered at the yamen two days later, on May 23, to demand the abolition of the temple tax, which had been increased from 10 percent of the property's worth in 1909 to 30 percent in 1910.[91] Furious when the magistrate had further announced that 30 percent of the property would be sold instead of taxed in order to finance new public schools, the monks and priests nonetheless did nothing until the other villagers had taken action on their own behalf. When presented with the priests' demand, Magistrate Zhu agreed to it as well.

The following day, however, Zhu reversed his strategem of appeasement. He requested government troops, had several dozen monks and priests arrested, and ordered the blacksmith to make several hundred pairs of handcuffs immediately. The magistrate made no attempt to clarify the public granary accounts or to replenish shortages within the ten days promised. Instead, he advised those implicated in the affair to stay out of sight. When it was learned that the arrested monks and priests were being tortured brutally and that one had died of wounds thus incurred, fear and suspicion were added to an already tense situation, and villagers began to arm themselves for self-defense.[92]

When Prefect Wen Qi arrived from Dengzhou to investigate the local crisis, several *shezhang* prepared a petition that they planned to present to him. As he was leaving Laiyang on May 30 after conferring with Magistrate Zhu, 50 to 60 of the 108 *shezhang* from Laiyang county stopped the prefect's sedan chair to submit their petition on the villagers' behalf. Wen glanced at the paper and tossed it to the ground. A detour brought the *shezhang* again in front of the prefect's oncoming sedan chair, but again they were spurned in their attempt to communicate with him. The next day the villagers learned that Magistrate Zhu had telegraphed for forty soldiers stationed nearby to move into Laiyang to arrest Qu Shiwen.[93] Relying for military support on central government troops stationed throughout the province, the magistrate and merchant tax farmers depended on political connections with such higher officials in the bureaucracy as Prefect Wen in order to secure that support.

On June 2, five thousand villagers, vowing to oppose Wang Qi and his associates, established a rebel encampment near Jiulihe (Nine Mile River), about a mile to the west of Laiyang city. This site became the base from which assembled owner-cultivators and other rural people mounted resistance to county authorities. Magistrate Zhu responded by ordering the troops that he had summoned not to move against the crowd, and once again he attempted a policy of appeasement. Forty merchant firms in the city that were not associated with the reform managers volunteered to act as Qu Shiwen's guarantors in order to forestall violence. Jiang Ershou, a wealthy merchant and *shezhang* who did not directly support the protesters, also offered to act as Qu's guarantor and to mediate the dispute. Unlike the other *shezhang* who supported the opposition movement, Jiang possessed wealth that made him vulnerable to politically well-connected persons who were able to inflict ruinous taxation on those without county-level political influence. Because of his neutrality, Jiang hoped that he would be trusted by both sides as a mediator.

After another week of false promises and insincere attempts at appeasement, however, Magistrate Zhu still had done nothing to meet the demands he had accepted on May 21. On June 11, a crowd again demonstrated at his yamen. Seeing that the crowd was persistent, Zhu adopted a different tactic when he addressed the assembled villagers this time. Probably because the police bureau had been the most visible vehicle for the tax farmers' corrupt practices, Zhu decided to use Wang Jingyue, the head of the police bureau and a member of the political elite, as a scapegoat. Zhu told the people that Wang was responsible for all the new taxes and that the others involved in tax farming knew nothing about them. From what is known of the villagers' demands and experiences, it is unlikely that they took Zhu's statement as the whole truth. In any case, it was the last straw for the protesters, who had long been awaiting a peaceful settlement, and June 11 witnessed the first outbreak of activist violence in Laiyang.[94]

After reassembling at Jiulihe on June 11, the crowd passed through the city, destroying the residence of Wang Jingyue, who was very much hated for his role in squeezing rural taxpayers for unofficial taxes and for fabricating charges against them and their village headmen. In order to avoid damaging adjacent property, the protestors carefully dug up Wang's house, broke it into pieces, and carried the debris to the river bank to be burned. Wang responded by sending his son, Wang Tinglan, to contact Wang Qi and to go to Jinan, the provincial capital, to seek support. In the villages of Yuchitou and Yejiazhuang, the crowd also destroyed the residences of Gao Yufeng and Chen Yude. Gao had incurred the antagonism of the rural people for his role in reporting many of them to the magistrate for nonpayment of the increased deed tax, as a result of which heavy fines had been imposed and many of the owner-cultivators had gone bankrupt. Chen was a wealthy landlord. Having no degree status and not acting as an agent for Wang Qi's group, he was not considered a member of the political elite. He did, however, have vast stores of grain that he refused to sell during periods of grain shortages, instead lending them at an 80 percent interest rate.[95]

At the time of the destruction of Wang Jingyue's residence, several members of the county political elite fled to Jinan where they sought official military support. Censor Wang Baotian memorialized that several wealthy Laiyang notables were in Jinan where they "daily sent inflammatory petitions to high officials."[96] Shang Qinghan, a member of the Shandong Provisional Provincial Assembly, confirmed Wang Baotian's statement when he wrote that he had encountered his old acquaintance, Wang Qi, in Jinan shortly after Shang had read in *Jinan ribao* about the destruction at Laiyang. Shang also described Wang Qi's visit to a certain Sun Peinan, presumably a high provincial official, who Wang hoped would request the governor to dispatch troops to Laiyang. Sun instead advised Wang Qi to take his request to the leaders of the Provisional Provincial Assembly, which Wang did. Shang noted that despite the fact that the assembly was supposed to listen to public opinion, the rural people were unaware of this, and consequently only the voices of the wealthy and influential were heard.[97] Sun Mengqi, Laiyang's own representative to the assembly, approved of sending troops to Laiyang, saying that the problem had not been harsh measures, but rather too much leniency toward the populace.[98] Eventually a minority of five assembly members, including Shang Qinghan and Wang Zhixun, editor of *Jinan ribao,* resigned their membership because in their opin-

ion the assembly had failed to give the Laiyang case proper consideration. The assembly as a whole supported the governor's action of sending troops to suppress the revolt.[99]

Meanwhile at Laiyang, the final form of the protesters' demands was
issued on June 13. They were as follows:

(1) The land tax should be collected at the conversion rate of one
tael to 2,400 cash (i.e., the rate set by Yuan Shikai, former governor of Shandong, in 1901); surcharges should not be permitted;
copper coins should not be discounted in value, whether taxes
were collected in copper cash that was converted from rates set
in standard cash or in copper cash itself.
(2) Officials and elite members who fraudulently took grain from the
public granary or funds from the granary fund must bear com-
plete responsibility for repaying the amount they took and must
immediately distribute grain to the poor.
(3) Henceforth, not one single cash may be collected for any kind of
miscellaneous tax.
(4) The Education Society (*jiaoyu hui*) of the Self-Government Office (*zizhi ju*) should be managed by impartial and upright elite
members who are appointed by the public (*gongju*); if such people cannot be found, all such positions should temporarily remain
vacant.
(5) Police must not be allowed to enter the rural areas at will to
harass and disturb the countryside.
(6) The gentry and merchants of the city as a body should agree to
protect Qu Shiwen and see that he is not killed.
(7) The "degraded gentry and corrupt managers" should be ordered
to retire and should not be permitted to intervene in local affairs.[100]

On June 26 matters took a turn for the worse. Magistrate Zhu was
dismissed from office and was replaced by Magistrate Kuibao, who
immediately issued a statement calling for the arrest of Qu Shiwen and
his brother Qu Shigui. At a meeting to discuss whether to negotiate or
state a full uprising, Qu's sister-in-law reportedly said, "The government negotiated with the Buddhist monks didn't it? What came of that?
The monks were jailed and tortured and killed. We ought to learn from
what happened to them. The nuns see it this way. If we do nothing we
will be defeated, so we should rise up." To which Qu Shiwen replied,
"Only if everyone thinks so."[101]

Daotai Yang Yaolin ordered 300 troops into the county to make the
arrests.[102] Qu Shiwen fled to Malianzhuang, a town about fifteen miles

to the northwest of Laiyang city, where Lü Baohuang, an apparent sympathizer, offered to sequester Qu in his home until he was no longer sought by the government troops. After assuring Qu of his safety, however, Lü locked his house from the outside and went to the Gong Shun firm to inform Wang Qi of Qu's whereabouts. Wang Qi in turn informed Magistrate Kuibao and Taotai Yang, who sent 160 troops and 70 yamen runners to arrest Qu. Meanwhile, one of Lü's hired laborers (*gugong*) suspected Lü's intentions. Knowing that Qu was respected by the rural people and that he would be killed if arrested, he unlocked the door and told Qu to flee.[103] When the troops found Qu gone, they killed Lü Baohuang for turning in a false report, and began to plunder and rape in the village in their search for Qu. Villagers responded by sounding gongs and calling for people to assemble. The troops fired on the assembling villagers, wounding forty or fifty of them and killing seven. The crowd then armed itself with rakes and hoes and moved to attack the troops. The soldiers again opened fire, wounding approximately ten people, while one soldier was wounded.[104]

The Qu partisans, vowing that they would not disperse, regrouped at the Jiulihe. Here the Laiyang uprising escalated to the dimensions of a full-scale rebellion against the local magistrate and his tax farmers. Thirty to forty thousand people brought their own food provisions and rain gear and, in spite of a heavy downpour, spent the night of July 2 camped on the banks of the Jiulihe.[105] During the first two weeks of July, the Qu partisans, by the force of their organized members and their militancy, controlled the situation in Laiyang county. Tens of thousands of villagers mobilized through the *she* and *cun* networks to patrol the countryside and provide supplies. An elderly owner-cultivator who was on patrol explained that Qu Shiwen had circulated a notice (*chuanpai*) which read, "Whichever villages this notice reaches, every family in the village must produce one person either to patrol the roads or to deliver food."[106] The aged partisan went on to say that this was the busy summer hoeing season, and that "when our children went to do patrol duty earlier, we saw that this left the fields wasting; so we asked the young people to do the hoeing, and we [the older people] went on patrol. We have heard that in our county more than 100,000 people have been mobilized to seize the city, patrol the roads, and deliver food. Farming has been delayed, and if this goes on, food will be a big problem in the future."[107] When asked why he had become involved in the rebellion, the patrol replied, "We heard that there would be increased, heavy taxation; if you raise a chicken there will be taxes, if you raise a dog there will be taxes, even if you give birth to a child there will be taxes—also, for each *mou* of melons there will be taxes, and for each *mou* of peanuts there will be taxes."[108]

Laiyang city was in a virtual state of seige. Dr. C. W. Pruitt, a missionary physician, writing to the U.S. Consul John Fowler in Yantai on July 16, reported that a friend "from the country around Lai Yang says the estimated number of rebels is 100,000. They hold seige about the city for the purpose of killing the Mandarin and the gentry. Food is becoming scarce."[109] In a report of July 25, J. C. McNally, U.S. Consul in Qingdao, referred to the "beseiged city of Laiyang which for several weeks has been in the hands of the rebels."[110] During the seige, Li Lanzhai, a student passing through the Laiyang area on his way home from Beijing, went to Qu Shiwen's headquarters in hope of mediating a settlement between the rebels and the government. Having been given directions by the partisans, Li arrived at Qu's headquarters to find Qu dressed in a bamboo rain hat and white trousers rolled up to his knees. Qu stood eating scallions wrapped in a pancake. When approached by Li with the suggestion of mediation, Qu curtly replied, "Nothing can be arbitrated," and hurried on his way.[111]

On July 7, official troops under the command of Deputy Commander Ye Changsheng from Lingshan and Brigade General Li Antang from Dengzhou reached Jimo, thirty miles to the south of Laiyang. A correspondent for the *North China Herald* in Qingdao reported in the July 15 issue that "detachments of troops are coming down daily from Tsinanfu, 800 having come down on the seventh by rail to a point about 200 li from Laiyang."[112] A Jinan correspondent reported on July 9 that some 2,000 troops had been dispatched to Laiyang, writing that "fifteen hundred left here on July 7 and 500 more were sent from Weihsien."[113] By July 12, the Qingdao correspondent reported that there were 2,400 troops on the scene. The rebellion continued in full force as the partisans attempted to capture Laiyang city. Martial law was declared within the city, and hired firefighters guarded its walls. On July 10, a minor skirmish took place at Shuigoutou when villagers from thirteen *she* in the area planned an attack on the elite families of that town.[114] Meanwhile, the Qingdao correspondent wrote that although reports from Laiyang were very meager, "At all events the resistance is manifestly of a very determined character."[115]

The Laiyang rebellion abruptly came to a tragic end on July 13. Early that morning, government troops moved from Shuigoutou to Mashanbu near the partisan encampment at Jiulihe. It was reported that four cavalry intelligence officers had been captured by the rebels and killed.[116] Although these reports later proved to be false—the four had actually deserted and had been captured while plundering and sent to Qu—the official troops responded by shooting villagers; only then did the partisans retaliate by killing the captives.[117] General Li Antang then ordered the bombardment by cannon of the rebel encampment at Jiulihe, the ensuing attack claiming the lives of more than three hundred people. Governor Sun Baoqi was later to justify this massacre as a proper response to the partisans' killing of the calvary officers.[118] It is clear, however, that the rebels, unable to reach a settlement with the local officials, were determined to pursue their demands in the hope of bringing their cause to the attention of higher authorities, who, they hoped, would then act to redress their grievances. Given this stalemate, only a military contest could resolve the situation.

After the brutal destruction of human life at Jiulihe, the troops continued their attack. Eight hundred residences, including Bolinzhuang, Qu Shiwen's native village, were burned, as were Liujiatuan, Yujiadian, Mashanbu, Zhoujiatuan, Yaogezhuang, and Taizizhuang. The troops gathered pots, pans, and work ladders to be used later as evidence that the Qu partisans were forging weapons from scrap iron and possessed scaling ladders for the seige of Laiyang city. It was reported also that they had artillery, which actually consisted of a few crude cannons left over from local defense against the Nian rebels in the 1860s.[119] The partisans were, in fact, very poorly armed, and this largely accounted for their defeat. Qu Shiwen escaped, but the villagers had paid heavily and their cause was lost.

Later in July, several dozen of the Laiyang city merchants who were not supporters of Wang Qi travelled to Beijing where they hoped, perhaps with the aid of the Shandong Landsmann's Association (Shandong lüjing tongxiang hui), a group of Shandong merchants and officials resident in Beijing, to request an imperial audience and bring charges against Governor Sun Baoqi for his flagrant attacks on the Laiyang people.[120] Although possibly sympathetic to the protest movement, these city merchants, some of whom may have been degree-holders, had no impact on the development or leadership of the protest. Their influence was confined instead to the aftermath of the uprising and to the pursuit of a settlement that would diminish the power of Wang Qi and his associates. Unwilling to risk major financial losses, the city merchants had tolerated the encroachments directed by Wang Qi against them, which were minor compared with those experienced by the rural residents. However, they moved quickly to unseat the county political elite once the uprising had collapsed and charges could be brought against those responsible.

By September Laiyang was quiet, and the throne considered the affair closed. The Shandong Landsmann's Association in Beijing, however, which as early as July 14 had sent representatives to investigate the rebellion, continued to press Prince Qing, the head of the Grand Council, for the dismissal of both Governor Sun and Wang Xu, vice president of the Board of Justice and cousin of Wang Qi. Planning to enlist the support of the Shandong Provisional Provincial Assembly in these efforts, the association also repeatedly called for action against Wang Xu, who had been Wang Qi's principal backer in Beijing and who had perhaps influenced Sun's decision to send troops.[121] The possibility of preexisting hostility between the association and Wang Xu at the level of Beijing politics is suggested here. Although direct evidence is lacking, it is also possible that the association was backed by the court fraction against Prince Qing.

In mid-September, the Landsmann's Association requested that the throne investigate the Laiyang affair in order to discover and dismiss the persons responsible for protecting the corrupt county elite. While the chief censor, Zhang Yinglin, refused to memorialize on behalf of the association, Censor Hu Sijing, acting on his own initiative, memorialized that Governor Sun had done nothing to ensure a better future in Laiyang and that it was likely that trouble would break out again.[122] Governor Sun did offer his resignation several times, but in the end he remained in office, perhaps, as reported by *Shibao,* because he was related to Prince Qing through their children's marriage.[123] Finally, in response to the persistence of the Landsmann's Association, an imperial edict was announced on November 7, 1910. Magistrate Kuibao, Daotai Yang Yaolin, and Prefect Wen Qi of Dengzhou were dismissed. Brigade General Li Antang was asked to resign, and Wang Qi, Wang Jingyue, and Ge Guixing were deprived of their degree status.[124]

In the aftermath of the Laiyang rebellion, there was a broad spectrum of assessments as to what had happened there. While Magistrates Zhu Huaizhi and Kuibao, Taotai Yang, and Prefect Wen had all taken the traditional position that the Laiyang disturbances were the work of "local bullies and bad elements," Censor Wang Baotian and Governor Sun Baoqi both traced the source of trouble to the local network of corruption, which included merchant tax farmers and local official personnel.[125] A minority group within the Shandong Assembly followed this line of analysis and also moved cautiously toward the view that the partisans had legitimate grievances and demands.[126] Wang Zhixun, editor of the *Jinan ribao,* which reported extensively on the Laiyang incident, stressed the reasonableness and respectability of the Qu partisans' demands.[127] The Shandong Landsmann's Association in Beijing also defended the Qu partisans and went so far as to claim that Qu Shiwen was a spokesman for public opinion (*yulun*) and that a government that considered itself a constitutional body should listen to rather than suppress such expressions of popular grievances and local problems.[128] The experience at Laiyang also led some writers, including Liang Qichao's friends who published the periodical *Guofeng bao* (National Customs), to suspect that for China constitutional reform could have a destructive side and could lead to popular rebellions and collapse. Reform in the hands of corrupt elites could be robbery—worse than no reform at all.[129]

New Policy reforms did continue at Laiyang after the suppression of the rebellion. Once again, however, local history becomes vague. Although Wang Qi was deprived of his degree status, it is not known if he continued to exercise influence. Elections were held in early 1911, for city self-government officials and in mid-1913 for representatives from the rural districts. The magistrate's office presided over the county's self-government assembly. Of all those elected to these positions, the only name connected with the 1910 affair is Jiang Ershou, the wealthy grain merchant and *shezhang* who had remained neutral during the uprising.[130] As to how self-government was financed or what role the police bureau played, nothing is known. However, it is recorded that in the fall of 1911, Qu Shiwen returned to gather partisans and mount a new resistance, attempting an alliance with Guo Funian, a rebel leader from the Zhaoyuan area near Laiyang. As in 1910, the results were unsuccessful. Qu made one final attempt in 1914, when he secretly reentered the Laiyang area, now under growing Japanese influence. This time, however, his efforts to organize for revolt ended tragically with his capture and subsequent execution at Yantai.[131] There is no information as to what the issues in either of these later conflicts were or who the targets of revolt may have been. If the city merchants who opposed Wang Qi had become involved in the New Policy programs, they had perhaps not remedied the commoners' grievances against these reforms.

In 1914, Qu Shiwen, a man of sixty-five years with a lifelong career of defending the poor, sat in a Yantai jail awaiting execution. The state that convicted him found his death necessary if "order" was to be maintained and "modernization" pursued. Qu's two sons, Qu Hongyan and Qu Hongchang, who participated in the uprising were also arrested and executed.[132]

Contemporaneous Activism in Neighboring Counties: The Situations at Haiyang and Zhaoyuan

While the situation was unfolding in Laiyang, an antitax movement began in neighboring Haiyang county to the east of Laiyang on the coast of the Shandong Peninsula. Up to ten thousand rural people mobilized through village and *she* networks of communication under the loosely connected leadership of Song Xuanwen (1853–1915), Gao Qiwang (1848–1910), and Wang Ling (1874–1910). At the same time, in Zhaoyuan county to the north of Laiyang, Qu Shiwen's destination in the aftermath of the suppression of the Laiyang, Guo Funian (1877–1819), a local rebel leader, joined in support of Qu's uprising without generating a movement within Zhaoyuan.

In Haiyang, a main source of contention was the low exchange ratio set by the yamen clerks and runners for copper coins (*tongyuan*) in which new taxes and surcharges were levied under the pretext of New Policy reforms. This problem has been discussed in connection with the Laiyang grievances and was a factor in all of the rural activism of the post-Boxer decade. According to the regulations of the Board of Revenue in Beijing, land tax was to be collected half in copper coins and half in standard cash.[133] In 1907, the Shandong finance commissioner announced that, "the official collection of land tax should take into consideration the local conditions; the magistrate should discuss the supply of copper cash with the local gentry and people, and come to an agreement on what percentage is to be paid in standard cash. Moreover, for those areas in which the supply of standard cash is short, there should be a plan that avoids difficulties for the rural people."[134] Because of the extreme shortage of standard cash in Haiyang, Magistrate Wu of Haiyang in 1908 set the levy at 30 percent in standard cash and 70 percent in copper cash. The rural nonelite households, however, believed that 30 percent in standard cash was still too high. As a result, *shezhang* and *xiangzhang,* representing the interests of the commoner taxpayers, petitioned for a lower rate in standard cash. After reviewing the situation, Magistrate Wu announced that land tax could be paid in either copper cash or standard cash. This policy was reversed in 1910, however, when Magistrate Fang declared on taking office that the 30–70 ratio would be reinstituted. The required payment in standard cash was to be converted to copper cash at an exchange ratio disadvantageous to the taxpayers, resulting in an increased expense that the owner-cultivators considered to be an unofficial surcharge.

The *she* and *xiang* headmen, who repeatedly petitioned for land-tax payments in copper cash only so that taxpayers would not lose on the conversion rate, were led by a rural resident named Song Xuanwen, who was definitely progessive in his views, but not as willing to take the risks that Qu did in Laiyang when the decision to go beyond further negotiations had to be made. Orphaned at age ten, Xuanwen was raised by relatives who were poor. His uncle, however, made sure he was educated for seven or eight years, after which Xuanwen purchased a lower degree (*jiansheng*). When Xuanwen was seventeen, his uncle died and he could only study on his own. He worked as a litigation agent (*song gun*), a function usually performed by lower degree-holders, and eventually was able to purchase forty to fifty *mou* of land and build a thatched house three *jian* in size. He married, and he and his wife had four sons and three daughters.

Song Xuanwen was very open-minded. He believed in male/female equality and saw to it that his daughters were all educated in the classics as were his sons. He was one of the earliest supporters of the anti-foot binding movement in Haiyang. He was also especially critical of the corrupt local officials who flourished under the Qing rule. Hoping to contribute to improved local conditions, he and his son Song Xunji (1874–1923) raised funds for Haiyang's first factory in 1908.[135] When he heard of the government's plan to levy new miscellaneous taxes in 1908, he knew that the officials were planning to "make meat and fish of the people." By 1910 with the announcement of the New Policy in Haiyang, Song Xuanwen told the local magistrate that the people could not bear the extra burdens.[136] The *laobaixing* (commoners) of Haiyang regarded Song Xuanwen as a person of high standing, and he distributed grain without charge to families in need in years of poor crops.[137] In March 1910, Song ordered *xiang* and *she* headmen not to deliver taxes to the city, and on May 25, he was arrested for agitating against the payment of taxes according to the new formula. There are unfortunately few details available concerning Song's activities between the time of his initial agitation and his arrest.

From May 27 to 30, Prefect Wen from Dengzhou was in the Laiyang/Haiyang area to investigate both disturbances and to consult with the two magistrates. As Prefect Wen was leaving Haiyang, Song Xuanwen's son Song Xunji attempted to present a petition on his imprisoned father's behalf, but, as at Laiyang, Wen merely looked at the petition before throwing it to the ground. On being informed that the younger Song was absent without permission from his duties as teacher at Dengzhou normal school, Wen had him arrested, which led another son, Song Zengji, to assume leadership of the movement.[138]

Early in June, Song Zengji called a meeting at Wangshishan to make plans for action against the local authorities. The owner-cultivators and village leaders who attended organized themselves into a "party" (*dang*) and distributed leaflets that set a date for people to go the city to seek the release of both Song and his son. The leaflet read in part: "Enter the city and create a disturbance at the hall of the yamen; break open the jail and reverse the case in order to save Song Xuanwen father and son. For anyone who does not follow, disaster will fall on their village."[139] Magistrate Fang, learning of the Song partisans' plan, sent semiregular troops and runners to arrest the ringleaders before the announced date of the public demonstration.[140] With their plan of action threatened, several tens of thousands of people gathered on June 6 in advance of the set date and surrounded the county seat. The villagers marched through the west gate and attacked the yamen buildings, but as they reached the center of the city, police troops opened fire, killing four people. More people entered through the west gate, which was being held open by the protesters, and together they marched to the jail and freed the Songs.

While the Song partisans were storming the county seat and presenting their demands, Gao Qiwang (1848–1910) and Wang Ling emerged as grassroots leaders who took a more direct approach to reclaiming rural resources. Gao was a poor peasant who had educated himself so that he could eventually read literature such as *Shui hu zhuan*, *Sanguoyanyi*, and *Xiyouji*.[141] Gao and Wang led one thousand people in twenty-nine incidents between June 6 and into August to confiscate grain supplies and exact cash payments from wealthy *she* and *xiang* headmen who had been involved in embezzling public grain funds and collecting New Policy taxes. While Song Xuanwen represented the interests of the politically powerless property owners, Gao and Wang acted on behalf of the propertyless and the destitute. Their opponent, however, was the same corrupt administrative and commercial elite (*fushen*).

Once the Songs had been released, the protesters returned to their original concerns. During the next several days, they waited for Magistrate Fang to act on the following demands:

(1) The county granary with its 8,000 *shi* of grain should be immediately opened for distribution to the poor people.

(2) The land tax increase of 360 cash per tael should be canceled, and copper cash used as tax payment should not be discounted in value.

(3) Those agents who had exacted 8,000 taels in taxes for the police bureau and the new government research office should be ordered to forward the money to the magistrate's office immediately.

(4) Since orders had been received to abolish the mounted couriers (*macha*), contributions for this purpose should no longer be collected.

(5) Temple property should be used by the *xiang* themselves for establishing primary schools, and government education authorities should not be permitted to have schools on this property.

(6) The records of collections and disbursements of theater and shop taxes over the past years should be made public.

(7) Since all past disbursement for New Policies had been abuse ridden, henceforth upright gentry should be selected by the public (*gongju*) for posts concerning New Policies.

(8) The practice of taking more money than is due on the deed tax should immediately be abolished.

(9) With regard to those people who were shot by troops, since they were not bandits, their names should be legally cleared.[142]

These demands indicate that it was the abuses of the New Policy reforms, rather than the reforms themselves, that were the taxpayers' targets. The abuses not only imposed financial hardships on the rural people, but also encroached upon the traditional prerogatives of the intervillage local systems. The Song supporters wanted to be able to check potential abuses by overseeing any new schools that were established, making taxes a matter of public record, and publicly selecting New Policy managers, rather than allowing this authority to fall into the hands of the already entrenched county political-elite network.

According to a report in *Dongfang zazhi,* Magistrate Fang ordered some of the wealthy elite families to distribute grain and cash to the protesters. The wealthy elite families of the Shude and Renshu ancestral halls (*tang*) in the eastern *xiang* were required to pay 3,500 strings of cash, and wealthy degree-holder (*fushen*) Zhao Shide of Wei village was required to pay 2,500 strings of cash. When other members of the elite (*shenshi*), including Liu Shuntian, Miao Zhen, and Wang Wenxuan, heard of the demands to divide grain and distribute money, they left their homes. Their residences and property were destroyed, however, and their grain stolen. The magistrate in this case was not as firmly committed to support for the county elite. Apparently not relishing the situation that confronted him, Fang had requested a transfer from his post at Haiyang. After hearing that his request had been granted, he did nothing to either meet the villagers' demands or stop the confiscations in the rural areas, thus incurring the hostility of both the Song partisans and the wealthy members of the elite.[143] Song Xuanwen encouraged Gao to find a safe hiding place and helped his own sons escape to Yantai and Dalian. But Gao chose to stay and try to fight.[144] Once the new magistrate took office, he immediately hired spies and sent agents to arrest Gao Qiwang and two of his cohorts, Wang Ling and Zhang Ming. They confessed to their part in the confiscations and were decapitated on the spot.[145]

Events at Haiyang did not reach the large scale of tax resistance that occurred at Laiyang. Fewer villagers were involved, and the situation did not escalate to a seige of the county seat. Neither the reform managers nor the commoner community at Haiyang were as united as their Laiyang counterparts. While taxes had been collected by Haiyang political elite for the purpose of funding a new police bureau, no appointments had yet been made to this office, and it was therefore not yet an arm of a highly centralized reform-oriented organization. Among the commoners, the *shezhang* were divided in their support for the tax resistance, and many of them aided the wealthy degree-holders (*fushen*) who managed funds for reform programs. A split in the commoners' leadership at Haiyang also revealed the lesser cohesiveness of the antireform movement there. Although having the same opponents among the county notables, Song Xuanwen and Gao Qiwang represented a division in the rural populace between the moderately well-off owner-cultivators and the poor, often propertyless residents. This was perhaps indicative of the fact that Haiyang's populace was less homogeneous than Laiyang's predominantly owner-cultivator population.

Conclusions

While sharing issues and protest scenarios in common with many cases of anti–New Policy movements during the post-Boxer era, the history of Laiyang is unique for the high level of detail that had been preserved on protest leaders and local conditions. The documents on the Laiyang protest allow us to see in great depth the terms in which farmers fought to maintain the entire web of cultural, political, and economic factors supporting the foundations of rural livelihood and leadership. The way of life that farmers defended and took pride in meant more than just getting by. It was a full social identity with a long and rich cultural past. It was also a practical means of collective protection, which the New Policy arrangements would destroy.

Participants in the Laiyang protest understood that the central government along with its local officials and associates were most responsible for any threats to rural livelihood they experienced during this period. Whether through collaboration with or appeasement of foreigners, state policies to achieve the reforms required by the Boxer Protocol were perceived to be at the heart of the rural crisis. In keeping with these views, anti-Christian issues were subordinated to antigovernment greivances, and foreign sources of difficulties were considered a subcategory of administrative mismanagement and corruption. The only dividing line that held during this period of conflict was not a socioeconomic one, but a line drawn in relationship to the use of state authority. It was not a line between landlord and peasant or between the educated and the illiterate. For while present, both of these lines were crossed in the process of making alliances whether in favor of or in opposition to New Policy measures. The line of social conflict was between groups associated with those who used reforms to serve primarily themselves and groups that identified with those whose livelihood along with its cultural supports were most eroded by the swift currents of a new kind of commercial/political development that knew no moral limits.

In this struggle, the rural population was largely left to its own devices. Yu Zhusan's role and commitment to Qu Shiwen was critical, but the rebellion relied most heavily on the dedication of Qu and the cultural references cultivated within the workings of rural society's subsistence farmers. At Haiyang, the division between Song Xuanwen and Gao Qiwang, despite all of Song's good intentions makes clear the vital role that rural popular culture played in adding militancy to the protest. Neither the moderate reformers like Song, nor the revolutionaries among the Tongmenghui, who do not appear in the activities of these two counties, brought the depth of commitment to rural concerns that Qu Shiwen personified.

Notes

Epigraph: Liu Tongjun, ed., *Xinhai gemingqian Lai Hai Zhao kangjuan yongdong* (Antitax movements in Laiyang, Haiyang, and Zhaoyuan before the 1911 Revolution) (Beijing: Shehuikexue wenxian chuban she, 1989), 437.

1. Liu Tongjun, *Xinhai gemingqian Lai Hai Zhao kangjuan yongdong*, 425
2. Ibid.
3. "*Guan yu Qushiwen kangjuan touzheng qingguang de diaocha*" (An inquiry into the circumstances related to the Qu Shiwen antitax struggle) (an oral history given by Qu Hongjiang, Qu Guofu, and Tao Shouheng to Ren Zhixue), Bolin village, Laiyang, Shandong, April 19, 1984.
4. Ramon H. Myers, *The Chinese Peasant Economy: Agricultural Development in Hopei and Shantung, 1890–1949* (Cambridge: Harvard University Press, 1970), 223.
5. Myers, *The Chinese Peasant Economy*, 138, 151.
6. Jing Su and Luo Lun, *Landlord and Labor in Late Imperial China: Case Studies from Shandong*, trans. Endymion Wilkinson (Cambridge: Harvard University Press, 1978), 12.
7. Myers, *The Chinese Peasant Economy*, 224–27.
8. Albert Tévoédjrè, *Poverty, The Wealth of Mankind* (Oxford: Pergamon Press, 1979).
9. Zhang Yufa, *Zhong guo xiandai hua de qu cheng yanjiu: Shandong, 1860–1916* (Regional study of modernization in China, Shandong, 1860–1916) (Taibei: Academica Sinica, 1982), vol. 2, 644.
10. *Laiyang xianzhi* (Laiyang Gazetteer) (1935), 2.6:57.
11. Ibid., 2.1:38.
12. Zhang Yufa, *Zhong guo xiandai hua de qu cheng yanjiu: Shandong, 1860–1916,* vol. 2, 600.
13. Ibid., vol. 2, 588.
14. Liu Tongjun, *Xinhai gemingqian Lai Hai Zhao kangjuan yongdong*, 432.

15. *Laiyang xianzhi*, 2.6:56.

16. Ibid., 2.6:58.

17. Zhang Yufa, *Zhong guo xiandai hua de qu cheng yanjiu: Shandong, 1860–1916*, vol 2. 506–20.

18. Ibid., vol. 2, 726–37.

19. Ibid., vol. 2, 739.

20. *Laiyang xianzhi* (Laiyang Gazetteer) (1935).

21. Arthur H. Smith, *Village Life in China* (New York: Fleming H. Revell, 1899), 226–34; Martin C. Yang, *A Chinese Village* (New York: Columbia University Press, 1945), 174; Ch'u T'ung-tsu, *Local Government in China under the Ch'ing* (Stanford: Stanford University Press, 1962), 328, n. 99.

22. R. F. Johnston, *Lion and Dragon in Northern China* (New York: E. P. Dutton and Company, 1910), 155; Yang, *A Chinese Village*, 175–76; Ch'u, *Local Government*, 2.

23. Liu Tongjun, *Xinhai gemingqian Lai Hai Zhao kangjuan yongdong*, 11.

24. Ibid., 10.

25. Wei Zhongxian,"Qu Shiwen yu Laiyang canggu shimo" (The whole story of Qu Shiwen and the Laiyang granary), in *Xinhai gemingqian Lai Hai Zhao kangjuan yongdong*, ed. Liu Tongjun, 362–64.

26. Liu Tongjun, *Xinhai gemingqian Lai Hai Zhao kangjuan yongdong*, 424.

27. For another discussion of the Laiyang case, see James Braig Manwarren, "Rural-Urban Conflict in Shantung: The 1910 Laiyang Tax Uprising" (M.A. Thesis, Arizona State University, 1976). For briefer references to the Laiyang case, see John Lust, "Secret Societies, Popular Movements, and the 1911 Revolution," in *Popular Movements and Secret Societies in China, 1840–1950*, ed. Jean Chesneaux (Stanford: Stanford University Press, 1972), 169; and David S. Buck, *Urban Change in China: Politics and Development in Tsinan, Shantung, 1890–1949* (Madison: University of Wisconsin Press, 1978), 67.

28. *Laiyang xianzhi*, 2.2:53; Shandong lüjing tongxiang hui, 6.

29. Liu Tongjun, *Xinhai gemingqian Lai Hai Zhao kangjuan yongdong*, 432.

30. Ibid., 439.

31. Ibid., 442–43.

32. Ibid., 444–46.

33. Ibid., 434–35.

34. Chester C. Tan, *The Boxer Catastrophe* (New York: Columbia University Press, 1955) 36, 43–44; Siang-tseh Chiang, *The Nien Rebellion* (Seattle: University of Washington Press, 1954), 27–30; Joseph Esherick, *The Origins of the Boxer Uprising*, 45–54.

35. Liu Tongjun, *Xinhai gemingqian Lai Hai Zhao kangjuan yongdong*, 436–38.

36. Ibid., 12, 426–27.

37. Both Qu Shiwen and Yu Zhusan are described in written sources as taking up the responsibilities of *shezhang*, but it is not clear if Qu and Yu were formally recognized as *shezhang* by the county government, as evidently were each of their fathers. County historians at Laiyang told me clearly that Qu Shiwen and Yu Zhusan were not *shezhang*. In the written sources and those

based on oral histories, Yu Zhusan sometimes refers to himself as a *shezhang*, while Qu Shiwen does not. Qu and Yu were affectionately called "Great Uncle" (*daye*) by most people. In addition, Qu Shiwen is referred to as *zongzhihui* (commander in chief) by his supporters.

38. Kung-chuan Hsiao, *Rural China: Imperial Control in the Nineteenth Century* (Seattle: University of Washington Press, 1960), 419.

39. Kung-chuan Hsiao, *Rural China*, 321.

40. Ibid., 497.

41. Albert Feuerwerker, *Rebellion in Nineteenth-Century China* (Ann Arbor: Center for Chinese Studies, University of Michigan, 1975), 75.

42. Chung-li Chang, *The Chinese Gentry: Studies on Their Role in Nineteenth-Century Chinese Society* (Seattle: University of Washington Press, 1955), 138–39.

43. Zhang Yufa, *Zhong guo xiandai hua de qu cheng yanjiu: Shandong, 1860–1916*, vol. 2, 663–66. In Shandong, during the years 1644–1861 (218 years) there were 3,139 degree-holders at the *juren* and *jinshi* levels. From 1862–1903, there were 705 (41 years). Most counties had one to twenty higher degree-holders.

44. Zhang Yufa, *Zhong guo xiandai hua de qu cheng yanjiu: Shandong, 1860–1916*, vol. 2, 664–65.

45. Robert Redfield, *The Little Community and Peasant Society and Culture*, Book 2 (Chicago: University of Chicago Press, 1956; second impression, 1961), 41.

46. Sidney D. Gamble, *North China Villages: Social, Political, and Economic Activities before 1933* (Berkeley: University of California Press, 1963), 50.

47. Emily M. Ahern, *The Cult of the Dead in a Chinese Village* (Stanford: Stanford University Press, 1973), 84.

48. Hsiao-tung Fei, *Peasant Life in China: A Field Study of Country Life in the Yangtze Valley* (New York: E. P. Dutton and Co., 1939), 109.

49. Liu Tongjun, *Xinhai gemingqian Lai Hai Zhao kangjuan yongdong*, 426.

50. Gamble, *North China Villages*, 51.

51. Hsiao-tung Fei, *Peasant Life in China*, 108.

52. Ahern, *The Cult of the Dead in a Chinese Village*, 84.

53. T'ung-tsu Ch'u, *Local Government in China under the Ch'ing* (Cambridge: Harvard University Press, 1962), 2.

54. R. F. Johnston, *Lion and Dragon in Northern China* (New York: E. P. Dutton and Co., 1910), 155.

55. Reverend Bishop Bashford, retired, "General Survey, 1911," in *The China Mission Year Book*, ed. Rev. G. H. Bondfield (Shanghai: Christian Literature Society for China, 1912), 14.

56. Bashford, "General Survey, 1911," 13–15

57. Martin C. Yang, *A Chinese Village: Taitou, Shantung Province* (New York: Columbia University Press, 1945), 190.

58. Martin C. Yang, *A Chinese Village: Taitou, Shantung Province* (New York: Columbia University Press, 1945), 190.

59. Zhang Yufa, *Zhong guo xiandai hua de qu cheng yanjiu: Shandong, 1860–1916*, vol. 2, 850.

60. Shandong lüjing tongxiang hui, 10–11.

61. Zhang Yufa, *Zhong guo xiandai hua de qu cheng yanjiu: Shandong, 1860–1916*, vol. 2, 497.

62. *Shibao*, August 19, 1910. Originally equivalent to *shengyuan*, *xiushi* was probably by this time a euphemism for the purchased *jiansheng*.

63. Shandong lüjing tongxiang hui, 7.

64. Ibid., 10–11.

65. Wang Zhixun, "Tiaocha Lai, Hai luan shi baogaoshu," 28.

66. Shandong lüjing tongxiang hui, 9.

67. Zhang Yufa, *Zhong guo xiandai hua de qu cheng yanjiu: Shandong, 1860–1916*, vol. 2, 601.

68. T'ung-tsu Ch'u, *Local Government*, 182, 191.

69. *Laiyang xianzhi*, 2.2:53; Shandong lüjing tongxiang hui (Shandong landsmann's association), ed., "Laiyang shibian di tiaocha baogaoshu" (An investigative report on the Laiyang disturbances), in *Shandong jindai shi ziliao* (Sources on Shandong's modern history) (Jinan: Shandong renmin chuban she, 1958), 6, 10–11. This report was also published in *Shuntian shibao* (The Shuntian Times) August 13–29, 1910. It was later compiled in *Jindai shi ziliao* (Materials on modern history), no. 1 (1954), 26–47.

70. Shandong lüjing tongxiang hui, "Laiyang shibian di tiaocha baogaoshu," 7, 10–11.

71. Wang Zhixun, "Tiaocha Lai, Hai luan shi baogaoshu" (Report on an investigation into the Laiyang and Haiyang disturbances), in *Shandong jindai shi ziliao*, 28.

72. David S. Buck, *Urban Change in China: Politics and Development in Tsinan, Shantung, 1890* (Madison: University of Wisconsin Press, 1978), 27.

73. Shandong lüjing tongxiang hui, "Laiyang shibian di tiaocha baogaoshu," 12; Wang Zhixun, "Tiaocha Lai, Hai," 28.

74. For a discussion of counties where magistrates initially controlled the reform process with little popular resistance, see Stephen R. MacKinnon, *Power and Politics in Late Imperial China: Yuan Shi-kai in Beijing and Tianjin, 1901–1908* (Berkeley: University of California Press, 1980), 155; and Sidney D. Gamble, *Ting Hsien: A North China Rural Community* (New York: Institute of Pacific Relations, 1954), 125, 160, 165, 188, 238–39, 286.

75. Shandong lüjing tongxiang hui, 8; *Laiyang xianzhi*, 19, 2.2:51; also see Zhang Yufa, *Zhong guo xiandai hua de qu cheng yanjiu: Shandong, 1860–1916*, vol. 1, 376–78.

76. Shandong lüjing tongxiang hui, "Laiyang shibian di tiaocha baogaoshu" (An investigative report on the Laiyang disturbances), in *Shandong jindai shi ziliao* (Sources on Shandong's modern history) (Jinan: Shandong renmin chuban she, 1958), 7; *Laiyang xianzhi*, 2.2:45.

77. Shandong lüjing tongxiang hui, "Laiyang shibian di tiaocha baogaoshu," 12; Wang Zhixun, "Tiaocha Lai, Hai luan shi baogaoshu," 28.

78. David Faure, *The Rural Economy of Pre-Liberation China: Trade*

Expansion and Peasant Livelihood in Jiangsu and Guangdong, 1870 to 1937 (Hong Kong: Oxford University Press, 1989), 64.

79. Shandong lüjing tongxiang hui, "Laiyang shibian di tiaocha baogaoshu," 7. For a discussion of copper cash (*tongyuan*) and standard cash (*zhiqian*), see H. H. King, *Money and Monetary Policy in China, 1845–1895* (Cambridge: Harvard University Press, 1965).

80. Faure, *The Rural Economy of Pre-Liberation China*, 206–7.

81. Shandong lüjing tongxiang hui, "Laiyang shibian di tiaocha baogaoshu," 8.

82. *Laiyang xianzhi*, juanmo 8.

83. Shandong lüjing tongxiang hui, "Laiyang shibian di tiaocha baogaoshu," 27.

84. Shandong lüjing tongxiang hui, "Laiyang shibian di tiaocha baogaoshu," 18.

85. *Laiyang xianzhi*, juanmo 8.

86. Shandong lüjing tongxiang hui, "Laiyang shibian di tiaocha baogaoshu," 18; *North China Herald*, July 29, 1910.

87. Sun Baoqi, "Zou chafu Laiyang, Haiyang er xian zhaoluan qing-xing zhe" (Memorial on the disruptive situation in Laiyang and Haiyang), in *Shandong jindai shi ziliao*, 44.

88. Hubeisheng zhexue shehui kexue hui lianhe hui (Joint committee of the philosophical society and science association of Hubei), ed., *Xinhai geming wushi zhounian jinian luwen ji* (A symposium commemorating the fiftieth anniversary of the 1911 Revolution) (Hubei: Zhonghua shuju, 1961), 564.

89. Liu Tongjun, *Xinhai gemingqian Lai Hai Zhao kangjuan yongdong*, 11.

90. *Dongfang zazhi*, no. 6, 1910: 80.

91. *Dongfang zazhi*, no. 8, 1910: 61.

92. *Shibao*, September 16, 17, 1910: Wang Baotian, "Zou Laiyang, Haiyang er xian xiang jishan bianpai da chen," 41; *Laiyang xianzhi*, juanmo 8.

93. Shandong lüjing tongxiang hui, "Laiyang shibian di tiaocha baogaoshu," 14, 19; Wang Zhixun, "Tiaocha Lai, Hai luan shi baogaoshu," 30.

94. Wang Baotian, "Zou Laiyang, Haiyang er xian xiang jishan bianpai da chen," 40; *Dongfang zazhi*, no. 6, 1910: 80.

95. Shangdong lüjing tongxiang hui, "Laiyang shibian di tiaocha baogaoshu," 13.

96. Wang Baotian, "Zou Laiyang, Haiyang er xian xiang jishan bianpai da chen," 41.

97. Shang Qinghan, "Shandong ziyiyu yiyuan Wang Zhixun, Ding Shiyi, Zhou Shulin, Zhang Jieli, Shang Qinghan cizhi yuan you baogaoshu" (Report on the reasons for the resignation of Wang Zhixun, Ding Shiyi, Zhou Shulin, Zhang Jieli, and Shang Qinghan from the Shandong Provisional Provincial Assembly), in *Shandong jindai shi ziliao*, 35.

98. Shandong lüjing tongxiang hui, "Laiyang shibian di tiaocha baogaoshu," 23.

99. Wang Zhixun, "Fu Wang Zhixun deng wuren duiyu ziyiju cishi liyou shu" (Letter of resignation from the assembly by Wang Zhixun and five others), in *Shandong jindai shi ziliao*, 40; Shang Qinghan, 37.

100 *Dongfang zazhi*, no. 6, 1910: 80. For reference to exchange ratio set by Yuan Shikai, see Shandong lüjing tongxiang hui, "Laiyang shibian di tiaocha baogaoshu," 7.

101. Liu Tongjun, *Xinhai gemingqian Lai Hai Zhao kangjuan yongdong*, 428.

102. Shandong lüjing tongxiang hui, "Laiyang shibian di tiaocha baogaoshu," 15; *Dongfang zazhi*, no. 7, 1910: 92.

103. Shandong lüjing tongxiang hui, "Laiyang shibian di tiaocha baogaoshu," 15–16; *Dongfang zazhi*, no. 8, 1910: 62; Chen Guilong, "Zou chaming Shandong Li, Hai liang xian zishi qingxing ju shifu chenzhe" (A memorial on the distressing facts of the Laiyang and Haiyang uprisings in Shandong), in *Shandong jindai shi ziliao*, 50.

104. Wang Zhixun, "Tiaocha Lai, Hai," 31.

105. Shandong lüjing tongxiang hui, "Laiyang shibian di tiaocha baogaoshu," 16; Wang Zhixun, "Tiao Lai, Hai," 31; *Laiyang xianzhi*, juanmo 9.

106. Li Lanzhai, "Duiyu Laiyang Qu Shiwen shibian wo suo zhidao de yi linbanzhao" (What I know of the Laiyang Qu Shiwen rebellion), in *Shandong jindai shi ziliao*, 61.

107. Li Lanzhai, "Duiyu Laiyang Qu Shiwen shibian wo suo zhidao de yi linbanzhao," 61.

108. Ibid.

109. National Archives Microfilm Publication, United States (1910) Roll No. 7, Despatch 1031, Enclosure No. 13, July 16, 1910.

110. National Archives, Letter to W. J. Calhoun, July 25, 1910.

111. Li Lanzhai, "Duiyu Qu Shiwen shibian tiaoju jingguo luguang," (An attempt to arbitrate in the Qu Shiwen rebellion), in *Shandong jindai shi ziliao*, 62.

112. *North China Herald*, July 15, 1910.

113. Ibid., July 22, 1910.

114. Shandong lüjing tongxiang hui, "Laiyang shibian di tiaocha baogaoshu," 16, 20; *Dongfang zazhi*, no. 8, 1910: 62.

115. *North China Herald*, July 29, 1910.

116. *Laiyang xianzhi*, juanmo 9; Sun Baoqi, 54.

117. Shandong lüjing tongxiang hui, "Laiyang shibian di tiaocha baogaoshu," 17.

118. Sun Baoqi, "Zou chafu Laiyang, Haiyang er xian zhaoluan qing-xing zhe" (Memorial on the disruptive situation in Laiyang and Haiyang) in *Shandong jindai shi ziliao*, 54.

119. Shandong lüjing tongxiang hui, "Laiyang shibian di tiaocha baogaoshu," 17, 26.

120. *Shibao*, July 29, 1910.

121. *Shibao*, July 21, July 31, September 17, 19, 1910.

122. *Shibao*, September 19, 29, 1910.

123. *Shibao*, September 22, 1910.

124. Imperial Edict in *Shandong jindai shi ziliao*, 58.

125. Wang Baotian, "Zou Laiyang, Haiyang er xian xiang jishan bianpai da chen," 43; Sun Baoqi, "Zou chafu Laiyang, Haiyang er xian zhaoluan qing-xing zhe," 55, 57.

126. Shang Qinghan, "Shandong ziyiyu yiyuan Wang Zhixun, Ding Shiyi, Zhou Shulin, Zhang Jieli, Shang Qinghan cizhi yuan you baogaoshu" (Report on the reasons for the resignation of Wang Zhixun, Ding Shiyi, Zhou Shulin, Zhang Jieli, and Shang Qinghan from the Shandong Provisional Provincial Assembly), in *Shandong jindai shi ziliao*, 36.

127. Wang Zhixun, "Tiaocha Lai, Hai," 30.

128. Shandong lüjing tongxiang hui, "Laiyang shibian di tiaocha baogaoshu," 26–27.

129. *Guofeng bao* (National Customs), 1910: 4, 7.

130. *Laiyang xianzhi*, 2.1:39–41.

131. *Laiyang xianzhi*, juanmo 9.

132. Ma Gengcun, "Xinhai gemingqian de Laiyang kangjuankangshui de douzheng" (The struggle to resist taxes in Laiyang on the eve of the 1911 Revolution) in *Shandong sheng lishi xuehui* (Shandong province historical studies), vol. 4, (Jinan: Shandong sheng lishi xue hui bian, [Shandong province historical institute staff], 1982), 99.

133. Wang Zhixun, "Tiaocha Lai, Hai," 33.

134. Ibid.

135. Liu Tongjun, *Xinhai gemingqian Lai Hai Zhao kangjuan yongdong*, 447.

136. Ibid., 448.

137. Wang Zhixun, "Tiaocha Lai, Hai," 32; Sun Baoqi, "Zou chafu Laiyang, Haiyang er xian zhoaluan qing-xing zhe," 45.

138. Sun Baoqi, "Zou chafu Laiyang, Haiyang er xian zhaoluan qing-xing zhe," (Memorial on the disruptive situation in Laiyang and Haiyang) in *Shandong jindai shi ziliao*, 45.

139. Sun Baoqi, "Zou chafu Laiyang, Haiyang er xian zhoaluan qing-xing zhe," 45.

140. Wang Baotian, "Zou Laiyang, Haiyang er xian xiang jishan bianpai da chen," 41.

141. Liu Tongjun, *Xinhai gemingqian Lai Hai Zhao kangjuan yongdong*, 452.

142. *Dongfang zazhi*, no. 6, 1910, in *Xinhai geming*, 468.

143. Ibid.; Wang Zhixun, "Tiaocha Lai, Hai," 35.

144. Liu Tongjun, *Xinhai gemingqian Lai Hai Zhao kangjuan yongdong*, 449.

145. Sun Baoqi, "Zou chafu Laiyang, Haiyang er xian zhaoluan qing-xing zhe," 56.

Bandit Stronghold: from *Water Margin*

Source: *Shuihuzhuan* (Water Margin). Beijing: Renmin wenxue chuban she, 1992.

Shuihu zhuan
(Water Margin)

Shuihu zhuan (Water Margin) is a collection of stories set in the twelfth century and originally written down in the form of prompt books used by market town storytellers. Shi Naian (Shih Nai-an) and Lo Guanzhong (Lo Kuan-chung) are credited with writing the novel version of these stories in the fourteenth century. The stories tell of the exploits of Song Jiang (Sung Chiang) and his band of thirty-six major heroes and seventy-two minor ones, including two well-known heroines. The outlaws have a hideout at Mount Liang in Shandong province from which they engage in causes to challenge all varieties of corruption and oppression, whether it come from the hands of abusive officials, petty landlords, or unprincipled bandits who prey on people. The world of the *Shuihu* rebels is filled with violence and the earthy details of daily life, making these tales a favorite of market town audiences. Unlike *Sanguoyanyi* (The Romance of the Three Kingdoms), *Shuihu zhuan* is not an historical novel. Song Jiang (Sung Chiang), the leader of the band, and possibly one other character are the only ones with a documented presence in the historical record.[1] More perhaps than any other classical Chinese novel, *Shuihu zhuan* embodied reflections of popular rural culture. As the stories, their characters, and scenarios circulated among villagers, professional storytellers, and novelists with an educated audience in mind, the stories themselves became contested ground with layers of socially differentiated interpretive viewpoints. The following excerpt is a transitional passage from the life of Ch'ao Kai, who represents a more materialistic strain within the bandit community. The scenario involves harsh action taken by Ch'ao against corrupt petty official, Ho T'ao and his superior, the provincial governor, who have sent soldiers to harass and make excessive demands upon the villagers of Chi Chou Fu. This selection also tells of the acclaim such exploits

93

gained for the *Shuihu* bandits who consequently found many seeking to join their mountain stronghold and swear allegiance to their cause of social justice.

Excerpt

The four leaders were Ch'ao Kai and the three brothers Yuan. The man seated on the boat was Kung-Sun Sheng who had prayed to Heaven for a wind and had obtained it. These five men had led ten fishermen in the attack on the soldiers, and had succeeded in killing them all in the reeds, or in the water. There was only one man left and that was Ho T'ao, the thief catcher, who was lying in the bottom of a boat, tightly bound like a dumpling. Yuan the Second picked him up, and put him on the bank. He then cursed him saying, "You stupid reptile! You have deceived and injured the people of Chi Chou Fu. At first I thought of cutting your corpse into ten thousand pieces. But now I want you to return to Chi Chou Fu, and tell that thief, the governor, that the three brothers Yuan, or even Ch'ao Kai are not to be slighted with. We do not go to your town to borrow grains, but if he comes to our village it will result in his death.

"We are not afraid of a small governor, who has an order from the royal tutor to arrest us, because if Ts'ai himself comes here we shall only cut about thirty holes in his body. If we release you, you must not attempt to come here again. You must tell that sham official that he had better not have another dream like this one. There are no roads here, but I will get my younger brother to show you a way."

Yuan the Seventh got a small light boat, and placing Ho T'ao on board took him to a place where a road started, and then said to him, "You can get away by this road. All the men who came with you have been killed so is it not nice for us to let you go in this way? When the governor sees you that asinine thief will laugh at our weakness. I now beg that you will let me have your two ears as a keepsake."

Yuan the Seventh took his sword and cut off both ears of thief catcher Ho T'ao. He then cut his bonds, and left him on the bank.

Ch'ao Kai, Kung-Sun Shen, the three bothers Yuan, and the ten fishermen embarked on seven small boats and left the anchorage of the Shih Chieh Village, and went to the Li Family Village. There they found the boats that had brought Wu Yung and Liu Tang. Wu Yung asked how the affair with the soldiers had terminated, and Ch'ao Kai told him all the details. Wu Yung and all the men were very much pleased on hearing the news. They then placed their boats together in one place, and went to the inn to find Chu Kwei, the Speedy Courier. When Chu Kwei saw so many people arriving and assuming that they wanted to join the bandits he went out to meet them. When Wu Kung had told him the news Chu Kwei was much pleased, and saluted each person individually. He them invited them to come and wait upon the guests. He then took his bow and shot an arrow that had a whistle attached to it, into the reeds. As soon as the whistling arrow reached its destination a boat carrying a number of bandits came forth, and was sculled toward the inn. He then wrote a letter giving the names and number of the heroes who wished to join the bandits, and handing this to the boatmen, told them to take it at once into the stronghold. A sheep was then slaughtered and cooked for the assembled men.

They passed the night there, and early the following morning Chu Kwei ordered a big boat and invited his guests to embark. They also took the boats that had brought Ch'ao Kai and his party, and set off for the bandits' stronghold. In a short time they neared the landing place, when they heard drums and gongs beating. Four small boats came out to meet them, and after the boatmen had saluted by exclaiming, "ngo," they retreated.

Upon reaching the landing place called the Golden Sand Bund, all the fishermen and other men were told to remain in that place. About ten bandits were there to conduct the leaders to the stronghold. At the barrier, Wang Lun with the other chiefs was awaiting them, and they all saluted Ch'ao Kai and his fellow leaders.

Wang Lun said, "I have heard the great fame of Ch'ao Kai, the Heavenly King, like the sound of thunder in my ears. Today I am greatly honored by you entering our straw stockade."

"I am quite uneducated," sai Ch'ao Kai, "and am very rough. Today I want to hide my incapability and am willing to be a subordinated follower of yours, I hope you won't reject my application."

"Don't talk like that, " said Wang Lun. "Please come into our stronghold where we can discuss matters."

They all went up the mountain.[2]

Notes

1. C. T. Hsia, *The Classical Chinese Novel: A Critical Interpretation* (Bloomington: University of Indiana Press, 1980; previously published by Columbia University Press, 1968), 83.

2. Shi Naian, *Water Margin*, trans. J. H. Jackson (Hong Kong: Commercial Press, Ltd., 1963) vol. 1, 241–43.

3

Zunhua, Zhili:
Camel King Wang at the Foot
of the Great Wall

In 1909 the officials established a police office. . . . The tax burden
on the *nongmin* (small farmers) became heavier, and people could
not maintain their livelihood. At this time Yang Xiu, Wang Congman and others saw that the people's livelihood was difficult . . .
and they began to organize *lianzhuanghui* (village associations).

—oral history given by Zunhua villagers, 1959

"It is said that among ancient men long ago there were a few who died
in the interest of humanity. Today such people are also few. Qin Erxiong of Shangdian was such a person of simplicity and great will."[1]
So began a memorial that the peasant activists of twenty villages around
Shangdian compelled the county magistrate to have engraved on a ceremonial bell and publicly displayed in order to absolve Qin and others
of any charges of wrongdoing in their efforts to oppose government
plans in 1908 for a new tax on southern Zunhua fruit orchards. Oral
history accounts record that the immediate problem had begun in the
late Guangxu period (1875–1908) of the Qing Dynasty. At that time,
the central government's exactions were already felt to be a burden
damaging people's livelihood. Peasants paid a three-*fen* tax on goods
they bought and a two-*fen* tax on items they sold. With every transaction, the trend toward excessive taxation seemed to grow more onerous.
The southern region of Zunhua in an area of twenty villages centered
around Shangdian, known as the eastern eight *bao*, had extensive fruit
orchards. In the early 1900s, draught conditions had adversely affected
productivity of the region. In the best of times, the area was not especially fertile. As one local saying put it, this area is so poor that "even
the rabbits do not leave their shit here."[2]

By autumn of 1908, it was clear that weather conditions during the

growing season had been better than in the past several years, and small
owner-cultivators were expecting a relatively abundant harvest. They
were not about to lose their surplus to increased taxes. Oral history
accounts that provide the narrative for this protest identify Liu Zhenduo
as a central target of the farmers' unrest. Further identified by his reputation in the county as a bad seed (*huaizhong*), Liu worked with the
yamen personnel in charge of tax collection. Seeing the opportunity
to collect additional tax revenue, Liu with the approval of the county
magistrate called a meeting of the *nongmin* to announce plans for a
miscellaneous tax on local fruit crops. Before long, an incident took
place in which a person from Shangdian who was taking two baskets of
pears to sell at Shaliuhe was stopped on the road by Liu who then
pressed the fruit seller for taxes. This irregular, haphazard approach
caused great dissatisfaction among the rural people. In response, they
began to organize among themselves. Qin Chenming of Shashangdian
led a delegation of farmers to the magistrate's office where they presented their case. Having approved Liu's plans earlier, the magistrate
did not respond to the grievance. Instead he confirmed that the *nongmin*
must continue to pay the fruit tax.[3]

When Qin Chenming returned to Shangdian, everybody knew that
the magistrate and his yamen underlings were determined to press for
taxes. They also knew that their meager livelihoods would suffer. To
address this situation, Qin, his son Qin Erxiong, and others formed a
leadership group that mobilized more than three thousand people from
twenty-eight villages.[4] They decided that they would resist taxes even
to the point of death. If the government sent official troops to arrest
people, the *nongmin* would sound gongs and beat drums to bring people
together to resist the soldiers.

One evening, as soldiers rode into the Shangdian area, the official
search for Qin Chenming and Qin Erxiong began. Qin Erxiong was standing outside his door and refused to go with the soldiers. One soldier then
attacked Erxiong drawing a sharp knife across his intestines. Erxiong,
according to eyewitnesses, showed no immediate signs of pain. People
carried him to Xindian for medical attention. Realizing that the magistrate
would immediately send more soldiers to arrest Qin Chenming and his
son, people sounded the gongs and gathered one or two hundred farmers
carrying spears and hoes and marched to Xindian. Meanwhile, the soldiers blocked the exits at the inn where Qin Erxiong and his sons rested.
People surrounded the place in large numbers. Looking around, the soldiers could tell that they were outnumbered, so some of them retreated.
In their attempted retreat, four of the soldiers were caught by the people.
Inside the inn, Qin Erxiong, now safely in the hands of his fellows, for
the first time realized how badly he was wounded. Those near him saw a

lot of blood and knew Qin was weak. The next day Qin's intestines protruded through his wound, and there was nothing anyone could do. The bleeding continued, and on the following day he died. According to an oral history given years afterward, protesters recalled that in retaliation for Qin's death, they made the four soldiers they had captured drink large quantities of cold water as a kind of torture.

News of Qin Erxiong's death spread very quickly throughout the eastern eight *bao*, and those who supported the protest gathered in large numbers. Erxiong's father immediately went to the yamen to file a legal suit. The magistrate knew that in a case where a soldier had killed a person the case would be tough to handle. On the day the settlement was issued, the magistrate went by sedan chair to Shadian to announce the finding. A large group assembled and the magistrate said, "This wound that Qin Erxiong suffered was self-inflicted. At the yamen . . ." But the crowd would not allow him to continue. With rising anger and contempt the crowd drew near. "Not possible," someone shouted. "Someone killed him. Someone took his life." "The magistrate does not speak the truth," called someone else. And finally, "Get him!" A loud sound, resembling that of a swarm of agitated bees, rose from deep within the crowd. The person in front of the crowd was Qin Erxiong's mother. She waved the sole of a cotton hand-stitched shoe she has been making and began to beat the magistrate on the head.[5] His hat fell off. His soldiers retreated. The magistrate could save himself only by running away.

Beyond the above account recorded by Tian Zhihe from villagers at Shangdian in 1961, little more is known of the details surrounding this protest. Brief notes indicate that some local individuals did mediate in the conflict and that some of them even went to Beijing to file a suit on Qin Chenming's behalf. Eventually another magistrate from Fengguo county and a military official ordered the Zunhua magistrate to pay a large sum, five thousand *kuai* according to one account, to Qin's family and to compose a memorial for Qin absolving him of any wrongdoing, stating clearly that Qin's actions were in the interest of justice, and giving honorable mention to all of the villages that had supported the protest.

It is this memorial for Qin Erxiong that makes this case most memorable. Without it would Tian have known about this event at all? Among the various ways that rural protesters claimed space in local memory, this one carried some extra weight. Continuing from the lines quoted at the beginning of this chapter the memorial bell displayed on a tripod read:

> The people sought to reject a proposal for a fruit orchard tax, and Mr. Qin on the fifth day of the twelfth month in 1908 used his life to stop the taxes.

This tax will not be levied on the people (*xiangmin*) again. Qin's merit is
hereby recorded and carved on a ceremonial bell. His life was as great as
Mt. Tai and higher than the North star. People already honor him for his
meritorious virtue (*gongde*). Mr. Qin's valor will be handed down forever
by this record and will never fade.[6]

In the 1908 case at Shangdian, dissident villagers successfully asserted their moral and economic interests. For those in northern Zunhua
county who would raise the banner of rebellion in 1909 against New
Policy reforms, the Shangdian story stood as recent evidence that resistance to injustice was a reasonable choice if the right conditions prevailed. There were other incidents of recent memory as well that might
have contributed to anti–New Policy dissent. A Boxer attack in 1900
raised issues not only of local corruption and excessive taxation but
also of foreign presence and its effects.

In 1878, an American Protestant missionary by the Chinese name of
Da Jirui purchased one hundred *mou* of land outside the south gate of
Zunhua city. A church was built on this land, and in 1885 Protestant
mission work in the county expanded to include an elementary school.
Under the slogan "Support the Qing, destroy the foreigner," the Zunhua Boxers in June 1900 destroyed the Protestant church.[7] They also
slaughtered two foreign priests and eighty-seven Christian converts. In
order to lift the Boxer seige of the foreign legation in Beijing, the armies of eight nations entered China by way of Tianjin. By the end of
September, the invaders with the help of county officials were moving
through Zunhua on mopping-up missions. Foreign troops, assisted by
Zunhua county officials, ruthlessly killed Boxer units and destoyed
Boxer locations at Shimen (Stone Gate) to the west of Zunhua city.[8] A
shift in rural activist consciousness came clearly into focus at Zunhua
during the post-Boxer opposition to New Policy government reforms.

Popular Culture:
The Moral and Political Economy of Rural Relations

Suffering is not automatically experienced as injustice, for the perception of injustice is itself shaped by social context. It is also the case
historically that injustice only rarely leads to collectively organized resistance. As Barrington Moore has observed in his cross-societal study
of injustice, a potential injury is perceived by a group as just rather than
unjust if those in positions of authority convincingly present the injury
as part of a larger set of social principles required for society to function
at its best.[9] For example, the oppression of Chinese women, through

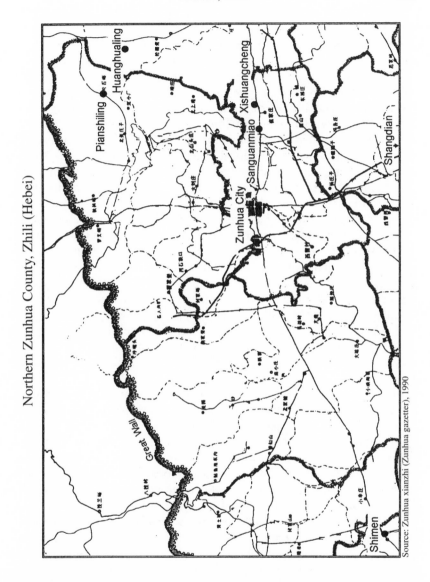

Northern Zunhua County, Zhili (Hebei)

Source: Zunhua xianzhi (Zunhua gazetter), 1990

foot mutilation was largely accepted as socially desirable because it was part of an aesthetic, philosophical, and marriage system that supposedly arranged for optimum harmony between the natural and social orders. So said those who effectively dominated family and political life for centuries, but not without challenge that would eventually in the late nineteenth and early twentieth centuries become audible. In the case of New Policy reforms, fiscal and administrative intrusions into the coun-

tryside were presented by subcounty managers as part of the program
for national strengthening, a larger goal to make hardship more tolera-
ble. In many counties across China, this was apparently not convincing.

Notions of reciprocity and resistance were culturally supported ideals
in rural China. Those with grievances against privileged members of
society had a specific set of values and behavoral norms upon which
they could draw. This cultural framework, which justified collective
action as well as shared standards for judging those in positions of authority, was necessary before local circumstances could give rise to political activism. Any articulation of grievances was dependent on common values in defining problems and their causes. Group consciousness
among villagers about methods of protest and standards for leadership
played a crucial role in the formation of anti–New Policy resistance.
Put another way, those persons who became involved in opposition to
New Policy reforms were already paticipants in a rural culture that held
that protest against injustice was both possible and necessary. Their
judgment that the actions of the reform managers and their functionaries were unfair evolved within a framework that gave social as well as
moral support to those villagers who chose not to accept the new policies passively. Such ideals had an emotional dimension rooted in the
popular culture of folktales and childhood memories as well as an intellectual component to bring immediate political and economic issues
into focus.

Of equal significance was the fact that the same ideals also gave
moral and social support to those among the more privileged who were
inclined to act out of a sense of social responsibility on behalf of standards they considered integral to overall societal well-being. Time and
again in the cases of opposition to New Policy reforms, figures from
the middle and upper social strata stepped forward to mediate, file suits
on behalf of protesters, or represent peasant perspectives to higher authorities. At Zunhua in 1908, pressure from peasant's as well as those
groups that took the case to Beijing were equally essential to the final
judgment against the local magistrate. At Laiyang, Jiang Ershou and
others of the middle merchant, landowner circles acted as guarantors
for Qu Shiwen. Members of the Shandong Landsmann's Association
played a sympathetic role in publicizing the peasants' plight. This willingness to act on behalf of near-subsistence farmers' interests was a
critical factor in the possible success of intervillage dissident movements. Sanctioned by prominent themes in both Chinese classical
thought and folk narratives, the ethical support for social responsibility
contributed to an environment in which the just redress of grievances
through collective action was a practical, realizable ideal.

State ideology itself provided many of the props that justified popular protest. The Mandate of Heaven, a cornerstone of classical political philosophy, maintained that the emperor held the right to govern only as long as he carried out Heaven's Will. The doctrine of Heaven's Will asserted that each person should be able to sustain a livelihood appropriate to his or her station in life and that harmony based on this just distribution of material resources should prevail. When misgovernment and corrupt practices upset the harmony, people were justified in overthrowing the ruler and installing a new person to carry out the Mandate of Heaven. The works of Meng Zi (Mencius) particularly emphasized this "right" of the people. By extension, the principle it embodied was applied not only to the emperor but to local government officials and to persons whose authority was identified with the magistrate's office. Many taxpayers who opposed the New Policy programs rallied behind the centuries-old slogans, "Officials compel the people to rebel" and "Officials oppress, the people rebel."

The process that Barrington Moore describes as the "creation of standards of condemnation for explaining and judging current sufferings" was an ongoing feature of the popular culture.[10] Many of the values applied to current circumstances had been transmitted from generation to generation in storytelling. Scenes from the *Romance of the Three Kingdoms* (*Sanguoyanyi*) and *Water Margin* (*Shuihu zhuan*) were widely read and were enacted in storytelling form at market towns and village gatherings. Arthur Smith, a nineteenth-century American missionary well acquainted with the rural areas, commented that "almost every hamlet can furnish some, if not many persons, who have acquired education enough to devour with delight the stirring stories of the past."[11] Such semiliterate individuals, in addition to countless professional storytellers, were key persons in transmitting the popular tradition of social protest. All children, regardless of their social class, grew up hearing these tales. Obviously not all rural inhabitants were equally inclined to view rebellion as the solution to unaddressed grievances. Opposite the activist's interpretation of Heaven's Will was a posture of fatalism and resignation, equally strong and more commonly assumed. The many ways in which protest was legitimized and encouraged, however, made it easier for one sector of the populace to respond with collective protest to misgovernment and the avaricious behavior of some local elite members. Chinese history carried a current of dissident practice within its rural society that made possible immediate and formidable responses to the activities of state-building, which in different national contexts beset many agrarian communities, some with fewer cultural resources for resistence at their points of contact with industrial growth.

The heroic deeds of the *Water Margin* characters preserved in their narratives familiar images of trusted leaders and rebel brotherhoods. For centuries after, they were first told and then written down in novel form, the *Water Margin* stories continued to describe the social and political world in which young Chinese grew up. The heroes portrayed in these stories and in others like them were typically semiliterate persons, neither well-to-do nor impoverished, often proficient in the martial or spirit arts, loyal to just authority, and frequently displaying a violent temper in the presence of injustice.[12] Such models of leadership walked not only the stages of village theaters but the lanes of village communities across China. The 108 heroes, including 2 heroines, depicted in *Water Margin* dwelled in a permanent stronghold deep in the Liangshan Forest. The women among their ranks were hero-bandits by virtue of the fact that they upheld the same standards and martial spirit as the men.[13] From Liangshan they emerged to save people from corrupt officials, ruthless criminals, and greedy landlords. Alongside a definite preference for hierarchical organization in the society of heroes was an egalitarian commitment to brotherhood in the fight for justice, even at the expense of family ties. Each of the residents at Liangshan Forest knew where he or she stood in this hierarchy and accepted the authority of the acknowledged leader. Loyalty was not, however, granted blindly. A leader could make mistakes, and the leader could be overriden in his or her views by a consensus among supporters. While the hierarchy was viewed as a necessary organizational tool that allowed the community to function, in decision making each hero's voice was important to the model of collective leadership inspired by an ideal of social justice.

Although themselves constituting an organized community, the rebel forces did not generally mobilize commoner organizations for the purpose of redressing grievances.[14] In these respects, the heroes were "social bandits" as Eric Hobsbawm has defined the term. In Hobsbawm's analysis, a person "becomes a bandit because he does something which is not regarded as criminal by his local conventions, but is so regarded by the state or the local rulers. . . . The population hardly ever helps the authorities to catch the 'peasants' bandit' but on the contrary protects him."[15] The social bandit then lives on the margins of peasant society, moving camp from place to place in the mountains and hills. In Hobsbawm's view the social bandit could assist peasant uprisings but could not lead them. In fact, "to be effective champions of their people, bandits had to stop being bandits."[16] They had to become peasants once again. Therefore, while the leaders of the anti–New Policy protests often took inspiration from the stories of the *Water Margin* heroes, they were themselves peasants and not bandits. Bandit groups were present at Haiyang and in other counties where protest developed, but they joined in support of peasant leaders based in the villages rather than as leaders themselves. At Laiyang, Qu Shiwen, a peasant leader thoroughly grounded in village life and exemplifying the ideals of the *Water Margin* heroes, had by the end of his life been separated from his community, forced by the state into hiding and the life of a social bandit. The line between the peasant and bandit was often blurred. And not all bandits were viewed by rural communities as socially progressive. Nian rebels at Laiyang in the 1860s attacked the public granary that Qu Shiwen and others would protect in the 1900s from avaricious New Policy managers. In the rural landscape of place-based politics, social class alliances were moveable around definitions of social well-being dependent on the perspectives of activists themselves.

In the moral economy of rural disputes over New Policy reforms, economic issues were a concern of real and growing urgency, but they were far from the only concern. After a period of rising expectations in the late nineteenth and early twentieth centuries, standards of living throughout China were suddenly threatened with a sharp decline from 1908 to 1911. Between 1885 and 1905, taxes had lagged farther and farther behind inflationary price rises. The value villagers received for their crops and handicraft goods at market kept well ahead of rising land tax and surcharge rates. The real tax burden decreased until around 1906–8, when taxes suddenly caught up with prices. At Chuansha, landowners were better off in the early 1900s than they had been in the 1880s. This was characteristic of the Suzhou-Shanghai area in general, where people felt better off in 1906 than they had in 1875 or 1850. Their gains, however, were severely curtailed in the 1908–11 period, when New Policy taxes were introduced.[17] In north China at Dingzhou (Dingxian), Zhili, where no opposition to New Policy reforms occurred, the same economic pattern prevailed. From 1875 to 1906, the taxpayers' burden decreased significantly relative to rising prices, while in the last years of the Qing Dynasty, taxes overtook prices.[18] Counties with anti– New Policy disturbances ran the full range from moderately wealthy to poor. The tax collection rate was no higher in areas where protest developed. In the province of Henan, for example, where the tax rates ranged from 1.15 to 2.36 units per tael of assessed land value, the rate at Mixian[19] was 1.15, at Yexian[20] it was 1.79, and at Changge[21] it was 1.93, all counties with antitax movements in the New Policy era. Furthermore, wealthier areas did not necessarily support reforms with greater ease than poorer areas. Even counties with high densities of wealthier families often had pockets of poorer farmers. Concerned about the economic consequences for rural China, an editor for *Shibao* commented that "if New Policy reforms have such difficulty in a prosperous area like Chuansha, how will they ever succeed in the more backwards and less prosperous areas of China?"[22] Although the economic component of the rural crisis was certainly present to precipitate the moral and political issues, none of the protesters in the cases considered were living on the brink of disaster. Similar to the situations studied by James C. Scott in the work on the moral economy of peasant societies, the protests initiated by Chinese farmers in opposition to New Policy reforms seldom if ever were an act of desperation taken in "moments of madness" in order to avoid imminent starvation.[23] Instead, peasants carefully calculated their interests on a collective as well as on an individual basis. The long-range interests of near-subsistence farmers were, therefore, an important consideration when groups measured the impact of reform programs. Each villager, while assessing his or her own interests in a given crisis, was also willing to support collective action if that support was mobilized by community leaders. The practice of mutual aid through intervillage associations and an awareness of the traditional forms of protest both contributed to a propensity for collective action. Although a focus on the individual as the basic unit of social action, as Samuel Popkin has suggested in his work on the "rational peasant," provides some insights into how dissenting Chinese villagers viewed political and economic changes in the post-Boxer decade, in the case of the anti–New Policy movements, community-based organizations such as intervillage associations and temple networks played a critical role in defining protest issues as a process of mediation among individual, family, and group interests.[24]

The political issue of who would control the new institutions and their financing was fundamental. If villagers lost control of their own locally raised funds, their spiritual and community centers, and the functions of their own village leaders, they would be more vulnerable to further economic encroachments. Other significant institutional features of Chinese society also contributed to the feasibility of successful protest. The state's low military presence throughout the country reduced the risks of initiating protest and escalating to violent attacks if grievances remained unaddressed. Participants in an uprising could be assured that at least several days would elapse before government troops requested by the magistrate could arrive in the county. This situation was, of course, changing from the time of the Taiping Rebellion, as the government introduced industrial technology to move troops around more quickly and provide them with greater fire power. By the time of the post-Boxer uprisings, the military situation was most disadvantageous for effective protest. In addition to the low military profile that had always facilitated resistance, there was the positive consequence of a system of general low government presence in the daily lives of local inhabitants. This meant that a vast area outside of direct official control existed in which informal social organizations and communication networks flourished, linking virtually every village household in a variety of associations.

In a nutshell, the primary interest of the peasant protesters was the maintenance of an ethical system of moral economy, which allowed their near-subsistence lifestyles to work. For this to happen, moral values had to be integral to economic behavior. Monetary profit had to be subordinated to overall social well-being. From everything the small and middle farmers could judge, this lifestyle although filled with hardship was the best they could imagine if they were to retain as much collective control as possible over their social and economic environments. The moral position that best protected their interests was: No matter what the justification, it was not right for those who already had so little to be asked to give more. Explicitly economic issues were a part of but also secondary to the moral and political dimensions of these situations. At Yexian, Henan, for example, where taxes rose from 130 to 320 cash per *mou,* a spokesman for the protesters saw the decision to take action in this way:

> Spending money like this is a small matter, but in the future once self-government is carried out and with the national debt the common people will have to pay for everything. Therefore at this time we absolutely must not agree to these plans. Officials and elite members are conspiring to compel the people to rebel.[25]

It was the trend toward burdensome taxation and the loss of locally based leadership, rather than the current new taxes and reform institutions, which were at the heart of the matter from the dissenting point of view. The maintenance of the status quo was not an end in itself for the protesters. Traditional attitudes did not prevent villagers from considering that new arrangements might serve their interests. The problem was in the nature and execution of the reforms themselves. One of the demands of the protesters at both Laiyang and Haiyang was that persons selected for self-government and police bureau posts be popularly respected. In counties where the reforms were carried out without opposition, persons selected at the village level of society were delegated a share of the decision making and management authority related to the reforms. But even this compromise was sometimes seen as a slippery slope toward the loss of village integrity. The protesters were anything but shortsighted. They showed a keen sense of political and economic shifts over the long term, and it was this trend that motivated their actions in the 1901–11 decade.

旧县城北城楼

Old Zunhua: North Gate Drum Tower

Source: *Zunhua xianzhi* (Zunhua gazetteer). Zunhua: Hebei renmin chuban she, 1990.

Rise of Anti–New Policy Protest at Zunhua

On February 5, 1910, a group of rural residents met at Gold Mountain temple (*Jinshan si*). Their collective decision was to proceed with the destruction of Police Chief Yue Weisong's residence and the confiscation of his grain and other possessions.[26] Magistrate Ye Sigao responded to the news of this gathering with concern. Carried by yamen runners, Ye rode in his sedan chair out through the city gate and along a country road to Gold Mountain temple. As carts and villagers passed him, he thought of what he might say to appease those peasants who were resisting the new miscellaneous taxes.

When he arrived he began to address the people who had assembled. "Abide by the law," he said. "Behave yourselves; pay taxes according to the regulations."

The rural people listened, but their indignation grew. "We hardly have food to eat. If you don't stop raising taxes, we would rather die than submit!"[27] The more people talked, the more angry they became.

Hoping to intimidate the protesters, the magistrate pressed on, "When the state (*guojia*) sends soldiers, what will you do?"

Listening to his words, the peasants grew even more intent on standing their ground. "If the soldiers come," they said, "then the soldiers come. We will not go away. When they come, we will fight."[28] Even the magistrate did not know what to say. The village leaders wanted the magistrate to promise that the New Policies would never be implemented in the east *xiang*. They demanded that he write a statement to this effect and stamp it with his official seal.

When it was clear that Magistrate Ye was unwilling to meet their demands, the crowd began to hurl insults at him. As a rural manager from the first *bao* of the east *xiang* attempted to pacify the villagers, the protesters pulled him to the ground and thoroughly beat him.[29] People then gathered in front of Ye's sedan chair, took his eyeglasses, threw them on the ground and broke them into pieces.[30] Unable to return to his sedan chair, Ye Sigao became fearful. He called out to Wang Congman, a leader of the crowd, and referred to him respectfully as Wang "Dalaoye" (great uncle).

Finally the magistrate said that the police tax would be reduced by 70 percent. People would have to pay only 30 percent. In one voice the people replied, "We don't have even one single cent, how can we pay?"[31] The group continued to surround the official and would not let him leave. Wanting to avoid trouble for himself, Ye replied, "Our office will send an official communication (to the higher authorities) and request an exemption."[32] But the peasants would not be fooled. Unable to free himself from the demonstrators for almost twenty-four hours, the magistrate was finally released when a Major Ge of a local Banner battalion arrived.[33] Ge proposed the same 70 percent reduction for the eastern *xiang*. People had work to do, so they took the Major's word. Once safely back in the yamen, Magistrate Ye stated that the agreement was not valid. What conditions shaped this conflict, and how effective were the farmers in their protest?

Located approximately ninety miles to the east of Beijing and just south of the Great Wall, Zunhua was in the wheat-growing region of north China. Administratively, Zunhua was designated a *zhou* until 1913 when it became a *xian*.[34] A foothill area, Zunhua included low mountains and plains. Animal husbandry, wheat, corn, gaoliang crops, and fruit orchards were sources of livelihood. Although 80 percent of Zunhua's population worked predominantly in agriculture, Tianjin and to a lesser extent Beijing constituted major commercial entrepôts in the marketing networks of which Zunhua was a part. Zunhua was also home to the prestigious Imperial Tombs of the late Qing emperors, including Kangxi and Qianlong and the Dowager Empress Cixi.

Ethnically Zunhua's population was more diverse than that of either Laiyang or Chuansha. Zunhua's proximity to the Manchus and other non-Han groups north of the Great Wall accounted for this demographic feature. A 1985 record showed eleven ethnic minority groups concentrated in thirty-five market towns in the northwest quarter of the county where they ranged from 4 to 86 percent of the population, making up 8 percent of the total county population.[35] Although we do not know exactly what the ethnic composition of Zunhua was in 1910, we do have an idea of the movement of people in this area from the earliest periods of China's history.

The Donghu people, a non-Han group, dwelled in the Zunhua area during the spring and autumn and the Warring States periods. After the Tang Dynasty, the Qidan (Khitan) and Nuzhen peoples, also both non-Han, dominated the area for more than 360 years. During this time, which included the rule of the Song Dynasty, Zunhua was first incorporated as a county and its local history begins at this point in the years 923–36.[36] Under Mongol domination during the Yuan Dynasty, some of the descendents of the Mongols moved into Zunhua. In the Ming Dynasty, members of the Moslem minority (Huizu) settled in Zunhua city and the town of Malanling. Afterward other Moslems from Shandong and Hebei provinces moved into the area. At the end of the Ming Dynasty during a peasant revolt, rebel leader Li Zicheng sent a delegation to Zunhua in March of 1644 to see what the situation was there in terms of support for his attack on the dynasty.[37] Shortly thereafter, the Ming armies sided with the Manchus to capture and decapitate Li, bringing the peasant rebellion across most of north China, including

Zunhua, to a close. Manchu rule under the Qing Dynasty thus began. With the Manchus on the throne in Beijing, their numbers began to increase significantly in Zunhua. A mausoleum for the Manchu rulers was laid out in 1663 in northwestern Zunhua. At this time, Mongols also increased their presence in the area as herders, and that corner of Zunhua became known as a "cattle pen." Finally in 1794, Manchu administrators and soldiers moved into the northwest in large numbers to manage and protect the Qing Mausoleum.[38]

Among the rural households throughout Zunhua, the primary divisions were based on economic and political status. Major households (*dahu*) commanded greater land and commercial resources than did the minor households (*xiaohu*). All households, major and minor, were grouped into units known as *bao*. Each of three of the county's large rural divisions (*xiang*) contained eight *bao,* and the fourth contained nine. The major households had residents in all the *xiang,* but they were most influential in the north *xiang* and in the county seat.[39] Among the minor household members and laborers who lived in different *bao,* an extensive network of Buddhist sects formed communication links.

The crisis regarding New Policy measures at Zunhua developed over a two-year period. In January 1909, the magistrate, in keeping with New Policy reforms, had begun to make preparations for the establishment of a police department at Zunhua. Of all the issues over which commoners and reform managers clashed, the establishment of police bureaus was perhaps the most sensitive. This reform introduced new coercive authority that interfered with both the economic and political integrity of subsistence ways of life. To assist him in carrying out his task, he called upon county notables (*shenshi*), including their associates, the rural managers (*dongshi*). The plan that they devised provided that the twenty-five *bao* of the east, west, and south *xiang* would be divided into twelve districts, and that the nine *bao* of the north *xiang* would be administered by the chief police bureau in the city. In the last week of May, police offices were established in each of the twelve districts. One of these districts, comprising the first, second, and third *bao* of the east *xiang,* was to become the center of opposition to the new bureaus. The Gold Mountain temple in the east *xiang*'s second *bao* was selected by the New Policy managers as the site for that district's police bureau.

It happened that this temple was a meeting place for a popular local Buddhist sect. Much of popular opinion quickly coalesced around the view that the new chief of police in Zunhua city, a wealthy notable (*fushen*) from the east *xiang,* was not to be trusted. Use of the temple and other issues were at stake. Many families were in severe debt to local merchant/landlords, a consequence of a series of bad harvests in recent years. These factors, in combination with the long history of unequal tax burdens, led many villagers of minor household status to conclude that "police chief Yue Weisong intends to let policemen come and disturb the rural people. They want to get money and become rich."[40] In the last week of June 1909, the villagers gathered and drove the local police chief out of the Gold Mountain temple and into the city. The magistrate, who was about to leave office, did not take any action against the crowd.

By the end of July, a new magistrate, Ye, was on the scene. He and the New Policy managers were anxious to expedite the establishment of police bureaus. In August, he ordered the local constables (*difang;* equivalent to *dibao*) to give instructions to the *bao* headmen that the establishment of bureaus should proceed. The police tax (*jingshui*) and the school tax (*xueshui*) were already planned. In the area around San-guanmiao (Three Officials temple), each village was to pay 19.7 *yuan* for the police tax and 17.22 *yuan* for the school tax. People felt that the government had its lackeys who would collect the taxes and profit themselves in addition. In the city, for example, there was Lao Yan who was head runner and in charge of arresting people. To the north of the city at Erliuzhuang, village headman Dai Erliu and others began to press the *nongmin* for money. Everyone knew that even at Lianxiaogu-ang, a Lao Zhan who was the servant of Dai Erliu had enough money to pay for the new tiled roof he was putting on his house.[41] Several thousand villagers responded with a march to the county seat. There they attacked the residences of the New Policy managers and the new schools and police offices in the third *bao* of the east *xiang*, doing minor but noticeable damage. Because the magistrate had to prepare for the Imperial Tombs ceremony, he let the matter go. After the ceremony, however, he ordered the reestablishment of the police bureau in the east *xiang* and the arrest of anyone who opposed it.[42]

The *nongmin* of three *bao* east of the city saw no shift in the local government position on the police tax and other reforms, so they began to mobilize themselves for collective action. They selected (*gongtui—* public selection) Yang Xiu of Sanguanmiao village, Wang Congman of Pianshiling village, Fu Shan of Huanghualing village, and Li Hailong of Xishuangcheng village as their leaders.[43] Yang Xiu was born in 1855 into a poor farming family, although in some villagers' view he was a little better off than the other three leaders.[44] From childhood he was known as an honest and daring individual who was well respected and felt comfortable with friends among the poor.[45] According to accounts in *Shibao*, Yang was also a temple leader (*sizhang*). Wang Congman was a farmer who owned two *mou* of land and worked as a crop-watcher and a butcher. He was known as the Camel King because he was tall and strong, and he had a large following in certain *bao* of the east, west, and south *xiang,* particularly among the irregularly employed (*wulai guntu*). He also managed a branch of the sect headed by Yang, and was himself associated with the Lianhua (Lotus Flower) temple south of the county seat. Although there was an outstanding warrant for Wang's arrest, relating to some other incident, no one was willing to make the arrest. Li Hailong and Fu Shan were both small farmers. A fifth person mentioned in some accounts was She Zeng, who was described as moderately wealthy. Possibly he was an owner-cultivator having relatively substantial landholdings but "minor household" status.[46]

Conflict over the police tax began to heat up again in early 1910. As police chief Yue continued to press for the establishment of police bureaus in the rural divisions, villagers made plans to stop his efforts. The four leaders made several visits to the yamen without any progress, so they began to organize *lianzhuanghui* (village federations) composed of several hundred to a thousand people who several times gathered at Gold Mountain temple in Chunshuling (Tree of Heaven) village to develop a movement to resist taxes.[47] Eventually more than three thousand people were mobilied from twenty-eight villages.[48] One person in each family that supported the protest was asked to join in disseminating informaton among the rural population in order to give public notice of their cause. Because the protesters were without weapons, they gathered people who knew martial arts and organized them into groups. In the eastern Sanbaomei village, a person in charge of that village for the *lianzhuanhui,* but not an official headman, circulated a *chuanpai* (wooden placque) saying that they should prepare for an emergency and be ready to fight.[49]

Later in February after the events already recounted on the fifth, county notables (*shenshi*) of each *xiang,* apparently constituting a sector of the elite not directly involved with reform programs, called a large meeting to discuss methods for avoiding disturbances. A few of them were willing to go to the east *xiang* to try to persuade the protesters to be calm. By May, more than half the villages in the county had presented petitions stating that they did not support the rebels. However, the villages of seven *bao* had joined the protest movement.[50] Shortly after a *dibao* had drawn up invitations that set a date for the wealthy households (*fuhu*) belonging to the first *bao* of the east *xiang* to meet and discuss plans for police bureaus, the protesters learned that the meeting was scheduled to be held in Sanguan temple. They thereupon occupied the temple, threw out the *dibao,* and used abusive language toward the *fushen* who arrived. During the second week of June, Magistrate Ye again ordered the rural managers (*shendong*) and wealthy county notables (*shenfushi*) to meet and reach an agreement. Several dozen met, Ye himself providing a meal. They set a date for establishing police bureaus, and stated that minor households would not be asked to contribute to the needed funds.

Despite these words, within a few weeks the head yamen clerk surnamed Yan was sent to the villages to the east of the city and attempted to collect taxes. According to accounts, he was very rude and arrogant. "Those who do not pay the police tax will be arrested," he said. The people immediately gathered and argued strongly on just grounds that Yan had spoken insolently, and so everyone in one action tied him up and put him in the Gold Mountain temple.[51] The other runners ran back to the yamen to tell what had happened. Ye then sent an official letter to the Gold Mountain temple requesting that the rural people free Yan and that they send their leaders to the yamen to discuss the matter of the police tax.[52]

Resistance did not subside. By July the magistrate ordered yamen runners to arrest the Camel King. The leaders of the protesting villages rang bells at the temple and gathered their forces. They captured six of the runners, took them to the Linhua temple, and then transferred them to the Gold Mountain temple. Wang Congman sent circulars to each village calling for one member from each family to join the rebel forces. According to some reports, up to twenty thousand persons assembled.[53] The runners who had been captured were badly beaten at this time, but their lives were spared when the rebels agreed to release them at the request of Major Ge, who was highly respected by the protest leadership. Evidently the excessive violence on the part of some of the leadership alienated some of their supporters. Nonetheless, the resistance continued in force.[54]

The magistrate, unperturbed by staunch peasant resistance in his area, made plans at this time to take a census, establish self-government offices, and conduct a survey for industrial enterprises. The east *xiang* had shown such fierce opposition to the police bureaus and was in such a state of chaos that no one dared to introduce these measures in that area. Nonetheless, rumors immediately began to circulate that the investigations were for the purpose of levying new taxes, and that there would be taxes on people, houses, livestock, chickens, dogs, wells, stoves—everything. If such exactions came to pass, the villagers thought, they would have no means of livelihood. Subsequently, Yang Xiu declared that he was visited in his dreams for three successive nights by Guanyin, the goddess of mercy, who urged him to relieve the distress of the people.[55]

In November 1910, Magistrate Ye was promoted to Daotai and a new magistrate, Yue, took office. A notable (*shenshi*) named He Rongguang who was not previously associated with the management of reforms made three trips to the east *xiang* to negotiate, proposing a compromise:

the villagers would select six people from among themselves to put on uniforms and be police, the police chief in the city would supervise them, and he would provide the money. The protestors, however, were unwilling to accept these terms, fearing that any arrangements that fostered new police forces controlled by the county elite would ultimately be to their disadvantage.

Finally, on the lunar New Year, January 30, 1911, Yang Xiu, Wang Congman, Fu Shan, and Li Hailong were invited to the magistrate's yamen for a banquet and discussion of the tax problems.[56] Yang Xiu understood that dealing with the *zhou* official would only create more trouble, but the main issue concerned the rural people's resistance to taxes, so he knew he had to go to the magistrate's meeting. Wang Congman and Fu Shan saw the situation and said they would go with Yang Xiu to protect him. Li Hailong would remain outside the yamen so that if there was any reason to summon the people, he could do it. Once inside, Yang Xiu could see that the magistrate's manner was insincere. They ate and drank wine and then Yue told Yang Xiu, Wang Congman, and Fu Shan that if they would go out and collect the taxes, he would make sure they were given good appointments. With stern voices the three refused. "No," they said, "we are completely with the *nongmin* who do not have enough to eat and cannot accept any of these proposals."[57] Yue immediately ordered their arrest. Outside, Li Hailong learned that the three had been arrested and immediately sent a *chuanpai* for circulation in the villages. In front of Chunshuling temple, approximately a thousand people immediately gathered. Li and the other protesters marched toward the county seat. When Yue heard this he immediately ordered that the city gate be closed. As people gathered outside the city wall, they chanted that the officials must cancel the police tax. By this time, up to ten thousand protesters were present. Wang Congman's wife was among them and called out until her voice was hoarse, "If you do not let us in we will not let food and wood into the city until you die."[58] The magistrate then ordered a brigade of the police to take positions with their weapons on the city wall. At this time, the *nongmin* had no military weapons, and when they heard gunfire come from inside the city walls and saw the police fire on the protesters, they began to retreat to the villages.

The next day, Yue sent armed men to surround Yang Xiu's home and destroy it. According to oral histories that provide many of the details of this narrative, Yang Xiu's wife escaped carrying her grandson and granddaughter to Baimaling village. The local people of Sanguanmiao village helped her as best they could. The houses of Wang Congman, Fu Shan, and Li Hailong were also destroyed and burned and their things were taken away. Their families all had to stay outside and their livelihood was ruined.

Yue was fearful that the people would try to enter the city to rescue the three, so the next night he sent them to Tianjin. Before long, Yang Xiu was sentenced to death. He was fifty-six years old. He took responsibility for the uprising in order to spare the lives of the younger men by proclaiming that, "the protest against taxes is a matter of the people's will. I am the leader. It has nothing to do with Wang Congman or Fu Shan."[59] Wang Congman and Fu Shan received sentences of five years and three years, respectively. The peasants of the eastern three *bao* who wanted to commemorate these struggles and honor their leaders asked the people who performed marketplace theater to make a shadow puppet play (*piyinxi*) based on the events. Wang Congman's wife and son told local historians in 1959 that people often cried when they went to see this play. Performed in Zunhua for two decades after the events of 1911, the shadow play dedicated to the memory and ideals of Li Hailong and others was lost in the 1930s when the Japanese in their invasion of north China entered Zunhua county.

Activism in Other Zhili Counties: Qian'an, Yizhou, and Longyao

East of Zunhua another disturbance developed in the county of Qian'an, just south of the Great Wall, where the land was stony and barren, and the people were generally farmers living near subsistence with market contacts. We have few reports on this case, and any oral histories that might have been recorded are unpublished and in the county archives, as was the case at Zunhua. In the summer of 1909, new miscellaneous taxes had been imposed, adding to the already heavy tax burden. Then at the beginning of September, Qian'an magistrate Liu ordered the self-government managers, who were also public affairs managers (*dongshi*) associated with the county degree-holders, to make a census survey outside of the city. While carrying out this task in the Lingkou area of the county, census takers Hu Xuehai, Shi Pengling, and Ling Yundeng, among others, extorted supplies from the villagers and levied extra fees on cattle. The opposition of the villagers grew and they began to organize village associations to resist.

Magistrate Liu consequently issued arrest warrants for the village leaders (*cunshoushi*) of Lingkou, including individuals of the Wang and Zhang surnames. Many village leaders were captured, and at the self-government managers' insistence, according to some journalists' reports, the magistrate ordered that they be questioned under torture.

When news of this reached the Lingkou area, each village sounded its gongs to call the people together, and ten thousand persons with Wang Xiu, also a village leader, as their guide, marched to the county seat where they demanded the release of the village leaders and the cancellation of the surcharges. By the time the villagers arrived to carry out negotiations, the reform managers had fled. Taking this as an admission of their abusive practices, the villagers destroyed the doors, windows, furniture, and utensils of the managers' residences, leaving the buildings themselves intact. When news of these attacks reached other areas where the managers had also coerced extra fees, ten to twenty thousand additional villagers organized to join those already in the city.[60] Unlike the case at nearby Zunhua, the events at Qian'an developed over a shorter time and ended in the villagers' favor in part because the local magistrate and his associates showed less persistence in their efforts. The exact reasons for this are unclear from the sketchy details available.

At Yizhou, sixty miles southwest of Beijing, villagers led by one hundred of their representatives sustained a month-long opposition to the authority of a few wealthy merchants and degree-holders who managed New Policy institutions and funds. The following is a brief account of the events.

By 1910, new schools, police bureaus, and self-government offices had been established throughout the county, and taxes had been rising. Because the local magistrate, Tang Zeyu, suffered from an illness causing frequent lapses of consciousness, he was replaced by his cousin, Expectant Magistrate Tang Hongyou, who had a reputation for being covetous and unconcerned with the people's welfare.

As at Laiyang, the reform programs were entrusted by the magistrate to a few prominent members of the county elite. Upon his arrival in Yizhou, the new magistrate placed all of the New Policy programs in the hands of "three or five" men who were distrusted by the commoner taxpayers. After opening a self-government office, two men, Zhang and Zu, both referred to as "gentry" (*shen*), sold all of the grain in the public granary fund for a total of thirty thousand cash and deposited this amount in their own accounts. On the pretext of levying fees for self-government, they also collected twenty thousand cash in miscellaneous taxes and kept these funds for their private use. While taking a census in the countryside during the second week of June, Zhang and others collected fees from each household. Added to these problems was the fact that Yizhou had not had rain for a long time and farmers, expecting loss of their crops, were unwilling to pay the regular taxes. Zhang claimed that the rural people, by withholding their tax payments, were obstructing the implementation of New Policy and should be officially interrogated.

In mid-June, the villagers of each *xiang,* having gone to the city to pray for rain, also went to the yamen to demand that no self-government fees be levied. Magistrate Tang was not available, so the crowd waited outside his yamen for several days. On June 27, villagers again gathered in groups and marched to the city, but Magistrate Tang still failed to appear to address the demonstrators. While in the city, some villagers noticed that the Kaiyuan temple had been taken over for use as a self-government office and that all of the Buddhist statues had been re-moved. In addition to the extra taxes and harassment by the reform managers, the villagers now deduced that the drought was due to the New Policy as well, reasoning that the removal of the statues to provide space for the self-government bureaus surely had angered the local dei-ties. The indignant villagers, directing all their grievances against one source, began to attack the residences of the self-government officials and the police headmen and created a disturbance at the self-govern-ment bureau. Hearing the commotion, the reform managers, also re-ferred to as "gentry," fled from the bureau offices. Soon after, the vil-lagers destroyed the bureau and several schools.

In the wake of this destruction, events continued to unfold. Magistrate Tang returned the official seal of office to his ailing cousin Zeyu, who then requested troops from Governor-General Chen Kuilong. Subse-quently, the financial commissioner sent a deputy into the area to inves-tigate the situation, and on June 29, government troops moved into Yi-zhou. By this time, village protesters had turned their attention to the destruction of an imperial hostel in the area. Meanwhile, one of the protesters, apparently a member of the less-influential county elite, sent a telegram to the Grand Council in Beijing informing the court that the causes of the disturbances were the coercive methods of the reform managers, insincere words of officials, and the obstruction of rain.

Shortly thereafter, a heavy rain fell and most of the farmers returned to their fields to cultivate a new crop. One hundred of their representa-tives remained at the yamen to present the following demands: (1) all the grain from the public granary must be returned; (2) they must never again send people to collect money; (3) the managers of self-govern-ment and the police bureaus should all be executed; (4) never again should schools and police bureaus be established; (5) the Buddhist stat-ues from the Kaiyuan temple should be returned to their original places; (6) the local official as far as possible must present the people's cause to the higher authorities and pray for rain until the ground is thoroughly soaked; and (7) the corrupt elite members who embezzled school, self-government, and other fees should have to repay them double. The de-tails of how this case was settled are unknown, but a telegram of July 30 from the Grand Council to Governor-General Chen discusses the necessity for suppressing the resistance and finding out if there were any disreputable people among the leaders.[61]

In general outline, the events at Longyao, Zhili, closely paralleled those at Laiyang and Zunhua in the development of centralized tax-collection firms and the subsequent formation of village level antireform alliances. The establishment of a functioning police bureau was also essential to the reform efforts in each of these counties. For Longyao, however, many fewer details are available.

Plans to establish police bureaus began at Longyao in 1906 when acting magistrate Lü Tiaoyuan proposed to finance the bureaus by collecting an education fee and by expropriating the funds of the village crop-watching societies. Villagers paid into these funds at the rate of one *sheng* (roughly a pint) per *mou* of winter wheat and two *sheng* per *mou* of summer crops. Not until 1908, however, under a new magistrate, did the merchants and lower degree-holders establish new schools and a police bureau. At this time, Cao Shufen was named chief of police, and he in consultation with other reform managers proposed many changes, including a self-serving alteration in the land tax collection system. Under the traditional system, village leaders had collected the land tax in the village and forwarded it to yamen underlings. The village headman was able to pocket some of the proceeds as payment for his services, and the village taxpayer could expect a tax reduction from his local headman in times of low crop yield or personal misfortune. With the reforms, taxes were to be delivered by taxpayers directly to the offices of the political elite (*shendong*) in the county seat. As another example of the oppressive power of the police bureau, officials acting under Cao's authority ordered the dismantling of illegal saltpeter distilleries in the northeast section of the county, where the land was high in sandy and impure carbonate of sodium, leaving the people without a means of livelihood.

In order to protest the change in land tax collection, village headmen demonstrated at the yamen, demanding that Magistrate Li Guofeng dismiss police headman Cao, and that recently collected levies be remitted. Villagers from the northeast, who had refused following the dismantling of their distilleries to pay taxes at the same rate as the rest of the county, joined that protest and returned with other villagers on March 18 to demand total exemption from new levies and permission to be allowed to resume processing saltpeter. Rural district managers (*qudong*) were sent by the magistrate's office to hold meetings in the villages to attempt to calm the situation, but the meetings never took place. Instead, county police officials with the magistrate's sanction arranged for government troops to move into the area, and fighting ensued between the two sides. Villagers destroyed the county police office and broke into the county jail. Troops killed nine people and wounded six, while the villagers wounded two soldiers and one of the police officials. As in so many cases of opposition to the New Policy reforms, the case at Longyao ended in military suppression by the government.[62]

Conclusions

The cases of anti–New Policy resistance in Zhili reveal evidence of the link between reform and the privatization of public resources. Embezzlement of granary, school, and self-government funds by tax-farmers who also became reform managers raised powerful resistance by communities of small owner-cultivators. The size of these movements was remarkable, including thousands of protesters mobilized through rural networks under village and intervillage leadership. Given the inclination of local lower degree-holders and wealthy merchants to coalesce around the New Policy reforms into new commercial networks, the struggle of even the most upright magistrates against these tendencies was often futile and of short-lived success at best in most cases.

As governor-general of Zhili from 1906 to 1908, Yuan Shikai attempted to select magistrates who would carry a commitment to reform into their assignments. At Anping in central Zhili, a newly appointed magistrate in 1908 reorganized the corrupt, poorly equiped police force in the county seat, regularized salaries, and introduced training programs. The bulk of new funds to pay for this program came from a land tax surcharge of fifty cash per *mou*, in addition to a new sales tax levied on certain shops and a tax on horse-tail hair. Village headmen were also given a role in selecting police officials for the rural branches and in determining how the levies would be collected.[63] However, given the already deteriorating conditions of administrative authority, including the short terms of office for magistrates, even the most heroic, well-intentioned efforts were easily overwhelmed. New political and economic opportunities presented by the New Policy reforms and shifts in investment possibilities created their own field of forces, so that over the long term few magistrates had the means to sustain effective reform. Where resistance was absent, place-based conditions, including the lack of accumulated grievances or the absence of strong lower degree-holder support for the reforms, might become key factors. At Mixian and Changge in Henan and Deqing in Zhejiang, local elites did calculate that the reforms would not be worth the risk of raising protest and creating disruption.[64] At Qian'an, discussed above, a weak magistrate and half-hearted reform managers fled at the first sign of rural resistance, giving the protesters a success, at least for the time being.

Increasingly, however, magistrates resorted to coercive measures to lay the foundation for compliance with new taxes and administrative reforms. Governor-General Yuan had such coercive authority, and after the fall of the dynasty and the devolution into warlordism, coercive methods became in some areas even more readily available. At both Yizhou and Longyao as well as Zunhua and other locations dissident practice faced a modernizing military capacity along with the move toward constitutional government.

Notes

Epigraph: Liu Erru, "Dong san bao kang jingshui douzheng" (The struggle of three eastern bao against the police tax), oral history recorded at Zunhua, 1959 (Zunhua Party Archives), an oral history recorded in 1959 by Liu Erru from among others Xu Jingshun (67 years old) and Xu Jingtai (73 years old); Yang Xiu's sons Yang Dizheng (61 years old) and Yang Liang (60 years old) at Sanguanmiao; Chen Youjin, Sun Yude, Li Shulian (78 years old) and Wang Dechun (74 years old) at Xishuangmiao village; Dai Fu (69 years old) and Wang Congman's son Wang Pingliang and Wang Congman's wife (78 years old) at Majiaguo village, Zunhua Party Archives, 3.

1. Tian Zhihe, "Zunhua dongba nongmin fankang shuiguojuan de dou" (Protest against fruit orchard taxes by the peasants of eight bao in the east of Zunhua county), oral history recorded at Zunhua, 1961, Zunhua Party History Materials, serial no. 26, document no. A20011.2.

2. Ibid., 2.

3. Ibid., 2–4.

4. *Zunhua xianzhi* (Zunhua Gazetteer) (Shijiazhuang: Hebei renmin chuban she, 1990), 10.

5. Tian Zhihe, "Zunhua dongba nongmin fankang shuiguojuan de dou," 5–7.

6. Ibid., 7–8.

7. *Zunhua xianzhi* (1990), 9–10.

8. Ibid., 10.

9. Barrington Moore Jr., *Injustice: The Social Bases of Obedience and Revolt* (New York: M. E. Sharpe, Inc., 1978), 50.

10. Ibid., 87.

11. Arthur H. Smith, *Proverbs and Common Sayings from the Chinese* (New York: Dover Publications, 1965), 87.

12. Shih Naian, *Water Margin*, trans., J. H. Jackson (Hong Kong: Commercial Press Limited, 1963) 24, 138.

13. Ibid., 666–67, 675.

14. Ibid., 162, 916.

15. Eric Hobsbawm, *Primitive Rebels: Studies in Archaic Forms of Social Movement in the 19th and 20th Centuries* (New York: Norton, 1965), 14, 15.

16. Ibid., 27.

17. Yeh-chien Wang, *Land Taxation in Imperial China, 1750–1911* (Cambridge: Harvard University Press, 1973), 116, 117, 123.

18. Ibid., 126.

19. Although described briefly and with few details, the Mixian protest provides an example in which the local notables lent active support to an antireform movement. For this reason, it is the exception among the cases here surveyed. It was much more common for the non-reform-minded elite either to remain neutral, as at Laiyang, or to attempt to negotiate on behalf of the magistrate, as did some of the Zunhua notables.

The available account of events is as follows. In order to finance a local self-government bureau, the clerks and runners had been collecting 120 cash per *mou,* and additional charges were planned. In April 1910, two thousand people, including the degree-holding elite not in charge of New Policy programs, marched to the county seat to present demands to the magistrate, who had just fled to the provincial capital. The crowd destroyed the gate of the main hall, but did not rob the granary or the treasury. Troops from a nearby government garrison sent into the area to keep the peace were immediately met with resistance from the rural populace. The magistrate of Zhengzhou telegrammed to the provincial offices that the Mixian situation was getting worse, with more people joining the opposition and refusing to disperse. The governor of Henan responded by ordering the local prefect to return to Mixian with the magistrate, bringing additional troops to quell the violence. Upon the magistrate's return, villagers began to scatter (*Dongfang zazhi* [Eastern Miscellany], Shanghai, 1910), no. 4.

20. Early in 1910, when planning began for the introduction of New Policy reforms at Yexian, county notables visited the countryside to attempt to persuade the villagers that self-government would be beneficial. The commoners, however, as in all of the above cases, were skeptical, and according to one account someone rose at a meeting to declare:

Self-government brings injury to the common people (*baixing*). Before the New Policy was carried out, the common people were content; now with self-government, police bureaus, and schools everything involves plans to get money from the people. Previously there were transport fees and official errand expenses in addition to the standard tax of 130 cash per *mou*; now the tax per *mou* has been increased to 320 cash, and the common people must give out more money. Giving out money like this is a small matter, but in the future once self-govenment is carried out and with the national debt the common people will have to pay for everything, therefore at this time we absolutely must not agree to these plans; official and elites are conspiring to compel the people to rebel.

According to the account, many of those present were sympathetic, although they said nothing at the time.

On December 26, the county political notables (*shenshi*) announced an increase in the wine tax and in six other local taxes, and the rural people were in an uproar. The reform managers, having no plan to deal with this situation, returned to the county seat to seek the advice of the magistrate, who could do nothing at the time. In each *xiang,* the rural people began holding small meetings to make plans for resistance. Ten to twenty thousand people gathered, indignant over the actions of the county political elite, while others began leaving the Yexian area to avoid being caught in the fighting. The demonstrators went to the yamen to negotiate a settlement, but government troops, which had already been requested, were sent in to suppress the uprising. As in so many counties where conflicts over reforms occurred, government troops were the final arbiters (*Dongfang zazhi,* no. 12).

21. In most north China cases of resistance to New Policy measures, the degree-holders and merchants participated in reform management and were attacked by commoner taxpayers for their activities. The case of Changge provides an exception to both of these patterns. At Changge, the notables (*shenshi*) declined to participate in the reforms altogether because they feared that the additional taxation would create disturbances. In contrast to Mixian, they did not actively support the opposition once it was underway. Because the notables refused to manage reforms, the magistrate and his clerks and runners became the principal targets of the antireform movement.

As of mid-1910, Magistrate Jiang had levied many new fees, including three hundred cash on each tael of grain tax to support the police bureau and seven hundred cash on each *mou* of land for other New Policy programs. Taxpayers expected this last levy would soon rise to one thousand four hundred cash per *mou.* No attempt had been made to take the census, but runners had repeatedly been sent into the villages to collect new fees.

Villagers called meetings to discuss the situation, and the following leaflet was circulated to plan for a larger meeting to decide on collective action:

> To the elders and brothers of each village and earthwall community: Magistrate Jiang has been responsible for sending the runners out to collect taxes seven times in this one year already and our people's strength cannot bear this. Magistrate Jiang has also increased the land tax (*diding chian*) and our people's livelihood is not protected. Frequently we have petitioned for exemptions, but the taxes were only made heavier; officials beat the runners for uncollected taxes and the runners beat the people in turn; in this way our people's personal property tends to be consumed by rapacious officials. In order to discuss the situation, we call a meeting at Five-Mile village. Everyone who does not come will be opposed.

On June 20, approximately six thousand persons marched in columns to the yamen after gathering at the east gate of the city for a brief meeting. Within a short time, the demonstration swelled to ten thousand persons. The magistrate meanwhile had fled and left yamen guards to protect the offices. The protesters destroyed the magistrate's inner chamber but entered neither the room where the official seal was kept, nor the treasury, nor the jail. This suggests that the demonstrators considered the matter to be a personal grievance against the magistrate, rather than a challenge to the political office that he held (*Dongfang zazhi,* nos. 4, 8).

22. *Shibao,* March 11, 1911.

23. James C. Scott, *The Moral Economy of the Peasant* (New Haven: Yale University Press, 1976), 204.

24. Samuel Popkin, *The Rational Peasant* (Berkeley: University of California Press, 1979), 251–53.

25. *Dongfang zazhi*, no. 12.

26. *Shibao*, March 24, 1911.

27. *Zunhua xianzhi* (Qinghua), 6:1046–47, 2. These materials in the Zunhua County Party Archives were intended for inclusion in the old Zunhua gazetteer. This selection titled "Yang Xiu" is paginated to reflect its intended place in the old gazetteer, which remains unpublished at the Qinghua University Library in Beijing.

28. Liu Erru, "Dong san bao kang jingshui douzheng" (The struggle of three eastern bao against the police tax), oral history recorded at Zunhua, 1959. Zunhua Party Archives, 1–10.

29. *Shibao*, March 24, 1911.

30. Liu Erru, "Dong san bao kang jingshui douzheng," 3.

31. *Zunhua xianzhi* (Qinghua), 6:1046–47. 2.

32. Ibid.

33. *Shibao*, March 24, 1911.

34. *Zunhua xianzhi* (1990), 10.

35. Ibid., 105–6.

36. Ibid., 7.

37. Ibid., 8.

38. Ibid., 105.

39. *Shibao*, March 14, 23, 1911.

40. *Shibao*, March 23, 1911.

41. Liu Erru, "Dong san bao kang jingshui douzheng," 1–2.

42. *Shibao*, March 23, 1911.

43. *Zunhua xianzhi* (Qinghua), 6:1046–1047, 1–2.

44. Liu Erru, "Dong san bao kang jingshui douzheng," 1.

45. *Zunhua xianzhi* (Qinghua), 6:1046–1047, 1.

46. *Shibao*, March 23, 1911.

47. *Zunhua xianzhi* (Qinghua), 6:1046–1047, 2.

48. *Zunhua xianzhi* (1990), 10.

49. Liu Erru, "Dong san bao kang jingshui douzheng," 2.

50. *Shibao*, March 24, 1911.

51. *Zunhua xianzhi* (Qinghua), 6:1046–1047, 3; also see Liu Erru, "Dong san bao kang jingshui douzheng," 4.

52. *Zunhua xianzhi* (Qinghua), 6:1046–1047, 3.

53. *Shibao*, March 24, 1911.

54. Ibid.

55. Ibid.

56. Ibid.

57. Liu Erru, "Dong san bao kang jingshui douzheng," 5.

58. Ibid., 6.

59. *Zunhua xianzhi* (Qinghua), 6:1046–1047, 4.

60. *Dongfang zazhi,* no. 9, 1910.

61. *Dongfang zazhi,* no. 8, 1910.

62. *Yuzhe huicun* (Beijing gazette), July 3, 1908, 8–9, in *Zhongguo jindai nongye shi ziliao,* (Sources on China's modern agriculture), ed. Li Wenzhi (Beijing: Renmin chuban she, 1957) 1:957.

63. Stephen R. MacKinnon, *Power and Politics in Late Imperial China: Yuan Shi-kai in Beijing and Tingjin, 1901–1908* (Berkeley: University of California Press, 1980), 157–59.

64. *Dongfang zazhi,* no. 4.

Peach Garden Oath

Source: *Sanguoyanyi* (Romance of the Three Kingdoms). Beijing: Renmin wenxue chuban she, 1992.

Sanguoyanyi
(The Romance of the Three Kingdoms)

Sanguoyanyi (The Romance of the Three Kingdoms) is an historical epic based on events that took place over a one-hundred-year period from 168–265 A.D. This was an era of political and military contention that witnessed the fall of the Han Dynasty and the rise of a Warring States period. Originally popularized by poets, storytellers, and play-wrights, the historically inspired narrative was written in novel form by Lo Guangzhong (Lo Kuan-chung) in the late fourteenth century. His intention to create an historically accurate rendition was only partially fulfilled, but he did consciously attempt to minimize the theatrical elab-orations appreciated by enthusiastic peasant audiences and deemed sources of superstition and crudeness by the conventionally educated. The theme of moral retribution in the workings of history was one ele-ment common to various renditions of the narrative.[1] As rival groups compete for power, three kingdoms led respectively by Ts'ao Ts'ao, Liu Pei, and Sun Ch'uan become the primary contenders. Early in the story, Liu Pei and his associates Kuan Yu and Chang Fei take an oath as sworn brothers to act in service to the emperor. Eventually a conflict develops between loyalty to the sworn brotherhood and loyalty to the emperor and the cause of restoring his power. The following excerpt describes the meeting of the brothers who then swear their loyalty in the well-known Peach Garden Oath.

Excerpt

The call was posted in Cho county, where it was seen by a young man of the district who, though no scholar, was broadminded and even tem-pered, taciturn yet ambitious, a man of character who was himself attracted to outstanding men. His height was considerable, his ears long lobed, his arms strikingly long, his eyes wide set and almost able to see behind him, his face like flawless jade, his lips like dabs of rouge. A remote descendant of a son of the fourth Han Emperor, High Brilliance, he bore the dynastic patroynym of Liu. His given name was Pei ("prepared"), and his formal name was Hsuan-te ("obscured virtue").

Many generations ago, his branch of the Liu clan had held a landed estate in Cho county, but their holding had been confiscated by the court on charges that they had evaded payments of tribute. Liu Pei's father, a government official, was cited by the court for integrity and filial devotion. He died early, however, and Liu Pei remained with his mother, serving her with unstinting filial piety. He supported their poor household by selling sandals and weaving mats.

The family lived in a village of Cho county called Double Mulberry because of the giant mulberry tree near their home. It was overy fifty feet high. Tall and proud, the tree seemed from afar like a canopy of a chariot. A fortune-teller had seen in it a sign that the family would produce a man of destiny. As a youth Liu Pei had played under the mulberry, saying, "I'll be the emperor and take my seat on this chariot." An uncle, struck by the figure of speech, had remarked, "This is no ordinary child."

Liu Pei was already twenty-eight when the provincial authorities issued the call for volunteers to fight the rebellions. The rebels were known as the Yellow Scarves. Their leader was Chang Chueh, a man who had failed the official examinations and retired to the hills to gather healing herbs. There he had met an ancient mystic, emerald-eyed and young of face, leaning on a staff of goosefoot wood. The mystic led Chang Chueh into a cavern and handed him three sacred texts.

"These are called the Essential Arts for the Age of Equality," the old man had said. "Now that you have them, propagate their teachings as Heaven's messenger to promote universal salvation. Use them for any other purpose and retribution will follow." With that, the old man transformed himself into a breath of crystal air and vanished.

Chang Chueh had attacked the text. He learned to summon the winds and invoke the rain and came to be called Tao-Master for the Age of Equality. When pestilence spread through the land, he traveled far and wide curing the afflicted with charms and potions. He styled himself Great Worthy and Good Doctor, and his followers, numbering over five hundred, bound up their heads with yellow scarves. They were as mobile as the clouds, and all could write the charms and recite the spells.

As his following grew, Chang Chueh set up thirty-six commands under his chieftains and began to prepare an insurrection against the Han. He and his two brothers assumed patriarchal titles and told their people: "The Han's fated end is near. A mighty sage emerges. Let one and all, in obedience to Heaven, in true allegiance, strive for the Age of Equality." And in the four quarters of the realm, the common folk bound their heads with yellow scarves and followed Chang Chueh in such numbers that the armies of the court would flee at the rumor of their approach. The court ordered all districts mobilized.

Reading the order posted in Cho county, Liu Pei sighed with indignation that traitors would attack the throne. Someone spoke roughly behind him: "What are the long sighs for? A hardy fellow like you should be giving his all for home and country."

Liu Pei turned to see a man even taller than he, with a blunt head like a panther's, huge round eyes, a swallow's cheek, a tiger's whiskers, a thunderous voice, and a stance like a horse in stride. To Liu Pei, who asked his name, he said, "My surname is Chang, my given name Fei ('flying'), my formal name Yi-to ('wings to virtue'). We've been in this county for generations and farm a bit of land, sell wine, and slaughter pigs. I was looking for men of adventure and, coming upon you reading the recruitment call, took the liberty of addressing you."

"Actually," Liu Pei replied, "I am an imperial relation, and I want to raise troops to destroy the Yellow Scarves and defend the people. I was reflecting on my limitations when you heard me sigh."

Chang Fei said, "I have resources that could be used to outfit some local youths. What if you were to join with me in serving this great cause?" Liu Pei was elated, and together they went to a nearby inn. As they drank, they noticed a striking fellow stop at the inn's entrance to rest.

"Some wine, and quickly," the stranger said. "I'm off to the town to volunteer." Liu Pei observed him: gleaming skin, glistening lips, eyes like the crimson phoenix, brows like nestling silkworms. His appearance was stately, his bearing awesome. Liu Pei invited him to share their table and asked who he was.

"My surname is Kuan," the man replied, my given name Yu ('plume'), my formal name Yun-ch'ang ('cloud-lasting'). One of the notables in our district was using his position to exploit people. I killed him and had to flee. I have been on the move these past five or six years. When I heard of the mobilization, I came to answer the call."

Liu Pei then told of his own ambitions, to Kuan Yu's great excitement. Together the three men went to Chang Fei's farm to talk further. Chang Fei proposed: "Behind the farm is a peach garden. The flowers are at their fullest. Tomorrow we must make offerings there to Heaven and Earth, declaring that we three join together as brothers, combining strength and purpose." To this Liu Pei and Kuan Yu agreed.

The next day they prepared their offerings, which included a black bull and a white horse. Amid burning incense the three men performed obeisance and spoke their vow: "We three, Liu Pei, Kuan Yu, and Chang Fei, though of separate birth, now bind ourselves in brotherhood, combining our strength and purpose to relieve the present crisis. Thus we may fulfill our duty to home and country and defend the common folk of the land. We could not help our separate births, but on the self-same day we mean to die! Shining imperial Heaven, fruitful Queen Earth, witness our determination, and may god and man jointly scourge whichever of us fails his duty or forgets his obligation."[2]

Notes

1. C. T. Hsia, *The Classic Chinese Novel: A Critical Introduction* (Bloomington: Indiana University Press, 1980; originally published by Columbia University Press, 1968), 35–36.

2. Lo Kuan-chung, *The Romance of the Three Kingdoms*, trans. Moss Roberts (New York: Pantheon Books, 1976), 4–9.

4

Weiyuan, Sichuan:
Heaven-Protected Liu Xiangting
among the Red Lanterns

In order to accomplish the unfinished business of Hong Xiuquan [leader of the Taiping Rebellion], in order to enable China to become a civilized and powerful country whose people can enjoy a free and happy life, the rebel forces in this uprising must kill the Qing officials in every county . . . and confiscate the wealth of the landlords and scholar-gentry.

—Li Shaoyi, rebel leader
1909, Dazhu, Sichuan

Liao received no special given name at birth. There seemed no reason to bother. She was simply known as the ninth child. Born in 1886 to a poor peasant family in Jintang county, central Sichuan, her prospects for surviving childhood were not good. If she persevered, her fate would be filled with suffering. Great hope did not accompany the ninth Liao child's birth. But by chance, and perhaps because she proved a gifted girl, the child grew to young adulthood. Along the way she, like many villagers in her area, perhaps with her mother or an aunt, we do not know, frequently visited the nearby major marketing center of Shibantan, just to the northeast of Chengdu, capital of Sichuan province. There she saw the local Red Lantern practitioner, Zeng Ayi, and soon became her student studying boxing, swordsmanship, and Red Lantern doctrines, known as *Hongdengjiao*.

Although not all Red Lantern members were women, the organizations primarily comprised young women between the ages of twelve and eighteen who trained in using swords and fans as weapons. Their male counterparts in the early twentieth century were known as the Boxers, or *Yihetuan*. Gendered divisions among rural dissident groups were not uncommon. The Taiping movement, for example, had also

131

practiced the separation of followers into male and female groupings, each with their own leaders and teachers. Among values shared by many rural dissent communities was opposition to footbinding, and true to this standard Red Lantern members did not bind their feet or arrange their hair in the local customary styles for unmarried women. Although appearing in the historical record before the late nineteenth-century Boxer movement, which began in rural Shandong, the Red Lanterns are at this point in historical research best known for activities contemporaneous with and following the Shandong Boxers. Addressed by the parallel titles used to designate leaders of the Boxer groups, such as "Senior Sister-Disciple" (*da shijie*) and "Second Sister-Disciple" (*er shijie*), Red Lantern leaders commanded widespread respect and were especially well known in the Sichuan area and other regions of west central China.[1] Stories of two famous Red Lantern leaders, Holy Mother of the Yellow Lotus (*Huanglian Shengmu*) and Azure Cloud (*Cuiyun jie*) were particularly popular. In each story, a young woman, powerful and beautiful, developed a fierce and abiding hatred of foreigners who mistreated a husband or father.[2]

By sixteen, the Liao child had become more accomplished than her teacher. Knowledge of her boxing skill and ability to "speak about the doctrine" (*shuofa*) spread far and wide through the marketing networks of rural Sichuan. The 1899–1900 Boxer uprisings in Shandong sent new waves of antiforeignism throughout the Red Lantern areas. Shortly thereafter, beginning in 1901, landlords and officials began to press for new taxes in the name of reform. Weary from the weight of corrupt practices by local landlords and officials and foreign economic and cultural intrusions, villagers already familiar with the Red Lantern teachings listened attentively to Liao's speech and assessed her martial skill and leadership qualities.

In 1902, the year of a major drought in northeast Sichuan, Liao led a Red Lantern uprising that claimed as its slogan, "Destroy the Qing, Expel the Foreigner."[3] Finally the Liao child had a special name. Her followers called her Liao Guanyin after Guanyin, the Goddess of Mercy, or sometimes Liao Jiumei, Ninth Sister Liao. By either name, she rose with a moment of collective inspiration from deep despair to strike a blow at some of the local manifestations of social oppression. Under her guidance, thousands of supporters and some units of the local Boxer groups moved toward Chengdu with intent to attack Christian and corrupt elite offices. Passing through market towns and villages along the way, they drew attention and fear from officials who quickly called for troops to begin a suppression campaign. In the government dragnet to arrest leaders of the unrest, Liao escaped the area. Many of her coleaders were not as fortunate. Large numbers met with imprisonment and execution because they dared in their own way and their own language to step forward on their own behalf. No one knows what happened to Liao Guanyin. She was not the only goddess of mercy to be sought in connection with this uprising and she was not the only woman.[4] Liao may have escaped to lead other Red Lantern uprisings, which rose to a crescendo in rural Sichuan during the years 1905 to 1907. She may have moved eastward or to the south to join in the anti–New Policy protests, which marked the late post-Boxer decade. Most certainly, however, Liao's story became another thread woven into the rural culture of protest in this area especially rich in its varied dissident networks.

Weiyuan county, site of Sichuan's major anti–New Policy activity seven years later, was in 1902 on the periphery of the Red Lantern activism centered in Jintang county, where Liao Jiumei was born.[5] Itself embedded in a matrix of Red Lantern centers, Weiyuan was an active Elder Brother Society (Gelaohui) center. Whereas Red Lantern views tended to focus on antiforeignism, Elder Brother groups targeted anti-landlord and anti-Qing issues in their analysis of local problems. These issues were interrelated, and villagers were well aware of this fact. Pushing against each other like currents in a rural sea, Sichuan Red Lantern and Elder Brother groups through ongoing contact debated and reassessed the sources of hardship and injustice in village life. In 1906, Wang Fengzhao of Weiyuan called for people to "study boxing and oppose officials," and several thousand people from Weiyuan joined with the Red Lanterns of Renshou and Jungxian counties to stage an uprising.[6] At Kaixian to the east of Jintang and Weiyuan, a 1907 uprising organized by Red Lantern leaders including Wu Sang (Mrs. Wu nèe Sang) clearly identified, in addition to Christian churches, official exactions and landlord corruption in the form of new retail taxes and new schools as the targets of their collective action.[7] When rebellion once again stirred in 1909 in Weiyuan, villagers who asked Liu Xiangting to lead their protest made clear their antiforeign sentiments, but new circumstances represented by the New Policy reforms and the census and taxes these reforms produced brought antiofficial and antilandlord issues to the foreground and Gelaohui associations supplied the primary organizational networks for the movement. The context for the dissident events of 1909–11 in Weiyuan was a history of rural protest with strong and multifaceted roots.

Heterodoxy and Ethnicity: Sources of Antigovernment Activism in the Making of Rural Dissent

Themes of heterodoxy and ethnicity played their way through the long century of rural activism from the White Lotus Rebellion in 1796 to the

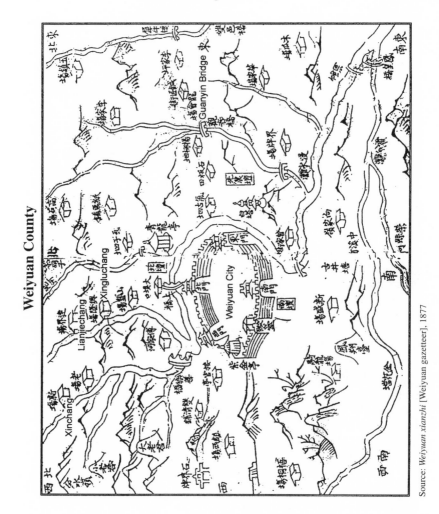

Source: *Weiyuan xianzhi* [Weiyuan gazetteer], 1877

Republican Revolution of 1911. Sichuan province was one area where these motifs were especially audible and recurrent. Home to heterodox White Lotus Buddhist sects and almost a dozen non-Han ethnic groups, including the Yi in the southern area across from Yunnan, the Miao to the east of Chengdu, and the Qiang to the northwest, Sichuan was also located just to the south of large Moslem populations that were ethnically Han but by religion a minority. Coexisting with the state and feuding among themselves when the state retreated from its own intrusive, aggressive postures, these groups nonetheless maintained antigovernment dispositions that were close to the surface of their respective political outlooks.

Among the ethnically Han rural groups, heterodoxy derived primarily from Buddhist sectarian activity sometimes associated with the White Lotus teachings but also embedded in rural customs of martial arts, supernatural beliefs, and healing practices. A "conversion-oriented" religious faith with strong populist and reformist characteristics, the White Lotus followed their own sutras and worshipped a supreme female deity known as the Eternal Mother.[8] Sect communities throughout north and west China practiced vegetarianism and healing arts, and established communication networks through a system of ties between teachers and students that formed what Susan Naquin has described as "chains of individuals across time and space."[9] "Strong vertical ties and a persuasive historical vision" that looked forward to a new age generated a powerfully imaginative and action-oriented rural project.[10] Within this framework, the sect's "extremely unusual openness to women as members and teachers betrayed the religion's heterodoxy."[11] The role of women in White Lotus communities inverted the "natural" social order as prescribed by state-sponsored orthodoxy, which drew from the philosophical commentaries cultivating classical social ideals. It is not clear from the sources how many women participated in the White Lotus sects or if, in some cases, they were the majority of sect members.[12] But documentation does reveal that of the women members whose backgrounds are known, 76 percent had men as their teachers and 24 percent had women as teachers. Women who taught had half women and half men as students.[13] A commander of government forces sent to suppress White Lotus-inspired activism in 1813 wrote that, "with these bandits who practice a sect, it was in many instances the women who taught the men. . . . The women are cunning and dangerous and this heterodoxy leads to rebellion. . . . Moreover, [in battle] our forces have so far killed more than one woman."[14] Consequently, the White Lotus did more than enough from the political perspective of the state to earn the label of "heterodox" (*xiefei*), a term not used for all peasant oppositional activity but reserved for those judged to be potentially most threatening to the status quo. Along this spectrum of dissent, the Taiping were also considered *xiefei*. The Triad secret societies of south China were not placed in this category.[15]

B. J. Ter Haar's work on the White Lotus teachings challenges common associations of rebellion with White Lotus activity. Examining judicial records through the dynasties in which rebel leaders were brought to trial, Ter Haar finds little that tied rebel activity to the teachings of Huiyuan and the original White Lotus Society beyond the readiness of officials to group all disturbances under one convenient label.[16] Instead, Ter Haar finds a rural society riddled with magic notions and great fears that were often associated with White Lotus teachings, creating an official discourse that falsely characterized White Lotus groups who in general did not become involved in political dissent. While the anti–New Policy cases considered in the present study contain no specific evidence of doctrinal ties to the White Lotus teachings, they are an example of how rural activism could draw eclectically on a mixture of lay Buddhist, alchemical, supernatural, and goddess views that had a diffuse and malleable reality in social behavior, enriching personal options, with or without orthodox religious roots.

Rural society had many more possibilities than are usually dreamed of in standard generalizations about Chinese gender roles. Far from the oppressed status conjured up by visions of orthodoxy labeled "Confucian," women in Sichuan and other parts of China sometimes found their way to membership in the ranks of lay Buddhist, White Lotus, and other secret society organizations. Women were often found among the ranks of religious sects (*jiao*) but were seldom included in secret society (*hui*) groupings. Long before movements for women's rights in Shanghai and other urban areas in the 1920s, however, some rural women had exercised leadership positions and a significant measure of equality with men in the folk religion associations that permeated country life. Father Leboucq, a French missionary in Zhili in 1875, was frightened by what he saw. Nervous about the possibility of a French Revolution or a Paris Commune-type event in China, Father Leboucq saw the potential for Chinese secret societies to play the role that Freemasons took up in France and for Chinese women to be the instigators of such social frenzy. He wrote:

> I do not know whether European secret societies admit women in their midst, but in China it is the harpies of the Water-Lily [White Lotus] who hold sway in the society. It is they who inspire and encourage the faint-hearted. Should the Water-Lily Society ever come to set up a Committee of Public Safety or a Commune. . . . it is certain that it would not lack women fire-raisers.[17]

Perhaps Father Leboucq's fears were insightful. Women were bound by oaths not to reveal their secret society membership to husbands or parents, unless they knew for sure that these relatives were also members. How many Chinese women lived secret lives beyond the confined daily routines of the household in which all roles were tethered to patriarchal authority? Women who joined a secret society before their husbands were supposed to be recognized by members as the primary managers of their households, an arrangement that was technically not in keeping with patriarchal norms but that was often described as the de facto situation in many families with or without secret society affiliations.

Rural activism, which drew on an amalgam of lay Buddhist, secret society, and supernatural practice, began to grow during the Qing in the late eighteenth century and continued its momentum into the nineteenth and twentieth centuries through the Eight Trigrams Uprising in 1813,[18] the Nien Rebellion from 1857 to 1868,[19] and finally the Boxer and Red Lantern activism of the 1898–1901 and later periods. Even as specific social issues shifted around landlordism, official corruption, political reform, taxation, and foreign religion, folk religion continued to be interwoven with the many designs of heterodoxy. *Bagua* and *Yihe*, specific forms of martial-arts boxing associated with study of the Eight Trigrams, itself an element in Daoist and Classical as well as White Lotus circles, were well-established features of peasant intellectual life from the casual practitioners who joined the Boxer movement toward Beijing in 1900 to the thoughtful rural political philosophers such as Lü Conglü, anti–New Policy leader at Laiyang.[20]

The Boxers and the Red Lanterns were especially active in Sichuan during the first decade of the twentieth century. In the aftermath of the defeat of Taiping Generals Li and Shi by the Qing armies, rural groups within Sichuan shifted to other means of continuing their struggles against the dynasty. In 1866, the Fujiao branch of the Red Lanterns, which was itself a branch of the White Lotus, rose to continue attacks on Qing officials. This Fujiao and Red Lantern activity in the Sichuan area of Pingshan county eventually expanded to include the area of Weiyuan, site of the 1909 anti–New Policy activism.[21]

Specific instances of anti-Qing activism by these heterodox societies on behalf of the rural population against landord and official abuses appear continuously in the historical record for the periods of the 1870s, 80s, and 90s.[22] The post-Boxer decade in Sichuan clearly demonstrates an evolution in rural thought. Under the slogan "Preserve the Qing, destroy the foreigner," Boxer activity spread throughout Shandong in 1900. After the defeat of the Boxers in Zhili and Shandong, Boxer groups moved into other parts of the country, including Sichuan. By 1901, Sichuan Boxer activity in Chongjing had modified that slogan to "Destroy the Qing, eliminate the foreigner, restore the Han."[23] Documented Boxer and Red Lantern dissent was recorded in the years 1902, 1905, 1906, and 1907.[24] Activity under the Boxer banner continued well into 1908 and continued to express this shift in political outlook. Both Boxers and Red Lanterns subscribed to antiforeign and anti-Qing views in such rhymes as the following:

> The emperor demands our grain.
> The foreign devils steal our treasures.
> But as long as we have our big swords,
> They'll get neither grain nor treasures.[25]

In addition to the Boxers and Red Lanterns, the Elder Brothers, or Gelaohui, was also active in Sichuan during the anti–New Policy era. Gelaohui expanded in the aftermath of the Taiping rebellion as the latter began to fail. Fundamentally anti-Manchu in outlook, the purpose of the Elder Brothers initiated by the Triads of the Yangzi valley was to continue the work of the Taiping by infiltrating the imperial army. As K. C. Liu and John Fairbank have written, "It was not by chance . . . that the phenomenal extension of the Ko Lao Hui in the lower and middle Yangtze [Yangzi] valley during the last third of the nineteenth century occurred in the same region which had witnessed the repression of the Taiping."[26] Demobilized soldiers, displaced farmers, and all those of the rural areas who continued to experience threats to subsistence livelihood were potential recruits to the continued struggle against the Chinese state. In 1870, the Gedihui leader Yang Zhurong (also known as Yang Yuchun) called a meeting at Kaishanli temple in Yien county of Hubei province along the Sichuan border that led to continued activism over local rural issues.[27] Similar incidents occurred throughout 1877 involving Guijiao, Gedihui, and Gele groups, all of which were interconnected with the Elder Brothers.[28] In 1884, Gelaohui associations organized another round of opposition to landlords and county officials, reaching a level of agitation that brought events to the attention of central authorities and into the historical record.[29]

Popular with the rural people in general, the Gelaohui at Weiyuan was especially active in the mining areas. A typical *xiang* (small rural administrative unit) or town might have four or five lodges known as *tangkou*, while a small place might have only two lodges. An interesting feature of the Elder Brothers was that their members were not primarily from the subsistence social strata. Instead, the Gelaohui was itself stratified by social standing. At Weiyuan, those of higher educational ranks, important landlords, scholar officials and even budding capitalists (*zibenjia*) would all enter into an upper lodge known by the name of the humaneness (*renzi*) league. Small landlords, small merchants, individuals who were self-employed, *nongmin*, and workers were not allowed to join the upper lodges so they usually entered a middle lodge, of which there were three known by the names of righteousness (*yizi*), decorum (*lizi*), or knowledge (*zhizi*). Those who could not enter the middle lodge would go into the lower lodge, which was designated by the characters for trust (*xinzi*). The name of each of these five lodges represented one of the classical virtues.[30] The middle "righteous league" was the central organization of the Gelaohui. This was the lodge to which Liu Xiangting, the leader of the Weiyuan protest, belonged. Among the elements in the lower lodge there was often a group that depended on extortion for its livelihood, and those in the upper lodge were often compelled to give them payoffs. For the Elder Brothers in the upper lodge such payoffs were no big deal. A well-to-do family's main objective in participating in the Gelao organization was primarily to know what was happening locally, to add to its own power and prestige, and to protect its own property. As of 1900, many elite families in the Yangtze valley already had at least one member in the Gelaohui to protect their family from other Gelaohui members and to maintain some leverage with the local magistrate.[31]

One of the most noticeable patterns that the Weiyuan case of 1909–11 illustrates is the lack of Tongmenghui (Revolutionary Alliance) connections to anti–New Policy activism despite the generally high level of Tongmenghui mobilization in the immediate area. After the establishment of the Tongmenghui in 1905, the Gelaohui developed direct connections with the Alliance, which extended outside of rural areas. In 1907, many Tongmenghui members resident in Japan decided to merge with the Gelaohui in preparation for rural uprisings the former hoped to cultivate for national revolutionary goals. Revolutionary Alliance member Jiao Dafeng had a brother who was prominent in the Sichuan Gelaohui. Jiao described the merger in this way:

> My eldest brother, who had a high standing in the Society of [Elder] Brothers in Szechuan, now on my recommendation became a member of the Revolutionary League. He was very pleased with my idea of the merge. In the latter half of 1907, through the assiduous efforts of the League members, the leaders of the secret societies . . . organized in Japan . . . the Society for Mutual Progress.[32]

In 1907, Tongmenghui activism occured at Jiangan and Luzhou counties approximately seventy miles to the southeast of Weiyuan. Tongmenghui members in this area spoke to the issue of overthrowing the Qing Dynasty in order to improve China's condition and made the case that in such a revolution the upper areas of the Yangzi River in Sichuan would play a crucial role. An uprising called at this time to capture the cities of Jiangan and Luzhou failed.[33] Similar activity in the Chengdu area proved unsuccessful. In 1909, Tongmenghui groups again planned a Sichuan uprising, this time to begin in Guangan county about 140 miles to the northeast of Weiyuan but to no avail. A situation that developed in the Jiading area (present-day Loshan county) about fifty miles to the west of Weiyuan provided the Tongmenghui with its next opportunity.[34]

In the late spring of 1909, just as the events at Weiyuan were beginning to take shape, a revolt of the Yi people in southwest Sichuan created a chaotic situation for local officials. Armies stationed around

Pingxian moved into the area, but the Yi were in a remote region difficult to enter. Commanders of these forces, who had secret ties to the
Tongmenghui, decided that rather than just sit with their troops on the
border areas between Sichuan and Guizhou provinces, they would make
use of their mobilized forces to stage an uprising. After contacting the
Tongmenghui in the region, together they planned an attack at Jiading.[35]
With thirty guns and three thousand bullets they first moved into Tong-
jiachang, a market town where a theater troup had gathered a large
crowd, inadvertently creating a perfect distraction while more than one
hundred Tongmenghui members under the leadership of Shu Eng
stormed the local militia storehouse, seized the supply of weapons, and
announced their uprising in the name of overthrowing the Qing.[36] Shu
Eng then gathered his forces at the town of Xinchang on the northwestern border area of Weiyuan county, which was administratively a part
of Jiading during the Qing Dynasty. There at Guanyin temple, Shu met
with his recruits to plan the next stages of the uprising at Jiading city.
Shu himself came down with a case of malaria and could not continue.
The Tongmenghui units moved on toward Jiading, however. On their
approach, the troops that were defending Jiading received reenforce-
ments and were able to block the Tongmenghui rebel units.

At this point, the rebels changed direction and moved toward Pingshan where they hoped to pick up additional support from local militias.
The troops from Jiading continued their pursuit from behind as Qing
forces began to move out from Pingshan toward the rebel groups. After
a day of fighting, the Tongmenghui units began to run out of munitions.
Large numbers of Tongmenghui recruits were wounded, arrested, and/
or executed. Some escaped to Shanghai. Others went to Guangdong.
More than 200 of the Tongmenghui's brightest and most talented members were killed in this incident.[37] Consequently, prospects for an uprising in the Sichuan area remained subdued until the time of the Protect
the Railway Movement in the summer and fall of 1911. Tongmenghui
member and resident of Jiepian, a market town in Weiyuan county, Hu
Yugai actively mobilized support for the Protect the Railway Movement
in his area. Hu and other Tongmenghui supporters also held meetings
in the Guandi temple in Xinchang just a stone's throw from Lianjiechang, Liu Xiangting's home town.[38]

With Tongmenghui activity including contact with the Gelaohui in
such close proximity to Weiyuan on all sides during the exact months
of the anti–New Policy protests, it is puzzling that there was no evidence of direct involvement with the census and tax resistance movement led by Gelaohui leader Liu Xiangting. The pattern of Tongmenghui presence without involvement in the opposition to New Policy
reforms was also apparent in other counties. As the details at Weiyuan

indicate, most Tongmenghui members were involved in the local new school projects and hence associated, even if falsely, with the New Policy. They also tended to be affiliated with the upper-class branches of the Gelaohui. At Weiyuan, the railway movement drew on Gelaohui members from the upper and middle lodges.[39] Anti–New Policy leader Liu Xiangting represented the interests of the middle and lower levels of the lodges. In other words, class divisions and political orientation more than lack of organizational presence inhibited a peasant/Tongmenghui alliance over New Policy–related issues.

In noncrisis times, which the post-Boxer decade was not, religious sects like those discussed earlier, and secret societies, such as the Gelaohui, functioned as mutual aid societies and/or racketeering agencies. As Jean Chesneaux remarked, "Their lawless activites were never clearly differentiated from the politico-social struggle."[40] The slogan "Strike at the rich and help the poor," motivated a considerable amount of secret society activity, not only in ordinary times, but also in periods of pending crisis. Although most village and intervillage associations had functions that were primarily either secular or religious, invariably both functions were present and complemented one another. Secular and spiritual issues were generally not separated. Rituals borrowed from folk traditions and intended to strengthen the protesters' resolve resembled secret society ceremonies. At Laiyang, Qu Shiwen and his fellow protest leaders took a blood oath reminiscent of secret society initiation rites. At Zhaotong, Yunnan, messengers who went from house to house with information on when people should gather to attack the county elite members carried a secret sign consisting of two pieces of coal and a feather, conveying that the message was of extreme urgency—"quick as a blazing fire and swift as the flying wing."[41] The use of such imagery and symbols was a commonplace feature of rural society and could be found in both secular and spiritual activities.

Max Weber described the Chinese outlook as an enchanted worldview in which the supernatural and the mundane freely interacted.[42] Frederic Wakeman refers to Chinese thought, whether in the elite or popular culture, as holistic.[43] Reason was not isolated from magic and superstition; both belonged to the repertoire of human means for explaining or changing the world. Daniel Kulp, studying Phenix village near Swatow in Guangdong, found that people's beliefs easily integrated these views. He observed: "In addition to the living community there are: the natural community, the spirits residing in natural objects; the spiritual or ancestral community; and the spiritual or historical community, folk heroes and saints. The spirits and gods are conceived as made favorable to man's fortunes by magical devices and ceremonies."[44] Phenix villagers offered prayers to the orchard spirits, hoping for a good harvest, and boatmen took care to appease the spirits of the wind, rain, and river.[45] At Taitou village in Shandong, not far from Laiyang county, villagers worshipped the King of Cattle and prayed to the Dragon King for rain.[46] The use of sophisticated formulas and techniques to divine the will of the spirits constituted the practice of *fengshui* (wind and rain), geomancy, which was commonly followed throughout China. Temples and temple associations were a physical expression of the secular-spiritual continuum that characterized rural life. Most of the villages in China had one or more temples dedicated to a wide variety of deities, including local gods and spirits as well as such Buddhist deities as Guanyin, the goddess of mercy, or Guandi, the god of war and culture. Classical, Daoist, and Buddhist beliefs blended into a folk religion with local variations. Although in most cases village headmen did not directly manage temple affairs, they did work closely with the temple priests, who received donations from the community to coordinate villagewide ceremonies.[47] C. K. Yang describes the dual function of temples:

> Temple fairs and noneconomic religious gatherings of the periodic and fortuitous types were organized around the gods in the public temples. In this role, the temples and their gods acquired the character of being the collective symbols of the interests and even the very existence of the community. As the vast majority of the temples were collective undertakings of local community groups or the larger community of the state, the temple was a visible expression of the community and its collective interests, and public worship in it represented a periodic mustering of the community for the demonstration of common beliefs and common interests.[48]

While each village had its own temples, there were also temples located at crossroads between villages and in market towns that served as intervillage community centers. Temple associations of both varieties were involved in anti–New Policy movements.

Temples were central meeting places in many antireform uprisings. The first meeting to discuss local problems at Laiyang was held at Tangjia temple, and the confiscation of temple property for self-government and new schools or police bureaus was often an issue. In some cases, protesters emphasized the spiritual side of this conflict. At Yizhou, Zhili, for example, villagers charged that because statues had been removed from a local temple preparatory to its establishment as a self-government office, the spirits had been antagonized and had consequently inflicted a severe drought on the area, threatening the farmers' crops. Their demands, in addition to items related to embezzled granary funds, increased taxes, and police bureaus, included the demands that the temple statues be returned to their original places and that the officials pray for rain until the ground was thoroughly soaked.[49] At Wuyang, Jiangsu, and Cixi, Zhejiang, temple-related issues also entered explicitly into the political and economic disputes over New Policy reforms.[50]

Intervillage temple organizations were central to the mobilization of protest at both Zunhua, Zhili, and Chuansha, Jiangsu. At Zunhua, temple leadership and village leadership were separate but closely intertwined. Yang Xiu, the leader of the local heterodox Buddhist sect, managed the Jinshan shrine, which had branch temples in villages throughout the county. Groups worshipping at these temples were known as associations (*hui*). When an individual joined a *hui*, he signed a written agreement (*hetong*) and received a marker with his name on it that was to be worn at the waist. Upon learning that Jinshan temple was slated for conversion to a new police bureau under the reform programs, members of the temple associations mobilized up to twenty thousand persons by circulating a notice in villages throughout the three large *xiang* in which the sect's influence was the strongest. Yang Xiu told his supporters that Guanyin, the goddess of mercy, had appeared to him in his dreams for three consecutive nights, telling him to relieve the distress of the people. In order to raise funds and to publicize the movement, the Wulong and Jinshan temples gave two dramatic performances, which they financed by pressing wealthy families for donations. As the protest developed, sect temples became resistance headquarters. A wide spectrum of persons participated, ranging from the unemployed to small and moderate owner-cultivators, all of whom shared minor household status and carried an extra tax burden because influential major households were able to evade taxes. Roughly 30 percent of the villages in the area of the protest gave active support to the demonstrations.[51]

In addition to the organizational aspects of temple associations, images based on supernatural beliefs were a powerful means of communicating about secular ideas in a semiliterate culture. Hostility and fear regarding elite-managed reforms were often stated in metaphors that drew freely from both the secular and spiritual realms. At Yixing, Jiangsu, rumors were circulated by the villagers that the persons whose names were taken in the census would be turned into iron to be used in building a bridge over the Yellow River.[52] In the Suzhou area, this metaphor for the life-threatening potential of the reforms was expressed in a different way: Persons recorded in the census would die as their names were crushed under the wheels of railroad cars.[53] At Weiyuan, Sichuan, fifty thousand to sixty thousand persons protested against increased taxation and census taking. Accustomed as were all Chinese villagers to interpreting signs and symbols for information about forces around them that influenced their well-being, the protesters understood the design of red dots and lines on the census plaques nailed to every residence to mean that their homes had in effect been turned over to the foreigners and that they would be forced to become Christians. With signs interpreted as affirmations of pending economic threat, all elements that were either new or foreign became suspect in the eyes of the vulnerable taxpayers.[54]

The methods of both magic and protest had their roots in the agricultural life of the Chinese villager. Although magical formulas, protest strategies, and agricultural techniques had different organizational forms, their application, which had the common goal of providing for the villagers' individual and collective well-being, shared similar approaches. Collective action, appointed leadership, discreet developmental stages, well-coordinated planning, acute observation of natural and social phenomena, and pragmatism were features common to the practice of magic, agriculture, and protest. Hsiao-tung Fei has observed that:

> Magic is not a spontaneous and individual action. It is an organized institution. There is a definite person who is charged with the function and possesses magical powers. Secondly, there is a traditional ritual to call in the supernatural intervention. Lastly, there are myths to justify the ritual and the ability of the magician.[55]

Agriculture also was an enterprise that was more collective than individual and that relied more on precise timing than on spontaneity.[56] Furthermore, just as the villagers carefully watched for signs telling them when to plant and followed exact methods for tending their crops, so they carefully watched the political scene and judged when action should be taken in keeping with the traditionally prescribed stages of protest, ranging from petitions and public demonstrations to attacks on property and persons. There was no proclivity for dramatic actions that could not achieve practical results, whether in the secular or spiritual sphere. It was common for village shrines to fall into disuse for years if prayers spoken there had not produced results, only to be revived at a later date to determine whether or not the spirits had returned. An informal village consensus monitored the ongoing effectiveness of local shrines.

The enchanted worldview of Chinese villagers did not in itself give rise to the anti–New Policy movements, but it did influence the way in which protesters organized and, to a greater or lesser extent, the style in which reform-related issues were articulated. This pattern is not different from the habits of people in other agrarian societies. One example from *Forest Rites* by Peter Sahlins explores how in the mid-nineteenth century peasants of Ariege, France, drew on features of local social organization and culture to articulate political grievances in ways that might at first seem bizarre. Transforming symbols from annual Carnival village festivities and folk beliefs about the spirits of the forest, young men in intervillage association disguised themselves as female figures, known as the the Demoiselles, and attacked forest guards, charcoal makers, and owners of ironworks who under the Forest Code of 1827 attempted to limit peasant access to the forest and in so doing disrupted existing peasant practices of forest gardening.[57] This especially well-detailed study of the Demoiselles recalls the many commonalities of agrarian societies in their struggles to sustain themselves in the face of centralizing political authority in the early industrial setting.

The activism of ethnic minorities played an important role in the nineteenth-century evolution of rural politics. A part of but also distinct from mainstream society, minority groups had an ongoing cultural distance from the Han majority, which embodied a political dimension. Conflict between ethnic minorities and near-subsistence farmers as well as cooperation between these groups against local officials were equally a part of the rural script. A presence in rural society with additional layers of conflict with authority, the ethnic minorities were sometimes a catalyst in the rural mix of factors precipitating heterodox activism. Numerous large- and small-scale instances of ethnic- and minority-based activism were another prelude to the transformation of rural protest during the post-Boxer decade.

Before 1850, examples of common ground between issues raised by minority groupings and non-minority rural activists were few. Living in separate villages with a distinctive lifestyle, Moslem communities in northwest China also subscribed to the conventional *sangang* norms for societal obligations and took the imperial examinations although they were limited by government regulations in promotion to the higher reaches of office holding. Village headmen in Moslem communities were government appointed, but like all such local appointments those who held these positions generally retained legitimacy by virtue of their ability to mediate on behalf of village interests. Government policy toward Moslems shifted in 1762 by imperial decree, which introduced discriminatory practices against Moslems. While Han Chinese who committed theft could be punished with a light flogging, Moslems for the same offenses were to be exiled to Yunnan or Guizhou and could also be condemned to wear the cangue for the remainder of their lives.[58] Moslem led antigovernment uprisings began two decades after this imperial decree and continued into the nineteenth century. While this line of conflict was between officials of the state and the Moslems, as the early nineteenth century developed signs of economic stress, Han Chinese and Moslem groups at the village level came into conflict with each other for local land and commericial resources. In the 1813 Trigram rebellion, rebel leader Xiao Hansan led a group to beat up and rob Muslims who had refused to join them.[59] Major Moslem uprisings such as the Panthay Rebellion in Yunnan in 1856–73 and Dongan Rebellion in Shaanxi and Gansu in 1862–73, often began as disputes between local Han officials and Moslem leaders or as conflicts among rival Moslem groups. In either case, the inclination of officials to move with severity against Moslem communities drew out the abiding conflict with state authority in each case. What the Moslem groups had already experienced, that the state and its agents could be a harsh source of demands and limitations on rural communities, the Han groups had yet to fully experience in the nineteenth-century set of circumstances. Not until the end of the century would these groups find common ground.

Parallel to the experience of rural communities in many parts of China, minority groups were also increasingly encountering not only the full brunt of government oppression but also the deleterious effects of foreign presence. In 1848, French missionaries tried to establish themselves among the Tibetan (Zangmin) religious groups. In 1860, they began establishing churches in the Yi minority area of Dechang and several other places. By 1910, there were more than twenty congregations and a hospital associated with the mission of the Lingshan area of Sichuan, and minority based resistance to foreigners and their religion had been evident for decades before.[60] The years 1865 and 1868 saw resistance to foreign religions in eastern Sichuan at Yangzhou. The Tujia and Miao minorities both participated in the events at Yangzhou. In 1873, at Batang against the backdrop of earthquake and drought, the Zangmin and Lamaists joined together to oppose the foreign religions. The Qing government sided with the French. There were similar incidents involving the French missionaries in the Batang area in 1881 and 1887.[61] A case in 1897 shows the first instance in this time period of cooperation between groups among the Yi minority and the Han population on issues of antiforeignism in the Lingshan area of Sichuan.[62]

Continuing into the post-Boxer era, both minority and Han rural activists found themselves marching to the same government yamens for redress of grievances and attacking the same Christian mission facilities even when outright cooperation among different activist groups was not part of the scenario. Their focus was on antigovernment and antiforeign issues and not on each other. This was the analysis to which both groups had arrived in the post-Boxer decade and nowhere was this more evident than in Sichuan where a high density of minority groups did and still do make their homes. In 1903, people of the Yi nationality in Xichang county attacked the county government.[63] A Miao uprising struck in 1904 at Nanbu county to the northeast of Chengdu.[64] In 1905, the Yi attacked Christians at Ningyuan, and at Xichang the Majia branch of the Yi again rose in attack.[65] Also in 1905, Tibetans attacked churches and killed preachers at Batang in western Sichuan.[66] Of course, the Manchus themselves were an ethnic minority and not a seamless one at that. Class differences among them could erupt into antigoverment activism as happened in Chengdu in 1907.[67] In 1908, the Ahou and Sujia branches of the Yi initiated an attack on American Christians in the area of Xichang. At Meiru they killed an American missionary identified as Mr. Burke.[68] The same year and again in 1910, Lamaists clashed with Qing troops at Baan in Sichuan.[69] In July 1909, more than three thousand Yi marched toward Meiru to attack Qing government offices, a case detailed above in the section on the Gelaohui in Weiyuan.[70] Today this area of Sichuan is a Yi minority autonomous region, a testament to the success and continuing difficulty of these groups' efforts to maintain their identity. In 1909, the Tongmenghui, the Revolutionary Alliance with Gelaohui members, did a report on conditions in the Jiading and Pingshan uprising area, in the immediate vicinity of Weiyuan county and noted the importance of ethnic minorities to the struggles against the Qing government and foreigners in this area.[71]

Certainly the prime example of cooperation between minority groupings and other rural organizations was the emergence of the Taiping movement, which left a legacy well into the New Policy era. Although the original leadership and community base for this movement was the Hakka population, ethnically Han but culturally a minority, villagers across the heartland of Han China had no problem joining in and making the movement their own as they rose to protest their local variation of the issues the Hakkas addressed in their attack on landlords, tax collectors, and officials. Something similar happened in the decade of 1901–11 as groups from among the ethnic minorities as well as heterodox associations stirred the same pot of rural dissent without this time merging into one movement. A place-based pattern of widespread rebellion was the character of the post-Boxer decade. Sometimes, however, they did stir it explicitly together as in the case noted above in 1897 with the Yi minority and Han groups joining forces. At Nanbu to the northeast of Chengdu in 1904, Miao tribesmen raised an attack and in 1905 also at Nanbu, Yihetuan leaders joined with Tongmenghui to organize an uprising.[72] Ethnicity and heterodoxy crossed in time and space and sometimes rose in unity against state misgovernance.

Weiyuan: Geography and Social Relations

Events in the Weiyuan area clearly bring together anti-Qing, antireform, antitax, and antiforeign perspectives into one rural resistance movement. In the development of opposition to New Policy reforms, diverse rural networks embedded in place-based politics mobilized strong antigovernment sentiments against the "New Policy road" taken by county and provincial elites seeking new opportunities for advancement. The Weiyuan case details rich pockets of sectarian and secret society sources of dissident practice directed specifically at administrative authority (*qiyuan*). The role of the Gelaohui at Weiyuan is especially revealing of the social class divisions that could emerge within one organizational structure.

Beginning with the land, Weiyuan was located in the south central region of Sichuan province. Adding to the land the social relations of the area, Weiyuan was a county of poor to moderate means, depending on one's place in the social order. Neither at the center of local activism nor isolated from it in the decades before the anti–New Policy uprisings, Weiyuan drew together threads of many activist elements grown from the interaction of the land and the social classes that lived there, producing one of the largest opposition movements of the post-Boxer era. Itself a densely populated, intensively cultivated region in West China, Sichuan province contained a highly productive area in the alluvial plain centered around Chengdu, the provincial capital. While rice was the main crop in the central basin, to the north and east dryland crops such as cotton, soy beans, and corn were grown in the hilly terrain. To the west of the Sichuan basin were the rugged mountains of the Tibetan plateau, supporting a sparse population and little agricultural activity.

Set in the foothills region south of Chengdu, Weiyuan was in 1909 administratively a part of Jiading (modern Loshan). The administrative divisions within the county included five rural areas (*xiang*). Xinxiang, in the northwest area, altogether had four market towns: Shanwangchang in the southeast, Xingluchang in the east, Xinchang due south, and Lianjiechang to the north. Of all the *xiang* of Weiyuan, Xinxiang was the most mountainous and least densely populated, making up less than one-fifth of the county's total population.[73] There was relatively little land available for cultivation in this *xiang*, and the forests were very dense. Recently a small enterpreneur had opened a charcoal-making operation in the area and constructed several earth furnaces in Lianjiechang and Qiaobangou about six miles away. In Lianjiechang, there were three furnaces, two in Qiaobangou. By the middle of 1909 only one furnace was still functioning.

Foreign presence and dynastic decline both had their impact on the economy and people's livelihood at Lianjiechang where already poor conditions worsened. Inflation, which was rampant throughout China after the introduction of foreign mints in the 1880s, was a significant problem in rural Sichuan. In 1890, one *liang* of white silver was equal to six hundred copper cash coins, known as *wen*. By 1908, the value of silver had gone up 64 percent, and it required one thousand copper coins to equal one *liang* of silver. In 1890, a *sheng* of large grain rice cost thirty *wen*, and by 1908 the same unit of rice cost fifty *wen*. The prices of everyday items of food and household goods rose during these years. To give another example, pork that sold for thirty-two *wen* per *sheng* in 1890 cost forty-eight *wen* in 1908.[74]

By 1909, Christian missionaries were an ongoing presence in Weiyuan's rural society. At Xinjie there was a Gospel Hall, and an itinerant priest taught in Lianjie, Shanwang, and Xinglu market towns. Villagers in the area tended to feel that local people who joined the Christian circles withdrew from paticipation in village and family customs, such as ancestral ceremonies, activities that cultivated common bonds among villagers for whom conflict always came readily. A frequent complaint was that conversion to Christianity promoted exclusive worship of the cross. This intrusion into rural culture, among the numerous others witnessed during these years, took on many manifestations, as the *nongmin* saw it. Foreign presence seemed to lead to a breakdown of the social order in which one's place in a hierarchy was as much a source of protection as a possibility for oppression. Under reforms associated with the foreign religion, new education, and electoral government, villagers who wanted to protect their version of the status quo were offended when, for example, students no longer seemed to call their teachers *laoshi* as custom and order required.[75] As the supports for group solidarity and protection provided by the status quo weakened, Christian presence at Weiyuan became a focal point for many of the changes deemed undesirable by some among the rural population. It was true that many of the educational and administrative changes had coincided with the arrival of the foreigners and their religion. All of this had an impact in the dynamics of place and politics. Having a viable way to take care of themselves and their interests was no small matter for the *nongmin*. A potent strategy required a social dimension that was connected to every aspect of rural economic, political, and cultural life.

Liu Xiangting's Leadership: Gelaohui Networks

According to the most detailed of the accounts we have on this case, in the fall of 1909 Liu Xiangting, a miner of farming-family origins, led a major uprising in opposition to both government reform policies and foreign presence in Weiyuan county. The center of the uprising was Lianjiechang, located fifty-five kilometers to the north of Weiyuan city. Liu Xiangting himself was born about the time (1862–63) the great Taiping general Shi Dakai marched his armies into Sichuan under the banner of the Heavenly Kingdom of Peace with its vision of justice that many peasants hoped would transform rural society. Liu Xiangting's family was from Lijiadang, twenty *li* (one *li* = one-third of a mile) from Lianjiechang. Before Xiangting's grandfather's time, the Liu family had divided its lands. Shortly thereafter, the family gradually declined. By the time Xiangting's father received his share of the land, the holding was of such little value that he had to sell his house to a wealthier branch of the family in order to survive. Xiangting's father then left and resettled in an area where he was able to afford a grass hut and a small piece of land on which he could grow three to five hundred *sheng* (one *sheng* = one liter) of grain. When an iron ore mine opened nearby and employed several day laborers, Liu's father hired on to supplement the family income. During most of Xiangting's youth, his father was primarily a farmer. At middle age, when his father's physical strength declined, he worked primarily at the mine and left the tilling of the land to his eldest son, Xiangting, and his second son, Fu'an. The elder Liu continued each day to take his ox to the iron mine at Qiaofangou where they both worked long difficult hours.[76]

Liu Xiangting lived and labored on the land into his adulthood. Like many in the area, Liu almost as a matter of course came to participate in the Gelaohui organizations of the mining region at Qiaobangou. The population of Qiaobangou compared with that of Lianjiechang was small, but there were four Gelaohui lodges (*tangkou*) in the area. Branches of the lodge were known as the Darenhui (great humaneness society), the Dayihui (great righteousess society), the Dalihui (great decorum society), and the Dazhihui (great knowledge society). Liu Xiangting became the leader of the Dayihui. Each leader, described as a "rudder handle" (*duobazi*), rose through the ranks in his lodge. The lowest ranks were numbered nine and ten. At the rank of five, one could become a lodge official known as assistant to the "rudder handle." Upon reaching the first rank, one achieved the title of honor known as "going to the mountain" (*chushan*). After "going to the mountain," if one showed competence and enthusiasm for the business of the lodge, one could then be elected "rudder handle" of the group. In 1909, Liu Xiangting was selected "rudder handle" of the Dayihui.[77]

Simultaneous with his position as "rudder handle," Liu Xiangting also was *jia* headman for his area. This designation was part of the *baojia* system of surveillance, which local government officials established in the rural areas and attempted to enforce periodically, especially during times of hardship when livelihood became more fragile, tax collection more difficult, and thoughts of resistance more prevalent. As rural conditions became stressful in the late nineteenth and early twentieth centuries, Weiyuan officials once again turned to the *baojia* system as a way they might hope to compel unwilling taxpayers to meet their obligations to the state. Four market towns—Shanwang, Xinglu, Xinchang, and Lianjie—were each designated a *bao* headman (*zongbao*) who would oversee two to four *tuan* leaders (*tuanshou*), who would in turn oversee several *jia* headmen (*jiazhang*). Each *jia* headman would be responsible for about one hundred people and would be chosen from among representatives selected by subgroups of ten within the *jia* unit. Liu had for many years prior to the New Policy incidents been publicly elected as the *jia* headman of his area.[78] Such government efforts had seldom been successful in the past and certainly had little chance of working as planned with someone like Liu Xiangting involved, who would most likely act on behalf of the interests of the people who had selected him. In effect, the *baojia* system became another network, originally of government auspices, which local groups including the Gelaohui could make their own.

Even before the anti–New Policy protests began, Weiyuan was the site of numerous rural incidents in the late nineteenth and early twentieth centuries. In 1864, the Fujiao branch of the Red Lanterns had been active in Weiyuan.[79] Gelaohui leader Liu Xiangting himself was involved in an 1908 uprising in Zezhou and Weiyuan, about which there are few details.[80] Jiading, a major area of sectarian activity, was simultaneously in revolt during the Weiyuan developments in 1909–10. With the events of the post-Boxer era and the emergence of the constitutional movement, the rural activism of the Weiyuan area, long in the making, took another turn in the spotlight of national history.

In 1909, a population census was to be taken in Weiyuan as part of the Qing government's program for self-govenment. Preparations began with the compilation of a census book and the attachment of a census plaque on each household door to reflect the officially recorded census data. The Weiyuan county government designated lower degree holders (*xiucai*) as "census headmen" and sent them out first to the market towns of Xinxiang to begin census collection. Under the headman were two assistant investigators. These investigators had offical power and were directly connected to the New Policy reforms. Compared with the other local headmen (*zongbao* and *tuanshou*), the census investigators had what many villagers considered to be a clearly identifiable "foreign style" (*yangqi*), most apparent in such things as articles of foreign clothing or foreign cigarettes, as was also mentioned in the documents on the case at Laiyang. The attitude of the census takers caught the *nongmin*'s attention as well. Census takers, according to local accounts, acted haughty and were sarcastic. They considered themselves superior to and more progressive than other local leaders, such as the *bao* headmen and the *tuan* leaders. In the view of most rural inhabitants, all of this added up to nothing more than further evidence that the census takers were part of the general Qing policy of capitulation to the foreigners, the term for which was *touyang*. The dissenting *nongmin* view contended that the foreigners recognized Qing weakness and sought to exploit it. The Qing rulers in this scenario were only too happy to have an ally in the foreigners with whom they could collaborate to strengthen their position. By extension the county reform managers, beginning with census takers, were involved in a similar maneuver on behalf of their own place-based interests. Popularly rendered, when foreigners finally had jurisdiction over all of Chinese society, ten families would have to share a vegetable cleaver and no one would be allowed to worship heaven or the ancestors.[81] In other words, rural people would be materially and culturally deprived.

A correspondent for the *North China Herald* confirmed this general analysis and assessment of local conditions. His impression was that the disturbance was of a large scale. He reported that tens of thousands of people participated in the antitax protest at Weiyuan. In sheer numbers this would have rivaled the anti–New Policy revolt at Laiyang, Shandong. The correspondent also noted that smaller disturbances occurred in the same month at Jiating and Yisiliu (Isiliudzin) districts. Details reported in this Shanghai-based newspaper conveyed that the disturbances were

> a reaction on the part of some against certain new methods of government and the new education being introduced, but the real cause was doubtless the increasing taxation.
>
> The rumour got abroad that this year all taxation would be doubled and being believed by many caused great discontent. Add to this the increasing cost of living and we have sufficient explanation of the restlessness.
>
> The excellent harvests of the last few years have kept the price of food quite reasonable, but other prices have greatly increased. For example, cotton, so much in demand in this land, has within two years increased sixty percent in price.[82]

In January of the same year, a correspondent in Weiyuan wrote that rice was cheap, and hunger was, therefore, not the cause of the movement in which government schools, chapels, and *likin* stations were destroyed.[83] In recent years, new taxes had been levied on fruits, vegetables, salt, rape-seed oil, and coal carried by small salesmen from one market town to another in the hope of making a small profit. In the fall of 1909, a census was taken and people feared additional levies. At this time a small board was nailed above residential doorways, and rumors began to circulate that three cash per night would be collected from every family member. A design on the plaque, painted red and consisting of horizontal lines and dots with a cross in the center, was interpreted, the correspondent's sources informed him, to mean that the houses would be turned over to foreigners and Christianity would be forced on the occupants. According to this local observer, there had been no visible antiforeignism in the area, but when anxiety was high over the prospects of increased taxes, any foreign presence came under suspicion. The census was taken after new schools had been established throughout the county and much temple property had been confiscated for this purpose. This pattern was similar to the New Policy experience across rural China. Counties neighboring Weiyuan experienced similar agitation over census-taking for self-government elections, but only the more mountainous district of Weiyuan experienced a full-scale uprising.

The "New Policy Road": Census and Taxes

When the census-taking began in the spring of 1909, *nongmin* of northern Weiyuan quickly realized they would have to mobilize an opposition. Stories of groups gathering across the region to collect new taxes and carry out reforms encouraged by foreigners made clear that this would be a major struggle. Villagers at first refused to leave the census plaques on their doors, reasoning that to do so might potentially place them under the foreigners' jurisdiction. Next a group of rural delegates went to Liu Xiangting's place to ask him to take up leadership as their *jia* headman. At first Liu replied, "You are opposed to foreigners and do not permit the census plaques to be nailed, I am not opposed to foreigners, but if you are all opposed, I will lead."[84] The people of Matouli next came to find Liu Xiangting. They were also opposed to the census and would not nail the census plaques to their doors. They hoped that Liu Xiangting as "rudder handle" would take the lead. Xiangting argued that the Gelaohui emphasized loyalty to the brotherhood, called *yiqi*, and that if the authorities were capitulating to the foreigners, then the principle of loyalty expressed by the elders required him to take up leadership to protect the people from this detrimental exercise of authority both foreign and Chinese.

The situation at Weiyuan also showed how political divisions often had family dimensions. Liu Chufan, the *zongbao* of Lianjiechang, was Liu Xiangting's brother from the main family. Liu Jixi was Liu Xiangting's nephew, who lived in Lijiadang and shared the family residence with Liu Chufan. The two families were equally strong and influential, but there was no harmony between them and each was always ready to do in the other. During the New Policy era, they were on different sides of the reforms. Liu Jixi attained his *xiucai* degree when he was a youth and had recently been appointed by the magistrate to be "head investigator" of the census taking. While many Sichuan reformers and revolutionaries were involved in efforts to develop financial institutions with major urban capital connections,[85] Liu Jixi's participation in the reforms was a more limited and local expression of the political shift viewed by himself and others as a way to combat foreign presence by developing foreign institutions under their own Chinese control. For his part, Liu Xiangting thought that Jixi was one of the disrespectful young bullies produced by the new conditions. He remembered that Jixi had failed to pay respect to his uncle at the Qingminghui, a spring festival to honor the ancestors. While Jixi tried to excuse himself by saying that he had been a little drunk, Xiangting was convinced that in fact Jixi had begun to form foreign habits and would eventually go over to the foreign camp and cease to recognize his ancestors.[86] Such rebellious offspring were a very serious affair. There was clearly a generational side to this conflict as well. The more Xiangting thought about this convergence of personal and political matters, the more indignant he became. He decided that whatever people opposed in this situation, he should take the lead in order to bring these trends to an end. When the villagers saw Liu Xiangting had agreed, they went throughout the area to talk to people, and gradually others came to support *jia* headman Liu. They started by going to see people with the same family name (*benjia*). Gradually the people of the whole *jia* came under his guidance. Meanwhile, the investigators began registering households. They hired carpenters to cut trees and make wooden plaques for the census.

One day, according to a composite oral history, similar to the ones taken at Zunhua, assistant census taker Luo Jiucheng asked Liu Xiangting to help with the census in his *jia*. Liu replied, "First cousin Luo, the small spring harvest is already eaten, the rains have not come, people's livelihood is insufficient, the sky does not look bright. Wait until after the big harvest to try the census again. People will be in their homes then and can open their doors and answer your questions."[87] The weather was very hot. Luo Jiucheng was moved by Liu's words and figured it was a good idea to change the time for the census. After the census assistant departed, Liu Xiangting reported on the situation to his brothers and the *nongmin* of his *jia*. The Gelao of Matou and the *nongmin* all were grateful to Liu. The assistant census takers came every few days, and Liu said again that the people had nothing to eat.

The *nongmin* nearby saw that the census was making no headway in Shiquewo and asked their own *jia* headman to join in the resistance. *Jia* headmen Jiang Meitang and Liu Songqiao followed the same pattern in dealing with the census takers. The census assistants were all old-timers whose families had lived in the area for generations. Liu Jixi finally said to the *jia* headmen, "The census is for compliance with foreign methods of constitutionalism, and the timetable for this is very strict. If the schedule is not kept, the government will be blamed."[88] This statement only confirmed the *nongmin*'s perspective that they were being asked to pay for the officials' capitulation to foreign ways. The officials, in the view of the *nongmin*, were all afraid of foreigners, and so they submitted to them and gave foreigners advantages over the people. Such advantages, they argued, would lead to a situation where eventually there would be foreign crosses but no incense for honoring the ancestors. Hardships would multiply for each succeeding generation until not one tree would be left for making burial sticks, and there would be no paper money to burn for ancestral ceremonies. Even the man who made his living cutting grass for fuel or making charcoal from wood would have no knife to earn his livelihood.[89] Such images vividly expressed the point of view that linked reforms to industrial capitalism with a gradual but certain destruction of the material and cultural supports of rural family life.

Writing on the spectrum of reformers and revolutionaries in Sichuan during the post-Boxer decade, He Yimin notes the language in which many of their publications described the dire straits of China's position vis-à-vis foreign presence. One journal of a Sichuan reform group expressed the opinion that China was faced with national destruction and racial genocide, comparing themselves with India, Turkey, and Poland, "the red man and the black man." The same journal advocated political reform and self-improvement in the style of Washington, Bismarck, and others rather than "rushing to make brave revolution," which would only help England and other foreign aggressors in China.[90] In the range of political voices at this time, these too missed the alliances across class boundaries that might have begun a dialogue on alternative routes to social well-being and self-strengthening.

As a next step to counter the reforms and their consequences perceived by rural dissidents as extentions of foreign encroachment and government corruption, Liu Xiangting called a meeting under cover of night. Jiang Meitang, Liu Songqiao, and the *nongmin* of their *jia* all came to participate. Except for the upper lodge with its wealthier members who did not join, everyone else attended. Head census taker Liu Jixi heard about the meeting and went to tell Weiyuan county magistrate De Shou. Because De Shou was a Manchu, he did not know the people's customs, so he did not know what to do. The only thing he could think of was to tell *zongbao* Liu Chufan of Lianjiechang to go and investigate.

After receiving a confidential letter from the magistrate, Liu Chufan realized the situation was not simple. On the one hand, he had heard many complaints over the months about Liu Jixi putting on airs and being disrespectful to the commoners. On the other hand, he remembered that Liu Jixi harbored anomosity for Liu Xiangting, so Jixi might be using the reforms as an opportunity to make trouble for Xianting by suggesting that Xiangting was involved in rebellion. Liu Chufan decided to reply to the magistrate with an evasive answer. He told De Shou that it was common for *jiazhang* to organize crop-watching activities to guard against thieves and that the Gelaohui meeting had been solely for that purpose as far as he could tell. Subsequently, the magistrate called for a reexamination, issued a few words of warning, and for the time being dropped the matter.

Members of the subbureaucracy at Weiyuan would not, however, let the matter rest once they detected a lucrative possibility. Although Magistrate De Shou rose to officialdom through the imperial examination system, he was considered very mediocre in handling business. When he was at the provincial level waiting for a position, some people who wanted to cultivate him as a political connection organized a group of private secretaries, gatekeepers, and cooks to accompany him to his new post. There they could have access to confidential information and be in a position to influence decisions. When the private secretary who led this group saw the secret reports by Liu Jixi on Liu Xiangting, he noted that they included such phrases as "mass gatherings, organizing alliances." Here, he thought, might be a case of sedition he could report.[91] As noted earlier, the capture of "revolutionaries" was one of the current best ways for officials to gain bureaucratic kudos and possible promotion or honorary mention. On the other hand, the reports made by Liu Chufan and his assistant Yang Fanqing were so unequivocal he could not be sure the charge of "revolutionary" would stick. In order to manipulate the situation for his own profit, the private secretary wanted to make sure that Liu Xiangting was acting in rebellion against central government policies. The secretary went to De Shou and told him that Liu Jixi had, in effect, charged Liu Xiangting with opposing the investigation of residence records, refusing to nail up the census plaques, opposing the foreigners' religion, and burning incense to form alliances. This, he suggested, was tantamount to a full-scale, anti-Christian disturbance. What the secretary knew but did not say was that a situation like this could be milked from many angles by a skillful bureaucrat, such as himself. The secretary argued to the magistrate that the first responsibility of the officials was to protect the foreigners, and that he should dispatch messengers directly to Qiaobangou and Shiquewo to look further into the situation.

For the sake of his own political future, De Shou could no longer just let things go. He called a meeting of his underlings and his private secretaries. These subbureaucrats had many connections through the *hongheipai* networks, a system of red and black plaques indicating ranks in a secret society, and they were consequently attuned to local rumors and developments. For example, they already knew that Liu Jixi had, in fact, secretly reported against Liu Xiangting. Wanting further details, they ordered their own people who were happy to make some extra cash for the midautumn festivities to go to Qiaobangou and Shiquewo to make investigations. The local farmers, however, would not give much information. Children and grandmothers who did not know any better told them a few things they had heard, but that was it.[92] It soon became clear to the yamen underlings that Liu Xiangting had a lot of sworn brothers and not much money, so there would be no point in trying to blackmail him with charges of rebellion. Consequently, this group of yamen subbureaucrats quickly lost interest in the case.

At other levels, however, the petty official corruption, which certainly added fuel to the peasant's discontent, continued. On the night of the eighth month, fourteenth day, runners sent by the magistrate and the census headmen traveled the road between Qiaobangou and Shiquewo hoping to arrest Liu Xiangting's son. When this seemed futile, they decided to change plans and blocked the road, stopping people from each direction. On the pretext of searching for Liu's son, they looked through people's goods. Because it was the middle of the autumn festival days, people had come to market to buy wine, meat, incense, rice, and tobacco. There were two to three hundred people behind the roadblock, but some of them escaped the inspection point. The poor who had little were allowed to leave unnoticed, but anyone carrying a bundle was ordered to stop, and their things were confiscated. The opportunity for corruption overtook their official assignment. Various forms of unjust profit making layered over one another in the making of rural conditions.

Liu Jixi, realizing that the investigation for New Policy reforms was not going well, began to wonder if his own standing as lower degree-holder with prospects for further advancement might be endangered. If even in his own area the census plan was not working, how could he hope to someday be a higher official? It was not easy these days to do one's job. He was reminded of the saying: "The officials govern and the people curse." But he also knew that his rival Liu Chufan, anxiously awaited his failure, and this spurred him to further action. A *xiucai* (lower degree-holder) at seventeen, Liu Jixi had every right to expect that he would advance further in officialdom. The abolition of the examination system in 1905, as part of the preparation for constitutional reforms and industrial technology, changed all of that. Liu Jixi, like many of his peers, had to reassess his career plans. He reasoned: "Now that the official examinations have stopped, if I fail to make an excellent record on the basis of the New Policy system, how can I climb higher in the hierarchy of officialdom?"[93] The "New Policy road" was the way to go. Liu Jixi decided he must go to speak to Liu Xiangting to try to turn the situation to his advantage. The following exchange is reconstructed from oral history sources:

Finding Xiangting back at work in the mine, Jixi broached the subject of the reforms by saying, "The census and the door plaques are important matters. From spring to autumn everything should be finished, but you in this *jia* have not even begun. What is going on?"

Liu Xiangting saw that his usually conceited and arrogant nephew was trying to make harmony, so he said, "We are poor households in this *jia* of Shiquewo. Each year almost every household has a grain shortage. All day from early morning to night everyone is out trying to find money for food. We cannot afford to waste the time staying at home filling out census sheets. It is the time of the small sowing. We have to wait until the end of the year. Then you can come to investigate. When we have food in our stomach then we can do the investigation well. If we do not plant now, we farmers will have no food to eat. If you were hungry, would you come to do the registration?"

Liu Jixi lost his patience and was anxious to get things done. Without bothering to give a detailed explanation, he asked bluntly, "Isn't it true that you oppose the investigation, that you refuse to put the number plate on your door, and that you gather people together for meetings at night so that you can hinder or obstruct the census work?"

Liu Xiangting answered, "Our *jia* has always fulfilled the quotas of our taxes, we have never owed taxes to the government. From generation to generation in which year did we fail to fulfill the tax? When the crops planted on the mountain are ripe, people may steal it, wild animals may damage it. Farmers plant grains with hard labor, how could they stand the loss? How could they suffer from the loss? *Qituan* (adminstrative authority) is supported by everyone if it is good. If it is not good, we must bring it down."[94]

Liu Jixi responded in a threatening way, "Now that the New Policy is just beginning, the magistrate and the assistant magistrate are all serious in their work. If they are late in carrying out instructions from the officials above, they will be severely reprimanded and perhaps sent to prison. In this situation, to stir up the masses in protest could have serious consequences." Liu Xiangting saw that Liu Jixi was talking in an approach known among the *nongmin* as the three-step method of pressuring from above. Xiangting said, "the census is rejected by all the households, and the number plates are opposed by everybody. If the government sends you to put up the plates, we will sharpen our knives and kill you as an example to everybody."[95]

Hearing the decisive answer given by Liu Xiangting, Liu Jixi felt

TABLE 4.1
Principal Actors in the Weiyuan Protests

Name	Role	Position
Protest Leaders		
Liu Xiangting	Leader of activists	*Jiazhang*; Gelaohui leader
Liu Mianzhai	Eldest son of Liu Xiangting	
Liu Fu'an	Second son of Liu Xiangting	
Liu Chufan	Brother of Liu Xiangting	*Zongbao* headman for Lianjiechang
Jiang Meitang	Second in command to Liu Xiangting	*Jiazhang*
Liu Songqiaò	Second in command to Liu Xiangting	*Jiazhang*
Liu Tiancheng	Forms alliance with activists after Liu Xiangting's arrest	Guizhou Gelaohui leader
New Policy Associates		
Liu Jixi	Head of census taking; newphew of Liu Xiangting	*Xiucai* degree holder
Pan Qingyun	Census taker	Teacher at Kuiwenguan school in Lianjiechang
Liu Binxian	Census taker	Teacher at Kuiwenguan school in Lianjiechang
Luo Jiucheng	Associate of the census takers	
Li Jinsheng	Initially supports and then betrays Liu Xiangting	*Jiazhang* of Tiefochang of Gaoling

Sources: Kui Yingtao, *Sichuan jindaishi goa* (Sketches in Sichuan modern history), 351; Zhou Shandao, "Ji yujiulingjiunian Weiyuan tianbaodayuanshuai qiyi" (Remembering the 1909 uprising of the heaven-protected marshal at Weiyuan), in *Sichuan wenshi ziliao xuanji* (Selected historical materials on Sichuan) no. 3, Chengdu: Sichuan renmin chuban she, 1962, 89-105; Zhao Erxun, Memorial to the throne, in *Xinhai geming qian shinian wen minbian dangan shiliao* (Archive materials on people's activism in the ten years before the 1911 Revolution) Beijing: Zhonghua shuju, 1985, vol. 2, #463, 800.

discouraged about persuading Xiangting to cooperate and instead returned to his arrogant manner, slipped into his sedan chair, and ordered the carriers to run. In this way, Jixi escaped to the big house at Liujiagou and did not dare to come out. After two or three days, he felt it was still not safe enough, so his sister's husband, Tang Yiquan, suggested that he escape to Zezhou.

Modernized Military against Rural Dissent

In the tenth month of 1909 by the lunar calendar, during the first ten days, Liu Xiangting consulted with *matou* leaders of the registration system. Jiang Meitang and Liu Songqiao, *jia* headmen, also attended the meeting. Together they decided that they had exhausted the tactics of retreat, delay, and deception, so the only way out was to use force to forestall the officials' plans. At the meeting, the group slaughtered an oxen, sacrificed to the gods, drank blood in wine, and worshiped in the hall of the Gelaohui. Interestingly enough, the family records and geneology contained in the *Haidi*, which was the record of the local Gelaohui, reportedly went all the way back to the Han Dynasty. Liu Shiliang had written this Han history, and it was known that through the generations of transmission the manuscript had come to include some unintended alterations, leaving space for adjustments of meaning in application to current situations. Exhilarated by their gathering, the group publically selected Liu Xianting to be the grand marshal and the keeper of the grand seal. As Governor Zhao Erxun of Sichuan who memorialized the throne on this case noted, it was illegal for Liu Xiangting to assume this title and was, therefore, a declaration of rebellion by Liu and his supporters.[96] Jiang Meitang and Liu Songqiao jointly held the assistant seal. They adopted names as set forth in the *Haidi*, the Gelaohui's charter.[97] According to the *Haidi*, these brothers of the Gelaohui divided the organization into five *ying* and four *shao*. Elder Brother *Chushang*, a title of position, served as the notary; *Sange*, another title of position, was the administrator; the *Wupian* was the personal relations contact. All of these positions were outlined in the *Haidi*.

By the time the plan for the battle was worked out, the dark of night had already passed and it was light outside. With guns and knives the people poured through the villages in order to catch the chief criminal, Liu Jixi, who it was suspected had probably surrendered to the foreigners. The protesters wanted to kill him as an example. They surrounded his house, but everyone said that Jixi was already gone. Those who had suffered directly at Jixi's hand, especially his tenants, wanted to take some action. They stayed overnight to watch their crops and the next morning decided on a plan, which they then presented to Liu Xiangting. They put a demarcation in the middle of Lijia and set the part of the house belonging to Liu Jixi on fire. Grains in the warehouse were shipped out for supplies to the rebel army. They went to Lianjiechang and burned the unfinished number plates in the area in front of the Guiwenguan, an old-style school. There were two teachers, Pan Qingyun, who slipped back home while the crowds were occupied, and Liu Binxian, who was also a census investigator but had actually done very little investigating because he was busy teaching. At first the people asked Liu Binxian to serve in the army, but in the end they put him under house arrest. Rich families in the area also left their houses.

Farmers from the country came with chickens and vegetables to express their gratitude to Liu Xiangting for saving them from having to put number plates on their doors. They sent people to confiscate the family wealth of investigator Luo Jiucheng and to kill him. But when Luo saw that the houses were on fire, he also escaped.

Marshal Liu Xiangting continued to live in Lianjiechang, where people from various *matou* and *jia* kept coming in to offer him service. It took three days to compile the list of these many volunteers. On the fourth day, they began their march toward the county seat of Weiyuan. It was October 11 during the rainy season, and the roads were muddy and slippery. It took a long time to cover the forty *li* before they reached Xinchang. There they found out through reconnaisance that Weiyuan was already preparing day and night for the encounter. The town gates were closed, and people kept watch on top of the city walls. They learned that several hundred militiamen (*mintuan*) had already pitched camp about thirty *li* away on the pass of Gufoting.

Marshal Liu Xiangting gave orders that camp could be set up on the Daoguanshan. Then he dispatched three teams, one went to check out some other locations, a second went to arrest and kill investigator Wu Shaoyou, and a third set out to burn the foreign church at Xinchang and to arrest both Huang Mingzhi and Xiao Zhiquan. Within half a day, all the three teams returned and reported. Wu Shaoyou had already escaped because he recieved advanced warning. The protesters did, however, manage to capture some of Wu's wealth. Wu's neighbors had pleaded with the protesters to delay burning Wu's houses so that their own houses would not catch fire. In response, the rebels only smashed Wu's residence leaving it in rubble.[98] As for the church, because of requests from the neighborhood, the protesters only smashed the church without burning it. Sichuan Governor Chao's memorial omitted any anti-Christian references in his report to the throne, portraying the dissent as more the work of conventional bandits than rural dwellers with a critical view of new policies and foreign religions.[99]

Xinchang *matou* sent their head representative and others to scale the Daoguanshan mountain to pay respects to and entertain Marshal Liu Xiangting. One of them who held no official title was retired Elder Brother Tang Linchang who had been in the army for quite a long time. He inquired about the causes of the uprising. Marshal Liu answered, "In the first place we want to get rid of damages to the people. We want to get rid of harmful officials who are harmful to the people, and we want to cancel the number plates on the doors. We want to drive away foreigners and kill corrupt officials. In all of this, we want to help the kind people by abolishing unnecessary taxes and heavy taxes. As to whether we will succeed, I do not consider that now. We don't care whether we will succeed or fail. We just want to do it." He added straightforwardly and sincerely, "My head has already been given to the bodhisattva on the god shrine for a long time."[100] By this Liu Xiangting meant that he was as good as dead and in effect had been prepared to die for a long time given his commitments and activities, an expression of the rural heroic ideal. Tang, who was already sixty years old, had not slept well for several days in his journey to find Marshal Liu. Because there were no accommodations on Daoguanshan, he took shelter from the wind and frost in an abandoned sedan chair. Exhausted and in low spirits, he felt he had no more strategic ideas to suggest. His only advice to Liu Xiangting was to coordinate more people who were familiar with miliary affairs so as to improve their prospects. First Tang suggested they should attack and take over the county town, next seize weapons in a rapid operation, then put up messages to appease the people so they could succeed. Marshal Liu did his best to retain Elder Brother Tang as his adviser, but Tang declined on the grounds of old age and ill health and he soon departed.

Marshal Liu's forces were engaged with militia troops thirty *li* outside of Weiyuan for several days. The rebel groups then withdrew to Lianjiechang where they gathered more guns and sabers and recouped for two days before marching to the northeast. Governor Chao reported that the protesters even dared to use cannons,[101] suggesting that the seriousness of their challenge to the authorities would be measured in part by the level of weaponry they employed. As they marched, Liu Xiangting, in honor of his position as marshal in charge of the resistance, was carried by four people in a wooden chair that had many long streamers of red silk to mark his status granted by his supporters. Liu was guarded by his eldest son Liu Mianzhai and his younger son Liu Fu'an, one on each side. The procession looked quite formidable as they proceeded through the countryside for fifteen *li* until they reached Zhonggongshi where they pitched camp for one day. Learning that the Zezhou area was not prepared for battle, the rebel forces continued to

Luoquanjing and made advance camp at the pass of the Beiji Mountains. A person of the surname Lei had been arrested at Lou Quanjing by the salt ground workers and peasants who then took their prisoner to Marshal Liu and asked for instructions on how to punish him. Marshal Liu ordered them to hold him in custody for the time being.

Liu Xiangting then immediately sent the Gelaohui officer for interpersonal relationships (*zhaojiguanshi*) to the nearby places Tiefochang, Gaolochang, Zoumachang, and Longjiechang to answer their urgent calls for assistance. Li Jinsheng, the *jiazhang* of Tiefochang in the Gaoling Mountains, led his troops to join Marshal Liu. With these actions the dissident movement became larger and more powerful. The prefectural officials of Zezhou dared not go out of the town. Liu Xiangting's troops marched on to Zoumachang, Gaoyangchang, Longjiechang, and Tiefochang. Together with the local poor peasants they raided the churches, burned the door number plates, attacked the investigators, sealed their warehouses, and confiscated rice for people and hay for horses. Along the way, Liu also contacted individuals who were familiar with military affairs or even those associated with the *Lüin* (Greenwood), outlaws of the Robin Hood style, to seek further strategic advice and support.[102] The fact was, however, that there had been no major fighting in the area for over a generation and those who had firsthand experience in military tactics were already advanced in age, senile, and fragile so that they had difficulty walking and moving. How could they suffer the hardships of participating in martial activities? From this point the movement began to dwindle. Fewer people came in and more people began to leave.

Once individuals responsible for the immediate hardships had been attacked restoring some sense of justice, the goals of the movement became unclear to many. In addition, the movement's loose organization began to undermine military effectiveness. Liu Binxian and Lei Yanguan, who were being held under custody, managed to escape in the chaos. Lei Yanguan, as it turned out, had strong connections with elite groups in Chengdu and Zezhou. Upon his escape, he immediately wrote to individuals associated with these groups and informed them that although Liu Xiangting had many people who supported him, they were entirely untrained, more like "hooligans" than effective soldiers. Lei stressed that there was not a single trained general among them and that they had many other weaknesses as well.[103] By informing on the dissident movement, Lei hoped to clear himself of any association with the rebels and curry favor with the authorities.

Internal division also contributed to the rebels' decline. Factional fighting led to clashes between Liu Zhancheng and Li Jinsheng.[104] Li Jinsheng, *jia* headman of Gaolingshan who had supported Marshal Liu, defected when he saw that without an effective military capability the dissident movement would fail. As a leader of the movement, Li might even face execution, so he feared for his safety and that of his family if the rebellion failed as he now anticipated. Betraying the cause and intending to protect himself, he stole important records from Marshal Liu's camp and brought them to Zezhou to sell.[105] The officials at Zezhou interrogated Li about the records and found that what he said matched their reports. Then the official in charge at Zezhou saw an opportunity for himself. He ordered the militias (*lianding*) under his jurisdiction not to wait for the soldiers from Chengdu but to go ahead and march to Louquanjing in Weiyuan. Local officials raised the militias as ordered, but the two to three hundred people who were mobilized were unenthusiastic about the mission, so they stalled and moved very slowly.

Marshal Liu's informants soon received reports that Zezhou would send troops to attack them. The more fainthearted among his supporters began to desert. Liu Xiangting, however, continued to prepare for battle. He sent troops to meet the enemy and prepared his battle line at Beijikan, where Liu's forces hid cannons and themselves in the shade of nearby trees for camouflage. Unfortunately, those who manned the cannons were farmers untrained in artillery skills, and their accuracy was poor. As the enemy moved forward, Liu's forces simply fired off a barrage in the general direction of the advancing troops. When the Zezhou militias heard the cannons and saw that no one was hit, they became braver. Picking up their rifles, they advanced more quickly. Liu Xiangting's eldest son, who was skilled with cannons, looked out from the rebel's fortified area to get a clearer view. He got off one well-aimed shot, firing the field cannon directly at the advancing militias causing them to retreat. But because the rebels were unable to launch a sustained attack, the Zezhou militias were not deterred. Equipped with modern rifles, the militias were able to send bullets whistling over the farmers' heads. Having never experienced the impact and sound of this ammunition, the farmers were frightened. Many were wounded. It began to rain, and confidence sank. Cries of "I'm shot, I'm shot," began to fill the air. Elders called for people to stand their ground, but panic set in and the farmers scattered.[106] Fortunately for the rebel forces, it was almost dark, and the enemy dared not push forward. Silence fell on the battlefield until the dawn of the next day.

When the sun rose, Marshal Liu's camp was empty. Most all the peasants had returned home. Now the Zezhou soldiers were dominant and brave. Accompanied by the sound of bugles, the Zezhou militias swept forward. Considering every civilian they saw a rebel soldier, they broke into houses and made trouble everywhere. The prefecture official ordered the arrest of Liu Xiangting and sent people to find out what had happened to Liu and his troops. For several days, however, there were no reports. Finally, the provincial army with two units of troops marched into the area. They also sought to capture Liu Xiangting. The magistrate of Zezhou, because he could not get any information on the whereabouts of Liu Xiangting, decided that Liu might already have escaped the boundaries of his *zhou* jurisdiction. In this case, the magistrate would probably not be able to make the arrest and get the promotion he hoped for from the situation, so he ordered the militias to retreat and return to Zezhou.[107] Zhang Shudang, however, who had been sent by the provincial authorities, had no such restrictions on him, so he marched his troops through the territory of Zezhou and pushed toward Weiyuan. His investigators swept over these territories in search of information on the whereabouts of Marshal Liu. No arrest was forthcoming, so his troops began to take gold and silver and other wealth before they returned to Chengdu.[108]

Liu Xiangting continued to be revered by the peasants who sent him wine and food daily. No one spoke of the failure of the uprising. Even his sons and ordinary commanders were scattered after the uprising. Until the collapse of the Qing Dynasty, some people in Yunnan province said they had seen his brothers. One brother changed his family name from Liu to Chen, another changed his to Li. One night in darkness at a meeting before everyone scattered, although a group of peasant brothers continued to defend the marshal, Liu Xiangting decided that the uprising had come to an end. He told everyone to make his own way, and he himself set out to do the same.

Liu slowly made his way to the Renshou area where he had never been and lived in a farmer's house until the winter was over. In the spring of the next year when the birds were chirping and the flowers were blooming, he went out to fish and by chance met a buffalo boy with whom he began to chat. Two days later, this boy heard something about Liu Xiangting. He remembered the fisherman he had seen and told several people about their meeting.

News got around and eventually reached the ear of an official named Wang Langan who saw the opportunity to collect some cash. Wang was known to the local people of his market town as, "Wang the Lawless Stick," because of his inclination to use his position of authority to make money out of every situation, usually through unjust practices.[109] Wang was delighted at this new prospect for making some cash. He went with his men, found the fisherman, and questioned him. According to local accounts, Liu Xiangting was not willing to play games, so he admitted his identity and was arrested. Wang Langan made some deals that brought him good fortune. Dressing himself in fine clothes and providing Marshal Liu with a bath and clean clothes, Wang set off with more than one hundred soldiers to march the two-day trip to Renshou.

When they reached Renshou, the county official also saw how he could play the situation to his advantage if indeed this was the real Marshal Liu. He sent some informants to Lianjiezhang to try to verify Liu's description. One month later, satisfied that they had made a positive identification, they sent Liu Xiangting to Chengdu where he stood trial for the rebellion at Weiyuan. Found guilty, Liu Xiangting was sentenced to decapitation. Before being executed, as was the modern custom, he was photographed. His picture and his head were hung in public at Lianjiezhang. His head was soon stolen, but his photo was taken to Xinchang and Luoquanjing as well for display.[110] Some people insisted that the person beheaded was not the marshal but somebody who looked a little like him.

Resistance did continue after Liu Xiangting's death. Many of Liu's determined supporters joined with Geloahui leader Liu Tiancheng of Guizhou province just to the south and formed an alliance.[111] Long-term strategy was unclear in these years of New Policy, but the issues raised generated an ongoing ebb and flow of rural dissent.

Cases in Guangxi:
Cenqi and Yongshun

To the south of Weiyuan, other cases of opposition to reform received public notice. Groups that were once resistant to the Taiping rebels now found themselves protecting the same local resources against the administrative banditry of New Policy managers. At Cenqi, forty miles to the southwest of Wuzhou in Guangxi province, the local magistrate in 1910 had begun to raise taxes for New Policy reforms. Toward this end he confiscated the Zhongshengtuan militia funds that were under the control of the Chen family. Many *tuanlian* (local militias) raised at the time of the Taiping Rebellion had been dismantled by the late nineteenth century, but scattered exceptions did exist and were often the targets of the New Policy search for revenue. At the same time, it should be noted, that in some counties the *likin* stations, also put in place as a measure to raise funds for the government's anti-Taiping campaigns, continued into the 1900s to be used locally to raise government funds. Since the *tuanlian* were last raised under official auspices to suppress the Taiping, it could be argued that the government had a legitimate right to transfer the use of any remaining *tuanlian* resources to other government sponsored programs such as the New Policy. Whether *likin* or *tuanlian* funds, government officials sought to absorb any available remnants of cash collection mechanisms.

Chen Rongan, head of the Chen lineage at Cenqi, did not see it this way. Chen himself had raised the local militia in the 1850s to protect his own villages from the Taiping rebels. Although officially sanctioned, the *tuanlian* were, as far as Chen was concerned, under the jurisdiction of those who raised them. His efforts to protect village resources during the Taiping rebellion were successful, and he became a local hero throughout the county. Now in his eighties, Chen once again came forward to protect his villages, this time not from rebels but from the expanding state authorities who considered Chen and his supporters to be the rebellious ones. While Chen, because of a different place-based history, did not claim the Taiping mantle for his activism, he did, like many other protest leaders, declare that "each grain of rice is as valuable as a pearl, and each stick of firewood is as costly as a stick of cassia."[112] The Chen lineage was well connected with members residing in Guilin who brought accusations against the Cenqi magistrate. In order to resist taxes and the usurpation of their *tuanlian* funds, Chen and the villagers built earthworks around their villages, just as they had done to protect themselves against the Taiping rebels. In response, the magistrate requested government troops.

Three to six hundred troops arrived under the command of Prefect Zhi Zhong. They set up two field Krupp guns and bombarded the earthwork defenses. No attempt was made to negotiate, and the cost in human lives was great. Up to a thousand villagers were killed in the attack. Chen Rongan was captured and executed on the spot. A British observer remarked that "the execution of an old man of eighty caused a great deal of comment and will doubtless be remembered against the officials by the peasantry who are half robbers and who bear their rulers no good will."[113] A sympathetic movement developed in neighboring Loting, Guangdong, but it was also quickly suppressed.

The officials and troops finally had the upper hand in Cenqi. A local observer commented, "One cannot help feeling some sympathy for these simple people. They appear to have no connexion with any revolutionists; but, mad with rage at the thought that once more their hard earned cash was to go into the coffers of the officials, they took a stand to defend themselves."[114]

In another recorded instance of opposition to New Policy, the magistrate at Yongshun county, forty miles south of Nanning, began raising new taxes in January 1910. At first in some villages he levied a tax on wine, sugar, and oil amounting to $200 a year. He was also considering a prohibition against opium smoking and gambling.

Villagers organized a protest, and several people were killed in the battle that ensued. When government troops took the field, sixty men were killed and forty were taken prisoner. Several bandit gangs active in the area joined forces with the tax protesters.

In June, the magistrate decided to levy a tax of $1,000 a year on the sale of fish. He turned to the elite members who already worked closely with his office to ask them to appoint tax farmers who could insure the collection of the revenue. When a first group of tax farmers was unable to surmount the difficulties encountered from hostile taxpayers, the council of elite members appointed another group of tax farmers.

While delegating tax-farming authority to those firms that proved they could produce the revenue quotas, the Yongshun magistrate retained control of new taxes and reforms. His associates among the elite who helped manage the collection of taxes for reform were unable to monopolize all new tax authority for themselves. The magistrate in this case was the sole initiator of new surcharges. As one observer wrote, "He [the magistrate] is apparently in the position where he can tax anything and everything only he must not annoy too many people at the same time."[115]

Conclusions

In the post-Boxer decade in Sichuan, rural challenges to the government came from groups organized by ethnic identity, lineage, sectarian affiliation, and/or secret society networks. These groups were fundamentally antiofficial, synthesizing a position that placed the New Policy reforms at the center of antiforeign, anti-Christian, antiofficial, and anti-elite views in defense of the rural status quo defined by dissident villagers.[116] While there is no evidence that these groups coordinated their efforts, they were active in areas at the same times. Legitimacy for opposition to government activities may have been all the clearer with different groups arriving at similar conclusions. Both ethnic and heterodox groups had, as Susan Naquin described, their own well-developed organizational habits ready to govern local society as "autonomous assemblies sharing common ideals and organizational features, but only loosely associated in normal times."[117] Often competitors for the same limited local resources, whatever these groups thought of each other, in their activist, antistate profile, they were equally onerous to and a drain on government programs attempting to garner new resources and support for modern nation-state building projects. Dissidents chipped away at the same state structure, and each took. By the beginning of the twentieth century, rural dissidents saw national and county officials, with new style reforms and new military capabilities, as the primary source of their problems.

In the dialogue between peasant activists and urban reformers and revolutionaries, the Gelaohui activity visible during the anti–New Policy protests in Weiyuan reveals some valuable insights into the multilayered social structure of this organization. Writing on the Gelaohui in late-nineteenth century Sichuan, Prasenjit Duara argues that the Gelaohui was predominantly antiforeign and that early revolutionaries like Tao Chengzhang began the process of appropriating features of the secret societies described by Duara as a "silent site for resolving critical ideological problems."[118] In the texts Duara examines, the Gelaohui may have been silent, but at Weiyuan the Gelaohui of the middle and lower lodges was very vocal and not fundamentally antiforeign in its outlook. Whereas Red Lantern participants, who clearly did not tend to have members from the elite families, were unambiguously antiforeign, Liu Xiangting had to be convinced to take up the mantle of opposition to foreign presence. Neither was his anti-Manchuism or antigovernment position pronounced. He was, from what we know, primarily trying to fill his charge as local leader by listening to complaints and analyzing the situation as best he could. The middle and lower lodges of the Weiyuan Gelaohui functioned essentially as mutual aid societies responding to the New Policy developments and evolving an analysis that connected antigoverment with antielite and antiforeign aspects of the rural crisis.

The difference between being anti-Qing and anti-Manchu is important. Peasant activists became anti-Qing when the higher officials did not respond to place-based grievances against county bureaucrats, abusive landlords, or foreigners and their Christian converts, but they were not anti-Manchu in word or deed. The Manchu magistrate at Weiyuan was not opposed because of his Manchu background, and the managers of reform were not only clearly Han Chinese but family relatives as well. There was little perceptual or analytical basis here for anti-Manchuism. Specifically anti-Manchu sentiments seem to have been primarily carried by the upper classes, perhaps from the anti-Manchu views harbored by officials at the beginning of the Qing, revived under the revolutionary banner of the Tongmenghui, and then connected to peasant activism, which out of its own matrix of concerns included attacks on county government and then higher levels of government when redress of their grievances was not forthcoming. The Tongmenghui revolutionaries conflated anti-Qing with anti-Manchu views, mixed these views with racial and social Darwinian notions, and in so doing obscured the differences of privilege and class status, which were at the heart of the protest led by Liu Xiangting and others.[119]

Chapter 4

Notes

Epigraph: Wu Yannan, "Xinhai geming yu nongmin wenti" (The 1911 Revolution and the peasant question), in *Jinian Xinhai Geming qishi zhounian* (Commemorating the seventieth anniversary of the 1911 Revolution) (Beijing: Xueshu daolunhui lunwenji, 1983), 497.

1. Ono Kazuko, *Chinese Women in a Century of Revolution, 1850–1950*, ed. Joshua A. Fogel (Stanford: Stanford University Press, 1989), 49.

2. Ono Kazuko, *Chinese Women*, 51–52.

3. In Qiao Zhiqiang *Xinhai geming qian shinian wen minbian dangan shiliao* (Archive materials on people's activism in the ten years before the 1911 Revolution: compiled from the Chinese No. 1 Historical Archives, Beijing Teacher's University History Department), vol. 2, (Beijing: Zhong Hua Shu Ju, 1985), 751.

4. *Xinhai geming qian shinian wen minbian dangan shiliao*, 751–754.

5. Qiao Zhiqiang, *Xinhai geming qiande shinian* (Ten years before the 1911 Revolution) (Taiyuan: Shanxi renmin chuban she, 1987), 35.

6. Zhang Li, *Sichuan Yihetuan yundong* (Sichuan Boxer Movement) (Chengdu: Sichuan renmin chuban she, 1982), 116.

7. Qiao Zhiqiang, *Xinhai geming qiande shinian* 15; also see, Kui Yingtao, *Sichuan jindaishi gao* (Sketches in Sichuan modern history) (Chengdu: Sichuan renmin chuban she, 1990), 349.

8. Susan Naquin and Evelyn S. Rawski, *Chinese Society in the Eighteenth Century* (New Haven: Yale University Press, 1987), 135.

9. Naquin and Rawski, *Chinese Society in the Eighteenth Century*, 136.

10. Susan Naquin, *Millenarian Rebellion in China: The Eight Trigrams Uprising of 1813* (New Haven: Yale University Press, 1976), 268.

11. Naquin and Rawski, *Chinese Society in the Eighteenth Century*, 136.

12. Joseph W. Esherick, *The Origins of the Boxer Uprising*, 51–52; Naquin, *Millenarian Rebellion in China*, 299–300.

13. Naquin, *Millenarian Rebellion in China*, 41.

14. Ibid., 42.

15. Ibid., 269.

16. B. J. Ter Haar, *The White Lotus Teachings in Chinese Religious History* (Leiden: E. J. Brill, 1992), 172, 212.

17. Jean Chesneaux, *Secret Societies in China: In the Nineteenth and Twentieth Centuries* (Ann Arbor: University of Michigan Press, 1971), 60.

18. Naquin and Rawski, *Chinese Society in the Eighteenth Century*, 136.

19. Siang-tseh Chiang, *The Nien Rebellion* (Seattle: University of Washington Press, 1954), 10–15.

20. Chester C. Tan, *The Boxer Catastrophe* (New York: Columbia University Press, 1955), 43–44. Also see, Naquin, *Millenarian Rebellion in China*, 13, 313.

21. Kui Yingtao, *Sichuan jindaishi gao* (Sketches in Sichuan modern history) (Chengdu: Sichuan renmin chuban she, 1990), 187.

22. Kui Yingtao, *Sichuan jindaishi gao*, 188–192.

23. Ibid., 357.

24. Ibid., 357–67.

25. Ono Kazuko, *Chinese Women*, 51.

26. John K. Fairbank and Kwang-ching Liu, eds., *The Cambridge History of China*, vol. II, Late Ch'ing, 1800–1911, Part 2. (Cambridge: Cambridge University Press, 1980), 598.

27. Kui Yingtao, *Sichuan jindaishi gao*, 189.

28. Cai Shaoqing, *Zhongguo jindai huidang shi yanjiu* (Historical research on modern Chinese secret societies) (Beijing: Xinhua shudian, 1987), 205–9.

29. Kui Yingtao, *Sichuan jindaishi gao*, 193–4.

30. Zhou Shandao, "Ji yujiulingjiunian Weiyuan tianbaodayuanshuai qiyi" (Remembering the 1909 uprising of the heaven-protected marshal at Weiyuan), in *Sichuan wenshi ziliao xuanji* (Selected historical materials on Sichuan), no. 3 (Chengdu: Sichuan renmin chuban she, 1962), 92.

31. John K. Fairbank and Kwang-ching Liu, eds., *The Cambridge History of China*, vol. II, part 2, 595.

32. Chesneaux, *Secret Societies in China in the Nineteenth and Twentieth Centuries*, 140–41.

33. Zhou Kaiqing, *Sichuan yu xinhai geming* (Sichuan and the 1911 Revolution) (Taibei: Academic Books Publishers, 1986), 22–23.

34. Ibid., 25–26.

35. Ibid., 26.

36. Ibid.

37. Ibid., 27.

38. "Xinhai Weiyuan baolu tongzhihui de wuzhuang douzheng," (Record of the Sichuan railway protection disturbances), in *Sichuan baolu fengyun lu* (Record of the Sichuan protect the railway agitation) (Chengdu: Sichuan renmin chuban she, 1981), 147–56.

39. "Xinhai Weiyuan baolu tongzhihui de wuzhuang douzheng," 150.

40. Chesneaux, *Secret Societies in China in the Nineteenth and Twentieth Centuries*, 61.

41. *North China Herald*, April 8, 1910.

42. Max Weber, *The Religion of China: Confucianism and Taoism* (Glencoe, Ill.: The Free Press, 1951), 196–203.

43. Frederic Wakeman Jr., *Strangers at the Gate: Social Disorder in South China, 1839–1861* (Berkeley: University of California Press, 1975), 133.

44. Daniel Harrison Kulp II, *Country Life in South China: The Sociology of Families, vol. 1, Phenix Village, Kwangtung, China* (New York: Teachers College, Bureau of Publication, Columbia University, 1925), xxvii.

45. Daniel Harrison Kulp, *Country Life in South China*, 285.

46. Martin C. Yang, *A Chinese Village: Taitou, Shantung Province* (New York: Columbia University Press, 1945), 190.

47. Sidney D. Gamble, *North China Villages: Social, Political, and Economic Activities Before 1933* (Berkeley: University of California Press, 1963), 121.

48. C. K. Yang, *Religion in Chinese Society* (Berkeley: University of California Press, 1961), 96.

49. *Dongfang zazhi*, no. 8, 1910, in *Xinhai geming* 3: 529.

50. *Shibao*, April 16, 1910; L. R. Barr, Ningpo Intelligence Report, January 1-April 30, 1910, F. O. 228/1762.

51. *Shibao*, March 23, 24, 1911.

52. *Dongfang zazhi*, no. 3, 1910, in *Xinhai geming* 3:389.

53. Herbert Gaffe, "Intelligence Report for the Quarter Ended June 30th 1910, Nanking," F. O. 228/1762.

54. *North China Herald*, January 14, 1910.

55. Hsiao-tung Fei, *Peasant Life in China: A Field Study of Country Life in the Yangtze Valley* (New York: E. P. Dutton and Co., 1939), 166–67.

56. Hsiao-tung Fei, *Peasant Life in China*, 144.

57. Peter Sahlins, *Forest Rites*. (Cambridge: Harvard University Press, 1994).

58. John K. Fairbank and Kwang-ching Liu, eds., *The Cambridge History of China*, vol. II, part 2, 211–243.

59. Naquin, *Millenarian Rebellion in China*, 142.

60. Kui Yingtao, *Sichuan jindaishi gao*, 166–67.

61. Ibid., 168–69.

62. Ibid., 169.

63. Ibid., 353.

64. Ibid., 362.

65. Ibid., 354, 363–64; *Minbian shi liao*, vol. 2, 756.

66. Kui Yingtao, *Sichuan jindaishi gao*, 363

67. Ibid., 355.

68. Ibid., 354, 367.

69. Ibid., 366, 368.

70. Ibid., 354.

71. Ibid., 354–355. See also, Zhou Kaiqing, *Sichuan yu Xinhai geming* (Sichuan and the 1911 Revolution) (Taibei: Academic Books Publishers, 1986), 26–27.

72. Kui Yingtao, *Sichuan jindaishi gao*, 362–63.

73. Zhou Shandao, "Ji yijiu lingjiu nian Weiyuan tianbao dayuanshuai qiyi," 89.

74. Ibid., 90.

75. Ibid., 93.

76. Ibid., 91.

77. Ibid., 92.

78. Ibid.

79. Kui Yingtao, *Sichuan jindaishi gao*, 187.

80. Ibid.

81. Zhou Shandao, "Ji yijiu lingjiu nian Weiyuan tianbao dayuanshuai qiyi," 94.

82. *North China Herald*, April 22, 1910.

83. *North China Herald*, January 7, 1910.

84. Zhou Shandao, "Ji yijiu lingjiu nian Weiyuan tianbao dayuanshuai qiyi," 94.

85. He Yimin, *Zhuanxing shiqi de shehui xinqunti* (Research on modern intellectuals and late Qing Sichuan society) (Chengdu: Sichuan daxue chuban she: 1992), 92–93.

86. Zhou Shandao, "Ji yijiu lingjiu nian Weiyuan tianbao dayuanshuai qiyi," 94.

87. Ibid., 94–95.

88. Ibid., 95.

89. Ibid., 95.

90. He Yimin, *Zhuanxing shiqi de shehui xinqunti*, 86.

91. Zhou Shandao, "Ji yijiu lingjiu nian Weiyuan tianbao dayuanshuai qiyi," 96.

92. Ibid., 97.

93. Ibid.

94. Ibid., 98.

95. Ibid., 99.

96. Zhao Erxun, "Sichuan zongdu Zhao Erxun zou pingding Weiyuan deng xian luanshi qingxing pian" (Facts of the suppression of the uprising in Weiyuan and other counties reported by Zhao Erxun the Governor of Sichuan" (Memorial to the Emperor), in *Xinhai geming qian shinian wen minbian dangran shiliao* (Archive material on people's activism in the ten years before the 1911 Revolution) (Beijing: Zhong Hua Shu Ju, 1985), #463, 800.

97. Zhou Shandao, "Ji yijiu lingjiu nian Weiyuan tianbao dayuanshuai qiyi," 99.

98. Ibid., 100.

99. Zhao Erxun, "Sichuan zongdu Zhao Erxun zou pingding Weiyuan deng xian luanshi qingxing pian," #463, 800.

100. Zhou Shandao, "Ji yijiu lingjiu nian Weiyuan tianbao dayuanshuai qiyi," 101.

101. Zhao Erxun, "Sichuan zongdu Zhao Erxun zou pingding Weiyuan deng xian luanshi qingxing pian," #463, 800.

102. Zhou Shandao, "Ji yijiu lingjiu nian Weiyuan tianbao dayuanshuai qiyi," 102.

103. Ibid.

104. Zhao Erxun, "Sichuan zongdu Zhao Erxun zou pingding Weiyuan deng xian luanshi qingxing pian," #463, 800.

105. Zhou Shandao, "Ji yijiu lingjiu nian Weiyuan tianbao dayuanshuai qiyi," 102.

106. Ibid., 103.

107. Ibid.

108. Ibid., 103–4.

109. Ibid., 104.

110. Ibid., 105.

111. Zhao Erxun "Sichuan zongdu Zhao Erxun zou pingding Weiyuan deng xian luanshi qingxing pian," #463, 800.

112. *North China Herald*, August 26, 1910.

113. "Intelligence Report, September 1910, Wuchow," F.O. 228/1765.

114. *North China Herald*, August 26, 1910.

115. "Intelligence Report, June 1910, Wuchow," F.O. 228/1765.

116. Kui Yingtao, *Sichuan jindaishi gao*, 187.

117. Naquin, *Millenarian Rebellion in China*, 268.

118. Prasenjit Duara, *Rescuing History from the Nation: Questioning Narratives of Modern China* (Chicago: University of Chicago Press, 1995), 116, 121–23.

119. In Sichuan province in 1911, a dispute over railway construction developed into a movement that embodied multiple class perspectives. Provincial gentry and merchants from Guangdong, Sichuan, Hunan, and Hubei had raised sufficient funds by selling railway bonds in 1911 to finance the construction of two southern trunk lines that would connect Beijing with Canton and Chengdu. Zhang Zhidong, who was in charge of the national southern trunk office, opposed the plan because it would strengthen provincial officials at the expense of a unified national railway. The central government, however, did not have sufficient funds from wealthy provincial merchants and was consequently forced to turn to foreign bankers for loans. In May 1911, when Beijing ordered the provincial railway companies disbanded, the outrage in Sichuan provincial elite circles was immediate. Newspaper headlines cried out that the Manchu government was selling Sichuan to the foreigners, students formed railway protection associations, and secret societies became active in the movement as well. In Weiyuan, those who raised local support for the movement were not participants or leaders in the anti–New Policy activism. Hu Yugai and Yang Zhaonan were both Tongmenhui members and also members of the more elite Gelaohui lodges, connected to provincial commercial interests. For further discussion see, *Xinhai Weiyuan baolu tongzhihu de wuzhuang douzheng* (The 1911 Weiyuan armed struggle to protect the railway movement), in *Sichuan baolu fengyun lu* (Record of the Sichuan protect the railway agitation) (Chengdu: Sichuan renmin chuban she, 1981), 147, 150.

Guanyin with Monkey Battling a Demon

Source: *Xiyouji* (Journey to the West). Beijing: Renmin wenxue chuban she, 1992.

Xiyouji
(Journey to the West)

Xiyouji (Journey to the West) is a story of four pilgrims who under the guidance and protection of Bodhisattva Guanyin (Kuan-yin) journey from China to India to bring back Buddhist scriptures. The events are based on the historical mission of monk Xuanzang (Hsuan-tsang), also known by his honorific title Tripitaka, who in the seventh century A.D. successfully but not without great hardship returned from India with over 600 valued Buddhist texts. Originally the work of storytellers, the comic, satiric, and popularly philosophic tales of Xuanzang and his companions Monkey, Pigsy, and Sandy originally displayed characteristics of the Indian, Persian, and Arabic literary and oral traditions with which China had significant contact through active trade routes at least until the late Ming Dynasty (1368–1644).[1] When public storytelling by monks was officially prohibited in the tenth century as part of the formal dismantling of state-sponsored Buddhism, marketplace storytellers proliferated to carry on the storytelling profession. No doubt the content and shape of the stories underwent some transformations at this time, perhaps they became more entertaining, earthy, and less moralistic. By the time Wu Ch'eng-en wrote these popularly generated tales into novel form in the sixteenth century, he had numerous sources, including some Yuan Dynasty plays from which to draw. In the following excerpts, Bodhisattva Guanyin (Kuan-yin) learns of Monkey's misuse of his powers to cause havoc in the heavens. She realizes that put to good use Monkey would be a powerful ally for the monk Xuanzang on his mission to India. Guanyin eventually enlists Monkey's assistance after he repents his misdeeds and commits himself to join the other pilgrims, Pigsy and Sandy, whom Guanyin has also recruited.

Excerpts

So the great Sage quietly rested, while the hosts of Heaven encompassed him. Meanwhile the Great Compassionate Bodhisattva Kuan-yin had come at the invitation of the Queen of Heaven to attend the feast. With her she brought her chief disciple, Hui-yen, and on arriving they were astounded to find the banqueting halls in utter desolation and confusion. The couches were broken or pushed aside, and although there were a good few Immortals, they had not attempted to take their places, but were standing about in noisy groups, protesting and disputing. After saluting the Bodhisattva they told her the whole story of what had occurred. "If there is no banquet and no drinks are going," she said, "you had better all come with me to see the Jade Emperor." . . .

"What about the Peach Banquet?" Kuan-yin asked, after the customary greeting had been exchanged. "It had always been such fun, year after year," said the Emperor. "It is terribly disappointing that his year everything has been upset by that terrible ape. I have sent 100,000 soldiers to pen him in, but the whole day has passed without news, and I don't know whether they have been successful!"

"I think you had better go down quickly to the Mountain of Flowers and Fruit," said the Bodhisattva to her disciple, Hui-yen, "And investigate the military situation. If hostilities are actually in progress, you can give a hand. In any case let us know exactly how things stand." . . .

Along the way Kuan-yin enlisted the help of another disciple, Sandy, whom she rescues from his meat-eating habits: "It was for sinning in Heaven," said Kuan-yin, "that you were banished. Yet here you are adding sin to sin, slaying living creatures. I am on my way to China to look for a scripture-seeker. Why don't you join our sect, reform your ways, become a disciple of the scripture-seeker, and go with him to India to fetch the scriptures? . . .

To another disciple, Pigsy, who had a taste for human flesh and would like to repent but who fears the Buddhists will starve him, Kuan-yin offers this adivce: "There is a saying," the Bodhisattva replied, " 'Heaven helps those who mean well,' If you give up your evil ways, you may be sure you won't lack nourishment. There are five crops in the world; so there is no need to starve. Why should you feed on human flesh?" . . . .

Meanwhile, the Buddha has finally subdued Monkey after unsuccessful attempts by the Jade Emperor and Laozi, the Daoist Immortal. Trapped beneath the Mountain of the Five Elements, Monkey has had 500 years to reflect on his behavior: Kuan-yin came down toward the place from which the voice seemed to come and at the foot of a cliff found the guardian deities of the palace, who after welcoming the Bodhisattva, led her to where Monkey was imprisoned. He was pent in a kind of stone box, and though he could speak he could not move hand or foot. "Monkey," cried the Bodhisattva, "do you know me or not?" He peered through a chink with his steely, fiery eyes and cried aloud, "How should I not know you? You are she of Potalaka, the Saviour Kuan-yin. To what do I owe this pleasure? Here where days and years are one to me, no friend or acquaintance has ever come to seek me out. Where, pray, do you come from?" "Buddha sent me," said she, "to China, to look for one who will come to India and fetch the scriptures, and as this place is on the way, I took the opportunity of calling upon you." "Buddha tricked me," said Monkey, "and imprisoned me under this mountain 500 years ago, and here I have been ever since. I entreat you to use your powers to rescue me." "Your sins were very great," she said, "and I am by no means confident that if you get out you would not at once get into trouble again." "No," said Monkey, "I have repented and now want only to embrace the Faith and devote myself to good works." "Very well, then," said the Bodhisattva, delighted. "Wait while I go to the land of T'ang and find my scripture-seeker. He shall deliver you. You shall be his disciple and embrace our Faith." "With all my heart," said Monkey.[2]

Notes

1. C. T. Hsia, *The Classic Chinese Novel: A Critical Introduction* (Bloomington: Indiana University Press, 1980; originally published by Columbia University Press, 1968), 7, 131.

2. Wu Ch'eng-en, *Monkey,* trans. Arthur Waley (New York: Grove Press, Inc., 1958), 63–84.

Lianzhou, Guangdong:
The Greenwood/Tongmenghui Alliance

To treat the people who resist as rebels is bad management. . . .
How can troops be sent? These people will be killed. The city gentry must be behind this request for troops . . . [the disturbance] is a
distillation of grievous spirits in the area.

—Daotai Zuo Shaozuo, 1910

Village women along the narrow streets of Caiyuanba in Lianzhou
county were witness to the flight of Dr. Eleanor Chesnut as she ran
quickly past open doors and courtyard gates. Some of the women and
their female relatives and children had over the years sought medical
help at the Presbyterian Women's Hospital where Dr. Chesnut had
treated many of them during her almost ten-year-long career as a medical missionary in South China. In 1904, the Women's Hospital, which
the foreign woman doctor managed, had treated over five thousand patients. The Men's Hospital in the same year had seen over seven thousand patients.[1] Once a week Dr. Chesnut, who was born in Waterloo,
Iowa, on January 8, 1868, and orphaned early in her infancy, traveled
ten miles on horseback to hold a clinic at Sanjiang, a market town to
the southwest of Lianzhou city. The doctor chose a spartan lifestyle for
herself, leaving gifts and most resources for use in the hospital and
church facilities.[2] Many of the women who watched her from their
doorsteps on that autumn day might have felt a mixture of confusion
and fear. Dr. Chesnut was on the run for her life.

Earlier in the day along the same village streets, members of one of
many local gangs had paraded shouting antiforeign slogans and carrying a skeleton along with internal body organs in earthenware jars, all of
which they had seized when attacking the missionary medical facilities.
Leaders of the procession beat a gong and called out that the foreign
devils were involved in killing children and stealing their body parts.

Into opened vessels, villagers peered to verify the presence of livers and lungs and other pathological specimens floating in smelly liquid substances—teaching specimens said the missionaries, evidence of foul play said the boisterous young men rythmically circling their arms and punctuating their message with measured strikes to the gong. Local officials and leading members of the community, some of whom had themselves converted to Christianity, attempted to quiet the disturbance, but the band of young men continued unabated in their parade through the village streets. Several thousand others aroused along the way joined in the protest against the foreigners and their apparently evil deeds. Perhaps the foreign lady doctor and the foul smelling, slimy human remnants in jars, the likes of which no one had seen before, were related to the problems so adversely affecting many people's living conditions in these early years of the twentieth century.

Pursued by an angry crowd that had just assaulted another doctor and attacked the mission hospital, Dr. Chesnut, who had studied at the Woman's Medical College in Chicago and was proficient in Chinese, stopped suddenly when the clamor seemed temporarily to fade behind her. Realizing that her route to the officials from whom she sought help at the government yamen was blocked, she knew her effort to seek assistance had failed. She could escape to temporary safety, but her devotion to a cause that had brought her to China in the fall of 1894 and to the commitment of her life to "Christ and China" led her back to the mission residences where her fellow missionaries were presently held in danger of their lives. After helping to plan a group escape from the compound, Dr. Chesnut and the others found themselves on the run through village lanes and country paths until they reached the Long Tao Buddhist temple and the caves into which the temple led. When the temple keeper demanded a fee for their entrance rather than instinctively offering shelter, the missionaries suspected unsympathetic attitudes and turned away only to encounter the angry crowd, which had just caught up with them. An exchange of words, gestures, and grimaces began. Individuals pled for their lives or at least the lives of the others, especially for the one child among them. Words and gestures volleyed back and forth. The air was thick with anger and fear. If a resolution was possible, it did not find expression in this atmosphere. The attack began. In a moment of time that hung heavy in humid air, blows fell and five missionaries were cruelly slaughtered. Tossed dead by their assailants into the Lianzhou River, Dr. Chesnut and the others lay lifeless as the cool waters washed over their still warm, limp bodies. News of Eleanor Chesnut's death along with four others including a child must have met with different mixtures of satisfaction and dismay among the residents of Lianzhou.

The first three missionaries to have arrived at Lianzhou shortly after 1889 had been Mr. and Mrs. Edward C. Machle (Ella May Wood) and Miss Louise Johnston. They had sailed to China together shortly after the Machles' marriage. Mrs. Machle and her eleven-year-old daughter, Amy, were among the five massacred at the Long Tao temple. Mr. Machle by a turn of fate managed to escape. Miss Johnston by chance was absent from Lianzhou during the massacre, having taken a country furlough. When she learned of the death of her dear friends and fellow missionaries, she did not ask for reassignment. Instead her devotion seems to have redoubled. Such commitment by missionaries was from their point of view a simple fact of life.

In the chapters of human history, Christian missionaries really were a breed apart. Being far from home and taking upon themselves tremendous hardships to change other people's ways of life and thinking was itself almost a supernatural undertaking. Evangelical zeal carried within it the potential to inspire awe, which easily became downright frightening. What were these people doing so far from their own homes in the market towns and villages of northern Guangdong? Why did they put their labor and money into building those large structures, the likes of which no one in Lianzhou had ever seen? And then there was the fact of those human body parts in glass jars. Perhaps there was something fundamentally foreboding, though also powerful, about these foreigners. The missionaries were by all accounts a center of power, a presence that might be of some use to those in local society looking for more ways into influential networks. Their presence could also be intrusive and irritating in their single-minded pursuit of self-righteous goals, offering little or no ground for compromise. In 1910 when anti–New Policy disturbances developed at Lianzhou, Miss Johnston was in charge of the area's mission schools, which had multiplied by that time and were under missionary-trained Chinese management.[3] Many of the reform managers who came under attack by the protest leaders had themselves been converted to Christianity by the work of Miss Johnston in the town of Sanjiang.

Reverend J. S. Kunkle graduated from Western Theological Seminary and was appointed to the Canton mission with John Rogers Peale in 1905. Reverend Peale and his wife, Rebecca Gillespie Peale, went ahead; Reverend Kunkle delayed for one year in order to accept a fellowship for study at Oxford University. When he learned of the murder of Reverend and Mrs. Peale just one day after their arrival in Lianzhou, Kunkle wrote, "I cannot help thinking that had I been more zealous, it would have been I that gained a martyr's crown, and a better than I spared for the work. Now I earnestly seek the privilege of taking the place of one of those faithful ones who have given their lives for the cause."[4] In 1910 Kunkle was on the scene at Lianzhou. He reported extensively on the anti–New Policy disturbances, and with remarkable sympathy toward the protesters.

Missionaries and Merchants in the Making of Anti–New Policy Protest

The messenger and the message were equally significant in the making of the Christian mission experience in China. The vast majority of the Lianzhou population was Hakka with Ju tribesmen in the mountainous areas of the county.[5] Ironically, the first introduction of Christian views into the Lianzhou area was carried by a young Chinese of Hakka descent from the Canton area. Hong Xiuquan, leader of the Taiping Rebellion, carried Christian-inspired ideas into Lianzhou, Guangdong, in 1844 on his tour to raise support for a rural rebellion he and others hoped would build a Heavenly Kingdom on earth, free of elite corruption and social injustice. Hong himself had been familiarized with Christianity by American Protestant missionaries working in Canton immediately before the Opium War after which that city and others were forced open to Western European and American missionary and merchant activity. A mix of ideas from the Chinese rural culture of protest, including folk Daoism, Buddhism, and secret society beliefs, along with an understanding of Old and New Testament ideas, Taiping ideology was revolutionary in its rejection of the political and social theory derived from the Chinese classical scholarship including the works attributed to Kong Zi (Confucius). Connected with resistance to local landlords and tax collectors who did not respect customary obligations to protect rural well-being, Hong's ideas gained widespread acceptance. Within this context, Christian ideas about social equality and rejection of political orthodoxy had a compelling and familiar logic.

By the time American Protestant missionaries themselves moved into the Lianzhou area initially in 1882 and then in 1889 to establish hospitals, schools, and a church, Hong Xiuquan's message was a recollection from the previous generation. We have no idea if any of the villagers who availed themselves of the mission's medical facilities or converted to Christianity made any association with Hong's movement, but such associations were certainly possible given the long-lived rural memory for Taiping events that carried into the post-Boxer decade. The messenger was different, and the mixture of protest and Christian ideas was also transformed by the political and social context. Adult membership in the Lianzhou city congregation numbered over 300 by March 1905, and a large and attractive new church building had been dedicated. Ac-

Lianzhou County

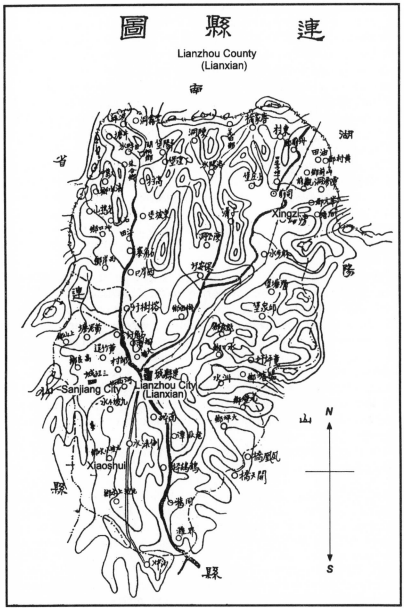

圖　縣　連

Lianzhou County
(Lianxian)

南

省

連

湖

陽

山　N

縣　S

Xingzi

Xiaoshui

Sanjiang City

Lianzhou City
(Lianxian)

Source: Guangdong quansheng difang ji yao (Guangdong provincial survey), 1934, vol. 3, p. 54

cording to missionary reports, a boys' boarding school and a girls' school flourished and there were numerous small groups of believers in the outlying villages.[6] Among those who attended these schools and sent their children were Li Ganshan, pastor of the Sanjiang church by 1910, and Mao Wenming, who managed one of the commercial firms in Sanjiang and by 1910 had also converted to Christianity.[7] Mao and others in Lianzhou combined Christianity as they understood it through the work of the local Protestant missionaries with ideas of constitutional reform. This context was certainly different in social class outlook and goals from the peasant-based movement with which Hong Xiuquan had combined his notion of Christian views.

The incident that took place in October 1905 was clearly related to the Lianzhou uprising in the fall of 1910 involving anti–New Policy issues. Not only were many of the individuals present in 1905 central to the events of 1910, but some of the conditions and specific grievances resurfaced in a more sustained and focused attack on the property of county elite members associated with reforms and foreign Christian presence.[8]

Sorting out the relationship between specifically anti-Christian and antiforeign motives seemed important to the Lianzhou missionaries in both 1905 and 1910. By separating the two, these observers offered a critique of western civilization and defined a version of Christianity that preserved the pursuit of justice and well-being Hong himself had seen as Christianity's core values. What the missionaries were unable to address was the disruption their outsider position so easily generated, especially when it was tied to the exercise of legal, commercial, and political authority that linked their message to developments detrimental to rural livelihood in the shifting societal formations of the early twentieth century.

The Presbyterians in their own investigation into the 1905 massacre concluded that,

> the irritation of the people was not particular to Lien-chou but that it prevailed to a greater or less extent in several other and distant parts of the Empire, shows that the real causes were general in their operation and independent of the individuals and their acts in Lian-chou. Missionaries and press correspondents at a score of widely separated places suddenly reported a tension of the Chinese mind and threats of trouble. The Chinese mind was stirred to a ferment independently of the missionaries, and conditions at Lien-chou needed only some slight pretext to break forth in fury.[9]

Cultural issues involved in the 1905 conflict and brutal attack at Lianzhou contained elements that could arouse antiforeign, anti-Christian fears. Such fears, however, were not automatically generated by foreign presence. Perceived group interest over any one issue and the individual personalities involved were crucial determinants in the reading of these cross-cultural interactions. According to mission accounts, the Presbyterian Church at Lianzhou appeared to be flourishing in the years leading up to the 1905 massacre. Even in retrospect the missionaries did not feel there had been reason to suspect currents of hostility that might be directed against them. Attendance at both the mission hospital and the church had risen steadily. No barrier kept many of the women and men of Lianzhou from seeking help for their medical problems at the mission compound. Those who had been successfully treated by the mission doctors over the years knew in their own bodies that good could come from whatever bizarre practices the foreigners might have. On the other hand when upon entering the hospital, the bands of young men acting as guardians of the community discovered anatomical and pathological specimens, including a skeleton and human body parts preserved in jars for use in medical instruction, they read them as evidence of the sinister and evil influence of the missionaries, which they had already decided was evil.

The ambiguity of perceptions as Lianzhou villagers and Presbyterian missionaries interacted with each other across a considerable cultural range was reflected also in the Board of Foreign Missions Report on the Lianzhou attack written by Arthur J. Brown. Reverend Brown clearly articulated the views that, "Mr. Peale had a revolver and was at first disposed to take it, but after consultation with the other missionaries, he left it in the house, feeling unwilling to begin his missionary career by any act of violence against the people whom he had come to save."[10] Reverend Noyes of Canton wrote: "By their death they have claimed Lien-chou for Christ and we must enter into this heritage. Don't have thoughts too hard against the Chinese."[11] And Dr. Machle, who himself had lost both his wife and his young daughter in the massacre, believed that: "The greater number of the 6,000 persons who witnessed the atrocities of the two hundred rowdies, thieves and gamblers are now very sorrowful that they even lent their presence."[12]

The Lianzhou missionaries did not jump to images of superstitious, backwards peasants who lacked morality and human decency. Quite the contrary, their response was level-headed even in the face of brutality to their own friends and family. They wanted no use of force or other retribution. For them the most important outcome was continued mission work. They did not as a group feel the 1905 attack was antimissionary or anti-Christian. In their minds it was antiforeign, a fine line perhaps, but one that they found it useful to draw.

The distinction between antiforeign and anti-Christian motives was, in fact, a recurring theme in missionary reports after the Boxer uprising of 1900. At the end of his major two-volume work, *China in Convulsion*, published in 1901, Arthur Smith, longtime missionary resident and observer of Chinese society wrote, "Unless China is essentially altered she will continue to imperil the world's future."[13] The Brown report on Lianzhou concluded in the same spirit. The people of Lianzhou needed Christianity. The massacre itself was proof of that in the missionary's view. Guns and other means of coersion would not bring about the transformation the missionaries thought China needed.

> From a variety of causes, the typical Chinese scholar regards all foreign ideals as inferior to those of the Chinese, and the effort to introduce them into China with the same mixture of amusement, contempt, and indignation which we should instinctively feel toward an organized attempt to import into a Christian land the religious system of Mohammed, to the displacement of Christianity. This is his most moderate and temperate view. When he becomes at all excited and intolerant, he views the advent of Western ways and moral teachings precisely as well-educated Westerners would the propaganda of Anarchistic tenets and the inculcation of Nihilistic practices among the people of our own land.[14]

Smith offers here a Christian critique of western civilization and in so doing draws a line between anti-Christian and antiforeign positions. Smith understands Chinese resistance to "Western ways" as an intelligent response to the situation in which Chinese find themselves. Resistance in this scenario is viewed as a necessary passage in fulfilling the evolutionary potential of humankind in the modern era. The possibility that western ways are flawed and that the Chinese have valuable qualities of their own to add to human progress is clearly indicated. In Smith's view, a view that resonated with the Lianzhou missionaries, Christianity combined with Chinese civilization would be superior to the present western civilization in which Christianity had built on the foundation of Roman civilization. Smith continued,

> But Christianity is itself an integral part of modern civilization, from which it can no more be dissociated than the rays of light and of heat can be untwisted from the sunbeam. The attempt on the part of the Chinese to expel from their Empire spiritual forces, is an uprising of the Middle Ages against the Twentieth Century. The effort on the part of some who have been cradled in Christian lands, in an unspiritual and a materialist age, to pinion and hand-cuff the disintegrating yet constructive forces of Christianity in their operation in China, is a futile struggle to reverse the tide of human development, and to arrest the slow but irresistible progresss of a law of man's spiritual nature. Let it be distinctly recognized that the development of Christianity in China will be and must be marked by con-

flict, perhaps not more so than elsewhere, but surely not less. It will undermine idolatry as it did in the Roman Empire, and upon the wreck of the
old will build a structure as much fairer than the Roman as the moral ideals
of the Chinese race are higher and purer than those of that ancient state.
When adopted, and even imperfectly put in practice, it may be expected to
alter the life of the court, as it has done in Western lands, inadequately
Christianized though these be. . . . Thus alone can the Empire be adapted
to the altered conditions brought about by the impact of Western civilization, with its Pandora Box of evil and of good.[15]

The Pandora Box of evil and good included among other things the
effects of industrial capitalism and the transformations it brought to the
role of commerce in rural life, elevating it above other social considerations and fostering a kind of exhalted materialism to which Smith referred. Clearly, this excessive materialism was one of the features Smith
and others hoped would be eliminated in the constructive interactions
between Christianity and Chinese culture. Yet, during the New Policy
era, it was the reform managers who were associated with foreign ways
and often Christianity as well, who were eagerly using these options to
develop paths for advancement that were seen as the modern route to
ends previously reached through the imperial examination system. The
materialism associated with the foreign reforms was unchecked to an
extent that generated exactly the kind of problem Smith and others saw
as a flaw in western society and that was undermining the best qualities
that he hoped to see preserved in China and added to human evolution
in the modern era. In brief, Smith had put his finger on the central
conundrum of modernity.

In material, commercial terms, Lianzhou was located in one of the
most productive agricultural regions in the country. Owing to a warm
and humid climate, many areas in the south and southwest had a year-
round growing season. The Pearl River delta in Guangdong province,
for example, a region highly commercialized by the nineteenth century,
produced two crops of rice per year and supported a major silk industry
to the west of Canton. Conditions varied a great deal, however, both
within a province and from one province to another. In contrast to the
densely populated alluvial delta plain of the Pearl River, northern
Guangdong was hilly and suitable for rice cultivation only in its valleys.
Vegetable crops were the main agricultural produce in this area. The
hilly northern area in which Lianzhou county was situated was one of
the least commercially developed areas in the province. A somewhat
remote county, 250 miles north and three weeks' travel by boat from
the provincial capital of Guangzhou, Lianzhou with a population of
about 300,000 by 1900 was nonetheless far from out of touch with

national and international developments.[16] Compared with the rich and
economically well-developed districts of the Pearl River delta, Lianzhou was less commercialized but not without its own commercial enterprises.[17] Lianzhou merchants and officials had networks through which
they maintained contact with Cantonese traders in the urban centers and
provincial capital. While villagers grew rice, in addition to tobacco,
sugarcane, and tea, rich hillside forests were a source of lumber as well
as a cover for the many bandit gangs that roamed the area.

Property relations became social and cultural terrain for contested
claims to local resources. Under New Policy auspices as we have seen
in numerous other cases, temples were claimed for new schools, new
government offices and new-style police bureaus. In a setting of scarcity, where a good life was possible but always vulnerable to erosion
by natural and social forces, small farmers sought fiercely to protect
their access to resources through customs based on community consensus. Any encroachment, no matter how small or temporary, was a potential danger of larger proportions. Missionary activity in Lianzhou
had begun with a property dispute. As Edward Rhoads points out in his
account, the Presbyterian mission did not succeed in acquiring property
in Sanjiang until 1890, at which time there was some opposition to the
foreigners' purchase of land but no concerted effort to block the sale.
When the mission attempted in 1895 to take possession of another piece
of land it had purchased, missionary Lingle "was mobbed by irate villagers and forced to withdraw."[18] Later, "pressed for a decision by the
American consul, the governor-general in September 1896 ordered the
local officials in Lienchow to stamp and validate the missionaries' deed
to the land."[19] During the construction of the mission hospital from
1897 to 1899, twenty plus villages expressed collective opposition to
the structure, but there were no actual attacks. At the time of the Boxer
Uprising in the north, the mission was placed under protection of the
county officials, missionaries withdrew from the area, and Elder
Brother Society groups (Gelaohui) became active in the area.[20] Again
in 1905 at Lianzhou there were property issues. An old man had promised not to construct a mat-shed on mission property the following year,
if Reverend Machle would overlook the structure this one time so that
villagers could accommodate musicians who were part of their celebration of All Souls' Day. What began as a small property dispute, with
the church initially being concerned about setting a precedent and very
adamant about its claims on Chinese soil, was resolved quickly to the
momentary satisfaction of all involved, only to be immediately transformed into a rush of antiforeign hatred by some dispossessed, volatile
young men. In 1910, the property issues would be raised by a broader

spectrum of the village population in connection with nationwide programs for county-level reforms.

A merchant-missionary-official alliance was often behind the reform process. Like many county governments of the post-Boxer era, Lianzhou officials experiencing a fiscal crisis born of rising costs and government expansion turned most easily to local members of the commercial and landed elite to manage new revenue collection projects. The need for new sources of leverage, available through association with foreign merchants and missionaries, was nurtured by the extra demands from above and the already fully utilized resources below. This alliance had been less present in 1905, when at the provincial level Chinese merchants were involved in nationalist discourses beginning with the anti-American boycott. Organized in response to the U.S. government restrictions on Chinese immigration to the United States, the boycott was an early expression of antiforeign sentiment within the newly emerged urban commercial networks. Writing on Sino-American relations before the First World War, Michael Hunt noted the role of the 1905 Lianzhou massacre in motivating President Roosevelt to take a more aggressive stance toward the Chinese government and the Chinese merchants. Roosevelt had in fact recently made some concessions regarding the Chinese exclusion aspects of U.S. immigration policy and wanted to make the point that this was not to be taken as a sign of weakness. Like many others, Roosevelt assumed that the massacre at Lianzhou was a product of the anti-American hysteria whipped up by the boycott committees. Although the boycott committees immediately denied any association with the events at Lianzhou, the effectiveness of the boycott in undermining American businesses in China encouraged Roosevelt to take a clear stand. He wrote that, "not only the Chinese people but the Chinese Government have behaved badly in connection with this boycott, and a boycott is not something to which we can submit."[21] American forces were to be increased off the China coast, and in December preparations were made for a possible joint army-navy expedition against the Canton.

> Spurred by the murder of five American missionaries at Lien-chou near the Hunan border, though it was unconnected with the boycott, President Roosevelt on November 15 ordered the U.S. Navy to "have as strong a naval force as possible concentrated on the Chinese shore, and as speedily as possible. Two weeks later, American gunboats and destroyers began arriving at Canton from Manila. However, despite the show of force, the boycott persisted.[22]

Foreign commercial presence in Lianzhou was limited and indirect. Five county-based commercial firms dominated in the area and any foreign goods entered the area through them. Local inhabitants were also very aware of international issues through letters that regularly passed between family members in the Lianzhou, South China, area and parts of California, Montana, Wyoming, and other regions where Chinese immigrants had settled. The Presbyterian Commission that investigated the massacre received testimony from several longtime resident missionaries fluent in Chinese. They agreed that posters, newspapers, and inflammatory literature all calling for the boycott of American goods earlier in 1905 had circulated widely throughout rural China, including the Lianzhou area. In addition, "The stories of the ill treatment of Chinese in the United States have gone back to China by letter and by word of mouth. The Chinese know how their countrymen have been butchered and their property destroyed in scores of American towns."[23] To the missionaries in Guangdong province, it seemed that every sizeable town in rural China recieved news from at least one of its residents in the United States. They concluded that any anti-Christian activity was primarily antiforeign.[24] The Presbyterian Commission insisted that the Lianzhou Catholic Church had a habit of enrolling "bad characters" and that the Chinese authorities were hestitant to take action against these individuals for fear of becoming embroiled with higher Chinese officials and the French Consul to whom the Catholic priests might appeal.[25] By the time local antigovernment and antiforeign issues had taken shape in 1910, this earlier stratum of views on things foreign was quite well-developed, and those who had sat on the sidelines in 1905 continued to read and think about those letters and their connections to what was happening with these foreign things in their own villages and towns.

In the New Policy incidents, local merchant associations prominent in the reforms were far from antiforeign in their outlook. This was a clear point of contention among various rural groupings. When provincial commercial and political interests shifted focus from boycott issues to reform, the alliance of things foreign and Chinese at the expense of subsistence farmers became pronounced. This connection was significant to those who protested the reforms as can be seen in dissident demands and analysis of local problems. Tax protester Yu Zhusan at Laiyang watched the yamen personnel associated with the reforms light up his American cigarette to communicate his status in the drift of things, and the villagers who convinced Liu Xiangting to take up leadership of the protest at Weiyuan were clear about the foreign contributions to their local hardships mediated as they were through the local leaders who played to the foreign presence for their own advantage. For the dissenting villagers there was no a priori connection in their view between landlord-merchant-official corruption and Christians' views or things foreign, but the association became an unavoidable reality as over the late nineteenth century and early years of the twentieth century, some members of the local elite and those with upwardly mobile aspirations combined their Christian faith and commercial networks with new opportunities for political advancement through what seemed to many of them to be the political parallel of western religion, constitutional government. By 1910 they were the most likely candidates for managers of the New Policy programs in numerous counties throughout rural China.

Revolutionaries and Reformers:
New Policy Roaders among Tongmenghui Members

In the year of the Lianzhou massacre, Sun Zhongshan established the Tongmenghui (Revolutionary Alliance) in Tokyo. Espousing primarily nationalist and anti-Qing political views, the young students who formed the backbone of this group held a variety of perspectives from anarchism to republicanism. A critique of modernity influenced by Tolstoy and Kropotkin ran through their range of views, but they also aspired to make China strong in the modern world and therefore partly on modern, industrial terms. Tokyo-based Chinese anarchists favored an agrarian base for self-strengthening, while the Paris-based anarchist groups envisioned advanced industrial technology as the foundation of the new society. Sun himself practiced Christianity and at the same time included socialist elements in his political vision. A critique of existing Chinese politics and society was part and parcel of this creative, albeit potentially confused, mix of social analysis. Many saw rural society with its conflicts as a base for their revolutionary movement. The vision of rural society that sought to harness rural dissent for revolution, almost always included transformation of that society itself. Issues surrounding the definition and extent of this transformation highlight social class as the critical factor in the dynamics of rural political discourse so apparent in these studies of anti–New Policy activism. In fact, it was the only factor that brought clarity of analysis and political direction to an otherwise infinitely flexible and workable combination of religious, social, and political possibilities.

Long Yizhen of Lianzhou, Guangdong, was one of the young men who had joined Sun Zhongshan's Revolutionary Alliance while a student in Tokyo. Like many who took up the revolutionary banner under the auspices of the Alliance program, Long returned to Lianzhou to help build a local base for the revolutionary movement. Within the context of Lianzhou politics, Long Yizhen was associated with one of the families identified with the inner-city (*chengnei*) circles.[26] This is significant because the core that managed preparation for the New Policy reforms was locally designated the outer-city (*chengwai*) group with its primary base of operations in Sanjiang, across the Lianzhou River from the county seat in Lianzhou city.[27] Once back in Lianzhou, Long Yizhen contacted his brother Yiyuan who had connections with a local secret society known as the Greenwood (*Lülin*).[28] This too was a common move on the part of Revolutionary Alliance members returning from Tokyo. Triad societies along with other secret society groups were active in the Lianzhou area, and Long Yiyuan had specific contacts with Greenwood leaders Li Guanmei, Shao Guzi, Ou Jinsheng, and Liang Beishui.

A second group of Tongmenghui members in Lianzhou were centered in Sanjiang city where the Presbysterian influence was greatest. Mo Huixiong, a graduate of the local school, joined the Revolutionary Alliance in 1908. Mao Wenming of Sanjiang city and Huang Xusheng of the inner-city elite in Lianzhou county seat had both converted to Christianity and gone to Guangzhou where they attended an English school. Together they traveled to Hawaii to do missionary work. There they joined the Revive China Society (*Xinzhonghui*), eastablished by Sun Zhongshan in 1894 and a forerunner of the Revolutionary Alliance with its anti-Qing outlook. Huang Xusheng later went to Hong Kong to help establish a branch of the Revolutionary Alliance.[29] The two groupings of Revolutionary Alliance members in Lianzhou had different local bases and different routes by which they had entered the early revolutionary movement. When the 1910 anti–New Policy conflict developed, the Long brothers and Greenwood leader Li Guanmei among others were at the center of opposition to the reforms, while the reforms themselves were undertaken by commercial firms with inner-city allies but with family-based ties in Sanjiang. One month after the 1911 Revolution took place nationally, Mo Huixiong and pastor Li Ganshan led an effort to separate Lianshan from Lianzhou and to make Sanjiang the capital city of the new county with themselves as the local officials.[30] Divisions among local Tongmenghui members based on different social class alliances and local competition were already apparent in the post-Boxer, New Policy decade and would plague the Guomindang into the 1920s and beyond.

Long before the events at Lianzhou in 1910, Sun Zhongshan considered Guangdong, among all of China's provinces, to be the key to successful revolution. As early as 1895, Sun worked with secret society groups to plan a terrorist attack on the government headquarters in Canton (Guangzhou), the provincial capital of Guangdong. He hoped that this event would touch off uprisings throughout the province that would eventually spread to the rest of the country and result in the overthrow of the Manchu government. The Canton plot was suppressed before it got under way, but Sun's judgment that Guangdong was seething with unrest was sound.

Several abortive uprisings coordinated by Sun and his associates tapped but failed to utilize fully the widespread rural discontent of southern villagers. By 1900, taxes were even higher in the Canton area than they had been five years earlier, and instability in the countryside, which encouraged farmers to join secret societies, had increased. Again Sun planned an uprising, this time at Waizhou, in coordination with peasant groups, and again the attack was premature because of makeshift organization and inadequate propaganda that did not take full advantage of local divisions and conflicts.[31] After gaining the support of student groups with whom he founded the Revolutionary Alliance in 1905, Sun was ready to launch yet another effort to mobilize rural dissatisfaction for revolution. This attempt ended in the suppression of the Ping-Liu-Li uprising in Hunan in 1906.[32] Despite these failures, Sun was not easily discouraged from pursuing the potential that he saw for major change in the conflict between commoner communities and members of the political and economic local elites. There was one last effort to coordinate uprisings across southern Guangdong. The revolution that Sun anticipated was to begin at Qinzhou, Guangdong, in 1907.

In the area between Qinzhou and Lianzhou in southwest Guangdong, not to be confused with the Lianzhou in northwest Guangdong, was a group of three sugar-growing villages known as the San Na because the names of all three villages shared the character "Na." The inhabitants of these villages were of Hakka ethnicity. Many of them belonged to the Black Flag secret society, and there was a long history of villager resistance to both French military forces and Chinese officials in these areas.

In the early 1900s, villagers attacked local officials who had increased various taxes. According to a report by Reverend Bach, an American stationed in the area, the officials pardoned some of the secret society headmen on the condition that they pay large sums of money to the officials. After paying the required amount, these secret society headmen were appointed as military officers. Persons who could not pay the amounts demanded were beheaded.

In the spring of 1906, villagers and officials made peace with each other, but when new prefects and officials were appointed in 1907, the levies again began to rise. Daotai Wang of Hanzhao issued an edict stating that the villagers of San Na would have to contribute eighteen thousand taels to support a public school in Hanzhao. San Aogui, a former secret society headman who had purchased his freedom and become an officer, was sent by the Daotai along with 300 soldiers to collect the money. The tax was to be collected as a levy on sugar, the principal crop produced in the district.

Villagers formed an association to protest the tax. Lai Xian, a degree-holder from Nalai village, assumed leadership, proclaiming himself emperor and issuing edicts that explained the villagers' grievances and declared their intent to capture the area from corrupt officials. Other demands were that rice prices be lowered, that merchants conduct business as usual, and that foreigners not interfere in the battle between villagers and officials.[33] This scenario was a familiar part of the rural tradition of commoner protest. It was a scenario that, in past periods of dynastic decline, had led to the development of warlordism and eventually the founding of a new dynasty.

The situation in the Qinzhou/Lianzhou area had thus reached crisis proportions when Sun Zhongshan decided to coordinate a series of uprisings around events in this district. Between February and May 1907, Sun made plans with student revolutionaries and secret society leaders to mobilize protesters into one united front. Uprisings would simultaneously take place at Qinzhou, Lianzhou, and Huanggang. This, the organizers hoped, would be the spark that would ignite a revolutionary conflagration. Minor attacks and skirmishes continued throughout this preparatory period.

In early May, armed confrontation broke out, and government troops came to the aid of the local officials. In less than two weeks, the tax protesters were forced into retreat. They scattered to the nearby hill areas, from which they continued to launch guerrilla attacks on the local officials and their associates. This style of fighting continued into September, at which time the villagers beheaded a district subprefect who had executed a wealthy villager for refusing to pay the additional taxes. One local observer aptly commented on the state of affairs that "disturbances of this nature are not so much antidynastic as directed against the local authorities due to their exactions and the utterly miserable methods of local government."[34]

The uprising at Huanggang, which was to have been timed to coincide with those at Qinzhou and Lianzhou, went off prematurely and was also suppressed. Although forced to begin the uprising earlier than planned because of security leaks, rebel forces, composed of villagers, secret society members, and local braves (*yong*), did succeed in capturing Huanggang city. They governed the county seat without opposition from the inhabitants until government troops arrived and overwhelmed the rebels' military capacity. An American observer wrote, "As long as the rioters were in possession, perfect order was maintained, and beyond levying money contributions on the well-to-do inhabitants, I have not heard of any complaints as to their proceedings or conduct."[35]

The Qinzhou and Huanggang uprisings were similar to other disturbances in south China during the first decade of the twentieth century. They had an organization, a logic, and a purpose independent of both the radical students who sought to harness their forces for national revolution and the secret societies that became tangentially involved or were sometimes vehicles for the expression of local disputes. A U.S. Consul stationed in Canton noted the increased incidence of protest and linked many of these demonstrations to census-taking, which accompanied the initial stages of New Policy reform. He wrote in October 1910:

> Not in years have robberies, piracies, clan-fights and rioting been so frequent in south China as now, or has such a feeling of general discontent shown itself among the people. . . . The rioting that has recently taken place in several districts within the Kwang Tung and Kwang Si provinces has been principally caused by the taking of the census, which people feared was the first step towards the imposition of additional taxes.[36]

The rural crisis, which Sun Zhongshan hoped would be the start of a revolutionary process, was intensified by the New Policy reforms, and his own revolutionary party at ground level in Lianzhou was divided in its approach and goals.

Prelude to Protest: Competition among Merchant Firms and Increased Taxation Lianzhou, Guangdong, September 1910–January 1911

By contrast with Laiyang, Shandong, where a single county elite network monopolized all economic and political affairs, at Lianzhou five elite networks competed with each other for control of the reforms.[37] Members of these networks were referred to as *shenshi* and *shendong,* indicating the degree-holding status of at least some of them. Each network formed a faction known as a *dang.* Two were located in the city, and one in each of the market towns Xingzi, Sanjiang, and Dongce. According to one informant interviewed by Daotai Zuo Shaozuo, who investigated the crisis at Lianzhou, there was not a single public-minded person among the elite members.[38] Mo Huixun, brother of Mo Huixiong, and Chen Songnian, tax-farming associate of Mo Huixun, were first to become involved in collecting census fees, ostensibly for new teachers' salaries. Deng Huanzhen, Zhu Songren, Huang Tingru, and Huang Zhiyi were all managers of the public granary and school mas-

ters and were known for their swindling. Local people had brought
grievances against them for past corrupt practices that had never been
corrected. In the view of the governor of Guangdong who memorialized
the emperor on this case, "the town *shenshi* and others were bitterly
hated by the local people for their sinister behavior."[39] Now the subprefect asked this same group to undertake preparation for self-government reforms.

The dominant *dang* consisted of a dozen persons who constituted one
of the city networks. Although other local families of influence were
located in the county seat, the groups that had a strong base in Sanjiang
had closest ties to the yamen official. According to a native of Hubei
who was a resident in Lianzhou and a member of the Lianzhou chamber
of commerce (*guan shanghui shi*), the leader of this city *dang* was a
certain Deng Shaozhen. Deng owned several thousand *mou* of land, and
early in 1910 had gained the subprefect's support for a plan to sell the
public grain supplies and deposit the funds thus obtained into accounts
controlled by members of his *dang*.[40] Close ties with the subprefect's
authority distinguished this *dang* from others in the area and provided
them with greater economic and political opportunities. *Shensi* Long
Yizhen and Long Yiyuan do not even appear in most accounts of the
anti–New Policy protest. They were in fact behind the scenes with Li
Guanmei and Mai Rongguang taking field leadership on behalf of their
own self-perceived interests.

Each of the five factions managed joint stock companies, or trusts
(*gongsi*), giving each network commercial as well as degree-holding
ties. The trusts were empowered by the subprefect's office to levy certain miscellaneous taxes.[41] Although each company listed one person's
name as the official tax farmer for a particular item, in fact many company members collected each of the taxes.[42] Within the dominant city
dang, for example, Mo Huixun, along with Chen Songnian and Ou
Yang, tax farmed the cow tax, while Ye Qisen and his brother tax
farmed the butcher tax. Each of these elite members was known for his
repeated misuse of both his tax powers and *shenshi* status with regard
to the rural people (*xiangmin*).[43] When new miscellaneous taxes were
introduced under the auspices of New Policy reforms, the city *dang*
headed by Deng Shaozhen was in the most powerful position to take
advantage of the reform programs and their finances.

Plans for the implementation of New Policy reforms began in early
1910. As a prelude to the election of local self-government officials,
county officials developed strategies for census collection. Wang Ling
had been sent by provincial officials to go to Lianzhou and set up a
postal office. He then became the postmaster.[44] Deng Shaozhen and
other members of the city elite (*chengshen*) were responsible for select-

TABLE 5.1
Principal Tax-Farming Networks at Lianzhou

Name	Status
Deng Shaozhen	Landowner; commercial firm owner; leader of the main city *dang*
Mo Huixun	Tax farmer (cow tax)
Ou Yang	Tax farming associate of Mo Huixun
Chen Songnian	Tax farming associate of Mo Huixun
Ye Qisen	Tax farmer (butcher tax)
Ye Qisu	Tax farming associate and brother of Ye Qisen
Huang Zhiyi	New school manager
Pan Fengyi	Colporteur for the local Presbyterian mission; *shendong*; census taker for local self-government reforms
Pan Fengyang	Census taker; *shendong*; brother of Pan Fengyi
Gu Zhixiang	Census taker; graduate of legal affairs who had presumably studied in Japan

Source: Zuo Shaozuo, "Lianzhou shijian riji zhailu" (Diary extracts of events at Lianzhou), *Jindai shi ziliao* (Material on modern history), 1955, no. 4, 70-84.

ing those who would take the census. Many of the persons selected were rural managers (*shendong*) who worked closely with the political elite of the city *dang*. Two Pan brothers, one of whom was a colporteur for the local Presbyterian mission, became census takers, as did Gu Zhixiang, a graduate of legal affairs who had presumably studied in Japan.[45] When the census was taken, and a wooden plaque (*dingmenpai*) was affixed to the door of each household detailing the number of occupants. At this time the census takers also collected a fee, which ostensibly was intended to pay teachers' salaries at the schools that the city elite had just recently established.[46]

The representation of these events in the local gazetteer argues the point that the door numbers were a postal address system for the convenience of the people. "Numbering the houses on a street is a practice in all countries of the world. So we can say that this is a manifestation of social progress. This is something that should have gone without meeting so much opposition."[47] According to American missionaries in the area, the rural people did not know that the census was a national project. One missionary wrote, "The special danger arises when such ignorance is accompanied, as here, by a loss of faith in their leaders. The ordinary distrust of officials was extended to include the gentry."[48] The official account confirms this impression: "They did no education to prepare the people for this. The citizens had always been oppressed and exploited by the local government, so they were always on alert against the government."[49] Villagers feared that a poll tax, coming on the heels of recent new levies on wine, pork, lumber, cows, and other items, was a portent of further tax burdens. In the villagers' view, "the taxes were as ferocious as tigers and as numerous as hairs. . . . The schools help the tiger to damage the people."[50]

On September 15, several weeks after the census taking had begun, village and *bao* (subprefectural subdivision) leaders mobilized villagers to march on Lianzhou city. The officials attempted to close the city gate, but in a massive effort, the marchers broke through the city gate; attacked several school buildings; as number of elite residences, including that of Deng Huanzhen brother of Deng Shaozhen; and the political elite's joint stock companies, including the Xiaotuanyue store and meeting hall. The protesters returned that night to destroy the wine distillery, the local real estate tax office, and the primary schools. According to a report in *Shibao*, the villagers wanted to destroy the mission church as well, but the river waters were high, so they could not get to it.[51] A total of ten buildings were damaged. An American missionary on the scene wrote, "In the weeks that followed, the whole region was kept in a state of excitement and alarm; an organization was completed and a propaganda carried out."[52] On September 21, local *shensi* Li Yabing and Xu Liujing were regarded as suspects and tied up by the protesters and beaten. Thier houses were burned.[53] Bandits from Yangshan county were gathering at the temple of Sifangyin and threatened to overrun the county seat.[54]

In the initial activism, Li Guanmei and Mai Rongguang emerged as the leaders of the commoners protest. It can be surmised from their female given names that both Li and Mai were of commoner status. Poorer families often gave their only sons female names in order to protect them from spirits who would do harm to male children. Skilled in the martial arts and locally famous as a tough and generous person who people trusted to mediate on their behalf, Li Guanmei of Hexi was about forty years old and had served in the army.[55] No further details regarding the status of Mai are mentioned by any of the local observers or investigators. The two did, however, represent a clearly defined interest group of commoner taxpayers. As one source observed, "The movement was a protest in the name of the people against increased taxation.

It objected to the offensive taxes already exacted for the new schools and took alarm at the prospect of their being increased. The gentry in charge of the schools were said to have appropriated the funds largely to their own use."[56]

Action against both the city elite's associates in the market towns and the members of the various market town *dang* began on September 23. Protesters destroyed the residences of census takers Pan Fengyi and Pan Fengyang and captured the former Pan, holding him for ransom. Over three thousand villagers participated in this action as they marched in three columns to Lianzhou middle school and the Yanxi senior high school where they smashed doors and windows and burned books.[57] According to a local observer, "The rioters in support of their claim to be ordinary citizens, representing the people, at first, carried on their work unarmed and took precautions against looting."[58] Protest organizers hung posters in the city and market towns calling for the capture of additional elite members. In response to the deteriorating situation, the subprefect ordered the cancellation of wine, rice caldron, butcher, and lumber taxes.[59] Villagers involved in the demonstrations launched several attacks against the elite members of Sanjiang market town and destroyed the new schools that the elite members had established. According to some reports, protesters were manufacturing weapons around the clock preparing for further battle.[60]

After the destruction of school buildings in Sanjiang market town on October 17, the protesters called for a meeting in nearby Beida temple. Rural leaders prepared a huge banquet and invited villagers to feast and discuss the local situation. A monastery at Shifangying village manufactured small bamboo tags with the name and several four-character phrases written on them.[61] Each household represented received, for a small fee, one of the bamboo plaques as a charm to counter the evil influence of the door plaques used in the census taking. Those assembled agreed that additional schools in the area should be destroyed and the elite members driven out. Elders chosen as protest leaders drew up a manifesto that referred to the golden age of the sage-emperors Yao and Shun, the traditional reference to a legendary time of good government and concern with public welfare.[62]

A week after this meeting, at which villagers had discussed the issues and charted a collective course of action, three thousand rural people from forty-eight *bao* around Lianzhou city carried guns and marched in nine units through the countryside to assemble their supporters. Li Guanmei led protesters from Hexibao, Shaochuibao, Liangzhangan, and Chuantang across the river to the county seat.[63] The assembled villagers proceeded to destroy the residences of Ye Qisen, Ye Qisu, and Huang Zhiyi, all of whom were associated with the city reform managers. The protesters also attacked the schools that Huang had established, destroying furniture and other items on the premises. Huang, for his part, took advantage of the chaos created by the attacks. He started a fire that destroyed his account books, thereby eliminating evidence that could have implicated him in the mismanagement of local fiscal affairs. Shortly afterward, he telegraphed the provincial minister of education and requested compensation for his losses.[64] Many of the city elite members left the subprefecture as soon as the fighting began.[65]

Subprefect Tang requested troops to suppress the disturbance, but Daotai Zuo Shaozuo disapprovingly remarked, "To treat the people who resist as rebels is bad management. . . . How can troops be sent? These people will be killed. The city gentry must be behind this request for troops."[66] He said further that the disturbance was "a distillation of grievous spirits in the area."[67] As the resistance grew, local secret societies and bandit groups joined the protesters' movement. On October 31, Sanjiang was attacked once again and held under seige by the protesters.[68] In early November, the rural people suddenly gathered in Shaoshui *bao*. They slaughtered pigs for a feast. Several thousand people were present. At this gathering they elected Li Guanmei as their leader and demanded that prefect Wu cross the river to meet him. Wu ordered his lieutenant to cross the river for the meeting. When the lieutenant saw the situation was about to boil over, he dared not stay and returned to his camp.[69] The vice officer of the Sanjiang defense could not carry out an effecive defense, so he reported to the province for assistance from Sanguan prefecture and together they made an attempt. At the same time, there was a campaign going on in Huaiji and other counties just across the border in Guangxi province, so the bandits traveled eastward from Guangxi to Guangdong in support of the rebellion in Lianzhou. Thousands of bandits poured into the area, built fortifications, and set up cannons in resistance. They attacked the official troops several times. Army commanders retaliated and took over the bandits' fortification. They killed eight bandits and captured six others who were put on trial and executed. Li Guanmei and the famous bandit Li Yaxing commandeered some riverboats and confiscated grain for their campaign.[70] According to some reports, the bandits were the first to fire shots. The conflict lasted for three to four hours before the bandits made a retreat. They refused to disband, however. Mai Rongguang gained the support of all the villages in Liusha for an attack on Lianzhou city. Several branches of bandits, five to six hundred strong, led by Ou Jinshen, Li Yashi, and Li Dongshi came over to Mai Rongguang's side for this rally.[71]

In the destruction that accompanied the second attack on Sanjiang, protesters demolished American Presbyterian missionary property.

Schools financed with fees levied by the various *dang* through their trusts were a primary target of the collective commoner violence. Because it had been years since the missionary schools were managed by an American, Miss Johnston, the protesters apparently assumed that these schools too were a part of the new program to extract additional miscellaneous fees from the taxpayers. The U.S. consul at Canton came to the conclusion that, "The attack on the Sam Kong school and chapel may be explained by the mob's thinking they were native schools, as they were wholly under the charge and direction of Chinese."[72] Missionaries in the area reported that this destruction "was due to the large mixture of foreign elements in the mob and to the excitement of the occasion."[73] The report goes on to note that in spite of the excitement, there was no looting, and targets were limited to property associated with the new school managers.

The protest was not simply a matter of conflict between the commoners and the "gentry." Differences among the gentry existed before the advent of New Policy reforms and were accentuated by those programs. During the initial establishment of new schools from 1903 to 1907, the market town elite networks had squeezed the commoners for taxes just as the city elite members had. With the introduction of plans for self-government in 1910, these *shensi* based outside the county seat but with connections to the subprefect became a new kind of political elite whose authority imposed even greater financial burdens on the commoner taxpayers. The protesters' main target was the property of the city *dang* headed by Deng Shaozhen, but, on two separate occasions, they also destroyed residences and schools belonging to the Sanjiang market town *dang*.

According to Wang Zhongfu, the postmaster who reported to Daotai Zuo Shaozuo on the Lianzhou incident, the dispute over the *dingmenpai* developed out of already existing hostilities among the various *dang*. The commoners became involved immediately afterwards.[74] Because the procedure of posting door placards was conducted by the city elite with the help of the yamen runners, it had worked to the disadvantage of both the various market town *dang* and the village taxpayers.[75] A *shenshi* known to be a degree-holder was among the market town *dang* members who opposed the posting of the *dingmenpai*.[76]

The market town merchants also made a bid for the sympathies, if not the support, of the foreign community in Canton. In a report to the *South China Morning Post,* they expressed concern for the safety of foreign property in Sanjiang and hastened to point out the important role that merchants had played in protecting European lives during the current crisis. They also noted the deplorable destruction of property suffered by elite members who had residences and businesses in Sanjiang and other villages outside the subprefectural city. The merchants went on to blame the protest entirely on the incompetence of the local civil and military officials, and the opportunism of the bandits who incited villagers already concerned that tax increases would follow the census taking.[77] Although satisfied to see their city rivals attacked by the rural taxpayers, the market town merchants were dismayed when their own *dang* members were also taken to task by the commoners for their exploitative behavior.

An American living in Lianzhou added this perspective to the discussion of the events at Lianzhou:

> Scholars of the old schools left behind in the new order of things are generally held responsible for inciting the people. The people, on their part, have had some just ground of complaint against the method of raising money for the schools through trusts. These trusts have had the power of levying a duty on every sale of such leading commodities as beef, pork and lumber. The people were further aroused by wild stories of increased taxation to follow the census.[78]

"Scholars of the old school" could refer to degree-holders not associated with any *dang* networks, or it could refer to the market town *dang* members. If the first definition is used, then there is evidence that a third sector of the local degree-holders was involved in the commoners' cause. If the second definition was the intended meaning, then it can only be concluded that the market town merchants' plan backfired when their own members came under attack. In either case, the developing disturbance became an opportunity for groups with diverse motives to serve their own interests.

By early December the resistance was almost three months old. More than one thousand villagers attended a meeting held at Xiaoshui *bao* on December 7 to discuss further courses of action. They decided that Li Guanmei should demand a meeting with Prefect Wu for the purpose of negotiating a settlement. Wu sent one of his majors to talk with Li and his supporters. However, since the major would not compromise and Li's forces were too large for the major to attempt to capture the rebel leader, negotiations broke down. On December 9, the prefect gave orders for troops to cross the river and enter the rebel territory.[79] In response, the villagers organized themselves into fighting units and formed an alliance with the local bandit groups led by Shi Shijiao and Li Yashi.[80]

A major victory for Li Guanmei and his fellow taxpayers occurred at Sanshuitong on December 11. Majors Chu and Huang led scout parties into the rural areas to clear out bands of rebels. Protesters had already captured many guard boats along the river and had cut off communications with Canton. When the troops reached Sanshuitong, rebel forces surprised them and inflicted heavy losses before reinforcements could arrive. Rebel units, encamped at a location they designated the "Square Camp," rushed to the battlefield in organized groups of ten to one hundred or more men. When support for the government troops finally arrived, six of the rebel leaders were captured and beheaded, and others were allowed to return home on condition that they persuade their supporters to disperse.[81]

By the end of December, the rebel forces had once again retreated to their base of Dalongshan[82] in the mountains, and there were no further major attacks. Li Guanmei, who had originally led the resistance to the *dingmenpai* and the new taxes, escaped and joined the bandits; his associate, Mai Rongguang, also fled the area.[83] The resistance lost momentum by January, but it was not because of a resounding military defeat. Provincial government troops in this case were poorly commanded and disciplined. They traveled in defenseless boats and took two weeks to arrive by water, on a trip that would have taken five days had they traveled by an overland route.[84] The protesters had successfully punished those persons against whom they had grievances, but were unable to maintain control of the area and to fulfill their plan of ridding the subprefecture of elite influence. Enthusiasm for continuing the effort eventually subsided. Li Guanmei was eventually betrayed by former supporters, captured on January 26, and executed.[85]

In the official settlement of this case, Zhang Qiling, governor of Guangdong and Guangxi, placed the blame on the Lianzhou subprefect. He had failed to explain the census investigation in advance to the populace, and he had chosen the wrong people to carry out the census. As a result of his negligence, people suffered. The vice subprefect at Sanjiang had not done enough to eliminate bandit activity in his area. Zhang Qiling recommended that the local elite be investigated and placed under strict surveillance. Once the area was calm, the census investigation could be put in the hands of other individuals and carried out. To restore order as quickly and effectively as possible, Zhang suggested that families who had suffered should be compensated. Missionaries were to be extended official protection, but because they were unhurt, no compensation was offered even though the American consul in Guangzhou had made the request.[86] In the spring of 1911, when the incident of opposing the door number plates had died down, the Lianzhou prefectural middle school and the Yenxi primary school resumed activity.[87]

Lianzhou was but one of a dozen recorded antitax uprisings in Guangdong from 1910 to 1911.[88] Protest also occurred at Dabu, Nanhai, and Jinan, among other districts, but there is little detailed information on these cases.[89]

Conclusions

Rural dissent drew both antiforeign and antigovernment themes into a place-based critique of New Policy ramifications for the rural political economy. The individuals who acted out hostility to foreigners in Lianzhou in 1905 came from among underemployed and unemployed youths. Local observers had, in fact, reported a visible increase in tension in the area just prior to the 1905 attack when in order to raise revenue for county reforms, the governor announced in 1903 his intention to introduce a new lottery system that would give the government a monopoly on gambling and close down many of the favorite local gambling places. In June 1904, local residents attacked and demolished one of the new lottery shops and demonstrated before the yamen offices to make their views known. In response, the subprefect cancelled plans for the lottery, and protesters were impressed with their success in the matter.[90] Emboldened by this success, young men from the same social groups moved in 1905 to destroy local institutions that embodied foreign presence and were linked to the government's need for additional revenue. Resistance to New Policy reforms continued to develop interconnected opposition to foreign presence and government reforms. Farmers and agricultural laborers became the core of the anti–New Policy movements, leaving other groups to join in rather than lead.

The cases of anti–New Policy protest in south China affirm the general picture of viable local communities throughout China struggling to sustain themselves through confrontation with similar political and economic dynamics emanating from the provincial and national levels throughout this period. The introduction of reforms stimulated both competition among local merchant firms and an increase in taxes on local consumer goods, but the responses to these changes varied depending on the local array of preexisting political alliances and socioeconomic groups. The following features summarize points of comparison and analysis that emerge in these county studies of rural resistance to reform: (1) the emergence of a new political elite against the backdrop of competition among local merchant firms, (2) competition between the political elite and the subbureaucracy for control of the collection of all taxes, (3) the moral and political issues that combined with economic burdens to fuel opposition to the reform measures, and (4) the component of independent commoner organization and leadership in alliances to check the expansion of elite power in the rural areas.

Competition among tax-farming firms at Lianzhou, Guangdong, for example, for the authority to collect new taxes was fierce and overt. The most powerful firms organized themselves into five separate networks. Initially each network or *dang,* several of which included degree-holders, collected fees to fund the establishment of new schools under its own control. Eventually, the city network that had the closest ties with the subprefect moved to claim more tax authority for itself, but it never possessed exclusive control of the fiscal and administrative aspects of reform. By contrast with Laiyang, Shandong, there was no history of financial cooperation and political dependence between the local subprefect and a single group among the local elite. Those who became reform managers at Laiyang monopolized county affairs in a patttern that tended to make open competition risky for the politically unprotected local merchants. In the pattern of developments at Yongshun, Guangxi, the political elite took advantage of its new authority not by collecting new taxes but by appointing tax farmers to do this work for it. Reform managers received the funds for the New Policy programs, but they did not have to assume the hazardous responsibility of collecting the new taxes and surcharges. No one group of tax farmers dominated. Instead, many groups competed for the authority to levy new taxes, and only those successful in raising the set amount were allowed to continue in this capacity.

Roles played by degree-holders also varied. Among the competing networks at Lianzhou, degree-holders were numerous, which was not the case at Laiyang. In spite of the larger number of merchant degree-holders at Lianzhou, they did not venture to establish principal business interests outside of the subprefecture, as did merchant degree-holders in the next case to be considered, Chuansha, Jiangsu. Lianzhou was a more remote county, whereas Chuansha had proximity to Shanghai. As a result, competition was stiffer within Lianzhou, and no one group gained the upper hand with respect either to the other commercial networks or to the subbureaucracy, which continued to exercise its interests by collecting the land taxes.

Persons who took up the leadership of protest against new taxes were placed by occupation and status at strategic points in local economic and political relations. Such persons articulated the interests of large numbers of rural residents. At Cenqi, Guangxi, for example, Chen Rongan, local militia leader and lineage headman, took up protest leadership when the county subprefect attempted to confiscate local militia funds for reform purposes. Occupying a key position as militia leader, lineage head, and local popular figure, Chen was personally inclined to lead the resistance to local officials and, for the same reasons, had widespread popular support. At Chuansha, where temple managers occupied strategic positions in the commoner community, and Laiyang, where *shezhang* and village headmen were the principal spokesmen for family and community interests, the same general pattern prevailed.

Rather than viewing these events simply as local response to national developments, I would like to consider these rural movements in the context of the history of place, an analytical framework emphasizing near-subsistence agriculturalists in their ecological and social relations. Only within such a context do the meanings of actions taken at great cost by Qu Shiwen, Li Guanmei, Liao Guanyin, and others reveal their full significance for their own setting and for the present. Activism within the history of place was an assertion against the encroachments of the dynamics set in motion by the introduction of New Policy reforms. A web of particular commercial and political relations structured life in a given county and linked it to conditions beyond the county. The nature of economic connections to major urban centers, density of degree-holders, and the patterns of county yamen politics among other factors were all a part of the configurations against which dissenting farmers struggled to continue to define themselves and their relationship to their natural and social environments.

Notes

Epigraph: Zuo Shaozuo, "Lianzhou shijian riji zhailu" (Diary extracts of events at Lianzhou), in *Jindai shi ziliao* (Materials on modern history) (Beijing: Kexue chuban she, 1955), no. 4, 72, 81.

1. Rev. Arthur J. Brown, D.D., *The Lien-chou Martyrdom* (New York: The Willet Press, 1905), 3.

2. Ibid., 20–21.

3. Ibid., 3, 20.

4. Ibid., 19.

5. Edward J. M. Rhoads, "Nationalism and Xenophobia in Kwangtung (1905–6): The Canton Anti-American Boycott and the Lienchow Anti-Missionary Uprising," in *Papers on China* (Cambridge: Harvard University, History Department, 1962), 167.

6. Brown, *The Lien-chou Martyrdom*, 5.

7. Huang Shaosheng, "Lianzhou guangfu qianhuo" (Lianzhou recovery) in *Xinhai geming yu Guangdong* (Guangdong and the 1911 Revolution), Ding Shencun, ed. (Guangzhou: Guangdong renmin chuban she, 1991), 26, 27.

8. Edward Rhoads in his study of this case concluded that the 1905 incident was a "spastic gasp of an anarchronistic xenophobia," similar to in his view of the Boxer uprising five years earlier. Rhoads, "Nationalism and Xenophobia in Kwangtung (1905–6)," 184.

9. Brown, *The Lien-chou Martyrdom*, 14–15.

10. Ibid., 9.

11. Ibid., 17.

12. Ibid., 19.

13. Arthur H. Smith, *China in Convulsion* (New York: Fleming H. Revell Co., 1901), vol. 2, 739.

14. Ibid., vol. 1, 77.

15. Ibid., vol. 2, 737–38.

16. Rhoads, "Nationalism and Xenophobia in Kwangtung (1905–6)," 167.

17. Edward Rhoads, *China's Republican Revolution: The Case of Kwangtung, 1895–1913*, (Cambridge: Harvard University Press, 1975), 8–11.

18. Rhoads, "Nationalism and Xenophobia in Kwangtung (1905–6)," 170.

19. Ibid.

20. Ibid., 171.

21. Michael H. Hunt, *The Making of a Special Relationship, The United States and China to 1914* (New York: Columbia University Press, 1983), 245.

22. Rhoads, *China's Republican Revolution,* 89.

23. Brown, *The Lien-chou Martyrdom,* 14.

24. Ibid., 15.

25. Ibid., 12.

26. Huang Shaosheng, "Lianzhou guangfu qianhuo," 25.

27. Ibid., see the cases of Deng Ganchen, 24, and Mo Huixiang, 25.

28. Ibid., 23. Lülin Uprising in 17 A.D.

29. Huang Shaosheng, "Lianzhou guangfu qianhou," 27.

30. Ibid., 25–26.

31. Harold Z. Schiffrin, *Sun Yat-sen and the Origins of the Chinese Revolution* (Berkeley: University of California Press, 1968), 243.

32. For a discussion of the Ping-Liu-Li uprising of 1906 see Joseph W. Esherick, *Reform and Revolution in China: The 1911 Revolution in Hunan and Hubei* (Berkeley: University of California Press, 1976), 58–65. Also see, Harold Z. Schiffrin, *Sun Yat-sen and the Origins of the Chinese Revolution,* 253.

33. National Archives, United States (Washington, D.C.), Numerical File of the Department of State, 1906–1910, no. 215; V. L. Savage, May 25, 1907; W. J. B. Fletcher, June 12, 1907; Reverend Bach to Bergholz, June 11, 1907. Rhoads, *China's Republican Revolution: The Case of Kwangtung, 1895–1913*, 110–11.

34. National Archives, 215/81, Bergholz, Canton, October 21, 1907.

35. Ibid., no. 215: Hansser to Bergholz, June 13, 1907.

36. National Archives, United States (Washington, D.C.), Records of the Department of State, 1910–1929, decimal file, no. 690: Bergholz, Canton, October 17, 1910.

37. For a brief discussion of the Lianzhou case, see Rhoads, *China's Republican Revolution,* 177–79.

38. Zuo Shaozuo, "Lianzhou shijian riji zhailu," 79.

39. Zhang Qiling, "Shu liang zongdu Zhang Qiling qi Lianzhou xiangmin kang dingmenpai" (Memorial to the emperor from Zhang Qiling the governor of Guangdong and Guangxi provinces on the resistance to the door plates at Lianzhou), in *Xinhai geming qian shinian wen minbian dangan shiliao* (Archive materials on people's activism in the ten years before the 1911 Revolu-

tion), comp. Beijing Teacher's University History Department (Beijing: Zhong-hua Shuju, 1985), no. 274, 479–480.

40. Zuo Shaozuo, "Lianzhou shijian riji zhailu," 74, 76.

41. Ibid., 70.

42. Ibid., 82.

43. Ibid., 76.

44. "Kangdingmenpai shijian" (The situation of resistance to door plaques) in *Lianxian zhi* (Lianxian gazetteer) section no. 7, miscellaneous records, 415.

45. Zuo Shaozuo, 74, 79.

46. Ibid., 76.

47. "Kangdingmenpai shijian," 415.

48. J. S. Kunkle, "The Lienchow Riots," *Chinese Recorder*, 42 (April 1911) 4:244.

49. "Kangdingmenpai shijian," 415.

50. Ibid., See also *Dongfang zazhi*, (Eastern Miscellany) (Shanghai), no. 11, 1910, 100.

51. "Lianzhou kangdingmenpai ta fengchao," in *Shibao* (The Eastern Times) (Shanghai), 11/5, 1910.

52. Kunkle, "The Lienchow Riots," 243.

53. *Dongfang zazhi*, no. 10, 100.

54. "Lianzhou kangdingmenpai ta fengchao," in *Shibao*, 11/5, 1910.

55. "Kangdingmenpai shijian," 415.

56. Kunkle, "The Lienchow Riots," 243.

57. "Kangdingmenpai shijian," 415.

58. Kunkle, "The Lienchow Riots," 244.

59. *Dongfang zazhi*, no. 12, 1910, in *Xinhai geming* (The 1911 Revolution) (Shanghai: Renmin chuban she, 1956) 3:370.

60. *Dongfang zazhi*, no. 10, 100.

61. "Lianzhou kangdingmenpai ta fengchao," in *Shibao*, 11/5, 1910.

62. Kunkle, "The Lienchow Riots," 244.

63. *Lianxian wenshi ziliao* (Historical records of Lian County), no. 4, 44.

64. Zuo Shaozuo, "Lianzhou shijian riji zhailu," 82.

65. Kunkle, "The Lienchow Riots," 244.

66. Zuo Shaozuo, "Lianzhou shijian riji zhailu," 72.

67. Ibid., 81.

68. Ibid., 74.

69. *Dongfang zazhi*, no 12, 110.

70. Zhang Qiling, "Shu liang zongdu Zhang Qiling qi Lianzhou xiangmin kang dingmenpai," 480.

71. *Dongfang zazhi*, no. 12, 110.

72. National Archives, decimal file, no. 723: Bergholz, Canton, December 23, 1910.

73. Kunkle, "The Lienchow Riots," 244.

74. Zuo Shaozuo, "Lianzhou shijian riji zhailu," 79.

75. Ibid., 83.

76. Ibid., 73.

77. *South China Morning Post*, November 12, 1910, 7.
78. National Archives, no. 723: Kunkle to Bergholz, November 28, 1910.
79. *Dongfang zazhi*, no. 12, 1910, in *Xinhai geming*, 3:371.
80. Zuo Shaozuo, "Lianzhou shijian riji zhailu," 78–79.
81. *South China Morning Post*, December 22, 1910, 5.
82. Zhang Qiling, "Shu liang zongdu Zhang Qiling qi Lianzhou xiangmin kang dingmenpai," 481.
83. Zuo Shaozuo, "Lianzhou shijian riji zhailu," 78–79.
84. Kunkle, "The Lienchow Riots," 244.
85. Ibid., 243. Also see, "Kangdingmenpai shijian," 415.
86. Zhang Qiling, "Shu liang zongdu Zhang Qiling qi Lianzhou xiangmin kang dingmenpai," 481.
87. *Lianxian wenshi ziliao*, 45.
88. Rhoads, *China's Republican Revolution*, 176.
89. Zuo Shaozuo, "Lianzhou shijian riji zhailu," 70–71.
90. Brown, *The Lien-chou Martyrdom*, 12.

6

Chuansha, Jiangsu:
Ding Fei and Her Vegetarian Sisterhood
in Resistance to Reform

Everything was to be taxed; even if a family gave birth to a child, it must pay a tax. They [the self-government officials] were going ahead with plans to collect new taxes which had already been discussed and settled upon; they had gone to the yamen to request a proclamation for taxes. Now because of the destruction, they are unwilling to begin taxes.

—Chuansha resident, 1911

Not until early spring 1911 does Ding Fei actually appear by name in the historical record as a leader of opposition to local New Policy plans. But the local vegetarian (*chicaidang*) sisterhood to which she belonged had existed for many years. The sisterhood was part of a network of lay Buddhist circles with a history in the area that went back to the mid-nineteenth century. Ding Fei was a widow. She may have joined the vegetarian sect after her husband's death; perhaps she staunchly refused to remarry, but we do not know that for sure. What we do know is that Ding or some other members of the sisterhood from Yugong temple made their way along the narrow pathways dividing planted fields of cotton in the early summer of 1903. Their destination was an intertemple meeting with vegetarians in neighboring Nanhui county where a recent incident had occurred involving two landlord sons who had lodged a complaint with the Nanhui county magistrate against local vegetarian halls. This was not the first time that the Chuansha/Nanhui vegetarians had come to blows with members of the local elite. For almost a decade now, members of the local temples had repeatedly found themselves embroiled in disputes with landlords, Zhang Bingyi among them. It often happened that the vegetarians' only way of periodically gaining redress of their grievances was to organize an attack on

213

landlord property. Problems and new sources of conflict seemed to multiply and worsen as the years passed. Now the landlord sons, some of
whom had just returned from studying in Japan, called the vegetarian
halls a bad influence and wanted to close them. Ding, or one of her
predecessors, very likely hurried on this day to meet with other vegetarian members of her lay Buddhist sect to plan a course of action.

The landlord sons about whom the vegetarians were concerned included Huang Yanpei (1878–1965), orphaned at a young age and raised
by relatives. Huang eventually became well known as an early advocate
of vocational education in China's modernization movement. Interestingly enough, in his autobiographical notes, he makes no mention of
the vegetarians whom county records say he visited in 1903. Huang's
relationship to popular rural culture was familiar yet distant and critical.
Born fourteen years after the defeat of the Taiping Rebellion, Huang
fondly recalled as a child seeing village theatrical performances of
events from the Taiping Heavenly Kingdom. He remembered listening
to people talk about the Taiping armies in the nearby area. One Taiping
song he especially liked had this refrain:

> The Taiping leaders entered Nanjing;
> Officials were driven to their deaths.
> The rich people's worries grew heavy;
> The poor people's lives were lightened.[1]

Huang understood, so he wrote, that the Taiping peasants had opposed
the Qing but had been unable effectively to overthrow "feudalism."
The peasant revolution was destined to defeat, he argued, because its
leaders were bound by "feudal" ideas and social relations.[2] And so it is
not surprising that Huang Yanpei early in his career discounted the rural
opposition to educational and political reform. In Huang's view, Ding
Fei and the vegetarians were a part of the problem, a part of the back-
wardness of China that the foreigners were so quick to point out and
that individuals like Huang were just as quick to reinforce in their repre-
sentations of rural China to the foreigners. Modern education, economic
development, and political reform were the answers to China's ills, as
far as Huang and others were concerned.

Far from seeking to suppress groups that included strong-minded and
socially active rural women, Huang depicted himself in his memoirs as
a champion of women's progress. And by some measure he was. At
the suggestion of Cai Yuanpei, Huang Yanpei and Zhang Zhihe had
established Chuansha's first elementary school in January 1903. Although his memoirs did not mention directly the longstanding conflicts
between local elites and groupings among the poorer classes, Huang

did record that because of local tensions, Zhang Zhihe, who came from a family of means, financed the school from his own resources in order to avoid popular opposition.[3] Because the elementary school did not admit girls, Huang with his brother immediately opened a separate girls' school to educate the sisters and female cousins of his own social class.

Several months after the Chuansha elementary school was in place, Huang along with Zhang Zhihe, Lu Jiaji, Gu Ciying, recently returned from Japan, and several people from Shanghai and neighboring Nanhui county decided to establish a lecturing society to promote new ideas. It was the summer of 1903, and the *Subao* case in Shanghai was in progress. The Qing government, seeking to crack down on revolutionary anti-Qing activity, had moved to close down the offices of the newspaper *Subao* and had arrested radicals Zhang Binglin and Zou Rong among others, charging them with insulting the emperor by using improper forms of address and taboo personal names for the Qing emperor.[4] A government communique sent to all county offices called for local officials to be alert for revolutionaries in their areas and to apprehend anyone engaged in spreading revolution against the Qing. It was not always easy to tell a revolutionary from a reformer. Both were involved in establishing new schools, lecturing societies, guilds, and various other new organizations.[5] It was a situation in which circumstantial evidence of revolutionary-like activity could make major trouble for an individual. While Huang mentions this situation surrounding the events of his arrest and death sentence in the summer of 1903, he fails to note his conflict with the vegetarian halls, which was the source of the crisis.

According to the Chuansha county gazetteer records, Huang had visited a vegetarian hall during the time he was establishing new schools and lecture societies. Taking gender segregation to be the norm for old and new institiutions, Huang voiced disgust at the sight of men and women sitting together at vegetarian meetings. Subsequently, he filed a complaint with the Nanhui authorities calling for the closure of these halls, which he deemed a bad influence on girls from good families. Someone, not identified by name in any of the sources, went to the Nanhui magistrate and said that Huang and the others were preaching the overthrow of the Qing Dynasty. Huang describes this person as a local bully who made trouble for Huang simply because it was the person's habit. A biographical sketch of Huang describes the person as one of Huang's relatives. Perhaps a disgruntled poor relation? The Chuansha gazetteer says that the vegetarians sought this person out because he had some connections at the yamen and might, therefore, be able to diffuse the case against the vegetarian halls. Huang, Zhang Zhihe, Gu Ciying, and Zhang Xiangsi were arrested. Persuaded that the four were revolutionaries sought by Shanghai officials, the Nanhui magistrate sentenced them to death until a Protestant missionary, William Burke, became involved in the case. The magistrate soon dropped the issue because he did not want to become embroiled with foreigners.[6]

Although thoughts and footsteps of the Yugong sisters through the Chuansha countryside in 1903 can only be surmised, the opponents they faced eight years later had much in common with the vegetarian's earlier adversaries. Zhang Bingyi, Zhang Zhihe, Lu Jiaji, and others were among those involved in the move to raise miscellaneous taxes to fund new schools, police offices, and self-government bureaus in early 1911.

Chuansha in the Yangzi Delta:
Cotton Production and Shanghai Connections

The lower Yangzi valley and vicinity was one of China's most densely populated and extensively commercialized regions. Included in this region was the Shanghai-Suzhou area and points west along the Yangzi River valley, as well as the Ningbo Plain and its neighboring counties in northern Zhejiang. An agriculturally rich region as well as a major commercial center, the lower Yangzi was well known for its high economic productivity.

Early in the nineteenth century, Shanghai was a regional trade center more than a major interregional point of exchange. At that time, it was Ningbo to the south of Shanghai that functioned as the major exchange point for the flow of goods between north and south China. Throughout the heavily trafficked lower Yangzi, waterways were important transport routes. Southern products arrived at Ningbo in large quantities and were repackaged into smaller units for their journey along canals into north China. In reverse, this process brought products going from north to south, and Ningbo flourished as a major financial trade center.

When treaty ports and the foreign trade were imposed on China after its defeat in the Opium War (1839–42), these economic patterns began to change. Shanghai, transmuted by foreign presence, increasingly became the hub of new commercial expansion extending inland to Nanjing and beyond. Owing to the shift from inland water routes to sea transport, Ningbo lost its major role in the north-south shipment of goods. During the late nineteenth century, Ningbo's long-distance trade declined, but its role as a regional trade center flourished.[7]

As changes took place at the macroeconomic level of society, rural areas in the lower Yangzi also generated some shifts in the local economy. Through the dense market network of the lower Yangzi, farmers

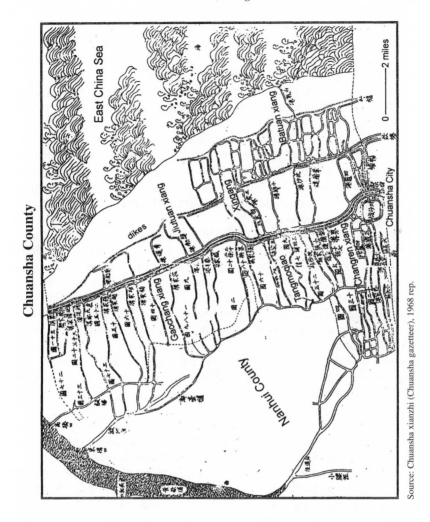

Source: Chuansha xianzhi (Chuansha gazetteer), 1968 rep.

found it profitable to specialize their activities and produce goods for market rather than strive for household self-sufficiency. In agriculture, specialization often followed climate and terrain. Hilly districts produced lumber, paper, and wax-tree oil, while foothill areas specialized in firewood, charcoal, and bamboo. In the flatlands, farmers set up cottage industries to supplement their income from rice cultivation or cotton production in those areas, such as Yuyao, Zhejiang, and Chuansha, Jiangsu, where the land was less suitable for rice growing. Cottage industries, including hats, embroidery, woven cotton fabrics, and fishnets, expanded to meet market demands as far away as Ningbo and beyond.[8]

Specialization and commercial agriculture gave farmers an additional measure of independence from the land and greater options in planning family strategies for economic well-being.[9] A peasant livelihood could be quite strong and resilient in this environment.

Owing in part to the prosperity of the lower Yangzi region, some families were able to support especially strong lineage ties. Single lineage villages were not uncommon, and lineage organizations were often the networks through which families managed both rural and urban enterprises. Wealthy lineage members typically owned business interests in major urban centers, such as Ningbo or Shanghai. While maintaining rural and urban residences, some heads of household practiced absentee landlordism, hiring managers to take care of their rural financial matters, including rent collection.[10]

Chuansha, a subprefecture of Songjiang prefecture, was located in a rich cotton-producing belt on the southeast coast of Jiangsu. Divided into five large rural divisions (*xiang*), one of which was a group of small offshore islands, Chuansha was crisscrossed by a dense network of waterways connecting numerous market towns in the area's bustling cotton exchange. The main artery of the subprefecture was a waterway lined on both sides with market towns. Tracts of land dotted with market towns and surrounded by dikes and water routes were dominant features of the Chuansha countryside. Of such importance were water routes in the landscape that the location of a rural residence in the subprefecture was often given in terms of the inlet (*gang*) on which it was situated, with no reference to villages.

Chuansha's hilly terrain was difficult to irrigate. Its proximity to the sea made much of its water salty. Because rice required more water and was less resistant to saline soil, farmers found it more profitable to grow cotton. By the eighteenth century, small farmers, usually husband and wife teams, grew cotton for the market on small plots of land that they owned and that they sometimes supplemented with land that they rented. As a group they were largely independent of landlord demands and had purchasing power for household goods and food stuffs in the market places.[11] Besides growing cotton and other crops for sale at market, small farmers in the Chuansha area also earned income from spinning and weaving. Rural women purchased extra raw cotton from merchants who ran business enterprises known as "cotton cloth shops." After spinning and weaving the cotton in their homes, the women returned to the market town to sell their finished products for the best price they could get. Statistics for the Songjiang area suggest that profits from commercial crops produced only about 50 percent of household income. Spinning and weaving provided the remainder.[12]

In the early nineteenth century, the Chuansha subprefect, in order to maintain the extensive waterways that were vital to the cotton trade, had granted authority to a group of rural project directors (*xiangdong* or *dongshi*) to keep the water routes in working order. According to Mark Elvin's study of neighboring Shanghai county, the rural project directors were typically elected from among a group of rural elite members, including landlords, merchants, and degree-holders (although degree status was not a prerequisite for inclusion in this group). The project directors' considerable influence included the power to propose taxes, which, upon approval by the subprefect, would be collected by the clerks and runners and forwarded to the directors. By this means, surcharges for water conservancy were added to the land tax, collected through regular tax collection channels, and then transferred to the directors. These surcharges were collected from merchants, including shopkeepers and pawnbrokers, and from the landlords as well as from small farmers.[13]

Examining the pattern of small-town formation and economic change in the Shanghai area from 1862 to 1909 Philip C. C. Huang finds that,

> some localities adapted to changing conditions by developing new handicraft industries. Chuansha county became a center of handicraft lacing; five of its existing towns thrived with the introduction of this industry, and three new ones sprang up around it. (Handicraft towel weaving, responsible for the rise of another of its new towns, Batuan, was also a new industry.)[14]

Chuansha was one of the areas where modern textiles did not eliminate all the old handicraft industries. An expanded supply of yarn actually stimulated hand weaving. Beginning in the early 1900s, poor peasant women of Chuangsha provided most of the labor necessary for the new towel weaving industry in the area.[15] Huang calls this pattern of economic development in the Chuansha and Yangzi Delta areas a case of commercial "involution," resulting in growth without development. In this environment, "merchants appear much more as extractors than as developers," and consequently, "in the first decades of the twentieth century, at least, peasant incomes barely kept pace with population growth."[16] The peasants' struggle to maintain their livelihood was fought without much leeway and in a field of rapidly changing circumstances fraught with new pressures on rural resources.

By 1910, Chuansha's highly commercialized rural society was stratified into the following groups: (1) landless poor who made a living at weaving, hunting, fishing, and odd jobs; (2) tenants and owner-cultivators who were heavily dependent on spinning and weaving and who grew cotton, some of which they sold for rice at market; (3) minor landowners who had more surplus but who were vulnerable to excessive taxation because they lacked the protection of the elite households; (4) farming households, which engaged hired laborers and which also managed small commercial enterprises under the protection of the elite households; and (5) major or elite households, including cotton-firm owners, other merchants, landlords, and degree-holders, who maintained rural residence but enjoyed urban political and commercial connections. Landlordism among these groups was strong only in the island *xiang,* which did not involve itself in the anti–New Policy protest. In the four main *xiang,* large landlords were few in number, and family holdings of even thirty *mou* of land were unusual.[17] Large fortunes acquired by some members of the major households were made in Shanghai commercial ventures.

Gender Relations:
Women's Oppression and Dissident Discourse

Rural women of farming families participated in the anti–New Policy activism in significant numbers. Because of their double oppression by class and gender, the documentation on rural women of poorer families, who in fact played highly active and vital roles in their households and communities, is even more fragmented than that of their male counterparts. Their strength in the dissident discourse derived in part from their general absence from public political life, making their appearance in that arena all the more vivid, startling, and unexpected when they stepped forward, often as irate mothers, household managers, and shrewd marketers. A case in point occurred at Xin'an, Guangdong, in 1910 when village women who regularly tended to household marketing and family budgets became involved in tax matters. A couple of brief accounts of the protest, noted as a curiosity more than anything else, rescue this incident from historical oblivion.

A census to be taken in June in Xin'an raised the suspicion among rural women that the magistrate was planning new taxes. The women had heard that once the door number plates (*dingmenpai*) were handed out, the scholar/officials (*shensi*) of the various areas would begin to levy taxes on each individual registered by the census. On the morning of June 15, several hundred women from Gumao village poured into census-investigator Jiang Yiji's house while he himself was out at a meeting in a nearby temple. The women, according to reports, scolded those present and made their case forcefully against the further posting of door number plates. Jiang and his associates by this time had nailed 103 plates, but when they heard of this disturbance at Jiang's home they ceased their activity.[18] The next morning when the chief census investigator entered the city, the women struck gongs to call a gathering. They went to the houses of the local *shensi*, delivered their demands boldly, and destroyed household property belonging to the *shensi* to underline the seriousness of their point. For several days after this incident, they organized support and collected funds of one *yuan* to five *mao* from each household to finance their movement.

By mid-July, thousands of village women in Xin'an county had organized and assembled at the magistrate's yamen to demand some assurance that the census would not lead to additional taxes. A local source reportedly commented that "the women are very ignorant and know little, but they know the value of cash and that the officials are always on the look-out to get it out of their pockets."[19] We know very little of how the women organized or who among them became leaders, but ignorant of the census and tax issues of the day they were not, and docile they were certainly not. Bandit gangs from Jiangang Mountain and other places joined to support the women. A woman named An Nanpo whose husband had just returned from Hong Kong gathered more than a thousand women at Beidi temple and formed an association to resist the authorities. They planted a seven-star flag and burned one thousand pieces of incense. An old woman addressed people assembled outside of the temple and marched with them to the flag ceremony. They also collected two *mao* in silver coins for the association to resist the authorities.[20]

For days the women continued to demonstrate at the yamen waiting for the magistrate to appear before them. When he finally did deign to speak to them, he spoke abusively to them and acted disinterested. The women drew close, slapped him several times, and demanded that he show them full respect by holding their meeting in his official yamen offices. Once in the magistrate's chambers, the women demanded an explanation of the census markings on their doors. The beleagured official stated that a census had in fact been taken but no new taxes were planned. Dissatisfied with the answer, and showing a familiarity with official matters, the women demanded that the magistrate put his words in writing and mark them with his seal. To ensure that the magistrate would not go back on his word, the women also demanded that 1,200 copies of the statement be made and distributed to the general public.[21] Under duress, the magistrate complied, and the issue was considered settled by the protesters, who returned to their villages, having taken care of the matter.

The magistrate, however, was not willing to let the matter rest. Having been treated in his view with such unwarranted disrespect by a crowd of rough women, whom he held in contempt, he issued warrants for the arrest of five women who had participated in the demonstrations. These five women were Mrs. Wen née Feng, Mrs. Zheng née Jiang, Mrs. Zheng née Yuan, Mrs. Wu née Fan, and Mrs. Wen née Huang.[22] Once these women were in custody, the magistrate ordered that they be tortured by being forced to kneel on chains with their arms tied behind them while they were beaten. When news of this reached the villages, thousands of women and men set out for the yamen to demand the release of the five women. People beat at the gates of the yamen for two days until the women were freed. The magistrate, meanwhile, fearful of the crowd, decided to close the city gates and request troops from Guangzhou. He stated in his request that the troops were needed because revolutionaries could take advantage of the disturbed situation.[23] When news of the approaching government troops spread throughout the area, protesters planned a retreat. They withdrew to north of the county where they collected their supporters and with spears and cleavers organized to continue attacks on the *shenshi* households in the area. The women and men destroyed and plundered a number of residences. As a consequence of this resistance, the campaign to put up door plates was suspended throughout the county of Xin'an.

News of the Xin'an women spread throughout the region. One official report noted that, "although this incident happened in a local place, its influence reached the whole province."[24] The "ignorant women" of Xin'an had their counterparts in almost every district of rural China. Closer to Chuansha, in the same month and year that Xin'an women called their magistrate to account for his authorization of census taking, people in the towns and villages around Suzhou, Jiangsu, became anxious about economic and political encroachments on their livelihoods. Less than a hundred miles from Chuansha, Suzhou and many other rural districts in the vicinity became the location of a rumor articulated in the form of a vivid metaphor. According to this metaphor, names taken in the census would be placed under railroad ties installed by the Chinese government and foreigners. When trains passed along the rails, their weight would crush the names and cause the death of the individuals whose names had been collected in the census. Shortly after the census was started, uprisings broke out simultaneously in several areas. Local power brokers who worked closest with the magistrate's office at Suzhou were described by observers as greedy and abusive of their authority. The leaders and participants in the resistance were mostly village women who, by one account, "attacked the small official of the place, pulled his queue, slapped his cheeks and broke the button on his hat."[25]

One of the layers of socially inflicted hardship within rural Chinese society was the subordination of women, creating for them an additional set of difficulties beyond their status as peasant householders. A definite pattern of women's activism was also very much a part of the rural story. Bound feet or not, women were a constant presence in family and village deliberations. Beyond the images of Chinese women that come to us filtered through the lenses of Chinese elite ideology in combination with Euro-American expectations with regard to gender issues, we know relatively little of the lives of such women.[26] In circumstances of perceived injustice, not all men participated in rural dissent, and neither did all women. But a well-defined current of women's dissident activism was always present alongside the terms of their particular oppression within Chinese society. The rugged environment of the farming household differentiated by gender, but the results for both women and men could be very cruel. In times of financial crisis, families might abandon newborn daughters to exposure and certain death or sell older girls into undesireable arrangements as concubines or servants. By social design, 10 to 15 percent of the male population was also routinely abandoned to a life without family, home, and heirs, a form of generational death from the Chinese familial perspective.[27]

In the story of China's peasant movements, women had a long history of organized participation and were often highly regarded for their initiative. White Lotus believers included women, and in some areas, women members were the majority of participants.[28] The Taiping too had separate women's units, and their demand for equal distribution of land was gender blind.[29] Women were quite capable of violence in opposition to abusive authority, and they often added their own style and strengths to patterns of protest, such as using fans in martial arts and avenging the mistreatment of husbands and fathers. The Red, Blue, and Black Lantern groups organized by women alongside the Boxer movement has already been discussed in connection with the anti–New Policy resistance in Sichuan. During the 1911 Revolution, there was an active Guangdong Women's Northern Expedition Army as well as women's military and medical units in the Shanghai area.[30] Perhaps some of them were from the Xin'an area or were inspired by stories of the Taiping women. During the defense of the granary at Laiyang when it was under attack by Nian rebels, women joined the *mintuan* (people's militia) mobilization and organized themselves into groups with thirty women to a *ban* and ten *ban* to a *lian* in order to supply the men on patrol with food.[31] Remarkably numerous, these examples are part of a pattern in the rural discourse on gender. Some women organized their own activities under their own leadership through the same marketing and temple associations as did peasant men. This provided a basis for their participation in social life including an awareness of local economic and political relations and a network for collectively responding

to problems. In areas where women were engaged in cotton or silk textile production and regular marketing for family household needs, these
associations were strong. Such conditions were not uncommon, and like
the Weiyuan area already considered above, many women in the Chuansha region of Jiangsu were also engaged in cotton textile production.

The post-Boxer decade was one in which many women in the urban
centers of China came into new realizations about their own situations.
This was the time when Qiu Jin, moved by the debacle of the Boxer
suppression in Beijing, decided with great difficulty to leave her family
life and devote herself to the cause of transforming Chinese society
through education and revolution. Returning from study in Japan and
joining the Tongmenghui, she began work in her home area of rural
Zhejiang. Women's education and training were among the issues
raised by both women and men in the emerging urban culture that
would give birth in 1915 to the New Culture movement. Numerous
women's journals flourished during these years and debates arose about
extending the franchise to women under the constitutional government
that would soon be in place. In the national boycotts of 1905 and 1906
against American and Japanese goods, respectively, urban women were
some of the primary participants. New foreign- and Chinese-owned factories in Shanghai and other cities employed rural women and children,
who often formed 50 to 70 percent of the labor pool. The labor movement of the May Fourth era would arise out of their activism. Common
ground among these women's groups had only vague social articulation
in this decade.

New Policy Reform at Chuansha:
The Makings of Conflict

The anti–New Policy activism at Chuansha was preceeded by a number
of recorded disturbances in the Yangzi Delta in 1910 at Ixing[32] and
Wuyang,[33] and in Zhejiang between Lake Tai and Ningbo at Tongxiang,[34] Cixi and Shangyu,[35] and Deqing.[36] In Nanhui county adjacent
to Chuansha, protest also took shape in March 1911. What distin-
quished the case at Chuansha was the visibility of rural women in the
protest and the relatively extensive coverage the case attracted in news
sources. In a list of rural activism in Jiangsu during this period compiled
by Wang Shuhuai in his study of modernization, the events at Chuansha
stand out as one of the three most extensive, and the best documented,
of thirty-seven attacks on New Policy–related institutions and officials
in different counties throughout the province.[37]

Initial plans for self-government in Chuansha had begun in the fall of

1909. At this time the first fees for self-government were levied. The Jiangsu Provisional Provincial Assembly resolved that self-government fees should be collected along with the tribute grain tax. At the spring harvest, twenty cash were added to each tael of assessed grain tribute, and in the autumn forty cash were added.[38] Furthermore, in 1909 the county notables petitioned the subprefect to request that a tax on tea and pigs be collected and used for the purpose of preparing for self-government. In March 1910, Chuansha Subprefect Chengan, who had taken office in April 1909, ordered rural director Wu Daben to oversee the establishment of self-government bureaus throughout the subprefecture. By November of that year a bureau was established in each *xiang,* and elections had begun for officials who would manage each bureau. As of December 1910, the self-government bureaus themselves were collecting the tea and pig taxes directly, instead of indirectly through the yamen subbureaucracy, as taxes had traditionally been collected.[39]

The Chuansha elite that managed New Policy reforms evolved from the group of nineteenth-century "rural project directors" (*xiangdong* or *dongshi*), which, as mentioned earlier, oversaw the maintenance and repair work on waterways vital to the local cotton trade. Elections for self-government positions were conducted in much the same manner as the selection of traditional rural project directors. Candidates were chosen from among the rural elite by a group of their peers. Further balloting for the elections in Changren *xiang* were scheduled when the uprising broke out in that area. The new directors attempted to levy taxes for self-government purposes just as the old directors had collected waterway conservancy fees. Eventually, however, the new directors sought to circumvent the yamen subbureaucracy of clerks and runners and collect taxes through institutions that they themselves controlled, such as their shops, their own commercial firms, or self-government bureaus.

Of the thirty-two officials whose residences were destroyed during the Chuansha uprising, sixteen had lower degree-holding status. All but two of these degrees were acquired by the regular examination route between 1877 and 1904. Of the remaining two, one was a military *shengyuan,* and the other was a *guoxuesheng,* equivalent to a *shengyuan.* Elite biographies in the Chuansha gazetteer include many men who were wealthy merchants, but social prestige and bureaucratic connections acquired through a degree or title were still coveted by the already wealthy. Gu Yiyuan, a subprefectural self-government assemblyman, an owner of two commercial firms, and a lower degree-holder (*guoxuesheng*) himself, saw to it that his son became a lower degree-holder.[40] The powerful Zhang lineage, which only a generation before had enhanced its prosperity through commerce in Shanghai, produced three self-government officials in 1910. Zhang Wenming was a self-govern-

ment assistant rural director (*xiangzuo*) who owned a cotton cloth firm
and a power loom workshop, which he operated in the courtyard of his
residence. Zhang Shouli, also of the Zhang lineage, was a subprefectural self-government assemblyman and military *shengyuan.* Zhang
Aihe was a subprefectural assemblyman.[41]

As rural directors became self-government officials, a division developed between these new directors (*xindong*) and the old-style directors
(*jiushi dongshi* or *jiudong*), who were not chosen as such officials in
1910. According to some sources, the old-style directors did not qualify
for the self-government positions because they were opium smokers
or were not interested in reforms. Bang Shoujin, one prominent *jiushi
dongshi,* was a landlord and a merchant, but unlike all of those who
became self-government officials in addition, Bang was not a member
of the Pudong Club, a merchant association of Chuansha residents in
Shanghai.[42] This association was the principal organizing unit of those
who were elected to self-government positions; their connections as degree-holders were important but secondary. From their meeting hall
above a bank in the South Market (Nanshi) area of Shanghai, the landsmann association discussed such matters as foreign banking, a fishery
established by self-government managers in Nanhui, which was meeting resistance from local fishermen, and the events at Chuansha.[43]

So close was the tie between the self-government officials and the
Pudong Club, that when those officials whose residences were destroyed by protesters were told to return to Chuansha for the settlement
of the case, the hostels and meeting rooms typically occupied by the
Chuansha elite at the Pudong Club were completely empty except for a
few servants and minimal staff.[44] In addition to their merchant interests
in Shanghai, a number of self-government officials owned commercial
firms that dealt in trading products of the lower Yangzi area. Several
officials were engaged in cotton textile manufacturing or related enterprises. With the advent of New Policy reforms in Chuansha, the old-
style directors in the city as well as in the countryside were displaced
through elections for self-government offices by a network of local elite
members who excelled in business.

Although only a few new taxes were actually collected for self-government in Chuansha by early 1911, the taxpayers had in fact been
experiencing a gradual increase in the land tax and miscellaneous taxes
for almost a decade. Kathryn Bernhardt, in her study of land taxes in
the lower Yangzi region during the post-Taiping era, finds that at Chuansha land taxes did not rise significantly until the early 1890s. Until the
turn of the century the real tax burden declined in all categories except
the cotton land tax. After 1900, taxes began to outpace prices and the
real tax burden rose significantly for most landowners with payment in

debased copper cash coins amounting to a 26 percent tax increase on rice land and a 27 percent increase on cotton land between 1897 and 1909.[45] Large landowners usually attempted to pass tax increases along to tenants in the form of higher rents. An examination of miscellaneous taxes shows that in 1902 a stamped receipt tax (*chuanpiao*) was levied, requiring each landowning household to pay five cash at each harvest for the purpose of funding schools. Of the proceeds from this tax, 30 percent were to go to the prefecture and 70 percent were to be kept by the subprefecture for local schools.[46] Between 1900 and 1909, total taxation in Chuansha had almost doubled.[47] This general picture of rising taxation lent credibility to the widespread fear that many new plans were under way to squeeze the commoner rural residents. A new prohibition decreed by the self-government officials against drying cloth on the street embankments led to speculation that the fines for violators would in fact amount to a tax on home-loom-woven cloth, since the weavers had no other place to dry their cloth. Similarly, it was feared that new fishing regulations, again legislated by the self-government assembly, would mean a tax on fishing as traditionally conducted by the local people.[48]

In spite of their growing political and economic influence, the self-government officials had not yet acquired control of the local tax collecting apparatus, which could have put muscle in their plans for new miscellaneous taxes. By early 1911, the subbureaucracy was still powerful. The yamen clerks and runners continued to supervise the chest into which land taxes were paid, thereby controlling the principal source of revenue in the subprefecture. However, a recent resolution of the Chuansha self-government assembly sought to change this arrangement by strongly suggesting that the self-government agencies take control of the land taxes.

Additional reorganization plans, designed ostensibly to eliminate subbureaucratic exploitation and corruption, also threatened the vested interests of the clerks and runners. According to Yao Wennan, an investigator for the Pudong Club, the Chuansha self-government meetings had adopted resolutions that called for (1) abolishing the positions of dike administrator (*tangzhang*) and "dike runner" (*tangchai*); (2) levying new commercial taxes; (3) prohibiting vegetarian meeting places; (4) abolishing the land-tax "chest fee" (*guijia*), which was the prerogative of the clerks and runners; (5) abolishing the customary fees for clerks and runners in Jiutuan *xiang* and Batuan *xiang;* (6) prohibiting gambling and opium smoking; (7) reorganizing control of land along the numerous creeks in Chuansha; and (8) abolishing the fees that *dibao* and *baojia* personnel had to pay to the clerks and runners to gain their positions.[49]

The self-government officials did not control a policing agency that could enforce new miscellaneous taxes and other new measures contemplated. Because of the difficulty in collecting taxes for the police bureau from shop owners, and probably because of the opposition of clerks and runners, Chuansha had not yet successfully established a modern police department, despite proposals to create one. Plans for a new police bureau began in August 1906, when Subprefect Changan asked Bang Shoujin, a merchant and old-style director, to oversee the establishment of a police office. Bang recruited local gentry sons as police officers and designated a drill ground at the Guandi temple. The project folded, however, owing to lack of funds. Again in October 1909, the subprefect ordered Bang and Gu Yiyuan, who later became a subprefectural self-government assemblyman, to arrange for drill instruction at the Guandi temple, which was later used as a self-government office. However, without funds, the police staff for the entire subprefecture dwindled to only eight people.[50] In the aftermath of the uprising, an advocate of self-government identified the lack of coercive authority to support reforms as the single factor most responsible for the initial failure of those reforms. He therefore proposed that militia units (*tuanlian*) be organized in conjunction with a national physical education program to train police forces, which would strengthen the proponents of New Policy reforms.[51]

Character of the Chuansha Uprising:
Its Organization and Logic

Women in Songjiang prefecture, where Chuansha was located, were extensively involved in the economic life of the area. This was particularly true of those women who were members of families with little or no land and of those who sought to live outside of traditional roles. In addition to working the land with their husbands, rural women did most of the home spinning and weaving of cotton yarn. Daily trips to the market towns to purchase new loads of raw cotton and sell their finished products gave rural women high visibility in the local economy. It also provided them with experience and contacts that extended beyond the family and village units. Salt production was another major industry in Chuansha and neighboring Nanhui county, and it was primarily women who were involved in the strenuous work of processing and transporting the salt.[52]

In addition to the economic side of women's roles at Chuansha, there were also important cultural dimensions of women's lives in local popular Buddhist beliefs. Many women and men in Chuansha and Nanhui were lay members of a Buddhist vegetarian sect (*chicaidang*) that up-held the principle of equality between men and women. Writing on themes in Chinese rebel ideologies, Yuji Muramatsu has noted the polit-ical threat with which officials associated vegetarian groups. Lay mem-bers worshipped and ate together, and were inclined to public criticism of the government when specific issues arose.[53] Consequently, the vege-tarians were both culturally and politically subversive within the ortho-dox framework of hierarchical human relations and obedience to au-thority. The folk Buddhist practice of worshipping female deities played an important part in establishing the spiritual authority of women vege-tarian leaders.

Vegetarian halls also functioned as mutual aid establishments for women who sought to live unmarried or to remain unmarried once they had been widowed. In the Chuansha-Nanhui area it was often difficult for families to find brides for their sons. The ratio of women to men in Chuansha in 1910 was recorded as roughly three to four.[54] As a result of the scarcity of brides and the refusal of some women to marry, the custom developed whereby the family of the prospective son-in-law had to pay a dowry and various other gifts to the family of the bride-to-be before she would be allowed to marry.[55] This was the reversal of the more common rural situation in which a daughter was an economic handicap to her parents, who themselves had to pay the dowry at the time of marriage. Widows also often refused to remarry, further con-tributing to the shortage of marriageable women. In both Chuansha and Nanhui, a practice called "to carry away the widow" (*guangshuang*) developed, whereby a family would pay a local bully to trick or force a widow to marry into its household.[56] It was perhaps as a means of counterattacking that so many widows joined together in vegetarian sis-terhoods. Ding Fei (Mrs. Ding née Fei), the initiator of the protest against New Policy reforms at Chuansha, was herself a widow and the leader of a sisterhood group within her larger following, which included both men and women.

Those elite members who compiled the histories of Chuansha and Nanhui considered the vegetarian halls to be blemishes on local cus-toms. According to them, the halls encouraged young girls from good families to think of wayward behavior, namely, nonorthodox lives as unmarried adult women. In fact, the recognition of the economic value of women's work and images of women from the folk Buddhist tradi-tions were woven into the local folk culture as a whole, creating close contact as well as friction between heterodox beliefs of rural common-ers who subscribed as lay members to the vegetarian sect and the atti-tudes of villagers who did not participate directly in sect activities. This is especially well-illustrated in the rich tradition of folk songs from the Chuansha area, which display remarkably proud and confident self-images of women as well as the envy and misery of the daughter-in-law. One song describes a goddess at work dressed in an apron of flowers:

> The goddess carries a small hoe;
> A turban of stars wraps around her head,
> An apron of flowers spreads over her stomach
> And drewdrops settle on her white breasts.[57]

The blending of White Lotus elements and local folk culture is evident here in the parallels between this song and the following passage from the Dragon Flower Scripture, which describes the children of the Eternal Mother:

> their heads [those of the son and daughter of the Eternal Mother] were surrounded with light, [on] their bodies [they wore clothes] of five colors, and with their feet they rode on two [magic] wheels[58]

Small girls are included in this imagery as well:

> Dressed in a blouse as white as the moon,
> A seven year old girl gazes at the fields
> With a small hoe in hand.[59]

Some of the Chuansha folk songs speak of unmarried daughters who are the pride of their parents and rivals to their sisters-in-law:

> The beautiful daughter visits her parents;
> Mother calls her "dear one,"
>
> Father calls her "little flower,"
> Elder brother calls her "younger sister,"
> And elder brother's wife calls her "troublemaker."
>
> The beautiful daughter opens the cooler
> And eats father's food.
> She opens the trunk
> And wears mother's clothes.
>
> The beautiful daughter does not
> Eat the white rice from elder brother's fields.
> She does not wear the wedding clothes
> From elder brother's wife's trunk.[60]

A Chuansha ditty designed to taunt unmarried women expressed the social pressure that was a part of the tensions surrounding the status of young women: "The adult unmarried woman weaves cloth; the smelly cow turns the mill."[61] Other hints of association with folk Daoist/Buddhist traditions also surface in these songs:

> Country girls are lazy.
> Weaving cloth,
> They are not happy;
> Burning incense,
> They are happy.
>
> Dressed in red shoes
> With green pull tabs
> And embroidered knee pants,
> The young women tie grasses
> Into bundles for fuel.
>
> They walk along the roads
> In lively, noisy groups
> Traveling to the Dragon Flower Pagoda.
>
> Inside the front door of the pagoda
> There are Daoists exercising;
> Inside the back door Buddhists exercise.
> Their exercised bodies are trim and slender,
> Their manly spirit is not good.[62]

Remarkably, it was also the local custom in the area to refer to Guandi, the warrior god, as Lao Taitai—"old woman."[63]

The spark that ignited the Chuansha protest in February 1911 was an attempt by the local self-government bureau of Changren *xiang* to take over for its own use several rooms in the Yugong temple, a local vegetarian community center. The initiator of the demonstration was Ding Fei, the widow who was the manager of Yugong temple, situated in the town of Tangmuqiao on the border adjoining Chuansha subprefecture and Nanhui county. When the self-government officials of Changren *xiang* first made known their intention to establish their bureau in the temple, the local common people and followers of Ding protested. Toward this end, they enlisted the aid of Gong Xiaojiang, a recently selected rural director from Nanhui, who was an owner of several hundred *mou* of land and who had connections with the Pudong Club. Gong gave the opinion that although the temple could temporarily be used as a self-government office, self-government regulations did not provide for permanent use of temple property. Gong thus sought to strike a compromise between the two sides. However, the Changren *xiang* offi-

cials maintained that the regulation did provide for permanent use, and
Subprefect Chengan sent a notice to this effect to Nanhui Magistrate
Lai, since the jurisdiction over the temple could belong also to Nanhui.
The commoners then attempted to persuade Gong Xiaojiang to take
their grievances to the subprefect, but Gong would not do this in view
of the official orders.[64]

Subsequently, when a self-government plaque was put up on the temple door, Ding Fei gathered her supporters for action. Among Ding
Fei's principal aides was Zhang Axi, a vegetarian from Nanhui. A hundred people, many of whom were women vegetarians, gathered and tore
down the self-government plaque on February 7, the day on which local
self-government officials had called a meeting at the Chengren *xiang*
office in preparation for further self-government elections. As a result,
Ding Fei was arrested, and one of her collaborators, Cao Asi, a local
constable (*dibao*), was ordered by the subprefect to be beaten. Imprisoned only a short time, Ding Fei bribed a runner to release her. She
immediately set about the tasks of vehemently criticizing self-government officials for their misbehavior and organizing vegetarian groups
to plan for a militant redress of their grievances.[65]

During the first week and a half that Ding Fei was at large, she sought
support from all of the nearby areas, and from the sixth district (*tu*) of
Nanhui county in particular. The sixth district was the meeting place
for the vegetarians during their Lotus Boat festival, which took place
in the second month of the lunar year, usually mid-March. Now the
vegetarians and their supporters called an emergency meeting in mid-
February to discuss the difficulties created by the self-government reforms and to decide on possible actions.[66] Subsequently, the sister
groups led by Ding Fei met at the Yugong temple to summon the aid of
Yulaoye, the patron deity of their temple, and to ask for three thousand
"spirit troops" to aid them.[67] Chuansha had also been one of the locations during the collective fear of 1876 in which rumor had it that paper
objects were brought to life by magical spells.[68] As a result of the vegetarians' militancy on February 7 and their subsequent activism, Subprefect Chengan had decided that the Yugong temple would not be shut
down, as had been suggested, but that the three other houses in the area
that were used for meetings by the vegetarians would be closed.[69] This
proposal did not appease the protesters, nor did it significantly interfere
with their efforts to organize an opposition to the managers of the New
Policy reforms.

Although the uprising was sparked by the dispute of the Yugong temple, self-government bureaus had already been established in three other
rural divisions without any apparent conflict. However, once Ding Fei
and the women vegetarians initiated an opposition, the discontent of

others became evident. Gu Aer, the manager of the Guandi temple where the Gaochang rural division self-government bureau had been founded, became the leader of attacks on self-government in his area. Referred to both as a director of community affairs (*dongshi*) and a temple director (*miaodong*), Gu was also respected as an arbiter of local disputes who held "court" in a teahouse where he also received presents for his services. Gu's income came from payments that the patrons made for oil used in the lamps at the hall of deities and from an incense shop which Gu owned.[70] Like Ding Fei, to whom people looked for spiritual advice, Gu was a well-respected member of his community with a close following. Each of these leaders had interests that were connected with the interests of a larger community. The self-government officials, through their new regulations and institutions and their opposition to vegetarianism, antagonized people from a diverse collection of occupations—cow salesmen who feared a tax on dairy cows, weavers who needed to dry their cloth on the open roads, and vegetarian sect members who were deprived of their meeting places. Once the uprising began, it spread quickly.

On the first and second of March, protesters attacked property related to self-government in Changren *xiang* and Gaochang *xiang*. By the third and fourth day of the uprising, the clerks and runners of the yamen subbureaucracy had also seized the opportunity to fan the flames of protest against self-government officials. On March 2, Li Songping and other clerks held a public meeting at Huigong temple, and the next day they met at the market town of Gongjin to persuade commoners from Jiutuan and Gaochang to join in the uprising.

After the massive destruction of property on the evening of March 3, Subprefect Chengan sent clerks Lu Xirong and Li Songping into the countryside to calm the people. However, according to several reports, the clerks instead addressed groups of people and told them that they would be safe if they destroyed offices, schools, and gentry residences in the countryside, but that if they came into the city to destroy buildings, the clerks would not be able to guarantee their protection. Nevertheless, Li also pointed out that Zhiyuan Hall, which was located in the city, must be destroyed in order to eliminate the root of the self-government problem. The Zhiyuan Hall had formerly been the meeting place of the gentry directors (*shendong*) who managed local public affairs in Chuansha subprefecture; it now became the center for the new self-government network. In addition, Li spread the word among the clerks and runners of the subprefecture that the self-government officials intended to abolish their customary fees.[71] This in fact was a part of the reformers' attempt to rationalize the local tax collection system.

Throughout the four-day-long uprising, demonstrators posted plac-

TABLE 6.1
Identifiable Participants in the Chuansha Uprising

Name	Occupation
Changren *xiang*	
Ding Fei	Rural temple manager; cotton cloth weaver
Gong Wojiang	
Zhang Axi	
Gaochang *xiang*	
Gu A'er	Rural temple manager; incense shop owner
Ye Guilin	
Batuan *xiang*	
Gu Asong	Coppersmith
Xi Akui	Carpenter
Huang Maolang	Rural shop owner (candy and fruit)
Jiutan *xiang*	
Xu Liushun	Marginally employed (hunter)
Zhang Fushan	Cow salesman
Li Songping	Yamen clerk
Lu Xirong	Yamen clerk

Others arrested: Chen Yejian, Song Juncai, Zhang Amu, Huang Jiashu, Fei Ahu, Zhu née Gu shi, Gu Ayi, Gu Tingxiang, Chen Zelian, and Big Xu Adi.
Source: *Minlibao*, April 3, 1911; *Shibao*, March 25, 1911.

ards in every market town of the subprefecture and all over the country-side, announcing the dates on which particular families would be at-tacked. Each commoner household was required to send one able-bodied man to fight on the rebels' side. For provisions, the protesters extorted food and money from wealthy households and shops.[72] By March 5, this organizational effort produced a force of two thousand people who were camped at Xingang, several *li* to the east of Tangmu-qiao, a market town.[73]

The property destroyed at Chuansha was estimated to be valued at

300,000 to 400,000 taels, but only a negligible fraction of this was plundered by the protesters. By and large, even according to the Pudong Club, the clothing, bedding, furniture, merchandise, school equipment, and personal belongings of the self-government personnel and their families were broken up and burned, rather than taken by the protesters for their own use. In the countryside where grain shops sold supplies at high prices, the people compelled the shopkeepers to sell grain at a fixed price of thirty cash per *shi* [133 1/3 lbs.]. Rural people of this area could afford to purchase grain at a price that they considered fair; their goal was not to plunder. Over the first four days of March, every grain shop in the subprefecture was sold out.[74]

The demonstrators at Chuansha carefully selected and demolished only that property that belonged to those against whom they had grievances. Residences to be burned were carried away to open areas where the fire would not interfere with other property. So consistent was this pattern in Chuansha as well as in other antitax uprisings that it amounted to a "ground rule" for rural protest. An eyewitness to the destruction of Ding Shiren's residence on March 3 identified Gu Asong, a coppersmith, and Xi Akui, a carpenter, as the principal participants in the crowd that assembled after Huang Maolan, a candy and fruit shop owner, sounded the gongs to people to gather. The crowd emptied Ding's residence of all furniture, clothing, and household items and made a huge bonfire with them outside. Gu and Xi carried cans of kerosene to the site for the fire. Ding's brother, Pangui, whose residence was just to the right of Shiren's, also had his belongings and house destroyed. Before Shiren's residence was burned, it was dismantled and, according to another eyewitness, the main roof beam proved difficult to remove. Xi Akui came to the rescue, however, with his strength, his carpenter's knowledge of beams, and his saw. The Ding families, meanwhile, were forced to take refuge in a couple of thatched huts that they owned. The angry crowd wanted to set fire to the huts, too, but they were convinced by some neighbors that nearby property would be unjustly damaged.[75] In another instance of property loss, on March 4 in Jiutuan *xiang*, Xu Liushun, a hunter, and Zhang Fushan, a cow salesman, were identified as those most responsible for the destruction of Huang Jiajun's residence.[76]

In addition to striking a blow against new miscellaneous taxes, protesters also took this opportunity to settle some other grievances against the elite households. Although having no apparent connections with self-government, two merchants were singled out for attack by the demonstrators. In both cases, the crowd destroyed account books. In another instance Xu Zongmei's library of old books and his account book were destroyed when his residence was completely demolished and burned.

TABLE 6.2
Owners of Property Destroyed at Chuansha

Name	Position	Occupation	Degree
Changren *xiang*			
Zhang Shouli	Sub-prefectural self-government assemblyman		Military *shengyuan*
Xi Shou	*Xiang* assemblyman		*Shengyuan* (1904)
Shi Hui	*Xiang* assemblyman		*Shengyuan* (1892)
Chen Weishan	*Xiang* assembly chairman		*Shengyuan* (1900)
Wu Daben	Rural director *(xiangdong)*		*Shengyuan* (1877)
Sun Wenbin	*Xiang* assemblyman		
Gaochang *xiang*			
Zhu Shunsheng	Self-government elector *(xuanmin)*		
You Guifen	*Xiang* self-government assembly chairman		*Shengyuan* (1902)
Chen Yuanbing	Elector		
Chen Zhaogui	*Xiang* assemblyman		
Wang Chengxun	*Xiang* assemblyman		
Zhang Wenqing	Elector		
Wang Wencheng	Rural director		*Shenguyan* (1890)
Chen Youheng	Assistant rural director *(xiangzuo)*		
Zhang Zoushao	*Xiang* assemblyman	Commercial firm owner	
Gu Naihuang	*Xiang* assemblyman	Commercial firm owner	
Zhu Shunqing	Elector		
Zhu Boda	Local constable *(dibao)*		
Lu Bingzhong	*Xiang* assemblyman		

TABLE 6.2 (CONTINUED)

Name	Position	Occupation	Degree
Batuan *xiang*			
Xue Weilun	*Xiang* assemblyman	Dye shop owner	*Shengyuan* (1901)
Ding Shiren	Sub-prefectural Self-government assemblyman		*Shengyuan* (1877)
Ding Pangui			*Shengyuan* (1883)
Gu Chengbu	*Xiang* assemblyman		
Bao Yiqing	Rural director		*Shengyuan* (1890)
Gu Shouxian		Commercial firm owner	
Gu Yiyuan	Sub-prefectural self-government assemblyman	Owner of two commercial firms	*Jiansheng* (purchased) *shengyuan*
Jiutuan *xiang*			
Lu Jiaji	Sub-prefectural self-government assemblyman; head of the bureau of preparations for self-government		*Shengyuan* (1889)
Xu Zongmei	Rural director		*Shengyuan* (1884)
Zhang Wenming	Assistant rural director	Cotton cloth firm owner; power loom workshop owner	
Gu Liang	*Xiang* assemblyman		
Huang Shangda	*Xiang* assemblyman		
Yang Zhenyong	*Xiang* assemblyman		*Shengyuan* (1893)
Huang Jiajun	*Xiang* assemblyman		
Zhang Zhihe	Sub-prefectural self-government		*Shengyuan* (1896)
Huang Xushan	Elector	Farmer	
Gu Yongjiang (residence unknown)		Commercial firm owner	

Source: *Shibao*, March 6, 1911; *Chuansha xianzhi*, 18: 6-9.

Xu was a self-government official and lower degree-holder, and although there were no specific references to any merchant activity in his family, his residence was described as especially elegant and richly furnished. The extent of the protesters' grievances against Xu was quite extreme, for he was the only individual personally attacked by the crowd.[77]

Several times during the uprising, protesters attempted to reclaim temple property taken over for use by self-government institutions. In one case, Gu Aer, the manager of the Guandi temple, along with his acquaintance Ye Guilin, assembled a group that moved the furniture of the local self-government office into the street, where it was burned. Afterward the crowd carved the characters "martial sage palace" (*wushenggong*) on a plaque and thus designated the temple for use only by Lao Taitai, the female warrior goddess.[78]

Throughout the disturbance, Subprefect Chengan took very little action, leaving most of the official decisions to his superior, Prefect Qiyang of Songjiang prefecture. After Ding Fei was arrested, Chengan had gone to the countryside to conduct an initial investigation. He was soon surrounded by villagers who destroyed his sedan chair and vehemently stated their demands, which included the release of Ding Fei. Chengan saw that he was caught between two determined and opposing forces, so he disappeared to Suzhou for more than ten days, thus undermining the self-government officials who needed the subprefect's pronouncements of support.[79] Although the self-government officials maintained an extensive network of bureaucratic connections, which included contacts with the governor-general of Liangjiang, the self-government officials' relationship with the crucial local official, the Chuansha subprefect himself, proved to be fragile.[80] The subprefect could not give self-government greater support principally because of his dependence on the yamen clerks and runners, without whom he could scarcely govern or collect the tax quota for his area. To be sure, the subprefect had approved many of the self-government officials' requests, including the collection of a few taxes through self-government offices. However, when the inherent conflict between self-government officials and yamen clerks at Chuansha developed into a crisis, even the subprefect's minimal support for self-government collapsed.

On March 4, troops sent from Shanghai at Prefect Qiyang's request arrived in Chuansha. The self-government officials of Chuansha had been requesting troops urgently since the first day of the disturbance, but Subprefect Chengan had hesitated to petition the higher authorities on their behalf. When Chen Jiren from Changren *xiang* and Cai Songfu, the assembly chairman of Batuan *xiang,* neither of whose property was damaged during the uprising, went to the yamen to discuss the disturbance with Chengan, the subprefect refused to see them. Instead he sent a messenger to say that everything was their fault and that they had implicated the subprefect in the trouble. Chengan also petitioned the governor, declaring, "The oppressive taxes of the gentry (*shenshi*) have given rise to the disturbance."[81] Once the troops had arrived in Chuansha, Subprefect Chengan was reluctant to use them on the self-government officials' behalf. When the soldiers under their commander's order prepared to go into the countryside, the yamen runners blocked their passage, and the troops were forced to circle around without having left the city.[82]

Although Subprefect Chengan would not order the use of troops, he did halfheartedly attempt to control the situation by making a few arrests. He also sent an old-style director (*jiushi dongshi*) named Huang to attempt to negotiate a settlement with the protesters. Hoping to establish rapport with the dissidents, Huang addressed a group of them and said, "I am of the old group (*jiudang*) too; won't you listen to me?" The crowd shouted back, "If you are with us why don't you join us and help destroy the buildings of the self-government officials?"[83] Such were the trials of Subprefect Chengan, whose political authority was torn between the subbureaucracy on which he depended to administer the area and the challenging forces generated by New Policy reforms, which he was obliged to see carried out. In addition, Subprefect Chengan had little credibility with the rural commoners for whom he was supposed to maintain a just and orderly government. The vacillation that this predicament encouraged, for the time being indirectly aided the forces that opposed self-government.

On March 5, Subprefect Chengan, accompanying Commander Wang Yunhua and Magistrate Hong Yusheng, who had been sent from a neighboring county by the Shanghai Taotai, began to investigate the Chuansha disturbance. As the party journeyed into the countryside, it came upon approximately two thousand protesters encamped at Xingang, where they were preparing a meal. After Wang moved his troops some distance away, Hong approached the people and asked what had caused the conflict. He was told, "The New Policy collected taxes that were too harsh. There was a house tax, a tea tax, a room tax, and a meat tax; in addition there were taxes on cows, sheep, chickens, ducks and also on home-loom-woven cloth. Everything was taxed, and the people were not able to sustain themselves."[84] Hong then attempted to reassure the people by saying that the house, tea, room, and meat taxes existed everywhere, and that if there were notices and receipts for these taxes, their legitimacy could be verified. Hong went on to tell the group that if the gentry directors (*shendong*) were overstepping these bounds, the commoners could petition and have the situation investigated. As to the cow, sheep, chicken, and duck taxes, Hong said that if these taxes had not been submitted by the self-government personnel to the regular officials for approval, the taxes would be remitted to the payers. The assembled crowd was skeptical that such checks could be effectively exercised on the self-government officials' actions.[85] This dramatic meeting between state officials and humble rural taxpayers yielded no remedy for the commoners' plight.

The Chuansha protest concluded without any major military encounters between the government troops and the rural people. Having achieved their goal of striking a blow at self-government and New Policy reforms in Chuansha, protesters began to scatter by the end of the first week in March. Many of the leaders fled to neighboring Nanhui and Shanghai counties. Self-government and provincial officials called for investigations that would lead to a settlement with the commoners and the yamen personnel so that self-government could be reestablished. In fact, self-government in Chuansha did continue into the early Republican period, and many of the officials who had suffered losses

TABLE 6.3
Buildings Destroyed at Chuansha

	Place (xiang)					
	Changren	Gaochang	Jiutuan	Batuan	Unknown	Total
March 1	3	1	0	0		4
March 2	5	0	0	0		5
March 3	1	14	8	8	1	32
March 4	0	7	6	7	1	21
Self-government bureaus	0	1	1	1		3
Schools	3	6	2	4		15
Residences	6	13	10	6	1	36
Businesses	0	2	1	4	1	8
Buildings torn down	8	0	2	3	1	14
Buildings burned	1	22	12	12	1	48
Total number of buildings destroyed	9	22	14	15	2	62

Sources: *Shibao*, March 6 and 11, 1911; *Chuansha xianzhi*, 23:9.

during the uprising returned as prominent officials after 1912.[86] The uprising in many ways served to draw out and destroy active opposition to self-government, which existed among the commoners and some members of the local subbureaucracy.

Immediately after the uprising, clerks and runners who were not purged from the subbureaucracy for participation in the uprising began to arrest people whom they suspected had supported the opposition to self-government. The clerks and runners also worked on the self-government officials' behalf to collect funds from the families of the protesters for damages that the officials had suffered during the uprising. The subbureaucracy itself now began to terrorize the rural population. Yamen runners arrested well-to-do members of lineages in which a relative had been involved in the destruction so that the self-government officials could be reimbursed for their property losses. Those families with property paid off the runners, and some had to sell everything to raise the funds. Those families without property were turned over to the higher courts for trial. Often runners would arrest someone other than the person whose name appeared on the arrest warrant. Women were the targets of arrests as well as men. Afraid to stay at home at night for fear of arrest, women went out into the fields to sleep.[87]

By early April 1911, a total of sixteen people had been arrested, including Ding Fei and another woman vegetarian, Mrs. Zhu née Gu. Gong Wojiang, Zhang Axi, Ye Guilin, and the two clerks Li Songping and Lu Xirong were also arrested.[88] The arrests were made most heavily among the vegetarians. Half of those arrested had given names that began with "A," taken presumably from Atai, the name of the founder of the local sect.[89] As a consequence of Prefect Qiyang's investigation, Subprefect Chengan was removed from office and fined two thousand silver dollars to pay for the schools that were destroyed. The case finally came to a close on June 22, 1912, when Gong Wojiang was garroted in a Shanghai prison.[90]

At Chuansha, as in Laiyang and other counties, taxes and reform continued as issues into the post-1911 period. Between 1912 and 1932, land taxes at Chuansha more than doubled with the steepest part of the rise coming in the last six years of that period. In 1926, miscellaneous fees were collected for welfare, police, household registration, water conservancy, and education. In 1933, new taxes were levied for public security, road construction, agricultural reform, self-government, and land surveys.[91] The New Policy period of the post-Boxer era was just the opening round of struggle for local resources and contention over the terms of social change in relationship to the demands of modernity.

Nanhui, Jiangsu: March 1911

On March 5, just after the last day of major destruction in Chuansha, a movement initiated by fishermen against New Policy managers developed in neighboring Nanhui county. As in Chuansha, many of the members of the Nanhui elite who managed the reforms lived in the rural areas and had contacts with the Pudong Club in Shanghai. They did not control the land tax collection, and they had very little influence with the county magistrate. The fishermen and farmers, on the other hand, organized themselves through temple associations that were very similar to the vegetarian groups along the Nanhui-Chuansha border. Women weavers were also involved in this protest, although in the case of Nanhui there are many fewer details.

During the first ten days of March, numerous anonymous placards were posted by the protesters. The self-government preparation office received a placard condemning both the prohibition of opium smoking and gambling, and the establishment of self-government bureaus and new schools. Other placards were posted announcing the dates on which certain residences owned by the county elite and certain schools that they had established would be destroyed. Because of the agitation in Chuansha, the New Policy managers and their associates in Nanhui were worried.[92]

There had also been a recent history of conflict between the commoners and the elite in Nanhui. In 1909, members of the county elite who later became involved in the management of reforms established several fishing companies. These companies set up bamboo barriers in certain inlets to trap fish, which, when full-grown, could not swim out to other areas where the local fishermen usually made their catches. The fisheries had effectively monopolized a local industry on which many people depended for their livelihood. The fish also ate the weeds in this part of the inlet and thus interfered with the farmers' collection of fertilizer for their fields. The rural commoners had complained about the situation many times but the magistrate had taken no action. The magistrate finally petitioned the prefect, who sent deputies to investigate the fishery, but by this time the fishermen had taken matters into their own hands. A Mr. Zhang, one of the local unemployed and odd-jobbers, offered to lead an attack on the waterway barriers erected by a fishing company at Liuzhao.[93] This plan was carried out and eventually became a central issue in the opposition to the New Policy institutions.

As the crisis developed, protesters delivered additional threatening messages that sent the reform managers into a state of panic. On March 8, a crowd removed the name tablets on both the Mingxin school and the local self-government bureau in Chenjiaqiao. Other placards continued to appear that gave the dates on which certain elite residences would be attacked. Many of the county elite members residing in the rural areas went to the magistrate to ask him to take action that would protect their property. Magistrate Lai, however, showed no sympathy. He was sarcastic toward and critical of the elite members, whom he thought were exaggerating their plight. He expressed the view that the threatening placards need not be taken so seriously. Meanwhile, as the persons who had been threatened continued to arrive at the yamen in search of protection, the doorkeeper and other yamen runners, much to the chagrin of the notables, collected their customary fees from all persons entering the yamen, as though all of this activity were business as usual. Some New Policy managers attempted to convince the protesters that they should postpone the scheduled date for attacks on their residences. March 15 had been set for self-government elections, but the self-government directors did not dare hold them in areas where there were rumors of pending violence.[94]

The protest leaders now began to take their first steps toward full-scale mobilization of the village communities. The leader, known only as Zhang, met at Shatu temple on March 19 with other protest leaders, including Zhang Jiesheng, Tang Shangda, and Tang Shunda. More than 100 people burned incense, took an oath of allegiance, and consulted the spirits in order to select the most auspicious date for attacking the various schools and residences. Zhang Jiesheng then led a procession from village to village carrying a flag, the writing on which declared that "Zhang Bingsheng is using a public cause to establish schools but actually he intends to take over temple property, which is not in accordance with public opinion."[95] Bands of fishermen joined with the leaders from the temple meeting to form the core of the protest organization.

On March 23, Zhang, the leader, gave the orders for Zhang Jiesheng and Tang Shengda to sound gongs and gather people. The leader himself twirled a seventy-two-pound pole, and others carried knives and weavers' shuttles. Several hundred people destroyed the fishing company at Liuzhao. They also removed the furniture from a school, confiscated the census books from the self-government bureau, and burned both the furniture and the books. Each of these places was housed in a building adjacent to the fishing company. The chamber of commerce whose members included the same New Policy managers was also attacked. Magistrate Lai, under increased pressure from the reform managers, finally agreed to send runners to the Liuzhao area, but he did not dispatch them until the next morning.[96]

The Nanhui disturbance quickly reached its peak and faded shortly thereafter. By March 27, a total of five fishing companies, two schools, one self-government office, one fire station, and one chamber of commerce had been damaged. The reform managers came to the conclusion that the magistrate was unreliable and that if their interests were to be protected they would have to organize militia corps under the auspices of the chamber of commerce, which they themselves controlled.[97] Evidently the New Policy managers had already acted on this thought, for when the office was attacked by demonstrators, eleven foreign-made rifles were seized. Meanwhile, a group described as the "peace-minded gentry" appealed to higher authorities for leniency toward the protesters, insisting that damage to the fisheries had been minimal, consisting only of destruction of the bamboo poles and nets that had been placed in the water. County elite member Gu Zhongyi, on the other hand, bypassed the authority of the magistrate and himself petitioned for troops. When the troops arrived on March 27, they attempted to disperse a crowd by firing blank shots. Schools were closed and students sent home, while a curfew was declared in the county seat. A battalion under the direction of the provincial commander-in-chief was sent to guard the city, but this did little to control the protest in the villages and towns. The protesters in the county seat had agitated long enough to make their point, and the presence of troops discouraged any further activism.[98]

Conclusions

The protest against New Policy reforms at Chuansha was distinctive because of the prominent role played by rural women. As initiators of the protest they remained active participants once other groups became involved. Women's role in the Chuansha dissent brings into view threads of women's activism that run through many of the other anti–New Policy protests and the fabric of rural society in general. At Chuansha place-specific economic and religious practices created public spaces within which women's collective activism became possible. Involvement in the market economy and participation in lay Buddhist networks were the pillars of support for daily livelihood and group-definition that made possible women's activism in Chuansha as a notable feature of the anti–New Policy protests.

The above cases from the lower Yangzi valley also add other dimensions to the patterns and variations found in these rural movements during the last years of the Qing. As in north and south China, county elites involved in commercial enterprises with relatively substantial holdings and political connections were most likely to become the managers of reform. The position itself conferred official, political status on lower degree-holders and merchants who previously had had only informal influence on county financial and administrative policies. With the discontinuance of the imperial examination system in 1905, the new road to political privilege seemed connected to these reforms. The terms *lieshen* (corrupt gentry) and *xindang* (new faction), so often used in official documents on these cases, became code for the conflation of gentry status with new commercial ambitions and official administrative authority achieved through the reforms. Many of the new-style elite did not have official degree status. They formed networks in which some members had lower-degree status, but commercial wealth was the operative feature of this new social class. For this group the New Policy road was the new way to advancement, and for many it led straight to the Republican Revolution.

Those commercial groups among the county elite designated as *shen-shi* who held back from the reform process sided in some cases with rural resistance to the New Policy developments. This group referred to in sources as the old-style party (*jiudang*) was a crucial and perhaps even more invisible social class than the peasants who led and enlisted in the dissident uprisings. Among the *jiudang* were those would not hestitate to squeeze taxpayers if given the opportunity. They simply were not as well positioned to take advantage of the reforms. But most often the term *jiudang* in these accounts connotes a position of resistance to the reforms based on specific notions about rural welfare. Individuals like Yu Zhusan at Laiyang, He Rongguang at Zunhua, and Mr. Huang and Bang Shoujin at Chuansha were mediators who potentially could have been enlisted to adjust reforms to place-based political and economic realities. They were individuals Zhao Erxun and others had hoped to involve in their proposals for subcounty level administrative changes. The split between the old-style and new-style county elite was a significant shift in the politics of place that the Republican Revolution would continue to reenforce and develop. When the revolution broke out and the revolutionaries had to govern rural society they turned not to those members who questioned the long- and short-term consequences of New Policy measures but to those who were already positioned to staff the new local governments under the banner of the Republican Revolution.

Reform managers in the counties considered in this chapter commanded very powerful economic interests, and yet they were largely impotent in their efforts to effect county political changes. Owning business interests located outside of the county in nearby urban centers such as Shanghai, Suzhou, Nanjing, Hangzhou, or Ningbo, these local elite members, although possessing some influence, had never cultivated strong ties with the magistrate's office, as had their counterparts at Laiyang, Longyao, or Yizhou in north China, where major commercial centers were fewer and at greater distances from one another. Consequently, in counties such as Chuansha, Nanhui, and Shangyu, the magistrate gave only halfhearted support to the efforts of the reform managers.

Magistrates in the lower Yangzi cases frequently pursued a more independent line of action when implementing reform programs. Rather than relying on a small circle of local elite members whom he favored to the exclusion of others, the magistrate often was immobilized between the opposing interests of reform managers and yamen subbureaucratic personnel. Obligated to carry out the reforms, but finding it difficult to do so without both disturbing public welfare and threatening various local-interest groups, the magistrate often failed to get reform projects off to a good start. This is illustrated in the cases at Wuyang and Ixing in Jiangsu.

The subbureaucracy was a strong, independent interest group in county politics. Initially, at least, much of the opposition to the reforms and reform managers came from the yamen clerks and runners, whose economic perquisites were threatened by the reorganization of county fiscal and administrative duties. Chuansha clerks and runners, for example, stood to lose their control of the land tax collection and their right to collect customary fees. In counties where clerks and runners were not directly threatened by reform measures, they continued to exert their traditional authority over tax collection. At Ixing and Guian, yamen clerks received the additional surcharges collected for reform programs and then forwarded these funds to the reform managers. In these cases, the reform managers gained new administrative authority but did not directly challenge the subbureaucracy's management of fiscal affairs. As the most visible agents of increased taxation in these instances, the yamen clerks bore the brunt of the taxpayers' hostility.

Whether allied with or against the yamen clerks and runners, commoner taxpayers who protested the imposition of new levies for reform programs in the Lower Yangzi region responded to the changes with vehemence and a sense of immediacy. There were very few attempts by the protesters to negotiate a settlement. Social groups within counties were polarized to the extent that discussion was not considered potentially productive. As a consequence, protest movements in this area quickly became violent and generally were of short duration.

When the Republican Revolution broke out in October 1911, the *shenshi* who had led the way to local self-government and new schools in Nanhui threw in their lot with the Shanghai revolutionaries who declared independence from the imperial center. Residents of Nanhui were instructed to wave the white flag of surrender when the revolutionaries arrived to oversee the transfer of authority. The Nanhui magistrate was to hand over his seals of office, his account books, and the funds held in the yamen treasury. When the Shanghai revolutionaries discovered that the magistrate did not have the sum his account books showed, they imprisoned him. Word spread throughout the towns and countryside. Those who had protested the New Policy reforms immediately saw the link between the local self-government officials and the revolutionaries and decided they wanted nothing to do with either. Along with some of the yamen clerks and runners, villagers marched to the county seat, rescued the magistrate, and burned down schools and self-governement offices. The attacks on the reformers and the revolutionaries continued sporadically in Nanhui.[99]

At Chuansha, when news of the revolution at Wuhan arrived, the *shenshi* in charge of local self-government decided to support the revolutionaries because they believed that the Qing forces would not be able to protect them if the revolutionaries marched into Chuansha county. Two members of the Chuansha *shenshi* traveled to Shanghai and received assurance from the military governor that they would not send an army to Chuansha. Back in Chuansha, the *shenshi* convinced Magistrate Liu to declare the independence of Chuansha from Qing rule, which the magistrate did on November 7. As Magistrate Liu was leaving the area, townsmen and villagers appeared in significant numbers to express their regret at his departure. If he and his predecessors had not been fully effective in their protection of commoner interests during the anti–New Policy demonstrations, it was still clear to many that the revolutionaries were not about to help with these matters either. In fact, the Republican government did not dismiss or replace any of the Chuansha local self-government officials.[100] From the dissident rural perspective, the continuity of power and its consequences for rural well-being could not have been clearer.

Notes

Epigraph: Yao Wennan, "Pudong tongrenhui gong tui Yao Wennan deng tiaocha Chuansha naoshi qingxing baogaoshu" (Report on an investigation of the circumstances of the Chuansha disturbances by the Pudong association's investigators Yao Wennan and others), in *Chuansha xianzhi* (Chuansha County Gazetteer, 1936), 23:10.

1. Huang Yanpei, *Bashi nianlai* (Eighty years past) (Beijing: Wenshi ziliao chuban she, 1982), 17.

2. Ibid., 18.

3. Ibid., 37.

4. Mary Backus Rankin, *Early Chinese Revolutionaries: Radical Intellec-

tuals in Shanghai and Chekiang, 1902–1911 (Cambridge: Harvard University Press, 1971), 92.

5. Ibid., 161.

6. Shang Ding, *Huang Yanpei*, (Beijing: Renmin chuban she, 1986), 27–29.

7. Yoshinobu Shiba, "Ningbo and Its Hinterland," in *The City in Late Imperial China*, ed. G. William Skinner (Stanford: Stanford University Press, 1977), 405.

8. Ibid., 401, 405.

9. Mark Elvin, "Market Towns and Waterways: The County of Shanghai from 1480–1910," in *The City in Late Imperial China*, ed. G. William Skinner (Stanford: Stanford University Press, 1977), 447.

10. Yoshinobu Shiba, "Ningbo and Its Hinterland," 435.

11. Elvin, "Market Towns and Waterways," 445. Also see David Faure, *The Rural Economy of Pre-Liberation China: Trade Expansion and Peasant Livelihood in Jiangsu and Guangdong, 1870–1937* (Hong Kong: Oxford University Press, 1989), 160.

12. Elvin, "Market Towns and Waterways," 447, 459.

13. Ibid., 465.

14. Philip C. C. Huang, *The Peasant Family and Rural Development in the Yangzi Delta, 1350–1988* (Stanford: Stanford University Press, 1990), 118.

15. Ibid., 120.

16. Ibid., 136–37.

17. *Chuansha xianzhi* (Chuansha county gazetteer, 1936), 5:14–20.

18. *Dongfang zazhi*, 8/25, no. 8, 225.

19. *North China Herald*, August 12, 1910.

20. *Dongfang zazhi*, 8/25, no. 8, 226.

21. *North China Herald*, July 22, August 12, 1910.

22. *Dongfang zazhi*, 8/25, no. 8, 1910, 226.

23. *North China Herald*, July 22, August 12, 1910.

24. *Dongfang zazhi*, 8/25, no, 8, 1910.

25. Herbert Gaffe, "Intelligence Report for the Quarter Ended June 30, 1910, Nanking," F.O. 228/1762.

26. For a discussion of these issues see J. Holmgren, "Myth, Fantasy or Scholarship: Images of the Status of Women in Traditional China," in *The Australian Journal of Chinese Affairs* 6 (1981): 147–70.

27. Faure, *The Rural Economy of Pre-Liberation China*, 200.

28. Susan Naquin, *Millenarian Rebellion in China: The Eight Trigrams of 1813* (New Haven: Yale University Press, 1976), 41–42, 151, 219, 299–300.

29. Ono Kazuko, *Chinese Women in a Century of Revolution, 1850–1950*, edited by Joshua A. Fogel (Stanford: Stanford University Press, 1989; originally published in Japanese, 1978), 7–15.

30. Rong Tieshen, "Xinhai geming qianhou de Zhong guo funu yundong" (The Chinese women's movement on the eve of the 1911 Revolution), in *Jinian Xinhai geming qishi zhounian xueshu taolunhui wenji* (Collected works from a symposium to commemorate the seventieth anniversary of the 1911 Revolution) (Beijing: Renmin chuban she, 1983), 664.

31. Liu Tongjun, ed., *Xinhai gemingqian Lai Hai Zhao kangjuan yongdong* (Antitax movements in Laiyang, Haiyang, and Zhaoyuan before the 1911 Revolution) (Beijing: Shehui kexue wenxian chuban she, 1989), 362.

32. The largest concentration of rural protests against New Policy–related reforms took place in the rich and densely populated area of Jiangsu and Zhejiang. Many of the incidents focused on opposition to census taking, which accompanied the first stages of reform measures. However, other issues and grievances against the reform managers were always the backdrop of such action.

At Yixing, poor crops had been harvested for several successive years, miscellaneous taxes had risen, and an unfavorable exchange rate had exacerbated the situation. New Policy managers, who had also begun recently to establish new schools, collected census data in March 1910. These persons were rural division headmen (*xiangdong*), many of whom had residences in the market towns, elite members (*shendong*), and rural managers (*dongshi*). When the census was taken, a fee of twenty cash was collected for each name registered. The census taking was also especially detailed, including both males and females of all ages. The hardships and fears engendered by the registration of all persons in every household contributed to the collective creation and circulation of a rumor that the birth dates of those men and women registered would be used to select people who would be made into iron ties for construction of a bridge over the Yellow River. This belief in supernatural forces and magic provided powerful images with which to articulate opposition to economic and political grievances.

In addition, on March 21 a notice was circulated in the east and west sections of Ixing stating that when the grain tribute tax was collected at the yamen tax chest, a self-government fee of forty cash would be collected for each *shi* of grain. Not only was an extra fee to be charged but the exchange rate that the farmers received at the tax chest would be worse than that which they received at the market place for their goods. Meanwhile, at the markets, rice was scarce and prices rose daily.

The villagers took action in this situation by sounding gongs to call village meetings and make plans to destroy the schools that had been established by New Policy managers and with which the census takers were associated. In six market towns, political elite residences, as well as schools and the education affairs office, were destroyed. During a brief interlude, a county elite member reported to the provincial treasurer that the demonstrators were determined and that some bandit groups had joined them. He went on to report that there were no plans to call for troops and that there should be some local relief work to resettle the people whose poverty led them to think of rebellion.

In the aftermath of the disturbance, reform managers abandoned efforts to carry out New Policy programs. At schools that had been damaged, the local *shenshi* removed the *xuetang* tablets, changing them to *shuyuan* signs, the traditional name for elite-managed old-style schools. Census books were taken from the schools and given to the representatives of the rural people. A guarantee was then drawn up that ensured the protection of the rural people from reforms for years to come. There are not enough details on this case to determine if the political elite had been conscientiously undertaking reforms under difficult economic circumstances, or if there had been abuses of the elite's new authority as well.

Source: *Dongfang zazhi*, no. 3, 1910.

33. In Wuyang, Jiangsu, which included Wujin and Danyang, there had been repeated disturbances since 1908 in which rural people had attacked the yamen court buildings. When the attacks on schools began at Ixing, unrest once again surfaced in the Wuyang area. Census takers who went into the rural areas in March 1910 immediately became embroiled in conflicts with the villagers. A Mr. Bao, who was the head of the self-government office in an area where friction developed, attempted unsuccessfully to talk with the people who had grievances. So fierce was the opposition of rural commoners to the extra fees collected by the census takers, and so real the fear that the census would lead to further taxation, that rural women in each of the first and sixth districts (*tu*) beat up the census taker who had come to their respective areas in the first district, injuring him quite badly. The protesters demanded the return of census records only from those self-government managers they did not trust. A Mr. Sun, for example, considered to have credibility and dignity, was not asked to turn the books over to the care of the villagers.

By March 1911, one year later, New Policy reforms still had not made much headway in the Wuyang area. On March 31, the prefect called a meeting of rural people and self-government assemblymen to discuss the problems involved in implementing the reforms. This meeting was held in the magistrate's court, over the opposition of some who felt it was improper to receive the rural people in such an official place. At the meeting, the magistrate asked the villagers' representatives to sign a bond promising that they would not interfere with self-government in the future. In exchange, the rural people would not be questioned about their attacks on the court in recent years.

Attempts continued to select persons who could manage self-government offices. When one assemblyman began to furnish a nunnery as a self-government bureau, the local populace demonstrated, and the assemblyman had to resign. In another case, Wang Daolai, known by officials to be a local bandit leader but nonetheless considered by them to be reputable, was asked to manage self-government in his district (*xiang*).

The self-government members who were rural division leaders (*xiangdong*), eventually met to discuss the slow progress of the self-government movement in their respective *xiang*. Demonstrations initiated by rural people had effectively checked the establishment of self-government offices, and the managers decided to resign as a body. The city self-government organization (*dongshi hui*) also dissolved itself. A second assembly was opened and a new *dongshi hui* elected. This group made three proposals: (1) a hospital should be established, (2) unused official land in the city should be turned over for self-government uses, and (3) temples in the suburbs of the city should be prohibited from storing coffins containing corpses. However, no progress was made with these measures.

Source: *Shibao*, April 5, 16, 20, 1911.

34. In 1908, opposition to new schools and higher taxes began in the Tongxiang area, a region riddled with secret societies and bandit gangs, many of which provided protesters with militia support units. While rural taxpayers in the neighborhood of Aza, a large market town fifteen miles from Tongxiang, had frequently requested land tax reductions because of poor crops, the magistrate proposed to increase the grain tax. In order to demonstrate their opposition to this proposal, and to the magistrate's inaction on their previous request, villagers marched through the countryside, blowing horns and announcing that one person from each family should join them in a protest at the yamen. For provisions, they demanded food and supplies from wealthy households. According to a British resident in the area, the protesters wore distinctive dress and were organized in bands of one thousand.

When the villagers reached Tongxiang, they attacked the yamen, demolished 100 houses and shops, and destroyed some American Presbyterian mission property that they mistook for a government school. Other residences and places of business were also attacked in the small towns around Tongxiang. At Haining, demonstrators destroyed a Catholic mission. An observer on the scene interpreted this as an attempt to embroil the Chinese officials with the foreigners. Demonstrators also attacked the railroad office and the post office. Government troops called into the area killed several dozen villagers. After this encounter, the troops, commanded by General Jiang Guidi and accompanied by the Mounted Artillery brigades of the 4th and 6th Divisions of the Beiyang Army, proceeded south toward other local disturbances.

A high official in Beijing who was a native of Tongxiang memorialized the Throne that the governor of Zhejiang should be ordered to identify and punish those members of the county elite responsible for the deteriorating situation at Tongxiang. An imperial rescript conveyed by the Grand Council commanded the governor of Zhejiang to pay compensation for the losses sustained by the native residents and missionaries in Tongxiang.

Once the tax protest was suppressed, bands of outlaws moved into the area. The bandits, often well dressed, would coerce shopkeepers in the market towns into selling them goods at prices that the bandits thought were fair. This community of outlaws had accumulated great wealth and was known to use the slogan "Level down the rich and level up the poor." Those who joined were well fed and well paid.

In January 1910, the same problem occurred. Crops were poor, and the grain tax was not reduced. Women and children first, and men later, demanded food at the homes of wealthy merchants who were also lower degree-holders (*fushen*). Local officials telegraphed the provincial government and requested troops.

Meanwhile, on January 24, some rural people tried to enter the city to pay their grain tax, but they were obstructed by another group from the rural areas that supported the tax protest. Several thousand people fought outside the city gates until the government troops arrived and fired on the crowd, killing one person and wounding two. The tax protesters then surged toward the city, broke through one of the gates, and went to the yamen to demand that taxes be remitted. In the city, they also destroyed the "people's convenience" granary. When the magistrate did not attempt to resolve the situation, the crown surrounded his yamen, plundered it until the building was empty, and then destroyed the structure. The following day, the rural protesters cut the telegraph lines and burned the east gate of the city.

Soldiers and peasants fought with each other throughout the day of January 26. In one incident, farmers tied two captured soldiers to one of their dead fellow villagers. The office of military affairs and the Taotai finally ordered the troops to shoot to kill. People began to disperse, but more than a dozen were arrested. The leader, on whom no detailed information is available, was beheaded. Throughout the fighting and earlier demonstrations, reporters on the scene noted both the well-organized behavior of the rural protesters and their competent leadership.

Source: North China Herald, January 17, 1908; *Dongfang zazhi*, no. 1, 1910.

35. Situated to the northwest of the Ningbo Plain, Ziji was an important cotton-producing center whose land was naturally irrigated by runoff from hills in the north of the county. Like Chuansha, Ziji was located near a major commercial center. Since it was common in the Ningbo area for major households residing in the countryside to have business interests in the city, this is likely to have been true of the Ziji area as well, although specific information to this effect is lacking.

The story at Ziji, according to the brief available account, begins with the levying of additional taxes to support the establishment of new schools. On April 19, 1910, a large group of people, arriving at a temple for their annual Qingming celebrations, discovered that the premises, always used for lodging on such occasions, were serving as a government school. Infuriated by the loss of property that had previously been at their disposal, and by the new taxes that they had been forced to pay for these schools, the villagers decided to destroy the school. Over the next five days, seven other schools in market towns were reportedly burned to the ground. A tax collector who was popular among the people was deputed to arbitrate a settlement.

While the disturbances at Ziji were taking place, similar outbreaks occurred in Shangyu in Shaoxing prefecture. Here a tax of 100 cash per picul had been levied on bamboo shoots, a commodity widely traded in the area. The magistrate had evidently approved the new levy, which was requested by the manager of a new school. Several thousand people came to the county seat to protest, and destroyed several official bureaus and a government-sponsored school. The magistrate appeased the crowd by arresting the school manager who had petitioned for the new levy, and the crowd of rural people eventually dispersed. An American missionary stationed at Shangyu described the events this way:

> We might have had an exciting time yesterday. . . . Some two to three thousand exasperated countrymen from the hill district south of the city had come with their carrying poles and props to enter a protest against unjust taxation for the support of the new schools. We heard the howling of the mob while we were having our dinner, but it died down again, and

we supposed the demonstration might pass off . . . but when we were in the midst of the Communion Service in the afternoon the mob, having finished the dismantling of the East Gate school proceeded to attack the one just back of our chapel, and we could distinctly hear the smashing of furniture and the crashing of window glass as we proceeded with the Service.

Source: L. R. Barr, Ningpo Intelligence Report, January 1–April 30, 1901, F. O. 228/1762.

36. In Huzhou prefecture, recent harvests had been poor and miscellaneous taxes were increasing. The tax protests in this area, which became most severe at Deqing, began at Guian. At Guian, disputes arose when the yamen clerks concealed information on the bad harvest in this district and demanded tax payments in full. The principal clerk in charge of the tribute grain had also caused deep resentment by demanding bribes and increasing surcharges. From Guian, protest movements spread to Wucheng and Deqing, where government troops were called in to suppress the disturbances.

At Wucheng, rural people organized for the purpose of obstructing the payment of taxes. An effective network of surveillance was operated by the protesters to enforce nonpayment of taxes. People were prevented from entering the city to pay taxes, and the protesters would demand food from the rural division (*xiang*) of anyone who did manage to pay taxes. If wealthy households (*fuhu*) paid taxes, their residences were attacked.

When the Wucheng magistrate heard of these actions, he telegraphed a request that troops be sent into the area. Judging that this was an inappropriate action taken against a legitimate cause, the villagers called a meeting, and the next day more than a thousand rural people from throughout the prefecture entered the city and demolished the yamen. The prefect declared martial law, and the next day provincial troops arrived while the demonstrators dispersed. The magistrate then ordered the county managers (*shendong*) to survey the households that had suffered crop losses. Those that had no harvest would pay no taxes; those that had taken in some harvest would pay 70 percent of the usual rate. The available sources do not reveal how this was executed or if it was to the taxpayers' satisfaction.

The largest tax protest in Huzhou prefecture at this time was at Deqing. On January 9, the magistrate opened the county granary for payment of taxes. Angered because their requests for tax reductions had been ignored, more than a thousand people entered the city to protest. The magistrate and the county elite members (*shenshi*) emerged from the city to try to persuade the people to be calm. The taxpayers, who were also referred to as farmers (*nongmin*), demanded that (1) the treasurer of the granary be punished for his manipulation of the tax collection, (2) those farmers whose fields had produced nothing not be required to pay taxes, and (3) those who had had some harvest be given a 30 to 40 percent tax reduction. The farmers in the northern *xiang* assumed leadership roles, while those in the eastern and western *xiang* joined in. The magistrate responded by requesting that the rural protesters send their representatives to the yamen, where he would discuss the matter of tax reductions with them.

The crowd would not disperse, however, so troops were called in with orders to shoot to kill.

Another tax issue directly involving New Policy reforms became evident on April 14 when rural taxpayers demonstrated their vehement opposition to the collection of surcharges for a new police bureau. Police headman Wu, singled out by the crowd and surrounded, carelessly brandished a knife, wounding several of the protesters. The people, now furious, moved to destroy the police bureau. They also completely destroyed a new school and forced the shops in the city to close. Merchants and county elite members (*shen*) decided that they should jointly petition the governor and request official aid. They argued that the police office was supposed to protect the yamen affairs, and since it had failed to do this, there was no point in collecting taxes to fund the police bureau. Instead, they argued, the old regulations should be followed and *tuanlian* should be established. Business resumed as usual the next day.

Source: *Dongfang zazhi*, in *Xinhai geming* (The 1911 Revolution) ed., Chai Degeng (Shanghai: Renmin chuban she, 1957), vol. 3, 440–41, 456–57.

37. Wang Shuhuai, *Zhongguo xiandaihua di quyu yanjiu, Jiangsusheng, 1860–1916* (A regional study of modernization in China: Jiangsu province, 1860–1916) (Taibei: Institute of Modern History, Academia Sinica, 1984), 205–7.

38. *Chuansha xianzhi*, 8:40.

39. *Minlibao* (The people's stand) (Shanghai), April 18, 1911.

40. *Chuansha xianzhi*, 3:13.

41. *Chuansha xianzhi*, 3:12; Yang Tingdong, "Tiaocha Chuansha naoshi qingxing bin" (An investigation into the circumstances of the Chuansha disturbances) in *Shibao*, May 25, 1911.

42. *Chuangsha xianzhi*, 21:2.

43. *Shibao*, March 12, 1911.

44. Ibid.

45. Kathryn Bernhardt, *Rents, Taxes, and Peasant Resistance: The Lower Yangzi Region, 1840–1950* (Stanford: Stanford University Press, 1992). 153–55.

46. *Chuansha xianzhi*, 1:20, 8:40.

47. Ibid., 3:26b–28a.

48. *Shenbao* (Shanghai daily news), March 10, 1911; *Shibao*, March 9, April 11, 1911.

49. Yao Wennan, *Chuansha xianzhi*, 23:11; *Shibao*, March 5, 1911; *Minlibao* (The people's stand), April 19, 1911.

50. *Chuansha xianzhi*, 21:2.

51. Hu Qixi, "Jinggao Chuansha fulao zhi chou shanhoushiyi zhe" (Comments of respectful warning by the Chuansha elders on negotiations to remedy conditions), *Shibao*, April 2–3, 1911.

52. *Nanhui xianzhi* (Nanhui county gazetteer) 20 (1927): 3, 4.

53. Yuji Muramatsu, "Some Themes in Chinese Rebel Ideologies," in *The Confucian Persuasion*, Arthur F. Wright, ed. (Stanford: Stanford University Press, 1960), 246.

54. *Chuansha xianzhi*, 14:3.
55. Ibid., 14:6.
56. Ibid., 14:16; *Nanhui xianzhi*, 20:6.
57. *Chuansha xianzhi*, 14:10 no. 2, 14:11, no, 13.
58. Daniel L. Overmyer, *Folk Buddhist Religion: Dissenting Sects in Late Traditional China* (Cambridge: Harvard University Press, 1976), 135.
59. *Chuansha xianzhi*, 14:15, no. 48.
60. Ibid., 14:12, no. 17.
61. Ibid., 14:11, no. 10.
62. Ibid., 14:6, no. 54.
63. Yang Tingdong, *"Tiaocha Chuansha naoshi qingxing bin,"* May 25, 1911. The full report was published in *Shibao*, May 21–25, 1911. It is also included in *Chuansha xianzhi*, 23: 12–21. For a related discussion, see Prasenjit Duara, "Superscribing Symbols: The Myth of Guandi, Chinese God of War," in *The Journal of Asian Studies* 47, no. 4 (November 1988): 778–95.
64. *Minlibao*, March 29, 30, 1911.
65. "Chuansha Changren Gaochang Batuan Jiutuan zizhi gongsuo bin Su fu wen" (Report to the governor by the Changren, Gaochang, Batuan, and Jiutuan self-government bureaus at Chuansha), in *Chuansha xianzhi*, 23:9.
66. *Shibao*, March 5, 1911.
67. Ibid., March 9, 1911.
68. B. J. Ter Haar, *The White Lotus Teachings in Chinese Religious History* (Leiden: E. J. Brill, 1992), 262–63, 272–75. As Ter Haar points out, "elite and non-elite alike shared the belief in evil magicians," 281.
69. *Shibao*, March 5, 1911.
70. Yang Tingdong, *Shibao*, May 25, 1911.
71. *Chuansha xianzhi*, 23:9; *Shibao,* March 11, 1911.
72. *Shenbao*, March 9, 1911; *Shibao*, March 8, 1911.
73. "Su fu pi Hu dao binbao Chuansha zizhi naoshi qingxing" (Shanghai Daotai's report to the governor on the circumstances of the Chuansha self-government disturbances), in *Shibao*, April 11, 1911.
74. *Shenbao*, March 9, 1911; *Shibao*, March 8, 1911.
75. Yang Tingdong, *Shibao*, May 24, 1911.
76. Ibid., May 25, 1911.
77. "Report to the Governor," *Chuansha xianzhi*, 23:9; Yang Tingdong, *Shibao*, May 25, 1911.
78. Yang Tingdong, *Shibao*, May 25, 1911.
79. *Shibao*, March 5, 1911.
80. County manager (*dongshi, shen*) Xie Jiushan went to Nanjing to petition the governor-general in person. The governor-general then sent a telegram instructing Prefect Qiyang to investigate the Chuansha uprising (*Shenbao*, March 10, 1911).
81. *Shibao*, March 9, 1911; contains a reference to "weaving women" who feared new taxes.
82. "Report to the Governor," *Chuansha xianzhi*, 23:9.
83. *Shibao*, March 8, 1911.

84. "Shanghai Daotai's Report," *Shibao*, April 11, 1911.
85. Ibid.
86. *Chuansha xianzhi*, 18:5–10.
87. *Minlibao*, March 31, 1911.
88. Ibid., April 3, 1911.
89. *Nanhui xianzhi*, 20:6.
90. *Chuansha xianzhi*, 23:8.
91. Bernhardt, *Rents, Taxes, and Peasant Resistance*, 208–10.
92. *Shibao*, April 4, 1911.
93. *Shenbao*, March 26, 27, 1911.
94. *Shibao*, April 4, 1911.
95. Ibid.
96. Ibid.
97. Ibid., April 6, 1911.
98. Ibid., April 5, 6, 1911.
99. Ichiko Chuso, "The Gentry and the Chuan-sha Riot of 1911," in *Kindai Chugoku no seiji to shakai* (The politics and society of modern China) (Tokyo: Tokyo University Press, 1971); also a paper delivered at the Eighth Annual Meeting of the Far Eastern Association in Philadelphia, 1956, 25–26.
100. Ibid.

Epilogue:
A Place in the Twentieth Century

China's rural dissident history of the post-Boxer decade was a unique feature of China's political and social encounter with modernity. Nowhere else in world history did such a loud chorus of rural dissent accompany emerging industrial capital. The New Policy reforms that became the focus of rural activism in this decade were intertwined with ongoing county administrative problems, which had worsened during the nineteenth century but that also predated the recent decline. Issues of local elite legal and fiscal excesses were recurring administrative and social problems throughout China's dynastic history. Devastation surrounding the Taiping rebellion and the new levels of commercialization to which bureaucratic political structures were compelled to respond in order to survive resulted in a situation in which by 1895, 49 percent of all county magistrates held purchased degrees, signaling a decline in the quality and the length of tenure of these local officials.[1] What made the post-Boxer decade of reform fundamentally different from earlier periods was the necessity of addressing political and technological forces generated by industrial centers, both within and outside of China.

During this period of state-building, the place-based culture of rural protest came to the fore under circumstances with which it had never before dealt. Place-specific combinations of boxer activism, secret society groupings, and intervillage associations brought forth a dissident rural analysis that drew on the anti-imperial government focus of the Taiping tradition and the antiforeign perspective that dominated the Shandong Boxer movement in 1900. Against the state's increasing need to homogenize local county/village life into units of self-government, new police, new schools, and a culture of industrial scientism, rural dissent asserted its difference and the cultural and social structures that

257

supported it. Variations that constituted the uniqueness of each instance of protest as well as some common patterns across counties have been noted in the preceeding chapters. By demonstrating the ultimate incomparability among specific expressions of rural opposition to New Policy reforms, this study has argued for a place-based reading that takes a particular "social space" in all of its cultural, geographical, and economic dimensions as a central reference point, rather than defining "the local" primarily in relationship to national state authority and reducing each instance of protest to a case study in which the state-building process is the whole.

Modernity, often associated primarily with the structures of industrial economic and political life, arose not only from those structures but *in the processes occurring between* the impulses toward the industrial reorganization of life and the critiques of those emerging organizational forms. The focus on this space has been vital to the analysis offered here. Criticism regarding the unchecked, socially destructive consequences of political and economic development have been as central to defining the modern era as initially was the factory system and later its global extensions. From the rural areas of France and England to the farmlands of the U.S. Midwest, the evolution of the modern era has been shaped in part by challenges to the consequences of industrial capitalist logic. In this respect, as movements of resistance, the late-Qing peasant protests were a part of, not apart from, modernity's definition both in and beyond China. Because Chinese society was structured in some ways not shared by Western Europe, the pattern of rural defense in China carried its own dynamism, strengths, and weaknesses. Patterns of early twentieth century rural protest in China are another voice in the well-established currents of dissent first heard at the origins of the industrial experience, primarily England in the early nineteenth century. Entering the discourse on industrial social relations and culture at a time when many critical voices within Europe had already been eliminated or silenced, Chinese peasants raised anew, from their own place-based perspectives, issues related to decision making, natural resources, labor, culture, and education.

Chinese patterns of political and economic change come into focus around the problems encountered in applying Jurgen Habermas's concept of the "public sphere" to China. Defined as social space for rational critical discourse located in the salons and coffeehouses of eighteenth century Europe and occupied by the bourgeoisie, the "public sphere," according to Habermas, negotiated between remnants of the absolutist state and the private interests of influential families to evolve social space for rational critical discourse. When the "public sphere" became more inclusive in terms of class and gender as groups fought to extend the voting franchise and legal rights in the nineteenth and twentieth centuries, the "public sphere" declined and failed to continue its role as a check on the growth of state power and instead increasingly became defined by the structures of industrial capitalism. The distinctive aspect of Habermas's definition of "public sphere" is its association exclusively with the commercial middle class, the bourgeoisie. Even in eighteenth-century Europe, however, rational discourse and critiques of the state included more than the middle class. Peasants, aristocrats, and workers all had their critical practices in relationship to state authority. In feudal Europe, unlike bureaucratic, imperial China, the commercial class also had a structural separateness that gave it a degree of independence and hence Habermas's focus on this group as an agent of change even during the decline of its own socially created terrain.

In imperial China, the "public" in terms of rational discourse and critique of autocratic abuse was defined across the social spectrum and perhaps had its most critical edge within the rural tradition of peasant protest. Chinese scholars were well known for not being able to launch sustained critiques of the political center, and merchants sought their interests through inclusion in the bureaucratic order more than through legal or political opposition to it. Government officials and merchants as a group had little interest in or ability to carry out thoroughgoing reform let alone outright resistance to government policies. Within the Chinese social context, the rural practice of protest constituted a highly developed critique outside of the institutional political circles. With high levels of social mobility, Chinese society had degrees of elasticity uncharacteristic of the feudal structures against which the eighteenth-century European bourgeosie sought to define its sphere. As Benjamin Elman has suggested, in China, private (*si*) was more likely to refer to the individual or to non-family-based voluntary associations whereas public (*gong*) tended to imply family networks that extended from the household to the village and market town, and even to the regional and national levels.[2] Rather than evolving into a block pattern of social classes, such as the one in which the Western European commercial middle classes, particularly in France and England, gained their distinctiveness, the norm in Chinese society was to define public interest across class and status divisions, boundaries that by social convention in China were not fixed and both could be and were often traversed. Family-based associations were not the basis of public activity in bourgeois society. Within the European pattern, the "public sphere" also did not include resistance to itself. In fact, the formation of this public sphere channeled resistance outward against groups holding hereditary claims to authority. Employing notions of equality and democratic decision making based on individual civil rights, the bourgeoisie claimed

for itself alone the space of rational discourse. From a Chinese historical perspective, this looks more like the emergence of a private class
than the evolution of a public sphere. Either Habermas's concept of
"public sphere" does not apply to Chinese social structures, or we must
consider that in China the public sphere inclusive of groupings across
social-class boundaries was configured differently. The possibility of
social mobility through education for men along with diffuse religious/
philosophical systems that did not narrowly define rationality and included "the right to rebel against unjust authority," shifted the critical
terrain in China to include the rural sector of public life and in the
process opened political discourse within this context to social groups
that the English polity largely excluded. Rather than simply apply the
European model of the public sphere to China, analysis of rural political
activism in early twentieth-century China requires the inclusion of non-
bourgeoise groups in conceptualizations of the public sphere.

Because relationship to landholding is a factor central to discussions
of ruralism in the industrial and postindustrial eras, it is not surprising
that the retention of landownership by significant numbers of peasant
farmers in China was critical to the social role they were able to play in
protests against state reforms. This pattern of widespread, small-scale
private ownership stood in marked contrast to the status of peasants in
feudal and early modern Europe. Rough estimates averaged over the
last centuries of imperial rule indicate that ownership was about 70
percent in north China and 30 percent in the south with mixtures of
tenancy and part-ownership making up most of the remainder. Because
the Chinese peasants continued to possess claim to the land no matter
how tenuous, they always had a vital resource for livelihood regardless
of how difficult nature made things. While nature took its toll, misuse
of bureaucratic legal and fiscal authority more often proved the primary
source of deprivation and the rise of tenancy, which invariably accompanied socially induced hard times. Networks based on self-defense
grounded in the rural culture of protest were strong, viable entities in
Chinese society, and peasants held on to them well into the twentieth
century. Consequently, in China the "public sphere" did include the
possibility of resistance to itself by embodying communities that functioned to restore sustainable peasant livelihood. When the structures of
the status quo shifted decisively under the advent of modern economic
and military forces, the community protected by the culture of protest
was threatened with extinction and the possibility of adjustment gave
way eventually to the need for alternatives. In this shift, the Chinese
peasant tradition of protest entered into the discourse on modernity.

The voice of rural dissent was not an obstacle to political and economic change, it was a challenge to the choices made by those who saw

themelves as cultural mediators looking for ways to accommodate and benefit from adoption and adaptation of modern institutions. Even those like Zhang Jian, who attempted to create a "self-reliant" model of modernization at Nantong in Jiangsu, fifty miles north of Chuansha, eventually failed because of inability to address issues raised by the New Policy protesters across China.[3] Central to this conflict were definitions of wealth and power. Drawing attention through their dissent to the social meaning of wealth was the rural protesters' most valuable contribution to the dialogue on modernity. Writing on development, ecology, and women, Vandana Shiva has noted that,

> Culturally perceived poverty need not be real material poverty: subsistence economies which satisfy basic needs through self-provisioning are not poor in the sense of being deprived. . . . This cultural perception of prudent subsistence living as poverty has provided the legitimization for the development process as removing poverty. As a culturally biased project, it destroys wholesome and sustainable lifestyles and creates real material poverty, or misery, by the denial of survival needs themselves, through the diversion of resources to resource intensive commodity production.[4]

While living in commercialized agrarian economic settings, Ding Fei, Qu Shiwen, and Liu Xiangting all articulated this same view in defense of the integrity of their own place-specific social and cultural practices. Cai Shaoqing wrote that peasant activism sped up the collapse of the Qing.[5] But it did more than this, it raised serious questions about the projects of modernity and suggested a search for alternatives. Others at the time recognized this issue of new forms of poverty generated by the reforms themselves. Liu Shipei, we recall, wrote in 1907, "Examining the situation after the New Policy we find that all those who benefited are capitalists of the new party (*xindang*). Most of the population will be worse off, more impoverished than before."[6]

Working on similar problems of village-level development in Africa and other parts of the world in later decades, Albert Tévoédjrè argued for what he called a "regime of strict economy" based on self-reliant development and integrated growth founded on genuine needs. Mao Zedong's policies, he noted, sought to move in this direction. Tévoédjrè's definition of "poverty in power" proceeded from the notion that the poverty of the people must be worked into the politics and policies of power. Power for its own sake or for an elite, ultimately destroys itself and the larger social and natural environments in which it moves. In his view, "Politics is not merely a technique to gain or keep power or run the economy from above: it is above all a people's ability to organize themselves so as to have the means of choosing, criticizing and reflecting on the aims to be pursued."[7] At the end of the twentieth century, the same positions defended by Qu Shiwen, Ding Fei, and many others at the beginning of the century are still clear to those who stress rural well-being in connection with development projects.

Those who acted out of the practice of protest in early twentieth-century rural China expressed a fierce mixture of emotional and practical commitment to a ruralism that dwelled firmly within a sense of limits and order giving structure to life. Emotional underpinnings of culture keep a history of place in order. Flexible within limits, the boundaries and commitments that keep emotional structures in place are also deeply rooted and larger than reason. The historical record leaves only residues of these emotions in the class-based violence of the New Policy period, in the religious fervor of European and American missionaries, in the images of "the other" negotiated between Chinese and foreign cultural interpreters, and in the wild sounding rumors that circulated the countryside telling of foreigners who would drain the life blood of peasants with rail lines and telegraph wires. Emotional structures generated powerful sources of resistance and resilience in support of sustainable livelihood set within place-specific social and environmental conditions.

In preindustrial societies worldwide, the poetry of rural life, not to deny its many hardships, was most often integrated without much self-reflection into the songs and activities of daily life, weaving together the emotional fibers of rural perceptions and sensibilities. In the English setting where the attacks of industry and capitalism were most swift and brutal, and where the counterattacks by Luddites and Captain Swingers and others were also present, there is a startlingly clear expression in actual poetic form of the deep rootedness of these rural sensibilities. Born in Helpstone in 1793, John Clare became known as the "Northhamptonshire peasant poet." Clare was, as literary scholar Robert Pogue Harrison has noted, "the most authentic and inalienable voice of modern literature."[8] An agricultural laborer displaced by the Enclosure and Engrossing policies of rural capitalism in early nineteenth-century England, Clare found himself unemployed and even when employed unable to survive on falling wages. Eventually Clare was compelled to relocate his family from the land on which he had grown up and to which he felt deeply connected. His sense of disorientation was so great that he began to lose his sanity and in 1837, two years before the outbreak of the Opium War between China and England, Clare entered an asylum never to regain mental coherence except in his poetry. Recurring themes in Clare's poetry were a celebration of nature's poverty and an unbearable pain at the realization of nature's vulnerability before those who would define nature as commercial, taxable real estate. Included in this pain that led to insanity was the realization of human vulnerability before those who would deprive people of their means to a livelihood on the land. As Harrison has so poignantly summarized Clare's vision, "The greatest threat to freedom was the loss of habitat."[9] Humans as well as the plant and animal kingdoms shared an ecosystem that was poor in a miraculous way, generously providing subsistence and beauty more often than not.

In this selection from one of Clare's poems titled "The Lament of Swordy Well," the peasant poet has the land itself speak of the ravages it is experiencing:

> My mossy hills gain greedy hand
> And more then greedy mind
> Levels into a russet land
> Nor leaves a bent behind
> In summers gone I bloomed in pride
> Folks came for miles to prize
> My flowers that bloomed no where beside
> And scarce believed their eyes.[10]

While Wordsworth and others expressed similar outrages on nature's behalf in the early industrial era, Clare's poetic sensibility is connected to intimate knowledge of and appreciation for a specific place with its particular flowers and social customs and hence to issues of livelihood, community, and social values.

Although the wild fields where flowers and creatures were free to find their place had long since disappeared from much of the heavily cultivated rural landscape in China, nature still shaped the rhythms of rural life; and the themes of local habitat, freedom, and the positive value of agrarian material culture were present in the settings at Laiyang, Chuansha, and other locales. Compared with their counterparts in England, the Chinese peasants had some significant advantages. They had established claims to the land and a strong matrix of supporting cultural practices that could not be quickly destroyed. The Chinese peasants did not experience industrialization with the front seat intensity that befell the English countryside. Because the educated classes in China were sometimes lumped together with Chinese peasants by racist and imperialist European views, something that was not a part of England's class experience under industrialization, those who became reform managers during the New Policy era often shaped their identity around qualities reflected in Euro-American political and educational ideals. This in turn gained them some favor with the foreigners who were anxious to see their own ideas reflected in the Chinese environment. This was a dynamic in the Chinese situation that also allowed the lines of conflict between rural dissent and political elite to emerge more vividly.

Beginning in the early 1920s with the work of individuals like Peng Pai in Haifeng County, Guangdong province, the Chinese Communist movement gradually became aware of the necessity of supporting agrarian society while also attempting to transform some of its social relations and integrate it into a national plan for industrial development. Mao Zedong's policies in the late 1950s and 1960s were radical efforts to push forward this project that was itself eventually undone by the goal of competition with industrial capitalism, whether found in the views of Mao's political opponents or in Mao's staunch opposition to those views. In 1955 when Mao identified the work of Wang Guofan among the poorer farmers at Zunhua,[11] he sought along with others to raise sustainable self-reliance to a national model. The context of defense against and indirect competition with transnational capitalism was a critical factor shifting a potentially valuable approach, selective assistance of modern technology to fulfill the recurring dream of the security, simplicity, and fullness of village life, to another end entirely, that of coordinating national industrial, military, and economic strength for standing in the international community. The long-standing rural vision of the Peach Blossom Spring Village[12] where peace and harmony prevailed amidst a self-sufficient agrarian lifestyle was stood on its head, in service to state planning rather than removed from burdensome demands of the state.

Today the Chinese government has internalized policies based on the notion of poverty as deprivation rather than prudent living. During the Maoist years, there was a struggle to find an alternative way to combine a rural focus with industrial development through socialist economic planning and social engineering. Just as the peasant tradition of protest pursued its goals through collective means, the policies under Chinese socialism recognized the same necessity. Individual to individual approaches provide insufficient protection for the environmental and social conditions that foster living within fair limits. Although plagued with its own problems, this alternative modernity also had its significant successes in economic development, educational opportunity, and health care delivery for the general population, all of which surpassed in the 1970s their current levels in the late 1990s. With the abandonment of the socialist project, flawed as it was, was also lost the opportunity to reexamine and possibly overcome the problems generated by past efforts to evolve forms of technological know-how and social organization appropriate to the creation of a public discourse in which on-site place-based self-defense is the focal terrain for media and market activity.

Even during and after the events of 1901–11, the political and cultural effects of industrial capitalist development were clearly not limited to the Chinese peasant experience. On the pages of *Guofengbao, Shibao, Dongfang zazhi,* and other Chinese periodicals, separated only by the turning of pages from articles on Laiyang, Chuansha, and Lianzhou, was coverage of peasant activism half a world away in the Mexican Revolution of 1910.[13] Asia/Pacific connections through business and political discourse were clear to the editors and readers of the press in Shanghai, Guangzhou, Beijing, and elsewhere in China. Parallels and perils suggested by the interconnection of developments in places like China and Mexico did not escape observers at the time and have continued to reemerge into the present. News from Renshou, Sichuan province in 1993 and Chiapas, Mexico, in 1994 carry themes from the rural story already in progress at the beginning of this century.[14] There is no doubt that China's situation vis-à-vis international powers was urgent in the post-Boxer decade. Perhaps the reformers and revolutionaries of the day could not afford to pay attention to the rural perspective, critical as it was and based in a fundamentally different approach to livelihood, community, and culture. But then sooner or later they or we could ill-afford not to pay attention to it. It is often said that history sets constraints on the possibilities of a moment and that to ignore those conditions is to invite danger or disaster. It is also perilous to fortify those constraints when they are held in place with expanding social injustice.

It is easy to empathize with historical actors like Qu Shiwen, Ding Fei, Liu Xiangting, and others. No matter how imperfect they were as individuals, their social location and their willingness to act on behalf of others tend to strike an empathetic cord. Representatives of a sector of the rural population with the least material surplus and the most to lose in any oppositional activity, these rural leaders and their supporters by their genuine inclusion in the study of county politics shift the ground of discussion. Empathy, as we know, however, achieves little if it merely serves to posit a contrary view, itself not to be confused with analysis. In this connection Peter Burke once wrote:

(although I consider myself a socialist and a historian) I'm not a socialist historian; that is, I don't believe in socialist history. I believe that to use history as a weapon in political struggle is counter productive. One comes to believe one's own propaganda, to overdramatise the past, and hence to forget the real complexity of the issues at any time. One comes to idealise one's own side, and to divide human beings into Us and Them.[15]

This study has focused on the stories of those whose perspective has been generally omitted or obscured in the rendering of the historical complexities that characterized the post-Boxer decade in China. Without idealizing actors to whom one extends empathy or adopting an Us/Them approach held by many of the participants to these local conflicts that did, in fact, have their own measure of drama and were then dramatized in folk culture, the stories of these rural actors, in their incompleteness and fragmentation, capture levels of complexity that might otherwise remain hidden, embedded in abbreviated accounts or reduced to footnotes. The perspective of rural dissent that emerges in these five studies and the numerous contemporaneous protests does not fill out or complement work on county, provincial, and national levels of reform activity during the post-Boxer decade, it fundamentally changes the ground of discussion. From the dissident vantage point, issues of social justice were as important as questions of how to meet foreign threats and challenges brought by industrial competition, in fact, they were seen as entirely integral aspects of the same conflicts connecting county problems to all other levels of politics. Consequences for livelihood cannot be set aside once the shift is made to include these complexities, and issues of livelihood inevitably raise questions of political control and cultural group definition. How to open the process of political and economic change to include these issues was the ultimate complexity raised by rural dissent.

Issues raised by the Chinese peasant protests at the beginning of this century still await an answer as the century draws to a close. Is there a viable contemporary critique of modernity that values and supports the small agriculturalist and rural livelihood? Is unchecked industrial capitalism a changeable feature of, rather than synonymous with, modernity? Perhaps as Bruno Latour has suggested in the title of his book, *We Have Never Been Modern*,[16] we need only reclaim our connections to the land, to life, and to poetry beneath the powerful overlay of reductionist rationality and alienated self to find new ways to proceed beyond the inequities and blind spots of the past. In the end, the stories of peasant resistance in early twentieth-century China take their place in the continuing evolution of place-based movements of individuals seeking social and environmental integrity.

Notes

1. Kwang-ching Liu, "Nineteenth-Century China: The Disintegration of the Old Order and the Impact of the West," in *China in Crisis*, Ping-ti Ho and

Tang Tsou, eds., vol. 1, China's Heritage and the Communist Political System (Chicago: University of Chicago Press, 1968), 115.

2. Benjamin A. Elman, *Classicism, Politics, and Kinship: The Ch'ang-chou School of New Text Confucianism in Late Imperial China* (Berkeley: University of California Press, 1990), 34.

3. Kathy LeMons Walker, "Merchants, Peasants, and Industry: The Political Economy of Cotton Textiles, Nantong County, 1895–1935" (Ph.D. dissertation, University of California, Los Angeles, 1986), 336.

4. Vandana Shiva, "Development, Ecology, and Women," in *Healing the Wounds: The Promise of Ecofeminism,* ed. Judith Plant (Santa Cruz, Calif.: New Society Publishers, 1989), 87–88.

5. Cai Shaoqing, *Zhongguo jindai huidang shi yanjiu* (Historical research on secret societies in modern China) (Beijing: Xinhua shudian, 1987), 40–41.

6. Liu Shipei, "Lun xinzheng wei bingmingzhi gen" (A discussion of New Policy as the root of people's suffering), in *Tianyi bao* (Natural justice), nos. 8–10 (1907), in *Wuzhengfuzhuyi sixiang ziliaoxuan* (Collected materials on anarchist thought) (Beijing: Beijing daxue qubanshe, 1984) 108. Also see, Liu Shipei, "Wuzhengfu geming yu nongmin geming" (Anarchist revolution and peasant revolution) *Tianyi bao*, 1908, in *Wushengfuzhuyi sixiang ziliaoxuan* (Beijing: Renmin chuban she, 1984) 158–62.

7. Albert Tévoédjrè, *Poverty, Wealth of Mankind* (Oxford: Pergamon Press, 1979) 103. See also 64, 98–101.

8. Robert Pogue Harrison, *Forests, The Shadow of Civilization* (Chicago: University of Chicago Press, 1992) 212.

9. Ibid., 215.

10. Ibid.

11. *Zhongguo nongcun de shehuizhuyi gaozhao* (Chinese agriculture's high tide of socialism), vol. 1, 3–5, 16.

12. This reference is to the fable by Tao Chien (365–427 A.D.) in which villagers live in a hidden valley cut off from the rest of world. They remain free of government influence to live peacefully and seek to protect their isolation. It has remained a metaphor for the village paradise in Chinese folklore and philosophy.

13. See "The Disturbance in Mexico," *Dongfang zazhi* 8, no. 1 (1911): 18; 8, no. 4 (1911): 21; "Truce in Mexico," *Guofengpao* 2, no. 8 (1910): 96.

14. See *China Focus*, 1, no. 3 (April 30, 1993): 5. In this report up to ten thousand peasants took part in a protest against excessive demands by government officials for miscellaneous fees. Renshou was involved in the 1909 New Policy protest at Weiyuan, Sichuan. *China Focus*, 2, no. 1 (January 1, 1994) carries an article about peasant disturbances in more than twenty provinces in the previous year with a range of issues from police and educational fees to forced magazine subscriptions and marriage insurance. For a discussion of contemporary village issues see Dev Nathan and Govind Kelkar, "Collective Villages in the Chinese Market," in *Economic and Political Weekly*, May 3 and 10, 1997. Regarding the uprising in Chiapas, Mexico, which came to international attention on January 1, 1994, many books and articles have been written. *First*

World, Ha Ha Ha! The Zapatista Challenge, edited by Elaine Katzenberger, discusses the land and justice issues in Chiapas in the context of global resistance to policies of economic colonization.

15. Peter Burke, "People's History or Total History," in *People's History and Socialist Theory,* Raphael Samuel, ed. (Routledge and Kegan Paul, 1981), 8.

16. Bruno Latour, *We Have Never Been Modern,* translated by Catherine Porter (Cambridge: Harvard University Press, 1993).

Appendix

Item #1: Anonymous placard posted at Shuang-liu county (fifteen miles southwest of Chengdu, Sichuan), April 1910

Translated by W. H. Wilkinson, consul-general at Chengdu, May 1, 1910

Source: F.O. 228/1758, Dispatch No. 33, May 3, 1910

I

The month is at the flower-dawn,
Farming is active;
Sudden rumours are rising
To men's agitation.

Don't say these are rumours,
Real trouble involves you.

His honour the Magistrate
Pretends to be sleeping,
But I'll now expound it,
Pay heed to what follows.

Foreign outlanders
With money in plenty
Are bribing our people.

Insensate folks listen;
Tell them there is money,

At once they are dazzled,
Tricked out like wild Daoists.

All around they talk loosely;
Some are in Business,
Sell needles, sell physic,
Change silk for worked slippers,
And women are dazzled.

This sort of cheapness
All do not comprehend it.

Yet lives are the forfeit,

'Tis hard in the telling.
When they meet with small boys,
They first cut off the privates.

'Tis horribly painful
And incense surceases.

The harm is not little
But mandarins reck not.

These sit in their yamens,
Caring only for pleasure,
Or bent on new dodges
Beyond telling, beyond telling.

There is yet one thing other
Tombs are rifled and in graveyards,
Coffins broken, corpses pillaged.

The thing is truly hateful.
Our very own forebearers
How have they offended?

When we ponder on these things
They seem brutally wicked,
If Heaven has eyes, why
Are these men not struck dead?

Alas for our villagers,
Who are so weak!

II

Eyes starting, heart aflame,
Find a solution.
Earnestly hoping now
All will unite, and,
Should such a thing happen
Join forces and seige them.

Our own village trainbands
Assemble and capture,
Not asking officials
But slaughtering promptly
Even if they use magic
They'll hardly escape us.

If you take them alive, then
Strip them stark naked;
Be sure on their bodies
You'll discover a plaster.

So cudgels won't kill them
But do not be flustered.

Get swords and spears ready,
Slice them and mince them,
Fling them dead in the river.

Rolled down to the sea caves,
When the Dragon Prince finds them
He'll deal them out justice.

III

Say this in earnest:
Unite your endeavors
Get ready your weapons,
Don't wait to arouse yourselves
Now is the time for it,
Living and dead will both profit.

GLOSSARY

Chinese characters are not given for names listed in Hummel's *Eminent Chinese of the Ch'ing Period* or for places included in Playfair's *The Cities and Towns of China*.

Atai	阿太	chuanpiao	傳票
		Chuansha	川沙
Baima	白馬	chushan	出山
baixing	百姓	Cixi	慈谿
ban zigeng nong	半自耕農	cun	村
bao	堡	cunshoushi	村首事
Bao Yiqing	包乙清	cunzhang	村長
baoban	包辦		
baojia	保甲		
baolan	包攬	Da Jirui	達吉瑞
baoshou	包收	Dabu	大埔
baozheng	包征	dahu	大戶
Batuan	八團	Dalihui	大禮會
Bolin	柏林	dang	黨
		Danyang	丹陽
Cai Songfu	蔡嵩甫	daotai	道台
Cao Asi	曹阿四	daqian	大錢
Cao Shufen	曹樹棻	Darenhui	大人會
Chahe	岔河	Dayihui	大義會
Changge	長葛	Dazhihui	大智會
Changren	長人	Dazhu	大竹
Chen Kuilong	陳夔龍	De He	德和
Chen Jiren	陳吉人	De Shou	德壽
Chen Songnian	陳松年	Deng Huanzhen	鄧煥楨
Chen Weishan	陳惟善	Deng Shaozhen	鄧紹楨
Chen Yajian	陳雅囝	Deqing	德清
Chen Yuanbing	陳元炳	dibao	地保
Chen Youheng	陳有恒	diding qian	地丁錢
Chen Yude	陳玉德	diding yin	地丁銀
Chen Zhaogui	陳朝貴	difang	地方
Chen Zilian	陳子連	difang tugun	地方土棍
Cheng'an	成安	youmin	莠民
chengshen	城紳	Ding (née)	丁費氏
Chenjiaqiao	陳家橋	Fei shi	
chicaidang	吃菜黨	Ding Pangui	丁攀桂
chuanpai	傳牌	Ding Shiren	丁世仁

273

Ding Shiyi	丁世嶧	Gu Ciying	顧次英
Ding Shiying	丁世英	Gu Liang	顧良
ding shui	丁稅	Gu Naihuang	顧乃璜
dingmenpai	釘門牌	Gu Shouxian	顧守先
Dongce	東冊	Gu Tingxiang	顧廷香
dongshi	董事	Gu Yiyuan	顧懿淵
dongshihui	董事會	Gu Yingjiang	顧瀅江
duobazi	舵把子	Gu Zhixiang	顧致祥
Du Jiujin	杜九金	Gu Zhongyi	顧忠宜
Du Shifu	杜世福	Guandi	關帝
		guan shanghui shi	管商會事
Fei Ahu	費阿虎		
Feng Guowei	馮國威	Guanyin	觀音
Feng Tongming	馮通明	gugong	雇工
fengjian	封建	Gui'an	歸安
fu	府	guijia	櫃價
Fu Shan	傅山	Guijiao	規教
Fu Xiang Yi	蚨祥義	Guo Funian	郭福年
Fu Yuan	富源	guoxuesheng	國學生
fugongsheng	副貢生		
fuhu	富戶	Haidi	海底
Furen wenshe	輔仁文社	Haiyang	海陽
fushen	富紳	He Rongguang	何榮光
		hetong	合同
gang	港	Hong Quanfu	洪全福
gangshuang	扛孀	Hong Yusheng	洪遹聲
Gao Qiwang	高起望	Hongdengjiao	紅燈教
Gao Yufeng	高玉峰	Hongheipai	紅黑牌
Gaochang	高昌	Hu Sijing	胡思敬
Ge Guixing	葛桂星	Hu Xuehai	胡學海
Gedihui	哥弟會	Hu Yugai	胡馭垓
Gelaohui	哥老會	Huang Jiajun	黃家駿
Gong Ju	公聚	Huang Jiashu	黃加樹
Gong Shun	公順	Huang Jintai	黃金台
Gong Wojiang	龔臥江	Huang Long	黃龍
Gong Xiaojiang	龔曉江	Huang Maolang	黃毛郎
Gongzhen	公鎮	Huang Minzhi	黃敏之
gongju	公舉	Huang Shangda	黃上達
gongsi	公司	Huang Song	黃松
Gu A'er	顧阿二	Huang Tingru	黃庭孺
Gu Asong	顧阿松	Huang Xushan	黃敘山
Gu Chengbu	顧成圃	Huang Xusheng	黃旭昇

Huang Yanpei	黃炎培	Li Xiushan	李秀山
Huang Zhiyi	黃志伊	Li Yashi	李亞石
hui	會	Li Zhisheng	李植生
Huigong	會公	Liang Beishui	梁北水
		Liang Muguang	梁慕光
Jiang Ershou	姜爾受	Lianhua	蓮花
Jiang Meitang	姜美堂	Lianzhou	連州
jiansheng	監生	lianzhuang hui	連莊會
jiaoyu hui	教育會	Liao Jiumei	廖九妹
jiazhang	甲長	Ling Yundeng	凌雲等
Jinan ribao	濟南日報	Lingkou	泠口
Jinshan	金山	Lingshan	靈山
jinshi	進士	Liu Binxian	劉賓賢
jiudang	舊黨	Liu Chufan	劉楚藩
jiudong	舊董	Liu Fu'an	劉幅安
Jiulihe	九里河	Liu Jixi	劉緝熙
jiushi dongshi	舊時董事	Liu Mianzhai	劉勉齋
Jiutuan	九團	Liu Shiliang	劉師亮
juren	舉人	Liu Shuntian	劉順田
		Liu Songqiao	劉松喬
Kaiyuan	開元	Liu Tiancheng	劉添成
kejuan	苛捐	Liu Xiangting	劉香廷
Kuibao	奎保	Liu Zhancheng	劉占成
		Liu Zhenduo	劉振鐸
Laiyang	萊陽	Liujiatuan	劉加疃
langshou	榔首	Liuzao	六竃
Lao Taitai	老太太	Long Yiyuan	龍裔元
laobaixing	老百姓	Long Yizhen	龍裔禎
Lei Yanguan	雷鹽官	Longyao	
li	里	(Longping)	隆平
Li Antang	李安堂	lougui	陋規
Li Ganshan	李干山	Lü Baohuang	呂保璜
Li Guanmei	李觀梅	Lü Bingzhong	呂秉忠
Li Guofeng	李國楓	Lü Conglü	呂從律
Li Hailong	李海龍	Lu Fengqi	魯鳳歧
Li Jinsheng	李金盛	Lu Jiaji	陸家驥
Li Jitang	李紀堂	(Lu Yiru	陸逸如)
Li Lanzhai	李藍齋	Lü Tiaoyuan	呂調元
Li Shaoyi	李紹伊	Lu Xirong	陸錫榮
Li Shoushan	李壽山	Lülin	綠林
Li Songping	李松平	Luo Jiucheng	羅九成
Li Xiuqing	李秀清		

Ma Yi'ang	馬亦昂	Qu Shigui	曲士貴
Ma Xiaoshan	馬孝山	Qu Shiwen	曲士文
macha	馬差	qudong	區董
Mai Rongguang	麥榮光		
Malianzhuang	馬連莊	Ren Zhixue	任致學
Mashanbu	馬山埠	renkou shui	人口稅
Miao Zhen	苗珍	Renshu	仁術
miaodong	廟董		
Mingxin	明新	Sanguan	三官
minzhuang	民壯	Sanguoyanyi	三國演義
Mixian	密縣	Sanjiang	三江
Mo Xuixiong	莫輝熊	Shandong lüjing	山東旅京
Mo Huixun	莫輝勳	tongxianghui	同鄉會
mou	畝	Shang Qinghan	尚慶韓
		Shangdian	尚店
Nanhui	南匯	Shangyu	上虞
Nanshi	南市	Shaoxing	紹興
Nian	捻	Shao Guzi	邵古仔
nongmin	農民	Shashangdian	沙尚店
		Shatu	沙塗
Ou Yang	歐陽	she	社
Ou Jinsheng	歐金生	She Zeng	社增
		shendong	紳董
Pan Fengyang	潘鳳陽	shenfushi	紳富士
Pan Fengyi	潘鳳怡	sheng	升
Pan Qingyun	潘青雲	shengyuan	生員
Pan Shouqin	潘守勤	shenshi	紳士
Pudong	浦東	shezhang	社長
		Shi Hui	施惠
Qian Jingshan	錢京山	Shi Jianru	史堅如
Qian'an	遷安	Shi Pengling	施彭齡
qianpu	錢鋪	Shi Shijiao	石士焦
qiangshuang	搶孀	Shiqiao	石橋
Qiaobangou	橋板溝	Shiquewo	石確窩
Qin Chenming	秦臣明	shoushi	首事
Qin Erxiong	秦爾雄	Shude	樹德
Qingming	清明	Shuigoutou	水溝頭
Qiyang	戚揚	Shuihu zhuan	水滸傳
Qu Guofu	曲國福	shuli	書吏
Qu Hongchang	曲洪昌	Shuntian shibao	順天時報
Qu Hongjiang	曲洪江	shuyuan	書院
Qu Laowu	曲老五	si	寺

sizhang	寺長	Wang Ling	王令
Song Juncai	宋俊才	Wang Qi	王圻
Song Juren	宋居仁	Wang Xu	王埩
Song Weikun	宋維坤	Wang Tinglan	王廷蘭
Song Xunji	宋塤吉	Wang Wencheng	王文澄
Song Xuanwen	宋煊文	Wang Wenxuan	王文宣
Song Zengji	宋增吉	Wang Xiu	王秀
songgun	訟棍	Wang Yunhua	王雲華
Songjiang	宋江	Wang Zhixun	王志勳
songsou	訟藪	Wang Zhongfu	王中府
suigongsheng	歲貢生	Wangshishan	望石山
Sun Baoqi	孫寶琦	Wei Longzhang	尉龍章
Sun Mengqi	孫孟起	Weiyuan	威遠
Sun Peinan	孫佩南	Wen Qi	文淇
Sun Wenbin	孫文彬	Wucheng	烏程
		Wu Daben	吳大奔
Taiping	太平	Wu Shaoyou	吳紹游
Taizizhuang	台子莊	Wu Yannan	吳雁南
tang	堂	Wujin	武進
Tang Hongyou	唐鴻猷	wulai guntu	無賴棍徒
Tang Shangda	唐上達	Wulong	五龍
Tang Shunda	唐順達	wushenggong	武聖宮
Tang Zeyu	唐則瑀	wushengmu	無生母
tangchai	塘差	Wuyang	武陽
Tangjia	唐家		
tangkou	堂口	Xi Akui	奚阿奎
Tangmuqiao	唐墓橋	Xi Shou	奚壽
tangzhang	塘長	xian	縣
Tao Shouheng	陶守恒	xiang	鄉
ting	廳	xiangdong	鄉董
Tongxiang	桐鄉	xiangmin	鄉民
tongyuan	銅元	xiangzhang	鄉長
tu	圖	xiangzuo	鄉佐
tuanlian	團練	Xiao Zhiquan	肖治權
Wang Baotian	王寶田	xiaohu	小戶
Wang Chi	王墀	Xiaoshui	小水
Wang Daolai	王道來	Xie Richang	謝日昌
Wang Chengxun	王承壎	Xie Youshan	謝酉山
Wang Congman	王從滿	Xie Zuantai	謝纘泰
Wang Fengzhao	王鳳朝	Xiguan	西館
Wang Jingyue	王景嶽	Xin'an	新安
Wang Langan	王灆杆	xindang	新黨

Xindian	新店	Yu Chunling	于春齡
xindong	新董	Yu Zanyang	于贊揚
Xingang	新港	Yu Zhusan	于祝三
Xingzhonghui	興中會	Yuan Feng	源豐
Xingzi	星子	Yuan Shun	源順
xinzheng	新政	Yugong	俞公
Xiucai	秀才	Yujiadian	于家店
xiushi	秀士	Yulaoye	俞老爺
Xiyouji	西游記	yulun	輿論
Xu Liushun	徐六順	Yuchitou	魚池頭
Xu Da Adi	徐大阿弟	Yuyao	餘姚
Xu Zongmei	徐宗美		
xuan min	選民	Zeng Ayi	曾阿義
Xue Weilun	薛維輪	zengsheng	增生
xuetang	學堂	Zhang Amu	張阿木
Yang Fanqing	楊氾清	Zhang Axi	張阿希
Yang Shaonan	楊紹南	Zhang Bingsheng	張丙生
Yang Tingdong	楊廷棟	Zhang Bingyi	張炳夷
Yang Xiu	楊秀	Zhang Fushan	張福山
Yang Quyun	楊衢云	Zhang Jieli	張介禮
Yang Yaolin	楊耀琳	Zhang Jiesheng	張介生
Yang Yuchun	楊玉春	Zhang Ming	張明
Yang Zhenyong	楊振鏞	Zhang Shangsi	張尙思
Yang Zhurong	楊竹蓉	Zhang Shouli	張守禮
Yantai	煙臺	Zhang Shunqing	張舜卿
Yao Weisong	岳維嵩	Zhang Wenming	張文明
Yao Wennan	姚文枏	Zhang Wenqing	張文卿
Yaogezhuang	姚各莊	Zhang Xiangmo	張相謨
yayi	衙役	Zhang Yinglin	張英麟
Ye Changsheng	葉長盛	Zhang Zhihe	張志鶴
Ye Guilin	葉桂林	(Zhang Fangmei	張訪梅)
Ye Qisen	葉其森	Zhang Zoushao	張奏韶
Ye Qisu	葉其蘇	Zhao Erxun	趙爾巽
Ye Sigao	葉嗣高	Zhao Naipan	趙乃泮
Yejiazhuang	葉家莊	Zhao Renshao	趙仁紹
Yexian	葉縣	Zhao Shide	趙世德
yitiao bianfa	一條鞭法	Zhaoge	趙格
Yixing	宜興	Zhaoyuan	招遠
Yizhou	易州	Zhengzhou	鄭州
yong	勇	zhiqian	制錢
Yongzhuang	永莊	Zhiyuantang	至遠堂
You Guifen	尤桂芬	zhou	州

Zhou Shubiao	周樹標
Zhoujiatuan	周家疃
Zhu Boda	朱伯達
Zhu (née) Gu shi	朱顧氏
Zhu Hongdeng	朱紅燈
Zhu Huaizhi	朱槐之
Zhu Shunqing	朱舜卿
Zhu Shunsheng	朱順生
Zhu Songren	祝嵩仁
zhuang	莊
zigeng nong	自耕農
zizhi ju	自治局
zongbao	總保
Zunhua	遵化
Zuo Shaozuo	左紹佐

Bibliography

Ahern, Emily M. *The Cult of the Dead in a Chinese Village.* Stanford: Stanford University Press, 1973.

Ainscough, Thomas M. *Notes from a Frontier.* Shanghai: Kelly and Walsh, Ltd., 1915.

Baber, E. Colborne. *Travels and Researches in Western China.* London: John Murray, Albemarles Street, 1882.

Barkan, Lenore. "Patterns of Power: Forty Years of Elite Politics in a Chinese County." In *Chinese Local Elites and Patterns of Dominance,* ed. Joseph W. Esherick and Mary Backus Rankin. Berkeley: University of California Press, 1990.

Bashford, Reverend Bishop. "General Survey, 1911." In *The China Mission Year Book,* ed. Rev. G. H. Bonfield. Shanghai: Christian Literature Society for China, 1912.

Bastid, Marianne. "Currents of Social Change." In *Cambridge History of China,* vol. 11, ed. John K. Fairbank and Kwang-ching Liu. Cambridge: Cambridge University Press, 1980.

———. "The Social Context of Reform." In *Reform in Nineteenth-Century China,* ed. Paul Cohen and John E. Schrecker. Cambridge: Harvard University Press, 1976.

Benjamin, Walter. "The Storyteller." In *Illuminations.* London: Fontana, 1992.

Bernhardt, Kathryn. *Rents, Taxes, and Peasant Resistance: The Lower Yangzi Region, 1840–1950.* Stanford: Stanford University Press, 1992.

———. "Elite and Peasant during the Taiping Occupation of the Jiangnan, 1860–1864." *Modern China* 13, no. 4 (October 1987): 379–410.

Bondfield, Reverend G. H. *The China Mission Year Book.* Shanghai: Christian Literature Society for China, 1912.

Brown, Arthur J. *The Chinese Revolution.* New York: Student Volunteer Movement for Foreign Missions, 1912.

———. *The Lien-chou Martyrdom.* New York: The Willet Press, 1905.

Buck, David D. *Urban Change in China: Politics and Development in Tsinan, Shantung, 1890–1949.* Madison: University of Wisconsin Press, 1978.

Buck, John Lossing. *Chinese Farm Economy: A Study of 2866 Farms in Seven-*

teen Localities and Seven Provinces in China. Chicago: University of Chicago Press, 1930.

Cai Shaoqing. *Zhongguo jindai huidang shi yanjiu* (Historical research on modern Chinese secret societies). Beijing: Xinhua shudian (New China books), 1987.

———. "Lun Xinhai geming yu huidang de guanxi" (On the relationship between the 1911 Revolution and secret societies). In *Jinian xinhaigeming qi shi zhounian* (Commemorating the seventieth anniversary of the 1911 Revolution). Beijing: Zhonghua shuju, 1983.

Chai Degeng et al. *Xinhai geming* (The 1911 Revolution), vol. 3, comp. Chinese Historical Association, 8 vols. Shanghai: Renmin chuban she, 1957.

Chang, Chung-li. *The Income of the Chinese Gentry.* Seattle: University of Washington Press, 1962.

———. *The Chinese Gentry: Studies on Their Role in Nineteenth-Century Chinese Society.* Seattle: University of Washington Press, 1955.

Chang, P'eng-yüan. "The Constitutionalists." In *China in Revolution: The First Phase, 1900–1913,* ed. Mary Clabaugh Wright. New Haven: Yale University Press, 1968.

Chang, P'eng-yüan (Zhang Pengyuan). "Jindai difang zhengzhi canyu di mengya" (Beginnings of modern local political participation—The Hunan example). *Bulletin of Historical Research,* no. 4 (April 1976), The Graduate Institute of History and the Department of History, National Taiwan Normal University, Taibei.

Chang Yü-fa (Zhang Yufa). "Qingmo Minchu di Shandong difang zizhi" (Local self-government of Shandong in the late Qing and early republican China). *Zongyang yenjiu yuan jindai shi yenjiu suo jikan* (Bulletin of the Institute of Modern History Academia Sinica), 6 (1977), 159–84.

Chatterjee, Partha. "Beyond the Nation? Or Within?" *Economic and Political Weekly,* January 4–11, 1997, 30–34.

Chen Chi-yun. "Liang Ch'i-ch'ao's 'Missionary Education': A Case Study of Missionary Influence on the Reformers," in *Papers on China,* Harvard, 66–124.

Chen, Xulu. *Xinhai geming* (The 1911 Revolution). Shanghai: Renmin chuban she, 1955.

Chen, Yung-fa. *Making Revolution.* Berkeley: University of California Press, 1986.

Chesneaux, Jean, ed. *Popular Movements and Secret Societies in China, 1840–1950.* Stanford: Stanford University Press, 1972.

———. "La Participation des classes populaires au mouvement national chinois (XIXe–XXe siècles)" (The participation of the popular classes in the national Chinese movement, 19th–20th centuries). Commission Internationale D'Histoire des Mouvements Sociaux et des Structures Sociales, *Mouvements d' independence et classes populaires aux XIX ^{e} et XXe siècles en occident et en orient,* tome II. Paris: Libraire Armand Colin, 1971.

———. *Secret Societies in China in the Nineteenth and Twentieth Centuries.* Hong Kong: Heinemann Educational Books, 1971.

————. "Egalitarian and Utopian Traditions in the East." *Diogenes* (1968): 76–102.

Chiang, Siang-tseh. *The Nien Rebellion.* Seattle: University of Washington Press, 1954.

Ch'ü, T'ung-tsu. *Local Government in China under the Ch'ing.* Cambridge: Harvard University Press, 1962.

————. *Law and Society in Traditional China.* Paris: Mouton, 1961.

————. "Chinese Class Structure and Its Ideology." In *Chinese Thought and Institutions,* ed. John K. Fairbank. Chicago: University Press of Chicago, 1957.

"Chuansha Changren Gaochang Batuan Jiutuan zizhi gongsuo bin Su fu wen" (Report to the governor by the Changren, Gaochang, Batuan, and Jiutuan self-government bureaus at Chuansha), *Chuanxha xianzhi, juan,* no. 23, 1936.

Chuansha xianzhi (Chuansha county gazetteer), 24 *juan,* Taibei reprint, 1936.

Clastres, Pierre. *Society against the State: Essays in Political Anthropology.* New York: Zone Books, 1987.

Cohen, Paul. *History in Three Keys: The Boxers as Event, Experience, and Myth.* New York: Columbia University Press, 1997.

Davis, Fei-ling. *Primitive Revolutionaries of China: A Study of Secret Societies in the Late Nineteenth Century.* Honolulu: University Press of Hawaii, 1971.

Dirlik, Arif. "Globalism and the Politics of Place." *Development* (1998): 41:2: 7–13.

————. "Civil Society/Public Sphere in Modern China: As Critical Concepts versus Heralds of Bourgeois Modernity." Zhongguo shehui kexue jikan (Chinese social sciences quarterly), no. 3 (summer 1993): 10–22. (published simultaneously in Chinese and English).

————. *Anarchism in the Chinese Revolution.* Berkeley: University of California Press, 1991.

————. "Vision and Revolution: Anarchism in Chinese Revolutionary Thought on the Eve of the 1911 Revolution." *Modern China* (April 1986): 123–65.

Dongfang zazhi (Eastern miscellany), Shanghai, 1908–1911.

Duara, Prasenjit. *Rescuing History from the Nation: Questioning Narratives of Modern China.* Chicago: University of Chicago Press, 1995.

————. "Knowledge and Power in the Discourse on Modernity: The Campaigns against Popular Religion in Early Twentieth-Century China." *Journal of Asian Studies* 50, no. 1 (February 1991): 67–83.

————. *Culture, Power, and the State: Rural North China, 1900–1942.* Stanford: Stanford University Press, 1988.

————. "Superscribing Symbols: The Myth of Guandi, Chinese God of War." *Journal of Asian Studies* 47, no. 4 (November 1988): 778–95.

Elman, Benjamin A. *Classicism, Politics, and Kinship: The Ch'ang-chou School of New Text Confucianism in Late Imperial China.* Berkeley: University of California Press, 1990.

Elvin, Mark. "Market Towns and Waterways: The County of Shanghai from 1480–1910." In *The City in Late Imperial China,* ed. G. William Skinner. Stanford: Stanford University Press, 1977.

Elvin, Mark, and G. William Skinner, eds. *The Chinese City between Two Worlds*. Stanford: Stanford University Press, 1974.

Engel, Barbara Alpern. "Women, Men, and the Language of Peasant Resistance, 1870–1907." In *Cultures in Flux: Lower-Class Values, Practices, and Resistance in Late Imperial Russia*, ed. Stephen P. Frank and Mark D. Steinberg. Princeton: Princeton University Press, 1994.

Escobar, Arturo. *Encountering Development: The Making and Unmaking of the Third World*. Princeton: Princeton University Press, 1995.

Esherick, Joseph W. *The Origins of the Boxer Uprising*. Berkeley: University of California Press, 1987.

———. *Reform and Revolution in China: The 1911 Revolution in Hunan and Hubei*. Berkeley: University of California Press, 1976.

Esherick, Joseph W., and Mary B. Rankin, eds. *Chinese Local Elites and Patterns of Dominance*. Berkeley: University of California Press, 1990.

Fairbank, John K. *The United States and China*. Cambridge: Harvard University Press, 1979.

Fairbank, John K., ed. *Chinese Thought and Institutions*. Chicago: Chicago University Press, 1957.

Fairbank, John K., and Edwin O. Reischauer. *East Asia: The Great Tradition*. Boston: Houghton Mifflin Co., 1958.

Faure, David. *The Rural Economy of Pre-Liberation China: Trade Expansion and Peasant Livelihood in Jiangsu and Guangdong, 1870–1937*. Hong Kong: Oxford University Press, 1989.

———. "The Rural Economy of Kiangsu Province, 1870–1911." *The Journal of the Institute of Chinese Studies of the Chinese University of Hong Kong*, 9, no. 2 (1978): 365–471.

———. "Local Political Disturbances in Kiangsu Province, China, 1870–1911." Ph.D. Dissertation, Princeton University, 1976.

Fei, Hsiao-tung. "Peasantry and Gentry: An Interpretation of Chinese Social Structure and Its Changes." *The American Journal of Sociology* (July 1946): 1–17.

———. *Peasant Life in China: A Field Study of Country Life in the Yangtze Valley*. New York: E. P. Dutton and Co., 1939.

Feuerwerker, Albert. *Economic Trends in the Republic of China, 1912–1949*. Ann Arbor: Center for Chinese Studies, University of Michigan, 1977.

———. *Economic Trends in the Republic of China, 1912–1949*. Ann Arbor: Center for Chinese Studies, University of Michigan, 1975.

Fincher, John H. *Chinese Democracy: Statist Reform, The Self-Government Movement and Republican Revolution*. Tokyo: Institute for the Study of Languages and Cultures of Asia and Africa, 1989.

Frank, Stephen P., and Mark D. Steinberg. *Cultures in Flux: Lower-Class Values, Practices, and Resistance in Late Imperial Russia*. Princeton: Princeton University Press, 1994.

Freedman, Maurice. *Chinese Lineage and Society: Fukien and Kwangtung*. London: The Athlone Press, 1971.

Friedman, Edward. *Backward toward Revolution*. Berkeley: University of California Press, 1974.

———. *Lineage Organization in Southeastern China.* London: The Athlone Press, 1965.

Gaffe, Herbert. "Intelligence Report for the Quarter Ended June 30, 1910, Nanking." F.O. 228/1762.

Gallin, Bernard. *Hsin Hsing, Taiwan: A Chinese Village in Change.* Berkeley: University of California Press, 1966.

Gamble, Sidney D. *North China Villages: Social, Political, and Economic Activities before 1933.* Berkeley: University of California Press, 1963.

———. *Ting Hsien: A North China Rural Community.* New York: Institute of Pacific Relations, 1954.

Gong Shuduo and Chen Guiying. "Cong Qing junjichu dangan kan Xinhai geming qian qunzong de fankang douzheng" (View from the Qing military department archives of the mass tax resistance struggles before the 1911 Revolution). In *Beijing Shifan daxue xuebao* (Beijing Normal University academic journal), no. 3 (1961): 1–13.

Great Britain, Foreign Office Archives. London: Public Record Office, 1905–1911. (1) F.O. 228, Embassy and Consular Archives, (2) F.O. 371, Foreign Office Correspondence.

Grove, Linda. "Rural Society in Revolution: The Gaoyang District, 1910–1947." Ph.D. Dissertation, University of California, Berkeley, 1975.

Guangdong chuansheng difang jiyao (Guangdong provincial survey), vol. 3, Taibei reprint, 1934.

"Guangdong Lianzhou xiangmin zishi xukai" (The disturbance at Lianzhou, Guangdong, continues) *Dongfang zazhi,* no. 11, 1910, 100/8722; also, no. 122, 1910, 108–9/ 18912–13.

Guofengbao (National Customs). Beijing: 1910.

Haar, B. J. Ter. *The White Lotus Teachings in Chinese Religious History.* Leiden, The Netherlands: E. J. Brill, 1992.

Habermas, Jurgen. *The Structural Transformation of the Public Sphere: An Inquiry into a Category of Bourgeois Society,* trans. Thomas Burger with the assistance of Frederick Lawrence. Cambridge: MIT Press, 1991, from the 1962 original.

Han Ju. "Xinzhengfu zhi jianshe" (The construction of new government). In *Xinhai geming qian shinian jian shilun xuanji,* vol. 1, part 2 (Collected essays on the ten year period before the 1911 Revolution). Beijing: Renmin chuban she, 1980.

Harrison, Robert Pogue. *Forests, The Shadow of Civilization.* Chicago: University of Chicago Press, 1992.

Harvey, David. *The Postmodern Condition.* London: Basil Blackwell, 1989.

He Yimin. *Jindai zhishi fenzi yu wangqing Sichuan she hui yanjiu* (Research on modern intellectuals and late Qing Sichuan society). Chengdu: Sichuan daxue chuban she, 1992.

Heeren, John J. *On the Shantung Front: A History of the Shantung Mission of the Presbyterian Church in the U.S.A., 1861–1940.* New York: The Board of Foreign Missions, 1940.

Hinton, William. *Fanshen.* New York: Alfred A. Knopf, Inc., 1966.

Ho, Ping-ti. *The Ladder of Success in Imperial China: Aspects of Social Mobility, 1368–1911.* New York: Columbia University Press, 1962.

————. *Studies on the Population of China, 1368–1953.* Cambridge: Harvard University Press, 1959.

Ho, Ping-ti, and Tang Tsou, eds. *China in Crisis. Vol. I, China's Heritage and the Communist Political System.* Chicago: University of Chicago Press, 1968.

Hobsbawm, Eric, *Primitive Rebels: Studies in Archaic Forms of Social Movement in the 19th and 20th Centuries.* New York: Norton, 1965.

Hobsbawm, Eric and Terrance Ranger, eds. *The Invention of Tradition.* New York: Cambridge University Press, 1983.

Holmgren, J. "Myth, Fantasy or Scholarship: Images of the Status of Women in Traditional China." In *The Australian Journal of Chinese Affairs* 6 (1981): 147–70.

Hsiao, Kung-chuan. *Rural China: Imperial Control in the Nineteenth Century.* Seattle: University of Washington Press, 1960.

Hsieh, Winston. "Peasant Insurrection and the Marketing Hierarchy in the Canton Delta, 1911." In *The Chinese City between Two Worlds,* ed. Mark Elvin and G. William Skinner. Stanford: Stanford University Press, 1974.

Hu Qixi. "Jinggao Chuansha fulao zhi chou shan houshiyi zhe" (Comments of respectful warning by the Chuansha elders on negotiations to remedy conditions). *Shibao,* April 2–3, 1911.

Hu Shengwu and Jin Zhongji. *Cong xinhai gemingdao wusiyundong* (From the 1911 Revolution to the May Fourth Movement). Hunan: Hunan renmin chuban she, 1983.

Hu Weixi. *Xinhai geming yu Zhongguo jindai sixiang wenhua* (The 1911 Revolution and Chinese modern thought). Beijing: Zhongguo renmin daxue chuban she, 1991.

Huang, Philip C. C. *The Peasant Family and Rural Development in the Yangzi Delta, 1350–1988.* Stanford: Stanford University Press, 1990.

————. *The Peasant Economy and Social Change in North China.* Stanford: Stanford University Press, 1985.

Huang, Ray. *Taxation and Governmental Finance in Sixteenth-Century Ming China.* London: Cambridge University Press, 1975.

Huang Shaosheng, "Lianzhou guangfu qianhou" (Lianzhou recovery). In *Xinhai geming yu Guangdong,* ed. Ding Shencun. Guangzhou: Guangdong chuban she, 1991.

Huang Yanpei. *Bashi nianlai* (Eighty years past). Beijing: Wenshi ziliao chuban, 1982.

Hubeisheng zhexue shihui kexue xuehui lianhe hui (Joint committee of the philosophical society and science association of Hubei), ed. *Xinhai geming wushi zhounian jinian luwen ji* (A symposium commemorating the fiftieth anniversary of the 1911 Revolution). Hubei: Zhonghua shuju, 1961.

Hucker, Charles O. *The Traditional Chinese State in Ming Times (1368–1644).* Tucson: University of Arizona Press, 1961.

Hummel, Arthur W., ed. *Eminent Chinese of the Ch'ing Period.* Washington, D.C.: Government Printing Office, 1943–44.

Hunt, Michael H. *The Making of a Special Relationship: The United States and China to 1914.* New York: Columbia University Press, 1983.

Ichiko Chuzo. "Political and Institutional Reform, 1901–1911," *Cambridge History of China,* vol. 11, ed. John K. Fairbank and Kwang-ching Liu. Cambridge: Cambridge University Press, 1980.

———. "The Role of the Gentry." In *China in Revolution: The First Phases, 1900–1913,* ed. Mary Clabaugh Wright. New Haven: Yale University Press, 1968.

Jiang Zuyuan. *Jianming Guangdong si* (A concise history of Guangdong). Guangzhou: Guangdong renmin chuban she, 1987.

Jin Zhongji and Hu Shengwu. *Xinhai geming shigao* (Historical texts on the 1911 Revolution), 3 vol. Shanghai: Shanghai renmin chuban she, 1985, second printing 1991.

Jindai shi ziliao (Material on modern history). Beijing: Kexue chuban she (Academic publishing association), 1954–55.

Jing Su and Luo Lun. *Landlord and Labor in Late Imperial China: Case Studies from Shandong,* trans. Endymion Wilkinson. Cambridge: Harvard University Press, 1978.

Johnston, M. A. *Lion and Dragon in Northern China.* New York: E. P. Dutton and Co., 1910.

Jordan, David K. *Gods, Ghosts, and Ancestors: The Folk Religion of a Taiwanese Village.* Berkeley: University of California Press, 1972.

Judge, Joan. *Print and Politics: "Shibao" and the Culture of Reform in Late Qing China.* Stanford: Stanford University Press, 1996.

Kearney, Michael. *Reconceptualizing the Peasantry: Anthropology in Global Perspective.* Boulder, Colo.: Westview Press, 1996.

King, H. H. *Money and Monetary Policy in China, 1845–1895.* Cambridge: Harvard University Press, 1965.

Kuhn, Philip A. "Local Self-Government under the Republic: Problems of Control, Autonomy, and Mobilization." In *Conflict and Control in Late Imperial China,* eds. Frederic Wakeman Jr., and Carolyn Grant. Berkeley: University of California Press, 1975.

———. *Rebellion and Its Enemies in Late Imperial China: Militarization and Social Structure, 1796–1864.* Cambridge: Harvard University Press, 1970.

Kui Yingtao, *Sichuan jindaishi gao* (Sketches in Sichuan modern history). Chengdu: Sichuan renmin chuban she, 1990.

———. *Sichuan xinhai geming shiliao* (Historical materials on the 1911 Revolution in Sichuan), 2 vol. Chengdu: Sichuan renmin chuban she, 1981.

Kui Yingtao, and Wu Yannan. *Xinhai geming shi* (History of the 1911 Revolution) 3 vol. Beijing: Renmin chuban she, 1980.

Kulp, Daniel Harrison II. *Country Life in South China: The Sociology of Familism.* Vol. I, *Phenix Village, Kwangtung, China.* New York: Teachers College, Bureau of Publications, Columbia University, 1925.

Kunkle, J. S. "The Lienchow Riots," *Chinese Recorder* 42 (April 1911): 243–44.

Laiyang xianzhi (Laiyang county gazetteer), 39 *juan,* Taibei reprint, 1935.

Latour, Bruno. *We Have Never Been Modern*. Cambridge: Harvard University Press, 1993.

Lefebvre, Georges. *The Great Fear of 1789: Rural Panic in Revolutionary France*. New York: Pantheon Press, 1973.

Lefebvre, Henri. *The Production of Space*. Oxford: Basil Blackwell, 1991.

Li Huaidao et al., eds. *Xinhai geming Jiangsu diqu shi liao* (Historical materials on the 1911 Revolution in the Jiangsu Region), Yangzhou Middle School Historical Compilations. Nanjing: Jiangsu Renmin chuban she, 1961.

Li Shu, ed. *Xinhai geming qianhou de Zhongguo zhengji* (Chinese politics before and after the 1911 Revolution). Beijing: Renmin chuban she, 1961.

Li Wenzhi, ed. *Zhongguo jindai nongye shi ziliao* (Sources on China's modern agriculture), vol. 1, 1840–1911. Beijing: Renmin chuban she, 1957.

Li Zhuran, ed. *Xinhai geming qiande qunzhong douzheng* (Mass struggle before the 1911 Revolution). Beijing: Renmin chuban she, 1957.

Lianxian wenshi ziliao (Historical records of Lian county). Guangzhou: Guangdong renmin chuban she, 1991.

Lianxian zhi (Lianxian gazetteer) undated.

"Lianzhou kang dingmenpai tafengchao" (Disturbance in Lianzhou against the nailing of door placques). In *Shibao*, August 10, 1910.

Lianzhou zhi (Lianzhou gazetteer) 1935.

Lin Huaguo. *Yihetuan shishikao* (Historical study of the Boxers). Beijing: Beijing daxue chuban she, 1993.

Lin Yutang. *The Importance of Understanding: Translation from the Chinese*. Cleveland: World Publishing Co., 1960.

Lin Zengping et al., eds. *Xinhai geming shiyanjiu beiyao* (Historical research on the 1911 Revolution). Changsha: Hunan chuban she, 1991.

Liu Benkui. "Xinhai gemingqian Shandong jindai chanye gongren jieji zhuangkuang" (The condition of Shandong's modern industrial working class on the eve of the 1911 Revolution). In *Shandong shizhi ziliao* (Shandong historical materials). Jinan: Shandong renmin chuban she, 1983.

Liu Erru. "Dong san bao kang jingshui douzheng" (The struggle of three eastern bao against the police tax), oral history recorded at Zunhua, 1959. Zunhua Party Archives.

Liu, Hui-chen Wang. "An Analysis of Chinese Clan Rules: Confucian Theories in Action." In *Confucianism and Chinese Civilization,* ed. Arthur F. Wright. New York: Atheneum, 1964.

Liu, Kwang-ching. "The Ch'ing Restoration." In *The Cambridge History of China,* vol. 10, *Late Ch'ing, 1800–1911,* part 1, ed. John K. Fairbank. Cambridge: Cambridge University Press, 1978.

———. "Wan Qing difangguan zishu zhi liao jiazhi" (The historical value of late Qing local officials' personal notes). In *Zhongyang yenjiu yuan chengli wushi zhounian jinian luwen ji* (Collected essays commemorating the fiftieth anniversary of the founding of Academia Sinica). Taibei: Academia Sinica, 1978.

———. "Wan Qing dufu quanli wenti shangque" (The limits of regional power in the late Qing period: a reappraisal). *Qinghua xuebao* (The Qing Hua journal of Chinese studies), no. 2 (July 1974): 176–223.

————. "Nineteenth-Century China: The Disintegration of the Old Order and the Impact of the West." In *China in Crisis,* ed. Ping-ti Ho and Tang Tsou, vol. 1, *China's Heritage and the Communist Political System.* Chicago: University of Chicago Press, 1968.

Liu Ping. "Ping Sun Zhongshan de nongmin guan" (Comments on Sun Zhongshan's view of the peasants) presented at *Sun Zhongshan yu Zhongguo xiandaihua* (Sun Zhongshan and Chinese modernization), Xueshu taolunhui (Academic symposium), Nanjing University, 1996.

————. "Qingmo nongcun 'minbian' sanlun (Discussion of rural "people's activism" in the late Qing). In *Jiangsu shehui kexue* (Jiangsu social science studies), no. 5 (1993): 94–98.

Liu Shipei (pseud. Shen Shu). "Lun xinzheng wei bingmin zhi gen" (A discussion of the New Policy as a cause of the people's distress). *Tianyi bao,* 1907, 10th month/30th day, *juan* no. 8, 9, 10, in *Wuzhengfu zhuyi sixiang ziliaoxuan,* vol. 1 (Selected materials on anarchist thought) Beijing: Beijing University Publishing Co., 1984.

Liu Tongjun, ed. *Xinhai gemingqian Lai Hai Zhao kangjuan yongdong* (Antitax movements in Laiyang, Haiyang and Zhaoyuan before the 1911 Revolution) Beijing: Shehuikexue wenxian chuban she, 1989.

Lo Shouzhang. "Qinxian sanna fankang tangjuan touzheng yu qin fang zhiyi" (Opposition to sugar tax). In *Guangxi xinhai geming ziliao* (Materials on the 1911 Revolution in Guangxi). Guangxi: Guangxi renmin chuban she, 1981.

Lojewski, Frank A. "The Kiangsu Tax Reductions of 1863: Ch'ing Fiscal Administration and Its Limitations," *Modern Chinese Economic History,* eds. Chi-ming Hou and Tzong-shian Yu. Taibei: Institute of Economics, Academia Sinica; distributed by the University of Washington Press, Seattle, now published in book form, 1979.

Lu Yao. "The Origins of the Boxers." In *Chinese Studies in History,* no. 20 (Spring/Summer 1987): 42–86.

Lu Zhanshan. "*Qiongbanzi de xinguangcai*" (New radiance of the bare sticks) in *Dangli bocai* (Party history collection), published by *Zhonggong Hebei sheng weidang li yanjiu shi* (Hebei province Communist party committee history research office) no. 68, November 1993: 34–38.

Lust, John. "Secret Societies, Popular Movements, and the 1911 Revolution." In *Popular Movements and Secret Societies in China, 1840–1950,* ed. Jean Chesneaux. Stanford: Stanford University Press, 1972.

Ma, Amy Fei-man. "Local Self-Government and the Local Populace of Chu'-uan-sha, 1911." Selected Papers from the Center for Far Eastern Studies, no. 1. Chicago: University of Chicago Press, 1975–76.

Ma Gengcun. "Xinhai gemingqian de Laiyang kangjuankangshui de douzheng" (The struggle to resist taxes in Laiyang on the eve of the 1911 Revolution). In *Shandong sheng lishi xuehui* (Shandong province historical studies), vol. 4. Jinan: Shandong sheng lishi xue hui bian (Shandong province historical institute staff), 1982.

MacKinnon, Stephen R. *Power and Politics in Late Imperial China: Yuan Shi-Kai in Beijing and Tianjin, 1901–1908.* Berkeley: University of California Press, 1980.

Manwarren, James Craig. "Rural-Urban Conflict in Shantung: The 1910 Laiyang Tax Uprising." M.A. Thesis, Arizona State University, 1972.

Mao Jiaqi. *Taiping tianguo shi yanjiu* (Historical research on the Taiping Heavenly Kingdom). Nanjing: Nanjing daxue chuban she, 1985.

Mao Jiaqi, Fang Zhiguang, and Dong Guanghua. *Taiping tianguo xingwang shi* (A history of the rise and fall of the Taiping Heavenly Kingdom). Shanghai: Renmin chuban she, 1980.

Marks, Robert. *Rural Revolution in South China*. Madison: University of Wisconsin Press, 1984.

Massey, Doreen. *Space, Place, and Gender.* Minneapolis: University of Minnesota Press, 1994.

McCord, Edward A. "Local Military Power and Elite Formations: The Liu Family of Xingyi County, Guizhou." In *Chinese Local Elites and Patterns of Dominance,* ed. Joseph W. Esherick and Mary Backus Rankin. Berkeley: University of California Press, 1990.

Meisner, Maurice. *Li Ta-chao and the Origins of Chinese Marxism.* Cambridge: Harvard University Press, 1967.

Meisner, Mitch. "Dazhai: The Mass Line in Practice." In *Modern China,* 4, no. 1 (January 1978): 27–62.

Meyers, Ramon H. *The Chinese Peasant Economy: Agricultural Development in Hopei and Shantung, 1890–1949.* Cambridge: Harvard University Press, 1970.

Michael, Franz. *The Taiping Rebellion.* Seattle: University of Washington Press, 1966.

Min Tu-ki. *National Polity and Local Power: The Transformation of Late Imperial China,* ed. Philip A. Kuhn and Timothy Brook. Cambridge: Harvard-Yenching Institute, Harvard University Press, 1989.

Minlibao (The people's stand], Shanghai, 1911.

Moore, Barrington Jr. *Injustice: The Social Bases of Obedience and Revolt.* New York: M. E. Sharp, Inc., 1978.

———. *Social Origins of Dictatorship and Democracy.* Boston: Beacon Press, 1966.

Mou Anjie. *Taiping Tianguo* (Taiping Heavenly Kingdom). Shanghai: Shanghai renmin chuban she, 1979.

Muramatsu, Yuji. "Some Themes in Chinese Rebel Ideologies." In *The Confucian Persuasion,* ed. Arthur F. Wright. Stanford: Stanford University Press, 1960.

Nanhui xianzhi (Nanhui county gazetteer). Taibei reprint, 1927.

Naquin, Susan. *Millenarian Rebellion in China: The Eight Trigrams Uprising of 1813.* New Haven: Yale University Press, 1976.

Naquin, Susan, and Evelyn S. Rawski. *Chinese Society in the Eighteenth Century.* New Haven: Yale University Press, 1987.

Nathan, Dev, and Govind Kelkar. "Collective Villages in the Chinese Market." *Economic and Political Weekly*, May 3, 1997, 951–63, and May 10, 1997, 1037–47.

Nivison, David S., and Arthur F. Wright, eds. *Confucianism in Action.* Stanford: Stanford University Press, 1959.

North China Herald, Shanghai, 1910–1911.

Ocko, Jonathan K. *Bureaucratic Reform in Provincial China: Ting Jih-ch'ang in Restoration Kiangsu, 1867–1870.* Cambridge: Harvard University Press, 1983.

Ono, Kazuko. *Chinese Women in a Century of Revolution, 1850–1950,* ed. Joshua A. Fogel. Stanford: Stanford University Press, 1989.

Osgood, Cornelius. *Village Life in Old China: A Community Study of Kao Yao, Yunnan.* New York: The Ronald Press, 1963.

Overmyer, Daniel L. *Folk Buddhist Religion: Dissenting Sects in Late Traditional China.* Cambridge: Harvard University Press, 1976.

Parish, William L., and Martin King Whyte. *Village and Family in Contemporary China.* Chicago: University of Chicago Press, 1978.

Parsons, Talcott, ed. *Max Weber: The Theory of Social and Economic Organization.* New York: The Free Press, 1947.

P'eng P'ai (Peng Pai). *Seeds of Peasant Revolution: Report on the Haifeng Peasant Movement,* trans. Donald Holoch. Cornell University East Asia Papers, no. 1. Ithaca, N.Y.: China-Japan Program, Cornell University, 1973.

Perkins, Dwight H. *Agricultural Development in China (1368–1968).* Chicago: Aldine Publishing Co., 1969.

Playfair, G. M. H. *The Cities and Towns of China: A Geographical Dictionary,* 2d ed. Shanghai: Kelly and Walsh, 1910.

Polachek, James. "Gentry Hegemony: Soochow in the T'ung-chih Restoration." In *Conflict and Control in Late Imperial China,* ed. Frederic Wakeman Jr., and Carolyn Grant. Berkeley: University of California Press, 1975.

Popkin, Samuel. *The Rational Peasant.* Berkeley: University of California Press, 1979.

Porchner, Boris. "Popular Uprisings as Class War: The Revolt of the Nu-pieds," In *The Peasantry in the Old Regime,* ed. Isser Woloch. New York: Holt, Rinehart, Winston, 1970.

Potter, Sulamith Heins, and Jack M. Potter. *China's Peasants: The Anthropology of a Revolution.* Cambridge: Cambridge University Press.

Pouliquen, Yves-Marie. "La Revolte de Lai-yang" (The revolt at Laiyang). *Echo de la Mission,* no. 79 (September 1910): 129–44.

Prazniak, Roxann. "Weavers and Sorceresses of Chuansha: The Social Origins of Political Activism among Rural Chinese Women." *Modern China,* 12, no. 2 (April 1986): 202–29. Also published in *Zhongguo shehui jingji shiyanjiu* (The journal of Chinese social and economic history), no. 1 1996: 68–76.

———. "Tax Protest at Laiyang, Shandong, 1910: Commoner Organization versus the County Political Elite," *Modern China,* 6, no. 1 (January 1980): 41–71.

Qiao Zhiqiang. *Xinhai geming qiande shinian* (Ten years before the 1911 Revolution). Taiyuan: Shanxi renmin chuban she, 1987.

Qing zhong qi wu shen bailian jiao qiyi ziliao (Materials on the White Lotus uprising in five provinces during the mid-Qing), vol. 4. Nanjing: Jiangsu renmin chuban she, 1982.

Rankin, Mary Backus. *Elite Activism and Political Transformation in China: Zhejiang Province, 1865–1911.* Stanford: Stanford University Press, 1986.

————. *Early Chinese Revolutionaries: Radical Intellectuals in Shanghai and Chekiang, 1902–1911*. Cambridge: Harvard University Press, 1971.

Rawski, Evelyn Sakakida. *Education and Popular Literacy in Ch'ing China*. Ann Arbor: University of Michigan Press, 1979.

————. *Agricultural Change and the Peasant Economy of South China*. Cambridge: Harvard University Press, 1972.

Redfield, Robert. *The Little Community and Peasant Society and Culture*. Chicago: University of Chicago Press, 1956; second impression, 1961.

Ren Zhixue, "Guan yu Qushiwen kangjuan touzheng qingguang de diaocha" (An inquiry into the circumstances related to the Qu Shiwen anti-tax struggle), an oral history recorded in Bolin Village, Laiyang, Shandong, April 19, 1984.

Reynolds, Douglas R. *China 1898–1912: The Xinzheng Revolution and Japan*. Cambridge: Council on East Asian Studies, Harvard University Press, 1993.

Rhoads, Edward J. M. *China's Republican Revolution: The Case of Kwangtung, 1895–1913*. Cambridge: Harvard University Press, 1975.

————. "Nationalism and Xenophobia in Kwangtung (1905–1906): The Canton Anti-American Boycott and the Lienchow Anti-Missionary Uprising," in *Papers on China*, Harvard 1962.

Robisheaux, Thomas. *Rural Society and the Search for Order in Early Modern Germany*. Cambridge: Cambridge University Press, 1989.

Rong Tieshen. "Xinhai geming qianhou de Zhongguo funu yundong" (The Chinese women's movement on the eve of the 1911 Revolution). In *Jinian Xinhai geming qishi zhounian xueshu taolunhui wenji* (Collected works from a symposium to commemorate the seventieth anniversary of the 1911 Revolution). Beijing: Renmin chuban she, 1983.

Rose, Gillian. *Writing Women and Space: Colonial and Postcoloniaal Geographies*. New York: Guilford Press, 1994.

Roth, Guenther. "Socio-Historical Model and Developmental Theory." *American Sociological Review*, 40, no. 2 (April 1975): 148–57.

Sahlins, Peter. *Forest Rites: The War of the Demoiselles in Nineteenth-Century France*. Cambridge: Harvard University Press, 1994.

Sangren, P. Steven. "Female Gender in Chinese Religious Symbols: Kuan Yin, Ma Tsu, and the "Eternal Mother." *Signs* (Autumn 1983): 4–25.

Scheiner, Irwin. "Benevolent Lords and Honorable Peasants: Rebellion and Peasant Consciousness in Tokugawa Japan." In *Japanese Thought in the Tokugawa Period: Methods and Metaphors,* ed. Tetsuo Najita and Irwin Scheiner. Chicago: University of Chicago Press, 1978.

Schiffrin, Harold Z. *Sun Yat-sen and the Origins of the Chinese Revolution*. Berkeley: University of California Press, 1968.

Schmidt, Peter R., and Thomas C. Patterson, eds. *Making Alternative Histories: The Practice of Archaeology and History in Non-Western Settings*. Santa Fe, N.M.: School of American Research Press, 1995.

Schoppa, R. Keith. "Rent Resistance and Rural Reconstruction: Shen Dingyi in Political Opposition, 1921 and 1928." In *Roads Not Taken: The Struggle of Opposition Parties in Twentieth Century China*, ed. Roger B. Jeans. Boulder, Colo.: Westview Press, 1992.

———. "Contours of Revolutionary Change in a Chinese County, 1900–1950." *Journal of Asian Studies* 51, no. 4 (November 1992): 770–96.

———. *Chinese Elites and Political Change: Zhejiang Province in the Early Twentieth Century.* Cambridge: Council on East Asian Studies Publications, Harvard University Press, 1982.

Scott, James C. *Weapons of the Weak: Everyday Forms of Peasant Resistance.* New Haven: Yale University Press, 1985.

———. *The Moral Economy of the Peasant.* New Haven: Yale University Press, 1976.

Scott, Jim. "Socialism and Small Property—Or Two Cheers for the Petty-Bourgeoisie." *Peasant Studies* 12, no. 3 (Spring 1985): 185–97.

Shandong jindai shi ziliao (Sources on Shandong's modern history). Jinan: Shandong renmin chuban she, 1958.

Shandong Lüjing tongxiang hui (Shandong landsmann's association), ed. "Laiyang shibian di tiaocha baogaoshu" (An investigative report on the Laiyang disturbances), *Shandong jindai shi ziliao* (Sources on Shandong's modern history). Jinan: Shandong renmin chuban she, 1958. This report was also published in *Shuntian shibao,* 8/13–8/29, 1910, and was later compiled in *Jindai shi ziliao,* no. 1 (1954): 26–47.

Shang Ding. *Huang Yanpei.* Beijing: Renmin chuban she, 1986.

Shang Qinghan. "Shandong ziyiyu yiyuan Wang Zhixun, Ding Shiyi, Zhou Shulin, Zhang Jieli, Shang Qinghan cizhi yuan you baogaoshu" (Report on the reasons for the resignation of Wang Zhixun, Ding Shiyi, Zhou Shulin, Zhang Jieli, and Shang Qinghan from the Shandong Provisional Provincial Assembly), *Shandong jindai shi ziliao* (Shandong modern history materials), 35–39. Jinan: Shandong renmin chuban she, 1958.

Shen Yün-lung. *Xiandai zhengzhi renwu suping* (Appraisals of modern political figures), part 2. Taibei: Wenhai, 1966.

Shenbao (Shanghai daily news), Shanghai, 1911.

Shiba, Yoshinobu. "Ningbo and Its Hinterland." In *The City in Late Imperial China,* ed. G. William Skinner. Stanford: Stanford University Press, 1977.

Shibao (The eastern times), Shanghai, 1910–11.

Shih Nai-an. *Water Margin,* trans. J. H. Jackson. Hong Kong: Commercial Press Ltd., 1963.

Shiva, Vandana. "Development, Ecology, and Women." In *Healing the Wounds: The Promise of Ecofeminism,* ed. Judith Plant. Santa Cruz, Calif.: New Society Publishers, 1989.

Shuntian shibao (The Shuntian times), Beijing, 1910.

Skinner, G. William. "Cities and the Hierarchy of Local Systems." *Studies in Chinese Society,* ed. Arthur P. Wolf. Stanford: Stanford University Press, 1979.

———. "Introduction: Urban and Rural in Chinese Society." In *The City in Late Imperial China,* ed. G. William Skinner. Stanford: Stanford University Press, 1977.

———. "Chinese Peasants and the Closed Community: An Open and Shut Case." *Comparative Studies in Society and History,* 13, no. 3 (July 1971): 270–81.

———. "Marketing and Social Structure in Rural China." *Journal of Asian Studies,* 24, no. 1 (November 1964): 3–43; vol. 24, no. 2 (February 1965): 195–228; vol. 24, no. 3 (May 1965): 363–99.

Skinner, G. William, ed. *The City in Late Imperial China.* Stanford: Stanford University Press, 1977.

Skocpol, Theda. *States and Social Revolutions.* Cambridge: Cambridge University Press, 1979.

Skocpol, Theda, Peter Evan, and Dietrich Rueschemeyer, eds. *Bringing the State Back In.* New York: Cambridge University Press, 1985.

Smith, Arthur H. *Proverbs and Common Sayings from the Chinese.* New York: Dover Publications, 1965.

———. *China in Convulsion.* 2 vols. New York: Fleming H. Revell, 1901.

———. *Village Life in China: A Study in Sociology.* New York: Fleming H. Revell, 1899.

Smith, Neil. *Uneven Development: Nature, Capital and the Production of Space.* Cambridge: Basil Blackwell, 1990.

Soja, Edward. *Postmodern Geographies: The Reassertion of Space in Critical Social Theory.* London: Verso, 1989.

South China Morning Post, Canton. November–December 1910.

Spence, Jonathan D. *The Death of Woman Wang.* New York: The Viking Press, 1978.

Starn, Orin. "Maoism in the Andes: The Communist Party of Peru-Shining Path and the Refusal of History." *Journal of Latin American Studies,* no. 27 (1995): 399–421.

Stockard, Janice E. *Daughters of the Canton Delta: Marriage Patterns and Economic Strategies in South China, 1860–1930.* Stanford: Stanford University Press, 1989.

"Su fu pi Hu dao binbao Chuansha zizhi naoshi qingxing" (Shanghai Taotai's report to the governor on the circumstances of the Chuansha self-government disturbances). *Shibao,* April 11, 1911.

Su Yunfeng, ed. *Zhongguo xiandaihua de quyu yanjiu, Hubei sheng, 1860–1916* (Regional research on Chinese modernization, Hubei province, 1860–1916). Taipei, Academia Sinica, 1987.

Sun Baoqi. "Zou chafu Laiyang, Haiyang er xian zhaoluan qingxing zhe" (Memorial on the disruptive situation in Laiyang and Haiyang), *Shandong jindai shi ziliao.* Jinan: Shandong renmin chuban she, 1958.

Sung Wook Shin, Tim. Concepts of State and People in the Late Ch'ing. Ph.D. dissertation, U.C. Berkeley, 1980.

Sweeten, Alan Richard. "Community and Bureaucracy in Rural China: Evidence from 'Sectarian Cases' (*chiao-an*) in Kiangsu, 1860–1895." Ph.D. Dissertation, U. C. Davis, 1980.

———. "The *Ti-pao* as Bottom-level Bureaucrat: Evidence from Local Criminal Cases in South China, 1860–1877," *Zhongyang yenjiu yuan jindai shi yenjiu suo jikan* (Bulletin of the Institute of Modern History, Academia Sinica), 7 (1978): 627–57.

———. "Women and Law in Rural China: Vignettes from 'Sectarian Cases'

(*Chiao-an*) in Kiangsi, 1872–1878," *Ch'ing-shih wen-t'i: Journal of the Society for Ch'ing Studies*, 3, no. 10 (December 1978): 49–68.

———. "The *Ti-pao*'s Role in Local Government as Seen in Fukien Christian 'Cases,' 1863–1869." *Ch'ing-shih wen-t'i: Journal of the Society of Ch'ing Studies*, 3, no. 6 (December 1976): 1–27.

Tan, Chester. *The Boxer Catastrophe*. New York: Columbia University Press, 1955.

Tao Chengzhang. "Longhuahui zhangcheng" (Regulations of the Dragon Flower Society). In Shu Hirayama, *Zhongguo mimi shehui shi* (A history of Chinese secret societies). Taipei: Guting shuwu, 1934.

Tawney, R. H. *Land and Labour in China*. London: George Allen and Unwin, 1932.

Tessan, Hiroshi. "Shinmatsu Shisen ni okeru hansho kuminchika to Kyukyo undo" (The semi-colonization of Sichuan in the late Qing and the anti-Catholic movement). *Rekishigaku Kenkyu* 6, no. 529 (1984): 17–33.

Tévoédjrè, Albert. *Poverty, The Wealth of Mankind*. Oxford: Pergamon Press, 1979.

Thaxton, Ralph A. Jr. *Salt of the Earth: The Political Origins of Peasant Protest and Communist Revolution in China*. Berkeley: University of California Press, 1997.

Thompson, E. P. "Eighteenth-Century English Society: Class Struggle without Class?" *Social History* 3 (1978).

Thompson, Roger R., trans. and intro. to *Mao Zedong's 1930 Report on Xunwu*. Stanford: Stanford University Press, 1990.

———. "Statecraft and Self-Government: Competing Visions of Community and State in Late Imperial China. *Modern China* 14, no. 2 (April 1988): 188–221.

———. "Visions of the Future, Realities of the Day: Local Administrative Reform, Electoral Politics, and Traditional Chinese Society on the Eve of the 1911 Revolution." Ph.D. Dissertation, Yale University, 1985.

Thorne, Susan Elizabeth. "Protestant Ethics and the Spirit of Imperialism: British Congregationalists and The London Missionary Society, 1795–1925." Ph.D. Disseration, University of Michigan, 1990.

Tian Zhihe, "Zunhua dongbabao nongmin fanfang guoshujuan de douzhen jingguo" (Protest against orchard taxes by the peasants of eight eastern bao in Zunhua county), an oral history recorded April 23, 1961. Zunhua County Party Historical Archives, serial no. 26, document no. A20011.2.

Tilly, Charles. *The Contentious French: Four Centuries of Popular Struggle*. Cambridge: Harvard University Press, 1986.

———. *From Mobilization to Revolution*. Reading, Mass.: Addison-Wesley Publishing Co., 1978.

Topley, Marjorie. "Marriage Resistance in Rural Kwangtung." In *Women in Chinese Society*, ed. Margery Wolf and Roxane Witke. Stanford: Stanford University Press, 1975.

United States, General Records of the Department of State, Record Group 59. Washington, D.C.: National Archives. (1) The Numerical File of the Department of State, 1906–1910, and (2) The Records of the Department of State relating to Internal Affairs of China, 1910–29, file no. 893, microfilm no. 329.

van der Sprenkel, S., *Legal Institutions in Manchu China*. London: Athlone Press, 1962.

Vlastos, Stephen. *Peasant Protests and Uprisings in Tokugawa Japan*. Berkeley: University of California Press, 1986.

Wakeman, Frederic Jr. *The Fall of Imperial China*. New York: The Free Press, 1975.

———. *Strangers at the Gate: Social Disorder in South China, 1839–1861*. Berkeley: University of California Press, 1966.

Wakeman, Frederic Jr., and Carolyn Grant, eds. *Conflict and Control in Late Imperial China*. Berkeley: University of California Press, 1975.

Walker, Kathy Le Mons. "Peasant Insurrection in China Reconsidered: A Preliminary Examination of the Jun Mountain Peasant Rising, Nantong County, 1863." *The Journal of Peasant Studies*, 20, no. 4 (July 1993): 640–68.

———. "Merchants, Peasants and Industry: The Political Economy of Cotton Textiles, Nanton County, 1895–1935." Ph.D. dissertation, University of California, Los Angeles, 1986.

Wang Baotian. "Zou Laiyang, Haiyang er xian xiang jishan bianpai da chen" (Memorial on the continuing disturbances in Laiyang and Haiyang), *Shandong jindai shi ziliao* (Shandong modern history materials). Jinan: Shandong renmin chuban she, 1958.

Wang Boyan. *Zhongguo jindai shi jianghua* (Talks on modern Chinese history). Jinan: Shandong renmin chuban she, 1957.

Wang Jiahai. "Lingxiu fengcai zhao ren wen: Wang Guofan de huiyi" (Leader's graceful bearing shines through public questioning: recollections of Wang Guofan). In *Dashidai* (Great era), published by the Hebei province party committee, 1993, no 8, 6–7.

Wang Shu-huai. *Zhongguo xiandaihua di quyu yanjiu, Jiangsusheng, 1860–1916* (A regional study of modernization in China: Jiangsu province, 1860–1916). Taibei: Institute of Modern History, Academia Sinica, 1984.

———. "Qingmo Jiangsu difang zizhi fengchao" (Riots against local self-government in Jiangsu during the late Qing period). *Zhongyang yenjiu yuan jindai shi yenjiu suo jikan* (Bulletin of the Institute of Modern History, Academia Sinica), 6 (1977): 313–27.

Wang Shijun, ed. *Qingzhongqi wusheng bailianjiao qiyi ziliao* (Materials on the White Lotus uprising in five provinces during the mid-Qing period), vol. 4, edited by the documents office of the Zhongguo shehuikexueyuan lishi yanjiusuo Qingshishi (Qing history office of the Chinese social sciences academy historical research institute). Nanjing: Jiangsu renmin chuban she, 1982.

Wang, Yeh-chien. *An Estimation of the Land Tax Collection in China, 1753–1908*. Cambridge, Mass.: East Asian Research Center, Harvard University, 1973.

———. *Land Taxation in Imperial China, 1750–1911*. Cambridge: Harvard University Press, 1973.

Wang Yü-ch'üan. "The Rise of the Land Tax and the Fall of Dynasties." *Pacific Affairs*, 9 (1936): 201–220.

Wang Zhixun. "Fu Wang Zhixun deng wuren duiyu Ziyiju cizhi liyou shu" (Letter of resignation from the assembly by Wang Zhixun and five others), *Shandong jindai shi ziliao*, 39–40. Jinan: Shandong renmin chuban she, 1958.

———. "Tiaocha Lai, Hai luan shi baogaoshu" (Report on an investigation into the Laiyang and Haiyang disturbances), *Shandong jindai shi ziliao*, 27–35. Jinan: Shandong renmin chuban she, 1958.

Watson, James L. "Hereditary Tenancy and Corporate Landlordism in Traditional China: A Case Study," *Modern Asian Studies*, 2, no. 2 (1977): 161–82.

Watt, John R. "The Yamen and Urban Administration" In *The City in Late Imperial China*, ed. G. William Skinner. Stanford: Stanford University Press, 1977.

———. *The District Magistrate in Late Imperial China.* New York: Columbia University Press, 1972.

Weber, Max. *The Religion of China: Confucianism and Taoism.* Glencoe, Ill.: The Free Press, 1951.

Wei Zhongxian. "Qu Shiwen yu Laiyang canggu shi mo" (The whole story of Qu Shiwen and the Laiyang granary). In *Xinhai gemingqian Lai Hai Zhao kangjuan yongdong* (Antitax movements in Laiyang, Haiyang and Zhaoyuan before the 1911 Revolution), ed. Liu Tongjun. Beijing: Shehuikexue wenxian chuban she, 1989.

Weins, Mi Chu. "Lord and Peasant: The Sixteenth to the Eighteenth Century." *Modern China* 6, 1 (January 1980): 3–40.

Weiyuan xianzhi (Weiyuan gazetteer) (Taibei reprint 1968, original 1877).

Willmott, W. E., ed. *Economic Organization in Chinese Society.* Stanford: Stanford University Press, 1972.

Wolf, Arthur R. *Studies in Chinese Society.* Stanford: Stanford University Press, 1979.

Wolf, Arthur R., . ed. *Religion and Ritual in Chinese Society.* Stanford: Stanford University Press, 1974.

Wolf, Eric R. *Peasant Wars of the Twentieth Century.* New York: Harper and Row Publishers, 1969.

Wolf, Margery. *Women and the Family in Rural Taiwan.* Stanford: Stanford University Press, 1972.

Wolf, Margery, and Roxane Witke, eds. *Women in Chinese Society.* Stanford: Stanford University Press, 1975.

Wright, Arthur F., ed. *Confucianism and Chinese Civilization.* New York: Atheneum, 1964.

Wright, Mary C. *The Last Stand of Chinese Conservatism: The T'ung-chih Restoration, 1862–1874.* Stanford: Stanford University Press, 1957; reprinted, New York: Atheneum, 1969.

Wright, Mary C., ed. *China in Revolution: The First Phase, 1900–1913.* New Haven: Yale University Press, 1969.

Wu Runliang and Liu Tongjun. "Yijiuyiling nian Laiyang, Haiyang renmin de kangjuankangshui douzheng" (The struggle to resist taxes in 1910 in Laiyang and Haiyang), in *Shandong shizhi ziliao* (Shandong historical materials). Jinan: Shandong renmin chuban she, 1983.

———. "Qingmo Laiyang kangjuandouzheng kaimo" (The late Qing struggle against taxes at Laiyang from beginning to end). In *Shandong sheng lishi xuehui* (Shandong province historical studies), vol. 4. Jinan: Shandong sheng lishi xue hui bian (Shandong province historical institute staff), 1982.

Wu Wo-yao. *Vignettes from the Late Ch'ing: Bizarre Happenings over Two Decades,* trans. Shih-shun Liu. Jamaica, N.Y.: St. John's University Press, 1975.

Wu Yannan. "Xinhai geming yu nongmin wenti" (The 1911 Revolution and the peasant question). In *Jinian xinhai geming qishi zhounian* (Commemorating the seventieth anniversary of the 1911 Revolution). Beijing: Zhonghua shuju, 1983.

"Wuzhengfu geming yu nongmin geming" (Anarchist revolution and peasant revolution). In *Wuzhengfu zhuyi sixiang ziliaoxuan,* vol. 1 (Selected materials on anarchist thought). Beijing: Beijing Daxue chuban she, 1984.

Xiao Gongqin. "Qingmo xinzheng yu Zhongguo xiandaihua yanjiu" (Late Qing New Policy reforms and research on Chinese modernization). In *Zhanlu yu guanli* (Strategy and management), no. 1 (1993): 61–66.

Xing Huanlin. "Xinhai geming zai Zhili" (The 1911 Revolution in Zhili). In *Hebei wenshi ziliao xuanji* (Selected historical materials on Zhili). Beijing: Hebei renmin chuban she, no. 5, 1981, 1–27.

Xinhai geming (The 1911 Revolution). Shanghai: Renmin chuban she, 1972.

Xinhai geming qian shinian wen minbian dangan shiliao (Archive materials on people's activism in the ten years before the 1911 Revolution), 2 vol. Compiled from the Chinese No. 1 Historical Archives, Beijing Teacher's University History Department. Beijing: Zhonghua shuju, 1985.

Xinhai geming si yanjiu beiyao (Research materials on the 1911 Revolution). Changsha: Henan chuban she chuban faxing, 1991.

Xinhai Weiyuan baolu tongzhihui de wuzhuang douzheng (The 1911 Weiyuan armed struggle to protect the railway movement). In "Sichuan baolu fengyun lu" (Record of the Sichuan protect the railway agitation). Chengdu: Sichuan renmin chuban she, 1981.

Yang, C. K. "Some Preliminary Statistical Patterns of Mass Action in Nineteenth-Century China." In *Conflict and Control in Late Imperial China,* ed. Frederic Wakeman Jr. and Carolyn Grant. Berkeley: University of California Press, 1975.

———. *Religion in Chinese Society.* Berkeley: University of California Press, 1961.

Yang Lien-sheng. *Money and Credit in China.* Cambridge: Harvard University Press, 1952.

Yang, Martin C. *A Chinese Village: Taitou, Shantung Province.* New York: Columbia University Press, 1945.

Yang Tingdong. "Tiaocha Chuansha naoshi qingxing bin" (An investigation into the circumstances of the Chuansha disturbances). *Shibao,* May 21–25, 1911.

Yao Wennan. "Pudong tongrenhui gong tui Yao Wennan deng tiaocha Chuansha naoshi qingxing baogaoshu" (Report on an investigation of the circumstances of the Chuansha disturbances by the Pudong association's investigators Yao Wennan and others). *Chuansha xianzhi* (Chuansha gazetteer), *juan* no. 23, 1936.

Yeh Wen-hsin. *Provincial Passages: Culture, Space, and the Origins of Chinese Communism.* Berkeley: University of California Press, 1996.

Young, Ernest P. "Nationalism, Reform, and Republican Revolution: China in the Early Twentieth Century." In *Modern East Asia: Essays in Interpretation,* ed. James B. Crowley. New York: Harcourt, Brace and World, Inc., 1970, 151–179.

———. "Politics in the Aftermath of Revolution: The Era of Yuan Shih-k'ai." In *Cambridge History of China,* ed., John K. Fairbank and Dennis Twitchett. New York: Harcourt, Brace, and World, Inc., 1970, vol. 12: 209–59.

Young, Marilyn B., ed. *Women in China: Studies in Social Change and Feminism.* Ann Arbor: Center for Chinese Studies, University of Michigan, 1973.

Yuzhe huicun (Beijing gazette). Beijing: 1908.

Zhang Li. *Sichuan Yihetuan yundong* (Sichuan Boxer Movement). Chengdu: Sichuan renmin chuban she, 1982.

Zhang Qiling. *Shu liang zongdu Zhang Qiling qi Lianzhou xiangmin kang ding-menpai* (Memorial to the emperor from Zhang Qiling the governor of Guang-dong and Guangxi provinces on the resistance to door plates at Lianzhou). In *Xinhai geming qian shinian wen minbian dangan shiliao* (Archive materials on people's activism in the ten years before the 1911 Revolution), 2 vol. Compiled from the Chinese No. 1 Historical Archives, Beijing Teacher's University History Department. Beijing: Zhonghua shuju, 1985, no. 274.

Zhang Xiaomei. *Sichuan jingji cankao ziliao* (Reference materials on Sichuan's economy). Shanghai: Zhongguo tushu zazhi gongsi, 1939.

Zhang Yufa. *Zhong guo xiandai hua de qu cheng yanjiu: Shandong, 1860–1916* (Regional Study of Modernization in China, Shandong, 1860–1916). Taibei: Academia Sinica, 1982, 2 volumes.

Zhao Erxun. "Sichuan zongdu Zhao Erxun zou pingding Weiyuan deng xian luanshi qingxing pian" (Facts of the suppression of the uprising in Weiyuan and other counties reported by the governor of Sichuan), a memorial to the emperor in *Xinhai geming qian shinian wen minbian dangan shiliao,* no. 463.

Zhengzhi guanbao (Government gazette). Beijing: 1908–1911.

Zhou Kaiqing. *Siquan yu xinhaigeming* (Sichuan and the 1911 Revolution). Taibei: Academic Book Publishers 1986.

Zhou Shandao. "Ji yijiulingjiunian Weiyuan tianbaodayuanshuai qiyi" (Remembering the 1909 uprising of the heaven-protected marshal at Weiyuan). In *Sichuan wenshi ziliao xuanji* (Selected historical materials on Sichuan), no. 3. Chengdu: Sichuan People's Publishing Co.,1962.

Zhou Yumin and Shao Yong, eds. *Zhongguo banghuishi.* (History of secret societies). Shanghai: Shanghai renmin chuban she, 1993.

Zunhua xianzhi (Zunhua gazetteer). Qinghua daxue collected materials, hand-written copy, 6:1046–47.

Zunhua xianzhi (Zunhua gazetteer). 1990.

Zuo Shaozuo. "Lianzhou shijian riji zhailu" (Diary extracts of events at Lian-zhou), *Jindai shi ziliao* (Material on modern history), no. 4 (1955).

Index

About the Author

Roxann Prazniak lives in Farmville, Virginia, where she is an associate member of the Martha E. Forrester Council of Women, a civic group working to improve educational opportunities in Prince Edward County since 1920.

She is the author of *Dialogues across Civilizations: Sketches in World History from the Chinese and European Experiences* and teaches at Hampden-Sydney College where she is Elliott Professor of History.